# VOLUNTARY ASSOCIATIONS

James Luther Adams

# VOLUNTARY ASSOCIATIONS

## A Study of Groups in Free Societies

Essays in Honor of James Luther Adams
*Edited by D. B. Robertson*

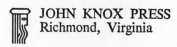 JOHN KNOX PRESS
Richmond, Virginia

LIBRARY OF CONGRESS CATALOG CARD NUMBER: 66-21648
© M. E. BRATCHER 1966
PRINTED IN THE UNITED STATES OF AMERICA
3371(WB)9950

# FOREWORD

*by Paul Tillich*

It is a great honor and joy for me that I have been asked to write a few introductory words to this book which is dedicated to the life and work of my dear friend, Jim Adams. Without him I would not be what I am, biographically as well as theologically. He received me graciously when I came to Chicago as a German refugee; he has studied my thought so thoroughly that I have sent to him all those who wanted to know about it, because he knows more about my writings than I do myself; he made the first translations into English of articles I had written in German; he helped me to get a publisher, and I have reasons to suspect that he did many more things for me than I ever have known.

Beyond this personal support, his thought and work have given me a deeper understanding of American Christianity. First and most important is the truth of which he is a living witness, that *agape,* Christian love, is not dependent on trinitarian or anti-trinitarian or other dogmatic traditions (he is a Unitarian), but on the divine Spirit, which grasps men of all creeds through the power which is manifest in Jesus as the Christ. The second thing I have learned from him is the emphasis on the practical, social as well as political, application of the principle of *agape* to the situation of the society in which we live. In this respect he represents the prophetic element in Christianity which much teaching in the churches badly neglects. I even may confess that I feel him as a "thorn in my flesh," when "the flesh" tries to ignore the social implications of the Christian message! He represents in his whole being a warning against a theology that sacrifices the prophetic for the mystical element, though both of them, as he and I agree, are essential for religion generally and Christianity especially.

The third point in which he gave me an example is his extraordinary knowledge of facts and persons and the preciseness and conscientiousness with which he works in all of his theological, sociological, and psychological investigations. There is humility in this attitude which I deeply admire. It is ultimately an expression of *agape,* which cares for the smallest, without becoming small itself.

But there is the other side of him which is equally astonishing: the largeness of interests and involvements in all sides of man's cultural creativity: in the arts as well as in the sciences. Again it is love, the *eros* towards the true and the beautiful, which makes it possible for him to unite intensive participation in these functions of the human spirit with his continuous concern for the practical problems of individuals as well as of the society. In theological terminology I could say that James Luther Adams is a living proof of the ultimate unity of *eros* and *agape* and for the possibility that this unity becomes manifest, however fragmentarily, in a human being.

# PREFACE

This book is an expression of gratitude for instruction, inspiration, and encouragement from students and friends of James Luther Adams. It is a result, too, of the contributors' shared belief with James Luther Adams in the historical and current relevance (scholarly and practical) of the general theory of associations. Our major theme represents a long-time concern of Professor Adams. This area of concern, to be sure, constitutes only one of several areas of research and reflection which have engaged his vigorous attention. Our concern in this collective venture, however, is especially related to free societies. There is also a shared assumption that only in free societies is the voluntary association a potent element of social vitality in public and community affairs.

Voluntary associations have had a long history. They have been a characteristic of democratic life in the West, and especially in the Anglo-Saxon world, since their great proliferation in the seventeenth century, a crucial century in the development of groups. The quality of our social and political life has been to a great degree determined by the virility of the myriad groups—clubs, organizations, and associations—alternately muddying and clarifying the spaces between the state and the family and between the state and the individual.

Historical developments receive substantial treatment in this collection of papers. The present situation also claims the serious attention of some of the contributors. But perhaps we raise and leave unanswered, in terms of specific treatment, such questions as these: (1) Do *all* voluntary associations represent a social gain or benefit? We of course would have to say "No!"* (2) Are the old war-horses (fighting

---

* A few selective examples of references to possible misuse or abuse of the association are these: Rice, C. F., *Freedom of Association*, Ch. VI; Petro, Sylvester, *The Labor Policy of the Free Society*, Ch. 6; Adams, James L., "The Political Responsibility of the Man of Culture," *Comprendre*, No. 16, 1956, particularly pp. 12-14; Cahn, Edmond, *The Predicament of Democratic Man*, p. 102; Horn, A. H., *Groups and the Constitution*, especially Chapters 6-7; Fellman, David, *The Constitutional Right of Association;* Boulding, Kenneth, *The Organizational Revolution;* Carney, F. S., "Towards a Christian Doctrine of Associations," *Quest*, Vol. II, No. 4, pp. 1-13, May 1958, in which Prof. Carney refers to "the fallen nature of associations"; Ziegler, Harmon, *Interest Groups in Ameri-*

groups) that battled for noble causes in the past still vital and relevant
in our society, or are they shells, dry and lifeless remains of what once
may have qualified as one of Hobbes's "worms" in the entrails?
Some of the papers in this volume suggest new possibilities in our
situation.

Our friend and teacher, J. L. A., has given much of his time and
energy and thought to putting life and relevance into a wide variety
and range of associations, as Max Stackhouse's biographical study
shows. To James Luther Adams there can be no proper disjunction between theological-societal faiths and presuppositions and the hot-
blooded act in politics and society, when this act is the considered, self-
conscious work of a group. The contributors to this volume are vividly
aware not only of J. L. A.'s venturesome involvement in civic, educational, and church activities; we know, too, of his irresistible emphasis
in his classroom work, in his direction of graduate research, and in his
extracurricular lecturing. Many readers will also know of his writings
on the subject, the latest being the Hibbert Lectures delivered in British and Continental universities in 1963. The *Leitmotif* of much of his
thought and labor is expressed in his variation on a New Testament
passage: "By their groups shall you know them."

There is something special which has to be said about J. L. A. as a
contemporary theologian and teacher: he manages consistently to
maintain with his students and associates a peculiar amalgam of friendship and scholarly engagement. All of us have been supported and sustained by this warm and creative kind of relationship.†

It is fair to say, I believe, that those of us who manage to corner
J. L. A. in times and places have been literally saturated with data
and references, and we sometimes find difficulty in following literally
all of his rich and enthusiastic suggestions! We have also felt that he was
rightly and relevantly "breathing down our necks" to the end that we
plunge not only into the documentary nooks and crannies but also into
the sea of action here and now. With J. L. A. we all share the view that
good intentions (or "reading a good book about it") is not enough. A
person must be "involved." This prefatory note may appropriately be

---

*can Society;* Hyde, D. R. and Wolff, Payson, "The American Medical Association:
Power, Purpose and Politics in Organized Medicine," *Yale Law Journal,* 63,
May 1954, pp. 938-1022; and one of the earliest is Channing, W. E., *The Works of
William E. Channing,* Eighth Complete Edition, Vol. I, 1848, in "Remarks on
Associations," pp. 281-332.

† We regret that we were not able to include in this volume papers submitted
by Professors Masatoshi Doi of Doshisha University, W. W. Schroeder of the
Chicago Theological Seminary, and John Hayward of Meadville Seminary;
omitted, too, is a paper, biographical in nature, by the late Leo Lerner, newspaper owner and long-time friend and fellow "social actionist" of J. L. A.'s.

concluded with one of J. L. A.'s favorite quotations from Goethe: "A tradition cannot be inherited; it must be earned."

To the Reverend Hampton E. Price and his staff at Gould Farm, Great Barrington, Massachusetts, I extend my thanks for encouragement at a crucial point in this venture.

It is with gratitude that we acknowledge also our indebtedness to the Staff of John Knox Press. At each stage of production the book has been given meticulous care.

D. B. Robertson

# CONTENTS

# SOCIOLOGICAL THEORY

# I / THE NATURE
# OF VOLUNTARY ASSOCIATIONS

*Karl Hertz*

In the introductory section of *Ethics and Bigness* the editors propose a number of generalizations which they believe to be valid. One of them defines public-interest decision-making as "a complex process of multi-lateral brokerage among legislators, and public executives, in and out of office."[1]

While the editors concern themselves primarily with the ethical dilemmas which confront the individual executive in this situation, obviously the problems to which they have addressed themselves have arisen within the context of a complex society in which large-scale organizations play a major role in ordering the lives of their almost countless members, adherents, clients, or customers. This situation poses for us the twin issues of the nature of the relationships which in fact exist among these organizations and of the kinds of norms which ought to govern these relationships. More accurately put, we need to discover, first, what regularities may be found within the succession of events and processes whose participants are giant organizations and their executives. We require, second, a normative theory of "organizations," their place in the social order and their rights and duties toward one another.

What we require we already possess. Indeed, we have possessed it in an explicit modern statement for a generation and in other forms for a considerably longer period of time, certainly as one basic theme of the Great Tradition of the West—at least since the Reformation of the sixteenth century.

The modern statement is found in the sociological writings of Robert M. MacIver. In *Community*[2] MacIver devotes considerable attention to exploring the relations between associations and the community. In *Society*[3] we have a more explicit formulation of what I shall call the MacIver doctrine. In this book MacIver singles out "the great associations" for special consideration, pointing out both the specific traits which differentiate them from simple, face-to-face groups and also the features common to them as a specific variety of group.

Thus far we are on familiar ground. But what comes next in Mac-Iver's discussion is often overlooked. Beginning with the preliminary distinctions and definitions and running through the specific discussion of the state is a series of consistent assertions about the role of "the great associations" in the social order. Thus MacIver tells us, "It follows from our definition that an association is not a community, but an organization within a community."[4] He continues, "The state is frequently confused with the community. In reality the state is *one* form of social organization, not the whole community in all its aspects."[5] He adds that it is "highly important" that we should realize "the associational character of the state."[6] What he says about the state he also applies to the church and economic organizations. These are the three major instances of "great associations."[7]

In the specific discussion of the state he returns to the same theme. "When we call the state an association we mean that it is a specific organization of society. We distinguish it thereby from the country or the nation on the one hand, from the unity of the social structure on the other."[8] What we have in the MacIver doctrine that state, church, corporation, and so on are associations within the community, not identical with it, is a doctrine of limited sovereignty. Implicit in this doctrine there is a basis for exploring the norms of "multilateral associational relations."

No one familiar with the history of political theory can deny the far-reaching implications of the above propositions. For what MacIver asserts without equivocation does more than challenge the concept of the absolute sovereignty of the state. By also identifying economic and religious associations as "great associations," he gives them places of equal importance and provides a theoretical framework for the discussion of the norms governing the relations among these "great associations." But at the same time, by seeing these associations as necessarily in relationship with one another, MacIver frees himself from any entanglement with laissez-faire theories of limited sovereignty as well as from doctrinaire commitment to an omnipotent state. As a matter of fact, his position cuts right through the usual neat dichotomy of liberal and conservative. What he contends for is, first, a particular view of the nature of "the great associations"; what he demands, second, is that we see the rights and obligations of these "associations" in the light of their constitutions and relationships.

MacIver's doctrine of the "great associations" is thus clearly a normative one; indeed, it may be considered one basic form of democratic social theory. This does not mean that MacIver ignores those historical examples in which the state has asserted far-reaching powers or that he overlooks totalitarianism. On the contrary, he says very explicitly: "But under no conditions which we can conceive, and certainly under no conditions which exist anywhere in the civilized world, is the state all-sufficing. . . . It is true that in recent times a form of state has arisen which claims to be totalitarian, and professes to co-ordinate and to control *all* the interests of its citizens. But the claim, in so far as valid, has been realized only by the forceful suppression of those interests and those groups that could not or would not be 'co-ordinated.' Moreover, in no instance has the end been wholly achieved."[9] Experience thus bears out what theory asserts. Indeed, the MacIver doctrine, whether applied to the state or to the other great associations, is a closely interwoven set of propositions about what these associations are and about what they ought to be.

The crux of the MacIver doctrine lies in the importance given to the "great associations" and the consequences of this emphasis for democratic freedom. In a not unlike manner Professor James Luther Adams has concentrated on the role of "voluntary associations," particularly religious associations and their contributions to both religious and political freedom. The concern which Professor Adams has shown for the left wing of the Reformation, specifically his interest in the Anabaptist doctrine of the church, has been both a theoretical and a practical one. While Professor Adams has explored historical connections in the sixteenth century, he has never lost sight of the problem of the freedom of the Christian man in the twentieth. Congregationalism as a form of ecclesiastical polity, the contract theory of the state, "the right of the people to assemble for the redress of grievances," the definition of an association as a group organized around the pursuit of common interests—these are great interrelated themes in the political struggles of the past centuries and major preoccupations in the literature of descriptive social theory and normative social philosophy.

Empirically we must point out that often the unqualified assertion of certain historical relationships (especially in filio-pietistic historiography) forces the careful student to question the too easy association between "freedom of association" as a norm and the existence of actually free societies. The assertion that the sovereignty of the state is limited does, after all, run contrary to what has been historically attempted more than once. Nor can one deny that the Christian church has often claimed to be more than a voluntary association of believers.

No criticism of either Adams or MacIver is intended in pointing out these difficulties. Both men have been acutely aware of them. But their concern with the theory of associations has focused attention on central issues with respect to social order in our day. Part of what differentiates social systems from the systems studied in physics, chemistry, biology, and so on, is that every historical society is not just a raw fact of nature but also the locus of a set of assertions about the "right ordering of human affairs." Our problem is not merely to validate descriptions, not even to state how values and facts may be related empirically; it is also and above all to ask whether the writ of law may be presumed to run beyond its original bounds, to inquire into the validity of norms of social order and of ideals of justice in human relationships. While it is a prime responsibility of social scientists to discriminate carefully between the "ought" and the "is" in the affairs of mankind, being careful not to confuse what must be separated, it is equally their responsibility not to separate what inherently belongs together, not to sever the vital connections which may exist between commitments to justice in human affairs and the kinds of social order in which justice can flourish.

What is required is first of all an enlarged statement of the theory of associations. What is at stake is nothing less than the conviction that a certain view of what it means to be a man, of what society is—indeed, what it means to believe that a man is a free, responsible, accountable person—requires the kind of social order in which the sovereignty of the great associations is indeed a limited one, in which certain structural characteristics define the relationships between the giant organizations within which human beings live out their lives in industrial societies. In essence, the associational theory, the belief that man is a responsible person, and a free society belong together.

The restatement is deliberately broader than MacIver's original assertion. It implies also the limited sovereignty of economic associations (this may not appear controversial) and equally the limited sovereignty of religious associations (one of the issues with which James Luther Adams has been constantly preoccupied).

Furthermore, the recognition of the interconnectedness of the normative and the descriptive draws attention to the basic issues. The normative content implicit in a sociological proposition may, if the proposition has wide acceptance, have empirical consequences of major significance. "If people define situations as real, they are real in their consequences." If people believe that "the mores can make anything right," not merely as a description of empirical affairs but also as the final word on questions of the morality of power—if, that is, they falsely convert the "is" into the "ought"—they may accept different kinds of political arrangements and tolerate political conduct which in earlier generations would have been spurned as "immoral."

It is not enough to assert that men may order their common existence in different ways and to discover, not surprisingly, that in each society men tend to cherish their particular form of social order. Nor is it enough to note that men may "feel free" under all those varying circumstances. One must also ask what *as a matter of fact* are the live options in any particular social situation, how much is included or excluded as optional, and how many persons actually are able to exercise these options. These are questions of fact, but they have far-reaching normative implications.

The problem of the interrelatedness of the descriptive and normative is much more complex than this illustration suggests. The point here is simply to draw attention to the issue.

In exploring the MacIver doctrine and some of its implications, my concern here will not be comparative; nor will it be to test the normative validity of the doctrine. Instead I shall take the doctrine somewhat for granted. Given the associational theory as a basic democratic theory, given that it has desirable consequences for human freedom, given that it is even in some measure descriptive of democratic practice, what are the antecedent historical conditions required to make it work? What is happening today? And what is the prognosis for tomorrow?

Here we need to be aware of certain ideological traps. "Limited sovereignty" is often the shibboleth of a certain kind of American conservative. Religious conservatives have also not infrequently made common cause with the political right, adding to their political primitivism their own doctrine of the role of religious associations in the community. On the other hand, while the "liberal" has talked of separation over against the churches, he has frequently espoused quite a different doctrine of the role of the political in other human affairs. Indeed, unless we recognize that "liberal" and "conservative" are now words that function primarily as ideological weapons and undertake a fresh re-examination of the issues, we shall probably be able to argue only for certain rapidly obsolescing political platforms.

At the outset we must recognize that objectivity in this context may not mean neutrality; it means recognition of one's own basic normative commitments. For there is no Archimedean point of leverage in the social sciences.

Specifically, we shall operate with a conflict model of society.[10] Society always involves the possibility that different modes of action may be available, that different groups may have opposite commitments in certain situations, and that the social process involves a continually moving and changing system of institutions. We espouse the associational theory in part because it offers built-in mechanisms for the ongoing processes of change. We see it in the possibility of a social order that can change yet maintain continuity with the past over against an order in which change is discontinuous (revolutionary).

Our social roles—citizens, scientists, church members—commit us to involvements and impose certain loyalties on us willy-nilly. But this is not all. For we begin with sociological presuppositions as well as normative ones.

There is a second theoretical perspective on the problems which the MacIver doctrine presents. Professor MacIver's distinction between "absolute" and "limited" sovereignty may be equated, in an approximate way, with communal and associational societies.

This distinction, in various vocabularies a part of the typological method, has recently reappeared in sociological literature in quite a different form. In Gerhard Lenski's provocative study of the role of the religious factor, he uses "communal" and "associational" involvements in religion as major variables. Not only is this distinction of major importance for his empirical analysis, not only is it rooted in the sociological work of Durkheim and Weber and thus part of the great tradition in sociology, but in his concluding chapter Professor Lenski uses his findings with respect to these two variables for some highly important reflections on emerging trends within American society.[11]

Lenski's distinction is not identical with MacIver's. For MacIver "community" refers to areas of social living "marked by some degree of *social coherence*." Its bases are *locality* and *community sentiment*.[12] In Lenski's work the communal is defined in terms of kinship and friendship relationships.[13] But his data show that the four religious communities can also be in some measure identified by neighborhoods.[14] In either instance, we are dealing with relationships that are integral rather than segmented, functionally diffuse rather than functionally specific. In an older language, we are dealing with the distinction between primary and secondary groupings.

One of the important consequences of Lenski's work is the discovery that in any particular institutional area the choice is not either-or. A person may be a highly involved Protestant (Catholic, Jew) in both the communal and the associational senses. Would it be amiss to speculate that the same possibility may hold true in economic and political relationships? Indeed, does not such evidence as ethnic identification with certain political parties, clubs, and territorial boundaries imply just such a double involvement? While the world of labor and business may seem to be the most rational, impersonal, and segmented of the spheres of organized social activity, does not the local network of business leadership, its involvements in country club and community fund, in college fraternity and secret orders, imply at least the continuing existence (however fragmentary at times) of a communal dimension here?[15] Is this perhaps a latent factor in the battle over discrimination? Perhaps the bitter smoke of personal outrage which hangs over many a country club and Greek chapter house is really an eloquent signal that what is at stake is not just membership in a prestige association but admission to a larger community held together by bonds both consanguinal and territorial.

We shall return to these questions below. We need for the moment to indicate some of the significance of the two dimensions. Lenski traced the implications of differential involvement for civil rights and political affiliation. One important finding he reported was that in a number of instances the communal involvement was associated with a conservative, anti-equalitarian position.[16] If we equate "communal" with Cooley's "primary group," we must question the romantic glorification of the primary group, the ideology of the small town as the repository of democratic virtues. (The Ann Arbor of Lenski is no longer a small college town; it is part of the vast Detroit metropolitan complex.)

Before exploring the implications of these distinctions any further, we need to recognize the troublesome nature of the word "community." For the most part probably (leaving aside the ecological use of community by Robert Park and his students), the specific defining characteristic of "community" has been the delimitation of spatial boundaries, territoriality. Those who are bound together in space, as neighbors, even in primitive societies, need not necessarily be bound together also by the web of kinship. The incest tabu indeed must disrupt in some degree the coincidence of kinship and residence. Yet both may also be appealed to within the same society as bases of solidarity. The traditional folk and peasant societies involved both consanguinity and territoriality. So, for that matter, at one point does the modern state: citizenship is conferred on those born of American parents and those born on American soil. In a more extreme fashion, Nazism united Blood and Soil in its ideology.

Thus the "communal" belongs to the "ascriptive solidarities" of the social life. The "associational" contrariwise implies "voluntarism." The two together are not contradictory but related dimensions, varying in degree, of the social order.

Our basic proposition, then, is that the essence of the associational is the voluntary. Here lies the structural connection with democratic theory. An associational society is one in which membership choices are possible, choices among political parties, economic groups, religious organizations, and so on. In addition, by implication, voluntary associations are organized to allow ultimate sovereignty to rest in the membership. Decisions are made from the bottom up—by citizens, stockholders, church members, and so forth.

A further implication is that an associational society is inherently pluralistic. For one cannot speak of choice unless there are alternatives. If, as Herberg has suggested, the various denominations have become essentially three religious communities and if each of these celebrates a variant of the one "American religion," then we have an "Establishment" in a much more far-reaching sense than the recent application of this term to white, Anglo-Saxon American Protestantism would imply. If, as Lenski suggests, these "communal bonds" are tight, if—as the creed of tolerance suggests—proselytizing is in bad taste, so that movement between the "communities" is not viewed as a matter of course, then associationalism is in a bad way.

Here our first question, about antecedent historical conditions, becomes germane. Many have found a major source of American freedom, especially religious freedom, in congregational theories of church government. We must, however, be careful how we assert our historical connections. Seventeenth-century Congregationalism is not identical with organizational pluralism. Indeed, we may even conclude that Massachusetts Bay was determined to have its cake and eat it too. The churches of the Bay were unquestionably organized as voluntary associations; no man was compelled to join a church; no one could claim birthright membership as an Englishman or become a member simply because he so desired. Membership required meeting the conditions of the church covenant. At the same time, however, the community was avowedly Puritan. It was a Christian community with a religious association of visible saints at its heart. In terms of community, the Bay Colony demanded assent to its precepts; in terms of association, its leaders recognized that sainthood could not be compelled. If one substitutes Protestant for Puritan, who can deny that many an American religious conservative would still desire this arrangement today? Is this not, in fact, what is now implied in the sudden popularity of the term "Establishment" in describing the white, Anglo-Saxon Protestant political and social elite in America?

In all fairness we must admit that what Massachusetts Bay avowed, pretending liberty of conscience since it did not compel church membership, Roger Williams challenged as offending liberty of conscience. There can be no free churches where only one church has public status, whether tax-supported or not. Nor can there be freedom of religion where men can disagree only in private. Nor can there be political freedom where only one party is recognized, a free market where there is only one seller or one buyer.

Colonial America was culturally homogeneous in a very large degree. Whatever may have separated Moravians and Presbyterians, Quakers and Anglicans, Lutherans and Baptists, these groups not only shared the common heritage of the Reformation but their American representatives also came largely from the more left-wing associational portion of the Protestant ecclesiastical spectrum. Denominational differences there were, and freedom of choice was a meaningful option within a larger consensus, but both differences and consensus existed within the framework of a larger cultural homogeneity.

This original situation has undergone drastic transformations. On the one hand, indeed, such doctrinal differences as were often still of basic importance to the nineteenth-century American Protestant—differences which in part account for the proliferation of sects and the flourishing of religious innovators—have largely disappeared in the growing similarity of outlook among ostensibly different denominational families. In wide reaches of American urban societies one can hardly recognize any singular distinctions remaining among Lutherans, Presbyterians, Methodists, or adherents of other major denominations.[17] But when choice becomes trivial, pluralism also becomes increasingly meaningless. On the other hand, while Protestants became homogenized, the population of the United States became increasingly heterogeneous. Thus from another vantage point the old question could again be asked. Furthermore, the concomitant changes in population size, industrialization, and urbanization brought new questions to the surface.

Is it far-fetched then to argue that the patterns and problems of Massachusetts Bay are still with us, that the debate between John Cotton and Roger Williams still goes on? For if the nineteenth century is the era of the glorious triumph of associationalism, as religious sects and denominations multiplied, as voluntary societies for the reform or the defense of a variety of causes flourished, as the corporation came into its own and political parties established their hold on national life, this triumph also had an obverse side. The chronic hostility toward the newcomers who streamed to America by the thousands in the nineteenth century revealed the limitations of the Protestant cultural establishment.

Belittle them as we may and condemn them on democratic grounds as we must, the nativistic movements of the nineteenth and early twentieth century did put their finger on a pattern of social change that was of increasing significance. One could assume with the advocates of democratic tolerance the eventual assimilation of the stranger in "the melting pot," and this assumption was widespread. By active missionary endeavor some of the "native" denominations attempted to win the

newcomers to the American churches, but for the most part these efforts failed, as did other efforts directed at homogenization of the population. In the early decades the newer groups often existed as ethnic
enclaves within the larger population, providing little if any real political threat to the national moral consensus. In the third generation,
however, as Will Herberg has pointed out, the process of transformation
has reached maturity. Within the national community we have three
subcommunities. In Herberg's analysis the emphasis falls on the consensus, on the American religion, which has grown out of the process of
change. Lenski's analysis documents and analyzes what Herberg has
discussed more impressionistically. The findings are paradoxical. For
on some issues the American consensus is more fully assented to by
those who are associationally highly involved,[18] presumably therefore
more explicitly committed to the religious tradition. In other instances,
the communally involved have accepted elements of the common cultural tradition. On the whole, however, we must argue that the cultural consensus has not reached as far as Herberg claimed; the possibility of four parallel communities—since Lenski rightly distinguishes
Negro Protestants from white—is not to be ignored. Thus the question
becomes: What are the conditions which must prevail in a free society
with heterogeneous traditions to maintain a single set of institutions in
which all participate freely?

We may expand our question with such subsidiary queries as, What
difference does increasing size make? What about bureaucratic structures? What about the centralizing tendencies in all kinds of organizations? How shall power be distributed? What happens to the nonconformist, the deviant, the political zealot, the religious prophet, the
economic radical? What about their followings? Will these be simply
marginal gatherings nibbling at the edges of vast uniformities? At best,
exotic sports of the new social order?

These questions (not all of which can be answered here) encompass
more than the dilemmas of religious pluralism. In politics, too, we have
seen the narrowing of the alternatives. Third parties have always had a
difficult time in the partisan arena. This is in itself no criticism of
pluralism, for dissenters, mavericks, radicals, and innovating spirits can
hardly expect to be popular heroes. What has happened, however, is
that both by structural change (imposing almost impossible conditions
for getting on the ballot) and also by a dominant cultural mood (dis-
approving those who ask unconventional questions), we have closed the
door on those who beckon us to see the world from a different perspective and to act in unfamiliar ways.[19]

The lack of vital public dissent is as apparent in business and the professions, in labor organizations and in that contemporary ideological stronghold of "voluntarism," private welfare, especially at the level of federated fund-raising. These are sweeping generalizations, of course, and deliberately so.[20] What is at issue is not whether discussion and debate occasionally occur, but that—to repeat what was said about political behavior—discussion and consensus are not "built into" the structure and culture of these major domains of our common life.

Indeed, many of the appeals to "voluntarism," to "freedom of association," and to the other catchwords of "associationalism" are today ideological rather than substantial arguments. Thus, as Michael Rogin has documented, the "voluntarism" of the old AFL served primarily as a means for defending a privileged group of skilled workers; it led finally to opposition to social legislation; in effect, the freedom of workers to organize was equivalent to a freedom to refuse to organize the masses, the commitment to "business [i.e., non-politically oriented] unionism" was a rejection of responsibility for the industrial worker. "Freedom of association" led to the exclusiveness of the elite.[21]

Similarly, most of the pleas for "right to work" laws were couched in the old voluntarist vocabulary; the advocates of these changes were presumably defending the freedom of the working man. Strangely enough, the same conservative defenders of "free labor" were able to write into law clauses compelling unions to represent non-members in grievance procedures as well as extending other collectively negotiated benefits to these same non-members.

In labor-management relations, however, the existence of conflict between the two organized elements of the economic order does ensure us some kind of public presentation of alternative courses of action. Within these groups, however, the dissenter often finds little room, whether he rises to speak in the union hall or at the shareholders meeting. The alternatives tend to be narrow; the pressures to go along with the organization are often overwhelming.

Furthermore, in greater or lesser degree, especially among those in either camp for whom the old vocabulary of voluntarism is still their organizational mother tongue, the existence of oligarchical control is combined with strong ideological resistance to interference from the outside. Thus any attempt from the outside, whether by legislation or by pressure of opinion, to secure structural changes confronts us with another facet of voluntarism, namely, its "private" character. Corporations are presumably "private enterprise," and labor unions "private associations." Their traditional spokesmen challenge the right of an outside authority, specifically a political authority, to set norms, define structural arrangements, limit patterns of action and the power of associations.[22] In associational theory, according to the MacIver doctrine, such intervention would mean that one "great association" exercised control in some degree over the affairs of another.

Specific situations will clarify what is at stake, indicate the range of appeal to "private association," and make manifest the ideological dimensions of the argument. Thus in states which have statutes providing for equal access to public accommodations for members of minority groups, we suddenly discover erstwhile commercial swimming pools becoming private clubs. The "members" must now purchase season tickets—in some instances single admissions are almost completely unavailable—and otherwise bind themselves to "club regulations." But one has difficulty seeing any other changes; the clubs are incorporated from the top down, the membership has no voting rights, and can even be suspended by action of the management or management's employees. These "clubs" are about as associational as many book clubs, record clubs, and other mass-marketing enterprises. But presumably as "private clubs" they are exempt from public accommodation statutes.

A more serious instance is the unofficial power wielded by local real estate boards. These presumably private associations, with their national code of ethics, in fact limit the freedom of action of the local realtor, especially in the field of open occupancy or mixed housing. We may well ask, by what legal right does a presumably private and voluntary organization exercise such power, with such long-run consequences for the good or ill of society?

The country club, the genuinely private club, belongs in some degree in a different category. But even here the question arises—exclusion from membership may be exclusion from power within the community. Further illustrations could be added, all of them touched with "the public interest." Medical societies and bar associations would be especially intriguing to analyze in terms of the categories of "private," "voluntary," and "freedom of association."

The fact that both structural characteristics and cultural norms are involved ought to warn us against a one-sided diagnosis of the ills of a pluralistic society. We cannot blame increasing size for everything; nor is officialdom necessarily diabolic. No doubt increasing size has contributed to the monolithic character of many organizations. For increasing size may beget bureaucracy, and bureaucracies tend to abhor conflict and controversy. In many large national organizations, including the churches, the necessity for proceeding through "channels," the use by the upper echelons of officialdom of the letter of the procedural manual, no doubt discourages many a would-be objector. The game is simply not worth the candle if it has to be played on the other fellow's terms, and if he has all the resources of the organization at his command.

An additional major factor in silencing dissent is, of course, the social norm of teamwork.[23] Let it be admitted, debate in the fullest sense of the word rarely flourishes at meetings of American voluntary associations. Organized opposition is the exception. An interesting case in point is the transformation of American charitable enterprises into philanthropic bureaucracies run by the established leaders of the community. Under a flood tide of slogans (and worse), we have now reached the point where individual enterprise on the part of local welfare agencies is almost the sin against the Holy Ghost.

Paradoxically, sometimes the enterprises of the majority thus fall by the wayside; thus in community after community Protestant leaders persuade their wives and the clergy not to press the issue of including Planned Parenthood Clinics in United Funds, since Planned Parenthood is controversial.[24] How often Negro militants are silenced by the Urban League and how much this may have to do with the slow pace of change in many Northern cities is another question well worth empirical study.

The norm of "teamwork" often appears as the natural companion of the bureaucratization of structure, i.e., the development of a hierarchically organized system of officeholders each with limited "expert" responsibilities. Nor is the logic of bureaucracy confined to the large-scale association; the small educational institution, the community hospital, the small business firm, and even the rearing of children[25] have followed the pattern of functional rationality which bureaucracy implies.

Structural change, i.e., bureaucratic associationalism, and normative innovation, "working for the team," may thus together constitute the essence of the problem for a bureaucratic society. The ideological appeals to "freedom" meanwhile mask the degree to which the order of things associational is rearranged into an order of things "communal," or, at least, the degree to which each of us is fitted into the available pigeonholes (religious, economic, political) within which careers may be pursued.

To assert over against this norm of teamwork a norm of dissent and factionalism is vulgar, if not downright unchristian and un-American; it is to suggest that the structural developments are not yet inevitable, that there is still room for "the dissidence of dissent, and the Protestantism of the Protestant religion." To do so is, of course, to pick the "wrong side." For the prevalence of the norm of "teamwork," a "good" word in the vocabulary of associationalism, militates most strongly against the development of "parties" within the bureaucratic organizations of our day. To organize support in advance for a proposal or a candidate is "bad form" in the churches, in college faculties, in welfare and benevolent organizations. Only in political parties is factionalism "tolerated," although never encouraged.

The situation of political parties and of trade unions—even, from a somewhat different perspective, of corporations—is modified by the fact that all of these are already in one sense or another "conflict organizations" and alternative choices exist. This is clearest perhaps in the instance of politics; it is somewhat meaningful in the trade union world, not in the sense that the unionist can get a job elsewhere but that at least for some there is a place in the ranks of management. It is symbolically true for the stockholder; he can sell his General Motors stock and buy Chrysler or IBM, but transactions of this kind have little in common with decision-making in the power struggle.

Not all of these considerations, of course, touch a major theme in the MacIver doctrine, namely, that the "great associations" exist alongside one another, that most of us are simultaneously involved in all three of them, and that a crucial issue is that of conflicting jurisdictions.

Put in the sharpest terms, what belongs to the internal structure of the association so far as decision-making is concerned and what belongs out in public? The older distinctions between the inner world of the spirit and the outer world of the law and related Protestant distinctions are hardly sufficient for the issue. In other words, which decisions belong to "the members only," and in which may outsiders intervene? Which actions are touched with "the public interest"? "Public interest" here means more than "of concern to political authority"; it means that other associations within the community have a stake in the decision. It means, therefore, that each association is also involved in "external relations" and that these relations define not only the conflicts and controversies going on at any time in the community but define also a sphere within which consensus is hammered out by conflict and coalition, negotiation and compromise, a sphere within which principles are always to some degree ambiguous, undergoing redefinition, being restated to reflect the changing relationships among the major associational groups.

What we need is an acceptable set of rules for carrying on these controversies, not attitudes which ignore and deplore, or "principles" which are ideological masks for the defense of privilege. We need a consensus on the rules of dissensus in a pluralistic society; we need a set of Marquis of Queensbury rules for the verbal fisticuffs and non-violent wrestling for power in which viable great associations must necessarily engage.

The necessity exists because conflict exists. Solutions which ignore conflict are therefore not acceptable. Attitudes which deplore the fact that labor and management have different interests, that Protestants and Catholics have differing stakes in certain legal enactments, that religious groups may find "the powers that be" hostile to religious interests—all of these, hoping to manufacture consensus artificially, to persuade all to a feigned loyalty to "the team," miss the essential point of the pluralist position.

That essential point once received a classic statement in American political theory. For, while the authors of *The Federalist Papers* did not speak directly in terms of an associational theory of the state, they recognized the existence of a plurality of factions (interest groups) within the body politic. In the tenth essay, Madison explicitly raises the question of factionalism and its relationship to liberty. His essential answer, still the pluralistic answer, is that the best safeguard against the usurpation of liberty by a single all-powerful faction is not the suppression of factions but their multiplication. Implied in this prescription is an open recognition that the social process will always include conflict and dissensus. This is a part of the price of freedom.

Pluralism must be built into the structure of our social order. It must be something more than a fond hope, a principle to which we pay lip service. *Structure must undergird dissensus.* Within the ranks of the trade unions the best example of a structured pluralism is found in the typographical union.[26] The two-party system, in which through a variety of legislative provisions, each party, even in its moments of defeat, retains some offices and some kind of foothold in public life, is another example of structured pluralism. The survival of "socialism" in certain American cities was probably largely due to the existence of a body of officeholders, the basic cadre for any political organization.

To suggest open "factionalism" in the churches, in some circles, is akin to blasphemy. But actually, differences of opinion already exist; indeed, organizational bases for "parties" are also available. The theological seminaries constitute one such base; strong congregations, another; regional synods would be a third. What is needed is to give recognition to what already exists and to provide some basic security—and provision for debate.

What is required then is not only the recognition of structural bases for pluralism but also the acceptance of dissensus as a value. The Congress of the United States and the state legislatures can somehow carry on even though much legislation of a crucial nature sometimes passes by only the smallest of margins—and politicians who have lined up on opposite sides of the fence and perhaps made violent speeches against one another can be seen to wine and dine together thereafter—because they accept the rules of the game. A legislative enactment decided by a single vote is as valid a law as one passed unanimously; a candidate elected by a fraction of a percentage point is still the legal officeholder—the country does not split apart, nor despite strong ideological differences do the political parties fall apart. Because along with the norm of dissensus, the politician accepts the norm of freedom of choice—and enough voters may change their minds to give him a majority the next time.

Some political decisions are, of course, irrevocable, but these are rarely the ones decided by a close majority. Pluralism implies the freedom of the individual to change his mind, his decisions, and his memberships. Because the politician has accepted the fact, built into the very institution of government, that alternatives are available, that there are two sides to every question, he manages to live with defeat as well as to rejoice in victory. Politics, American style—or democratic style—is probably a classic example of solutions to the problem of organization.

Politics illustrates another essential of pluralism. If competing choices are to be meaningful, the organizations which espouse them must have resources adequate for survival over a period of time. What keeps local county political machines going, even in the smallest rural counties, is that they have offices at their disposal—everything from precinct committeemen to endorsements on federal patronage. Unfortunately, local governments are not as well situated, and one reason for the decline of local responsibility lies simply in the lack of adequate financial resources to solve contemporary problems. These two considerations taken together suggest that only by developing strong bases of opposition is a vital pluralism possible.

Finally, and this word is directed particularly to religious organizations, unless free movement from one religious community to another is possible—a free movement resting on more adequate communications—and unless such movement represents a genuine choice among religious alternatives and not just a move in the status game, religious pluralism does not have much meaning. The real test of Christian tolerance is not that we sweetly agree with everyone and call every man brother because we see eye to eye with him, but that, although we disagree and disagree strongly and openly with our religious brother—and engage in full and free discussion with him—we nevertheless call him brother. This does not preclude ecumenism—but it does mean a recognition of limited sovereignty in all spheres, in order that man may never be simply the instrument of associations and the victim of power manipulations but that through his associations and through his use of power he might express what it means to be a free man.

A further proposition has been implicit in this discussion. Let us recognize, once and for all, that the problem of the "great associations" is not one of defining separate spheres enclosed by rigid boundaries within which each should operate. The "wall of separation" doctrine in church-state relations employs a misleading metaphor. Our rhetorical habits keep us from defining the problem correctly. Our concern is for the kinds of relationships possible among the great associations.

The church-state debate is a critical example. The basic premise of POAU, if taken seriously as a program of separation aimed at abuses as well as at Roman Catholicism, insists that within the framework of the national community all religious associations are essentially private ones and all private associations must be kept exclusively private. Its image of the state is that of neutral umpire. In effect, however, this may raise one great association to a position of dominance over another. Furthermore, there are a great many unexamined premises in the POAU position. If religion is really a private matter in the fullest sense, then we are all in the situation of the Protestants in Spain or the Christians behind the Iron and Bamboo curtains. Such "religion" may suffice for some, but it runs counter to one great strand of the Judeo-Christian tradition of the West, the continuing insistence of prophetic spirits that they may engage in a moral criticism of the social order, that they may demand structural change in the community. More than that, the POAU position suggests that religious convictions either have no public consequences or that "the devout" may not through political processes attempt to win public assent for their convictions. The historical record is against such a conception of the place of religion in American life.[27]

The vital question always is: given religious groups as one of the major associational domains within the community, how shall they be related to the other great domains, the political and the economic? Answers may vary with specific situations; different coalitions may form around different issues. But the ideological use of the separation doctrine—whether of the religious from the political, or the political from the economic—misses the essence of the American tradition; the American protest is against unilateral structural control of the one sphere of life by another, against totalitarianisms of the right or the left. The maintenance of *structural independence is a condition of freedom;* the maintenance of *vital relationships is equally a condition of meaningful freedom.*

The consequence of this position is simply that only if we accept as legitimate free and effective encounter, attended as necessary by controversy and partisan alignment, does the MacIver doctrine fit a heterogeneous society. For in the hurly-burly of three-sided conflict exist possibilities of providing organizational bases for dissent, of developing coalitions with respect to particular concerns, of effecting those rearrangements of position from time to time which will correspond to changing circumstances. Concretely, I am suggesting that Republicans and Democrats may differ in their appraisal of certain religious issues, just as Protestants and Catholics may differ on political issues; or as men with other associational allegiances may align themselves in other ways. We accept political differences as part of the "order of nature" in social affairs; I propose accepting these differences elsewhere as well.

All of this implies a conflict theory of society.[28] It implies a view of "human nature" as less than perfect. It rejects political Utopianism, moral perfectionism in religion, and all those forms of piety which tend to freeze the social order into conformity with any single philosophy or political blueprint. It openly views all positions—political, religious, and economic—as partial and biased, counsels skepticism about means, a willingness to work out particular situations pragmatically, a readiness for compromise and coalition. Its loyalties are to differences of opinion, to the freedom of man and his freedom to change his allegiances. Its doctrine is that institutions are made for man; to absolutize them is to forsake grace for works. But the Spirit still bloweth whither it listeth, grace may break through at any point, and institutions may shatter under its force; amidst the disorder of such conflicts and change, the freedom of man is secured.

Freedom thus requires structural diversity. Lipset and others have shown the import of this for trade union democracy.[29] Order in a free society requires that diversity and partisan differences be accepted as culturally legitimate. This is already true (with exceptions) in political life. We must work to make it legitimate in the other "great associations."

Two final considerations and a footnote on the Anabaptist doctrine of the church. One of the basic propositions which Georg Simmel put forth bears serious examination, namely, that the multiplication of disagreements contributes to stability.[30] Here is a theory of pluralism based on dissensus rather than consensus. Simmel's theory is not new; its classic political formulation is in the tenth essay of *The Federalist Papers,* referred to above. But Simmel's formulation generalizes it to cover all the major domains of our common life.

Practical realization of effective dissensus has other conditions. "Grass roots" responsibility cannot be meaningful unless resources are adequate. One reason for the transfer of functions from the courthouse to the state capitol, from the state capitol to Washington, is quite simply the inadequacy of local resources for the solution of local problems. These problems do not necessarily beset local religious organizations or trade union locals in the same way; but the same stipulation remains: resources must be adequate for responsible action.

The importance of the Anabaptist doctrine of the church—despite its tendency to slight the one holy, catholic, and apostolic church—was that its doctrine of congregational self-government created precisely the local source of responsibility which could provide the structural guarantee of diversity. Its tragedy has been twofold: one has been its abuse to foster divisiveness rather than diversity within a larger unity; the other has been the abdication of local initiative, the inertia of the faithful, until and unless officialdom prods them from above.

The pluralistic view of society is not only democratic; it is humanitarian in the largest sense, for it recognizes that the freedom of man is part of his essence. A national community which respects the basic dignity of man, a position implicit in the MacIver doctrine, a paramount element in James Luther Adams' concern with the Anabaptist doctrine of the church, will be committed to individual freedom, to institutional structures combining the communal and the associational in a continuing vitalizing tension and encounter. The encounters and controversies of strong men and strong factions who accept disagreement and debate as the natural state of the body politic will be the best hope for effective pluralism in a heterogeneous society.

# ASSOCIATIONS IN HISTORY: THEORY AND PRACTICE

# II / ASSOCIATIONAL THOUGHT
# IN EARLY CALVINISM

*Frederick S. Carney*

Frederic W. Maitland has commented that Otto von Gierke's relating of the state and the corporation (or collegium) in a single political doctrine is something of a stumbling block for the modern reader.
Yet "when all is said and done," Maitland observes, "there seems to
be a genus of which state and corporation are species."[1] This observation could well apply to the Calvinist political literature of the late sixteenth and early seventeenth centuries, as Gierke was well aware.
Moreover, the number of species constituting the genus within early
Calvinism can be enlarged even further by the addition of family, city,
and church, indeed, by all associations so far as they are relatively
stable and are seen from the standpoint of the political problem of
rule or authority.

Most modern discussions of Calvinist political thought have concentrated entirely upon the theory of the state and its relation to the church.
Seldom in the last hundred years has the more extensive framework of associations in general been examined. Thus other politically relevant associations, such as the family, collegium, and city,
have been largely neglected. If between these smaller associations and
larger ones there was for early Calvinists a continuity of basic principles
and appropriate procedures, as there seems to have been, then such
neglect has limited our resources for understanding even the state and
the church in early Calvinist thought. This essay is a modest contribution
toward the correction of this oversight.

There is, I submit, a distinct danger to be avoided in such an examination of the associational thought of early Calvinism. This is to concentrate one's attention upon questions addressed to the Calvinist political
literature which are not well designed to evoke its basic character. Unfortunately, Otto von Gierke's monumental studies in the history
and theory of groups, to which all serious students of associational
thought must finally pay their profound respect, fell prey to this dan-

ger.[2] He was deeply committed to the notion that the true association is a "group person" possessing a moral personality by virtue of its existence alone, and owes this existence neither to a fiction or concession from higher authority, nor to a contract or agreement among individuals or smaller associations. Because these early Calvinist writings, and especially the works of Althusius upon which he devoted such obvious affection, did not contain this notion of the group person, Gierke was finally required by the limitations of his own typology to consider them to be either individualist or absolutist in emphasis. He took the former choice because he read Roman private-law interpretations into their use of the concepts of society (*societas*) and covenant (*pactum*). But this was a mistake, as I shall attempt to make clear later, a mistake that he might have avoided had he not been predisposed to regard the group-person idea as the only conceptual alternative to what he felt to be the twin evils of individualism and absolutism into which the modern world had fallen.

Another instance of succumbing to this danger is John W. Allen's predisposition to interpret these writers according to whether they advocated obedience or resistance to rulers.[3] He believed that Calvin's position was one of obedience at almost all costs, while these later Calvinists were, depending upon who was ruling at any given time, mostly given to a theory of resistance. By this advocacy of resistance they were understood by Allen to have broken politically with Calvin, and to have borrowed decisively from the late medieval world.[4] Although Allen was quite properly reacting thereby against earlier attempts to democratize Calvin, his concentration upon this somewhat superficial question in politics led him, in my judgment, to misconstrue in a fundamental way the political thought both of Calvin and of these Calvinists. Unfortunately, a large number of modern political studies of early Calvinism have been unduly dependent upon the answers either Gierke or Allen obtained to questions that were not as helpful in getting at the materials to which they were addressed as they might have been.

There are three questions arising from my own studies in early Calvinism which seem to me to be the most important ones to ask. (1) Is there a common character of group life in all associations, and if so what is it? (2) What role does law perform in early Calvinist associational thought? (3) What significance is to be attributed to the frequent use of the social, political, or religious covenant in this thought?

Before proceeding with these questions, however, I want to say a word about primary sources. A vast quantity of relevant Calvinist literature is available for our purposes. I have selected thirteen books upon which to focus attention, twelve of which were originally published during the sixty-two-year period from 1556 to 1618. Perhaps the best known of these is the *Vindiciae contra tyrannos* written under the pseudonym of "Junius Brutus."[5] This work, which reflects the Huguenot agony in the decade immediately following the massacre of St. Bartholomew's Day in 1572, is especially interesting for its religious and political covenant theory. A shorter work of the same milieu is the anonymous *De jure magistratuum*.[6] This is generally attributed to Theodore Beza, the successor to John Calvin at Geneva. Two works by the celebrated French jurist Francis Hotman are included. The first is *Franco-Gallia,* a historical argument for French constitutionalism,[7] and the second is *Quaestionum illustrium,* a more properly jurisprudential volume.[8] In addition to these French writings, the Scottish literary humanist George Buchanan published in the same decade his widely read *De jure regni apud Scotos,*[9] and somewhat earlier the exiled English divine John Ponet produced his *Shorte Treatise of Politike Power.*[10] One of the richest volumes of Calvinist social thought is by an Italian theologian who taught at Strassburg with Martin Bucer, and later at Oxford and Zürich. This is the *Loci communes* of Peter Martyr Vermigli.[11] His interpretation of Romans 13 in his *Commentaria in epistolam S. Pauli ad Romanos* is also rewarding for our purposes.[12] Another Italian, Jerome Zanchius, who taught theology at Strassburg, Heidelberg, and Neustadt, wrote extensively on the relation of natural to divine law in his *De lege Dei,*[13] and on the family in his *Commentarius in epistolam ad Ephesios.*[14] But the culminating social theorist of this entire group of writers is undoubtedly Johannes Althusius of Herborn and Emden. His *Politica*[15] and his *Dicaelogicae,*[16] which pertain respectively to political science and jurisprudence, are of particular interest to us in this essay. Finally, I have included the Scottish preacher Samuel Rutherford's *Lex, Rex* because, although written almost thirty years after the latest of these other books, it reflects more of their spirit than it does of the rising individualism of his own time and place.[17]

## I

Althusius, the most systematic of the early Calvinist social theorists, began his best-known treatise with the following words: "Politics is the art of associating (*consociandi*) men for the purpose of establishing, cultivating, and conserving social life among them. Whence it is called 'symbiotics.' The subject matter of politics is therefore association (*consociatio*)."[18] After elaborating the general aspects of this thesis, he presents the five associations of family, collegium, city, province, and commonwealth as the all-inclusive parts of a single political doctrine.[19] His point is that there is a continuity of political principle and procedure, a common character of group life, in all of these associations.

Although none of our other authors gives explicit attention to all five of these associations, Althusius' point would have been accepted, I believe, by them. Zanchius writes in his commentary on Ephesians that subjection of wives to husbands, children to parents, and servants to masters is part of a general political doctrine that embraces the whole of human society, including the commonwealth.[20] Vermigli refers to a king as the father of his country, and says that he should act toward his subjects with a fatherly love.[21] Brutus argues that as a father in Christian lands has no power over his son's life, so a prince has no legitimate power to destroy or harm the commonwealth entrusted to him.[22] Beza compares the right of divorce by a wife from a husband who so abuses her as to defeat the very purpose of marriage with the right of a people to overthrow a tyrant.[23] The comparisons can also move in the other direction. Vermigli suggests, for example, that husbands should love their wives as an excellent ruler loves the commonwealth over which he presides.[24] The church also participates in these comparisons. The theocratic polity of ancient Israel is affirmed by these writers as an obvious standard for the commonwealth.[25] Zanchius also makes it a standard for the family.[26] A number of them maintain that as a council is superior to a pope, so the organized community is superior to its supreme magistrate.[27] Sometimes the superiority of a chapter to its bishop is appealed to as the proper analogy for the commonwealth.[28] Or the movement may be from family to church, as when Vermigli compares church government with a well-ordered household.[29]

The specific nature of this continuity of organizational principles among associations must now be more closely examined.[30] Gierke clearly saw this continuity in the political thought of Brutus, Beza, and especially Althusius. But he wrongly attributed it, in my judgment, to a common foundation of all groups in natural-law rights of individuals directly, and of associations indirectly.[31] This is not to say that Gierke approved of such a foundation. To the contrary, he set his own theory of the group person, which he felt to be the true German *Genossenschaft,* over against both natural-law individualism (with its achievement of larger wholes by contract) and authoritarian unity (based on images found, for the most part, in imperial Roman public law).[32]

I think we will be closer to the view of these early Calvinists if instead we conceive of associations as ways of living faithfully within, and thus of fulfilling, various aspects of human life. Associations are the places and occasions wherein we give ourselves to the glory of God and the welfare of the neighbor. They are the purposes that arise when men acknowledge fundamental human needs, and commit themselves to meeting them. Thus associations are teleologically oriented. The *tela,* however, are neither completely given nor completely arbitrary. They are given (or natural) in that there is a determinate structure to God's creation. They are arbitrary (or voluntary) both in their adaptation to time and place (human finiteness) and in their special arrangements for limiting and ameliorating the social consequences of man's corruption (human sinfulness). The constitution or basic structure of an association, then, is a function of the vocation that, through the combination of necessity and volition, the association serves. And rule or government of an association is to be judged by how well it contributes to this vocation. Most early Calvinists were as opposed to weak rule as to tyrannical rule, for both vitiated the vocation for which an association exists. And they preferred, whenever possible, to provide such structure for their associations as to avoid both abuses. It is in this sense that they were constitutionalists.

Althusius conceives the family as the more natural of private associations, possessing as it does "the same boundaries as life itself,"[33] and the collegium as the more voluntary in that it "need not last as long as the lifetime of a man."[34] Nevertheless, he recognizes both elements in each association. For, on the one hand, many aspects of family life rest upon the tacit or expressed agreement of its members, and, on the other, the collegium presumably exists to meet natural needs and should not be disbanded unless alternative means are available to provide them. He carries this integral relationship of necessity and volition into the public associations of city, province, and commonwealth. When we arrive at his discussion of the commonwealth, we are told that its end is, as that of other associations, piety toward God and justice toward the neighbor.[35] Furthermore, the communion of public life that exists within the commonwealth is the process by which the members "communicate everything necessary and useful to [this end], and remove and do away with everything to the contrary."[36] He thereafter devotes considerable attention to the kind of structure most likely to accomplish this vocation in the long run. In so doing, both contingent circumstances of time and place, and the corruptions of rulers and subjects, play major roles in his calculations. Although he is disposed toward strong rule in order best to accomplish the purposes of association, his highly articulated doctrine of the ephors is designed to indicate proper processes for limiting corruption and for overcoming it when it occurs.[37]

It has already been noted that our other authors were not as politically systematic as Althusius. Nevertheless, the same characteristics are, for the most part, either expressed or implied by them. Rutherford, for example, says that "as domestic society is by nature's instinct, so is civil society natural *in radice,* in the root, and voluntary *in mode,* in the mode of coalescing."[38] He thereupon proceeds to set forth a doctrine of the people in its relation to rulers which, while obviously addressed to the political struggles of mid-seventeenth-century England, has numerous parallels to that of Althusius.[39]

Buchanan argues that what the physician is to the human body the ruler is to the body politic. The end of each is the health of its charge.[40] But rulers also need restraints upon them to increase the probability that they will fulfill the purpose for which they exist. The following conversation is instructive.

> *Buchanan.* Will you allow me to make a brief abstract of what has been said? . . .
> *Maitland.* By all means.
> *Buchanan.* First of all, we ascertained that the human species was by nature made for society, and for living in community?
> *Maitland.* We did so.
> *Buchanan.* We also agreed that a king, for being a man of consummate virtue, was chosen as a guardian to the society.[41]
> *Maitland.* That is true.
> *Buchanan.* And as the mutual quarrels of the people had introduced the necessity of creating kings, so the injuries done by kings to their subjects occasioned the desire of laws.
> *Maitland.* I own it.
> *Buchanan.* Laws, therefore, we judged a specimen of the regal art, as the precepts of medicine are of the medical art.
> *Maitland.* We did so.
> *Buchanan.* As we could not allow to either a singular and exact knowledge of his art, we judged that each should, in his method of cure, follow the prescribed rules of his art than act at random.
> *Maitland.* It is safer undoubtedly.
> *Buchanan.* But the precepts of the medical art seemed not of one single kind.
> *Maitland.* How?
> *Buchanan.* Some we found calculated for preserving, and others for restoring health.

*Maitland.* The division is just.
*Buchanan.* How is it with the regal art?
*Maitland.* It contains, I think, as many species.[42]

But if the king fails in this duty through either neglect or oppression, if he consistently violates the prescribed rules for the health of the body politic, then the ephors (or optimates of the realm) are appealed to for corrective action. Indeed, this notion of the ephors, which derived among early Calvinists from Calvin himself,[43] is employed quite extensively throughout this literature.[44] Its function is one of making clear the seriousness with which public associations are expected to pursue, and as nearly as possible to fulfill, their fundamental purposes, and of indicating appropriate processes for correction when they do not.

In order to make the position of these early Calvinists as clear as possible, it may be helpful to compare them with their great contemporary Jean Bodin. Bodin shared with these Calvinists a profound interest not only in the state, but also in other associations. "The well-ordered family," he observed, "is a true image of the commonwealth, and domestic comparable with sovereign authority. It follows that the household is the model of right order in the commonwealth."[45] But Bodin's notion of what constitutes a well-ordered family differs from theirs. He was obsessed with the need for social unity, and thus assigns the father a power of life and death over his children. It is to be assumed, he says, that a father "would only commit such an act upon good and just grounds," but this provides no basis for a son to "defend himself and resist by force any unjust attempt at coercion on the part of the father."[46] The early Calvinist could not on principle agree with such absolutism in the family, nor with its implication for the commonwealth.

Likewise, there is a difference concerning collegia or corporations. Bodin was not opposed to collegia as such. To the contrary, he found them quite helpful. "The first princes and lawgivers," he wrote, "not yet having discovered how to keep their subjects in the paths of justice, founded fraternities, guilds, and communities; for the parts and members of the body politic being thereby brought into agreement among themselves, it would be easier to regulate the commonwealth as a whole."[47] But Bodin also held that the state may deny the right to exist to those collegia that are inconvenient to the sovereign ruler. "A corporation or a guild," he says, "is a legal right of communal organization, subject to sovereign power. The word legal implies that it is authorized by the sovereign, for without his permission no guild can be authorized."[48] Although Bodin begged for moderation by the state in dealing with collegia, and observed that "to abolish all such societies is to embark on a barbarous tyranny," he nevertheless noted that "it is also dangerous to permit all sorts of assemblies and fraternities whatsoever," and thereby indicated his belief that the right of particular collegia to exist remains in the hands of the state.[49] The position of the early Calvinists, on the other hand, was that a collegium that is not in principle illicit required no special fiat from the state for its existence.[50] Its own purposes, both natural and volitional, constitute its *raison d'être,* not its convenience to the state.[51]

The commonwealth or state provides a final point of contrast. The general dimensions of Bodin's position on the commonwealth is anticipated by his discussion of the family. The father with absolute power over his children, who should nevertheless exercise such power with moderation, becomes the archetype of the sovereign ruler in the commonwealth.[52] The early Calvinists, however, insisted that sovereignty (the political power that recognizes no human superior) rests with the people, not with the ruler thereof. The people is the owner of sovereignty, and the ruler exercises only a delegated authority. Such authority exists for the benefit of the people, not the people for authority.[53] *Salus populi, lex suprema*—the health of the people is the supreme law. The people, of course, is the organized community, and the right of sovereignty it possesses arises from the purposes for which the community exists. Gierke to the contrary notwithstanding, the people is not, for these early Calvinists, an assemblage of individuals bearing inborn rights, or of groups constructed on the basis of such rights. It is singular, not plural.[54] When confronted with Bodin's question as to how a king can govern those to whom he is also subject,[55] these Calvinists responded that the king is over individuals, but under the people (as the organized community). Thus an important distinction was employed between persons who were private citizens, and persons (such as the ephors) who served as officials of the organized community. Only the latter should take initiative in political action.[56]

Thus there would seem to be a common character of all associations in Calvinist political literature. This common character is neither individualist nor absolutist. It begins neither with the self-evident rights of individuals nor with the *a priori* authority of rulers. Rather it asks what is the vocation (or purpose) of any association, and how can this association be so organized as to accomplish its essential business. Authority (or rule) becomes a function of vocation; and great care must be taken to provide constitutional structures, both ideological and institutional, that authority not become unduly weak or corrupt. One can therefore properly say that Calvinist associational thought involves at its very roots both the acknowledgment of a high calling and the recognition of ever-present finitude and sin.

## II

The second task of this essay is to identify more precisely the contribution of law to man's associational life. One is impressed in reading this literature by its great emphasis upon law. References abound therein to natural law, to the Decalogue, to the Great Commandment, to divine law, to common law, to Roman law, to canon law, and to the proper laws of many nations, churches, cities, and collegia. I will attempt, first, to sort out the nature and functioning of these various species of law and, second, to identify what seems to be the general role law performs in the associational thought of early Calvinism.

There is some variation in the extent of the employment of natural-law doctrine by the Calvinist writers we are examining. Generally speaking, it can be said that Brutus, Beza, Hotman, Buchanan, Althusius, and Rutherford make very extensive use of it, while Vermigli, Zanchius, and possibly Ponet employ it more sparingly. For the former group of writers it has equal authority with the Decalogue and the Great Commandment, possessing as it does the same essential content and apparently being about equally available to contemporary Western man. The latter group also holds it to have the same content, but assigns it somewhat lesser authority because of the belief that man's sin has so clouded his reason as to make it less available to him. At the same time, the former group is more likely to emphasize its indicative qualities as pointing to what is observably present and cognizable in man's associational life, and the latter group its imperative qualities as expressing what has been planted in the minds of men and commanded of them from their birth.

The two groups are not actually very far apart so far as its political use is concerned, and Ponet's position regarding it may serve as something of a bridge between them. The law of nature, he writes, is "first planted and grafted only in the mind of man, then afterwards, because his mind was through sin defiled, filled with darkness, and incumbered with many doubts, set forth in the Ten Commandments, and after that reduced by Christ our saviour into these two words: Thou shalt love thy Lord above all things, and thy neighbor as thy self."[57] Later Ponet adds, "There is no man can deny but that the ethnics (albeit they had not the right and perfect true knowledge of God) were endued with the knowledge of the law of nature. For it is not private law to a few or certain people, but common to all: not written in books, but grafted in the hearts of men: not made by man, but ordained by God: which we have not learned, received, or read, but taken, sucked, and drawn out of nature: whereunto we are not taught, but

made: not instructed, but seasoned: and (as St. Paul saith) men's conscience bear witness of it."[58]

Common law is the term usually employed by these Calvinists to
express the shared content of natural law, the Decalogue, and the
Great Commandment. Sometimes it pertains merely to knowledge, but
often it implies both knowledge and inclination. As an example of the
latter, Althusius writes: "By the knowledge imprinted within us by God,
which is called conscience, man knows and understands law (jus)
and the means to be employed or avoided for maintaining obedience
to law. By this inclination, or secret impulse of nature, man is urged
to perform what he understands to be just, and to avoid what he
knows to be wicked. . . . In this common law (jus commune) is set
forth for all men nothing other than the general theory and practice of
love, both for God and for one's neighbor."[59] Then he adds: "Christ
set forth two headings of this common law. The first pertains to the performance of our duty immediately to God, and the second to what is
owed to our neighbor. In the former are the precepts and mandates
that guide the pious and religious life of acknowledging and worship-
ping God. . . . In the latter table are those mandates and precepts that
concern the just, and the more civil and political, life."[60]

Juxtaposed to common law is proper law, or the positive laws of
various states, churches, cities, collegia, and families. All proper law
ought to reflect and express this common law, however much adaptations may be made to physical conditions, social customs, and human
temperaments in various places and times.

When this common law is viewed as God's demand upon men and
associations, it is sometimes called divine law. Thus the content of
divine law is none other than that of common law. The content is now
perceived, however, as the general form or structure of one's response to God. But even common law, or one of its expressions,
can be understood in terms of this response to God. It is therefore appropriate for Rutherford to ask "who can deny the law of nature to be
a divine law?"[61] Likewise Zanchius is reflecting the same perspective
when he writes that "the law of nature is the will of God."[62]

Roman law is another category that is extensively employed by these
Calvinist writers. By Roman law I here mean the Corpus juris civilis
(Digest, Code, Institutes, and Novels) and the many medieval and
Renaissance commentaries upon various aspects of it. Brutus, Vermigli,
Althusius, and Rutherford drew especially heavily from it. Hotman
did also, but unlike the others he adopted an ambiguous attitude toward
it because of his strong preference for the customary law of France
which, he believed, was being undermined by the absolutist elements

adopted in France from the Roman law. Originally this Roman law was the proper law of the late Roman empire. But ever since its revival beginning in the twelfth century it had come to be employed increasingly as if it were an articulate body of common law. This is to say, it served as a meta-positive source of legal and political obligation. Of particular interest to us in this essay is the long-standing conflict among its interpreters between those who appealed to its absolutist concepts of empire for support of highly monarchist views of the state or commonwealth, and those who, following Bartolus, developed its theory of corporations (usually *universitates* and *collegia*) in constitutional directions and later applied this theory to all associations including the state. Gierke has commented insightfully on the manner in which political philosophy has thus grown out of law, especially in the "direct application of the ideas and rules of corporation law to the largest and highest communities."[63] It is important to note here that these Calvinist writers tended to follow the Bartolist approach, and in so doing to derive from this body of common law (assuming it can properly be called such) very concrete associational conceptions. The many references in these writers to Roman law are almost entirely to its more constitutional adaptations as opposed to its earlier and more absolutist constructions.[64]

Somewhat surprising is the attention paid by these Calvinists to canon law. All refer to it occasionally, and Brutus, Rutherford, Althusius, and above all Vermigli repeatedly appeal to it.[65] While canon law has the status of proper law for Catholics, it serves for the Calvinists very much as Roman law does, namely, as a written expression of common law. Especially appealed to are its discussions of the relation of the guardian (*tutor*) to his ward (*pupillus*) in the family and of the relation of an abbot to his chapter in the church, both of which relations are construed in constitutional fashion and established as authentic models for other associations. Brian Tierney's recent study of the role of corporation theory in the development of fourteenth-century conciliar thought understandably does not mention these Calvinists, but it does provide a valuable analysis of those aspects of canon law which particularly attracted their attention.[66]

So much for the various species of law in early Calvinist associational thought. I now propose to indicate the role of law therein. First, law is the expression of an objective rightness to be discovered and affirmed about man's associational experience. Such objective rightness can be discovered because it is assumed that there is a primordial essence of all true group life. The general form of this objective rightness that law expresses is neither absolutist nor individualist. Rather it is a tran-

scendent constitutionalism. When a seriousness of associational vocation (or high calling) is joined with a recognition of the grave possibilities of sin and finitude to disrupt the pursuit of this vocation, a
constitutionalism that can keep political authority (and thereby associational vitality) from becoming unduly corrupt or weak is a decided necessity. The expression of this objective rightness is both common and
proper. So far as it points to elements that are shared by all associations,
this expression is common law in one or more of its modes: natural
law, the Decalogue, and the Great Commandment, or even in a sense
Roman and canon law. So far as it adapts these shared elements of constitutionalism to the circumstances of time and space confronting a
particular association (whether a commonwealth, church, city, collegium, or family), it is proper law.

Second, law is the innate tendency of men and associations to be
constitutionally oriented, to be by nature motivated to live according
to the primordial essence of all true group life as well as according to
the special determinations of this essence in particular associations. This
second aspect of law is more prominent in Vermigli, Althusius, Buchanan, and Brutus than it is in the other writers. Nevertheless, they all
presuppose this second (or ontic) aspect as the precondition of the
first (or epistemic) aspect. Without it, law as the expression of objective
rightness would be an external and somewhat arbitrary imposition on
associational life. With it, law as the expression of objective rightness is the clarification of what men by nature seek.

Third, law is also the shape of man's response to God. As such, it is
divine law, which is nothing other than common law (and, in a secondary sense, proper law) understood as God's command. Because divine
law and common law share the same content, divine law (or the
theological aspect of law) is conformity to common law as a continuing act of faithfulness to God.

Needless to say, this presentation is an analysis of what these Calvinists mean ideally by law. They were also quite ready to recognize the
corruptive elements of law present in every association, and to attempt
to confront them with considerable realism.

### III

The final task of this essay is to assess the significance of the idea of
covenant (or contract) in the associational thought of these early Calvinists. Three forms of covenant are prominent, although not equally so
for all writers. The first is the social covenant, or the contract to live
helpfully and harmoniously together.[67] The second is the political
covenant, or the contract pertaining to the mode of government and

to the personnel who hold office therein.[68] The third is the religious covenant, or the contract between an association and God, or between its leaders and God, to maintain a faithful and just life.[69]

Many modern interpreters of this literature have assumed, wrongly in my judgment, that the Roman law conception of contract was determinative for these writers. Although these Calvinists made extensive use of many Roman law conceptions, they sometimes did so (as in this instance) only with significant qualifications deriving from their strong vocational orientation. Roman law had two basic branches, public and private. Public law pertained to all levels of civil government and, prior to Bartolist adaptations, tended to presuppose an absolutist authority on the part of the empire (or commonwealth) of which city and province were mere administrative units. Private law, on the other hand, pertained to the nongovernmental actions of individuals, especially in the economic realm. Contract (*pactum*) was fundamental to Roman private law as the means by which the partnership (*societas*) was usually initiated and maintained. This partnership was highly voluntaristic in that its existence rooted, for the largest part, in the continued willingness of the contracting parties that it should exist.[70] In the seventeenth century this essentially private law conception was borrowed by a number of political theorists, including Hobbes and Locke, and applied to the public realm in the sense of contracts of society and government. Thus all social and political life is seen as partaking somewhat of the model of a Roman private-law partnership. And it became easy for modern interpreters to read this later seventeenth-century development back into these earlier Calvinist writers. As a result, they are often interpreted as being more voluntaristic and individualistic in political thought than they actually were.

It is important to note, however, that Roman private law was not the only historical source for covenant, or contract, theory. Two others obviously influenced these Calvinists. The first was the Ciceronian notion of *societas* in which the more natural and given aspects of social life are emphasized.[71] The reference of *societas* here is to a social endowment rooted in the very nature of things, and within which every man must participate if he is to be truly human.[72] The prominent attention to Cicero (and other Stoics) in this Calvinist literature should restrain us from assuming too quickly that references therein to *societas* are to the Roman private-law notion.

The other, and even more important, source of covenant theory for the Calvinists was the Bible. The Old Covenant and the New Covenant are understood by them as relations of grace which men are called to accept, and which make a continuing demand upon the recipient, rather than as relations which men create by acts of their will, and which can be dispensed with as they choose.

These two alternative sources of covenant theory (Ciceronian and Biblical) influence the use by these Calvinists of the Roman law notion of *societas*. The following passage from Althusius is highly instructive: "The simple and private association (*consociatio*) is a society (*societas*) and symbiosis (*symbiosis*) initiated by a special covenant (*pactum*) among the members for the purpose of bringing together and holding in common a particular interest. This is done according to their agreement (*conditio*) and way of life (*vitae genus*), that is, according to what is necessary (*necessitas*) and useful (*utilitas*) for organized private symbiotic life."[73] Particularly to be noted is the manner in which the seemingly more voluntary elements are balanced, even in the private association, by the more natural elements. What is initiated by a covenant is both a "society" and a "symbiosis." This is not only according to "agreement," but also according to "way of life," which, being interpreted, means according to what is both "necessary" and "useful." Indeed, Althusius seldom uses the word *societas* to indicate the basic associational genus of which family, collegium, city, province, and commonwealth are conceived to be species. Rather he develops a new, and historically less loaded, word *consociatio* to express the balance he ascertains between the natural and the voluntary in his constitutional analysis of associational life.

Nevertheless, the notion of the voluntary is very closely tied up with the idea of covenant in these Calvinist writers. Basically, covenant is the agreement of an association, or its leaders, to conduct the life of that association in keeping with the primordial essence of all true group life, as well as with the particular expressions of this essence as adopted by the association in respect to the circumstances of its time and place. Thus the social and political covenants are agreements to conform to common law, and to establish and conform to such proper laws as shall seem best designed to express and fulfill the common law. And just as divine law is not different in content from common law, so the religious covenant is not essentially different in concrete intention from the social and political covenants. When the agreement of men to live according to what true group life requires is understood to be, above all, an agreement with God, then the form of the covenant is primarily religious.[74] It is in this sense that Brutus writes, "We honor our prince and love our neighbor because of and for the love of God."[75]

In concluding this essay addressed to the questions of the basic character of associations, of the role of law, and of the significance of covenant theory in the social thought of these early Calvinists, I wish to make one further observation. Events of major importance to Western man have occurred since these writers finished their labors. The two most important of these events may well be the decline of belief in a *Corpus Christianorum,* which belief they presupposed, and the rise of historical consciousness, of which they had very little conception. Nevertheless, the problems they posed may still be important ones today, even though they obviously require reformulation in order to enter into the dialogue of modern man. This is to say that among our most pressing needs today is a renewed understanding of the nature of associational life, of the role of law therein, and of the significance of the voluntary in the structures of our existence.

# III / THE RELIGIOUS BACKGROUND
# OF THE IDEA OF A LOYAL OPPOSITION

A Protestant Contribution to the Theory
and Practice of the Ecumenical Dialogue

*George H. Williams*

In the long history of Christianity as in the history of the Old Covenant People before it, in recurrent manifestations of renewal, reformation, dissent, schism, and heresy, we see innumerable variations of
two principles in tension: *loyalty* to the tradition of the community and
conscientious *opposition* in the name of selected and pre-eminent standards of that community. Opposition has often been registered in appeal to the original covenant, the basic Scripture, the universal tradition. Loyalty to and conscientious compliance with the consensus of
the Church is often expressed in terms of thinking with the mind of the
whole Church, both contemporary and historic. Although a *critical*
loyalty and a *conscientious* opposition need not be mutually exclusive,
it is evident that what has emerged as Protestantism has been disposed
to self-legitimate opposition even when this would result in the fragmentation of visible unity, not only in Western Christendom in the sixteenth century but within the several confessional communities that issued from the Reformation Era. In contrast, Roman Catholicism has so
emphasized the principle of loyalty, unity, and external order in the
tradition of both Petrine and imperial Rome that conscientious dissent
has been either surreptitiously sublimated in the proliferation of various orders or neutralized in the principle of inward assent or forcibly
ejected.

In the contemporary ecumenical situation, however, the importance
of both these impulses—conscientious, forthright opposition in deliberation and loyalty to the clarified mind of the Church—are being
more fully recognized on either side. Protestantism is surely more disposed to the claims of tradition than was formerly the case. Catholicism for its part has in the Second Vatican Council experienced the
wholesomeness of loyal diversity in conciliar debate.

It is the purpose of the following essay to reflect historically on the emergence of the political idea of a loyal opposition, specifically in the development of British parliamentary usage, and to suggest in the end the possibility of adapting the concept and even some of the procedure to the realm of the ecumenical dialogue. Evangelical liberty in the age of Martin Luther meant primarily individual freedom in Christ. Today this more individualistic evangelical liberty combined with the more corporate loyal opposition with its sources in the second reformation of the Church of England in the seventeenth century has considerable significance in the contemporary evolution of the modalities of the ecumenical dialogue. The essay is subtitled a *Protestant* contribution to the theory and practice of this dialogue for the reason that the emergence of the institution of loyal opposition in British parliamentary history has in fact a conciliar background and must be seen in part as a permanent political deposit of certain principles inherent in the royalist-parliamentary reformation of the Church in England in the sixteenth century and particularly of the Anglican-Puritan efforts at revisions of that reformation in the seventeenth century. The English parliamentary concept of His Majesty's Loyal Opposition has a long history, most of it political, but an earlier portion of it also ecclesiastical.

In honoring James Luther Adams, I wish to sketch the ecclesio-political history of the idea of a loyal opposition and then suggest some application of the concept to the present ecumenical dialogue. Although not an historian of the English Constitution, I hope that selected observations on one aspect of parliamentary development will be of interest to those knowledgeable in Tudor, Stuart, and Georgian history. As an ecumenist, I hope that my suggestions in the second half of the essay will be of interest to all those in any way involved in the great assignment laid upon Protestants ever since the entry of the Catholic Church into the ecumenical movement.

I believe that the idea of parliamentary polarization and a clarification of loyal opposition will have significance in an understanding of the relation between the conservatives (integralists) and the progressives (liberals) in the Catholic Church in their ecumenical and regional councils and the papally instituted appointive-elective, deliberative-legislative episcopal synod, in the measure that the monarchical role of the Pope is progressively clarified in the context of episcopal collegiality and the priesthood of the faithful (the apostolate of the laity). In the evolution of the British Constitution, the principle of opposition shifted from that between Parliament and monarch to that within Parliament itself. Similarly now that the authority of the Pope as unique spiritual sovereign is uncontested by Catholics (Vatican Council I), we may expect the gradual emergence *mutatis mutandis* of the principle of a loyal opposition within the deliberative episcopal college in regional and ecumenical councils. To be sure, most Catholics for the moment shy away from a term and usage that is almost uniquely an Anglo-American and genetically a Protestant concept.[1]

Thus a more immediate application of the concept of a loyal opposition will be in the clarification of the character of the Protestant-Catholic encounter and ultimately in the development of a Protestant theology, as it were, of committed interconfessional dialogue and ecumenical exchange.

To be sure, there is as yet no fully ecumenical council envisaged in which the Orthodox, Catholics, and Protestants would participate together. At present there is only the spreading "participation" of designated observers in the councils of the other ecclesiastical bodies. As anything more highly structured than this procedure is very unlikely in the foreseeable future, the "ecumenical council" envisaged in the following essay is in effect hypothetical. But it is being anticipated experientially in the ever-enlarging community of responsible ecumenists of all communions wherever they gather in ecumenical dialogue or trialogue, yearning for unity but critically loyal to the various traditions in which their lot is cast.

The following essay is divided into three parts. Part I is an introduction to the term "Loyal Opposition," with reference also to an episode of the Second Vatican Council which prompted the present inquiry. Part II is an examination of the religious presupposition of the English Reformation Parliament and the religio-political developments of the seventeenth century. Part III is a projection of the political institution of the loyal opposition into the realm of the ecumenical dialogue.

### I. INTRODUCTION: THE NINETEENTH-CENTURY ORIGIN OF THE TERM "HIS MAJESTY'S OPPOSITION"

As for the term "His Majesty's Loyal Opposition," it is characteristic of the English that verbalization of one of Britain's great concepts should have entered the vocabulary of world politics in the form of a sally of humor in the practical realm of domestic finance! The familiar phrase "His Majesty's Opposition" was coined in Parliament by the Speaker of the House, Sir John Cam Hobhouse, Baron Broughton. Under George IV on April 10, 1826, the House of Commons was debating the salary of the president of the board of trade. In the course of the debate the Speaker remarked that, for his part, he thought that the specific proposition was harder on His Majesty's opposition than on His Majesty's ministers, whereupon the House is recorded as having

laughed in appreciation of the turn of phrase. And almost immediately
Secretary George Canning, destined soon to become Tory Prime Minister, picked up the expression, remarking: "It [the proposal] originated, not with His Majesty's government, but with those whom the
honorable gentleman has [just] designated His Majesty's opposition."[2]
The second burst of laughter which followed Canning's appropriation
of Hobhouse's witty turn of phrase jocularly fixed it as a part of British
parliamentary vocabulary; and the leader today of Her Majesty's Opposition is, indeed, a salaried officer in precisely this capacity of *opposition* under the crown. It is assumed that he will work peaceably and
responsibly for the interests of the crown in his dual functions as critic of
the existing government and as leader of a potential, alternative government with different policies.

The idea and practice of a salaried leader of a loyal opposition is so
distinctively British that, of course, they who know it best have been
least articulate about its nature and theory. And, needless to say, four of
five recent studies of parliamentary opposition were written by
Germans![3]

What I shall later have to say about the idea of a loyal opposition in
the realm of ecumenical dialogue was prompted by an experience
shared with Professor Adams, both of us having served as Observers at
the Second Vatican Council, and notably by a certain episode at the end
of the second session.

On the next to last day of the second session, on December 3, 1963,
when Vatican II commemorated the four-hundredth anniversary of the
closing of the Council of Trent, a whole bloc of Observers, largely
representing the Lutheran and Reformed churches of the Continent,
declined on principle to attend, because the Council of Trent had
anathematized their Protestant forebears. An American Observer might
have pointed out that when Americans come to commemorate the two-
hundredth anniversary of the Declaration of Independence, we can be
sure that the British Ambassador in Washington will be affably prominent in the celebration. But the Continental Observers could not so
look upon the revolution of 1517 and the counter-revolution of 1563.
In contrast, all the Observers from English-speaking lands with others
felt just as strongly about the impropriety of being conspicuously absent.[4]

The differentiation of behavior among the Observers at the Council
may seem an insufficiently representative episode. It is adduced because it happens to have been the occasion for my reflecting on the
culturally conditioned psychologies of dialogue.

Who represented the authentic "opposition" on December third?

Some will reply: Those who stayed away from this particular celebration out of respect for their honored Protestant forebears. But it is the contention of the present essay to suggest that a no less truly loyal opposition was made up of those who out of courtesy and respect and openness to suasion kept their places as Observers, as on any other day of the Council session, whether they would agree or not with the points to be made.

As it happily turned out, the commemorative address by the cardinal patriarch of Venice was quite irenic. Moreover, there followed his allocution one of the most unusual events of the entire Council: two Lay Auditors came forward to address the Pope in solemn assembly. Particularly notable was the address of Professor Jean Guitton of Paris in his call for a theology of true diversity, both human *and Christian,* with the plea that the Roman Church might, through sacrifice on the purely human side, become truly catholic or universal.[5] Catholicism, with its theology of unity and ordered liberty, now rightly understands, he said, its ecumenical task in thinking through a theology of ecclesiological diversity.

Protestantism, one may add in contrast, having long made the best of diversity and pluralism, has for some time known that it must take up more seriously the theology of unity and do what it can in the new ecumenical climate with such scriptural affirmations as in Ephesians (4:3 f.) on the one body, one Spirit, and one Lord; with such scriptural intimations of primordial unity in Petrine faith as in Matthew (16:18); and with such scriptural prayers for unity as that of the only High Priest himself, as interpreted by John (17:21).

Since the concept of a loyal opposition, a precious legacy from the era of the Second Reformation in the history of the *Ecclesia Anglicana,* may have significance for the processes of an emergent unity in diversity, it is profitable for the ecumenist, as well as the ecclesiastical historian and the political theorist, to look again at this distinctive impulse in English reformed Christianity and, by derivation, in Anglo-American or British-American Christianity and polity.

II. RELIGIOUS PRESUPPOSITIONS OF THE REFORMATION PARLIA-
MENT AND ITS SUCCESSORS: FROM THE HOLY SPIRIT IN A CON-
CILIAR PARLIAMENT TO THE SPIRIT OF PATRIOTISM IN PARTY
DEBATE

The Churches of the Magisterial Reformation—Lutheran, Reformed, and particularly the Anglican and the Scottish—drew upon the theory of late medieval conciliarism, according to which the magistrates and the universities (the latter supported increasingly by royal or

princely endowments) constituted a loyal opposition to the central
authority in the Church.[6] But the ecclesio-constitutional assimilation of
conciliarism was quite different on the part of the reformed churches of
the Continent and of those in the British Isles.[7]

On the Continent the Lutheran churches never rejected outright the
possibility of a free General Council. But when territorial churches
were in fact reformed, it was under princes serving as emergency
bishops (*Notbischöfe*). Except for Hesse and certain city states the
synodal or conciliar role in reformation was abortive. But whereas the
Lutherans called for a National Council (loosely: a provincial synod)
and, never getting one except for the imperial Diet, settled for a territorial princely (or in Sweden, a royal) reformation, the Anglicans,
recognizing in principle a General Council, allowed Parliament (the
English counterpart of the imperial Diet) to serve provisionally but
effectively as a kind of National Council. In England (and Scotland)
the reformation of the whole of the realm gave the national Parliament
(or the national Assembly) the character of a regional council acting for
reform without tarrying for a General Council.

By reason of this historic coincidence the Reformation experience of
all denominations derivable from the established Kirk of Scotland and
particularly from the *Ecclesia Anglicana*—in the first instance, the
World Anglican Communion, but also including in the end Presbyterianism, Congregationalism, and Methodism—has been markedly different from that of the Reformed and the Lutheran churches of the
Continent. The difference (to put it in a phrasing that is admittedly
clearer than any single document of the British reformation) is that
England was reformed by a mixed parliament of episcopal and temporal peers and commoners who regarded themselves, in effect, as a
National Council. As heirs of the late medieval conciliar tradition, they
were confident that the Holy Spirit, in the conditions of a vexed and
divided Christendom, spoke through them for the healing of their part
of Christendom until such a time as a validly convoked General Council
could deliberate. The Henrician reformation presupposed that, pending
a properly called General Council, Parliament under the guidance of
the Holy Spirit could act for the whole body of England, which seen in
one perspective is the body politic and in another the body ecclesiastical. In effect, Parliament became the national synod of the *Ecclesia
Anglicana reformanda*.

The reformation in the kingdom of Scotland, it should be remarked
at this point, was in the end carried out and collectively embodied in
the national Assembly of the Kirk rather than in the disjointed Scottish
Parliament of the estates of the realm. This northern variation on the

conciliar theme, once the two parliaments had become one in the United Kingdom in 1707, only enhances the significance of religious pluralism in the evolution of the British concept and institution of a loyal parliamentary opposition. With the king of the United Kingdom a Presbyterian in Scotland and an Anglican in England, the old Reformation principle *cuius regio, eius religio* had indeed changed: His the region, *theirs* his religion!

This unobtrusive separation of the sovereign's personal religion and politics, however, only seemed to strengthen the religious factor in the evaluation of British political institutions. In a word, the British sense for the "spirit of the constitution," "public spirit," "the spirit of liberty," "party spirit" within the context of parliamentary debate, and the embryonic form, at least, of the later two-party system may, indeed, be traced back through the age of the first Hanoverian, George I, and his Whig Prime Minister Robert Walpole and the Tory theorist of the opposition, Henry St. John Viscount Bolingbroke; back to the Glorious Revolution of 1688; back through the Restoration, the Commonwealth, the Civil Wars, and the age of the first Stuarts; back finally to the Reformation Parliament, which considered itself the organ of the Holy Spirit working unerringly as through a national synod, for want—amid the pangs of reformation and the fragmentation of Christendom—of a recognizably valid General Council of the whole Church.

## A. *The Tudor Parliament as a Mixed National Synod*

The English Parliament made up of bishops, temporal lords, and commoners seemed to some theorists under Henry VIII exactly what the conciliarist Marsilius of Padua had in mind in his *Defensor Pacis* (1324) in defense of Emperor Louis of Bavaria, a mixed synod of clergy and laymen. By 1535 the *Defensor* had been translated into English with these programmatic words:[8] "All faythfull chrysten men are and ought to be called men of the churche, as well as those, whiche be not preestes, as those whiche be preestes."[9]

The lawyer Christopher St. German, a major Tudor theorist of the conciliar character of Parliament, in a treatise concerning the *Power of the Clergy and the Laws of the Realm* (1534), virtually repeated these words, making them his own when he wrote "that by the worde churche is not understande [sic] only the clergye, for they undoutydly make not the chyrche, for the hole congregation of Christian people maketh the chyrche."[10] St. German, holding the King supreme in temporalities and in the national Church, insisted that the King was "the Head, and most chief and principal Part of the Parliament,"[11] speaking always of the "King in Parliament" and not of the King by himself.

The nation ultimately, Parliament representatively, was in the Henrician theory the King's body politic *and ecclesiastic* as distinguished from his body natural.[12] St. German regarded Parliament so conceived as a national mixed synod, guided by the Holy Spirit, and as such incapable of error, in effect, infallible.[13] The King in Parliament, as it were, can do no wrong. As early as 1530, St. German in *Doctor and Student,* destined to be the basic handbook for law students in England up to the time of Sir William Blackstone, enunciated parliamentary supremacy and infallibility in these words: "[I]t cannot be thought that a Statute that is made by authority of the whole Realm, as well as of the King and of the Lords Spiritual and Temporal, as of all the Commons, will recite a thing against the Truth."[14]

It was the view of the extreme Tudor theorists of Parliament as an omnicompetent national synod that the king in succession to Constantine had the inherent right to call a council rather than the Pope.[15] So Thomas Boleyn, the Earl of Wiltshire, as early as 1530.[16]

Over against the claim that Parliament was a mixed synod, answering to the requirements of a reforming council for the nation in the tradition of Marsilius of Padua and Jean Gerson, were the Convocation of the clergy of the province of Canterbury and the less important Convocation or provincial synod of York with their traditional claim to the exclusive right to represent the Church in the sense of the *sacerdotium.* As early as the spring of 1532 Henry VIII had become aware of the competing claims of Convocation and Parliament, and he sent for the Speaker of the House and twelve members, informing them that he had just discovered a major constitutional issue—the anomaly of the bishops of his realm acting in two different kinds of representative capacity:

> We thought that ye clergie of our realme had been our subiectes wholy, but now wee haue well perceived [he said] that thei bee but halfe our subiectes, yea and scace our subiectes . . . [T]he copie of bothe the othes [oathes] I deliver here to you, requirying you to inuent some ordre that we bee not thus deluded of our Spirituall subiectes.[17]

By 15 May 1532, after anxious debate the Convocation of Canterbury, that is, the provincial synod of the Catholic province of Canterbury, handed in the document known thereafter as the Submission of the Clergy.[18] It was to be embodied two years later in 1534 in an Act of Parliament.[19] By this time St. German, in *An Answer to a Letter,* dealing with this and other statutes passed in 1534, went so far in his doctrine of parliamentary supremacy as to ask rhetorically:

> Why should not the parlyament, then, whiche representeth the whole catholyke churche of England expounde scrypture rather than the convocatyon which representeth onely the clergy?[20]

The answer of many Henricians was clearly that Parliament alone should represent the whole Church. Another of these extremists was Thomas Cromwell who, in his fearsome interrogation of one John More, receiver of the House of Sion and allegedly in contact with Robert Aske's rebellion in the North (the Pilgrimage of Grace, 1536), forced John More under duress to spell out the extremist presupposition of the Reformation Parliament, namely, that Parliament was an unerring synod equivalent to a General Council and never to be reversed by one. Asked Cromwell menacingly:

> What [now] is your oppynyon touching . . . generall Councell, where-unto some afferme and hold oppynyon that the holy goost is present and if the holy goost be present, how then can an acte of parliament of this Realme take away the force of the general Councell?

John More felt obliged to reply:

> Myn oppynyon concernyng the generall Councell is that an acte of parliament made in this Realme for the commenwelthe of the same ought rather to be obserued within the same Realme then any generall Councell. And I thynke that the holy goost is as verely present at such an acte as ever he was [in] any general Councell.[21]

The asseveration that the Holy Spirit is present in a political assembly is the Constantinian and late medieval conciliar legacy to the English Parliament in the age of reformation. No wonder that the Catholic envoy Bishop Gian Matteo Giberti of Verona would call Henry's Parliament a *conciliabulum*.[22]

The extremist views of Christopher St. German and Thomas Cromwell concerning Parliament's spiritual omnicompetence were not, however, fully shared by more representative architects of the Henrician establishment such as King Henry himself in his more responsible moods, Archbishop Thomas Cranmer, and the court chaplain and canonist Thomas Starkey. All three of these proponents of the *via media* between Continental Protestantism and Roman Catholicism, namely, royalist, episcopal Anglicanism, while they interpreted the English Parliament as, indeed, a mixed national synod, considered it *provisional,* ecclesiastically binding only *until such a time as a truly ecumenical or General Council might be called.*[23] Common to expo-nents of this more moderate view was the conviction, based upon fresh and far-ranging research, that the first ecumenical councils had been called by the emperors. With the Papacy itself most in need of reform-ing and with the Holy Roman Emperor a ruler of only a portion of Christendom, the right to call a General Council now seemed to de-volve upon all Christian princes, on the Emperor as but the first among equal sovereigns.

Insofar, of course, as Henry claimed the imperial dignity or it was claimed for him, he could in succession to Constantine and Justinian be said to have full competence to call a valid council for his own "imperial" realm.[24] And on the ground that the proposed (abortive) General Council at Mantua (1536) would not be truly free, Henry and his advisers called for princely reformations:

> Wherfore we thinke it nowe best, that euery prince call a councille prouincial, and euery prince to redresse his owne realme.[25]

A related anonymous tract on exegetical problems made the same point:

> The trouth is that none hath the authorite to expounde the doubtes of scrypture and to bynde the people to beleve that exposition but ye universal churche gathered by auctorite of kings and princes, or a particular churche gatherid by auctorite of the prince there, and the exposition of suche a particular church shall stande in effect tyll an universale general counsail be gatherid.[26]

Thomas Cranmer, signing "The Judgment of Convocation concerning General Councils" (1536), expressed a similar view, holding that the provisional national reformation would be subject to a validly called General Council:

> As concerning general councils . . . there never was, nor is, anything devised, invented, nor instituted by our forefathers more expedient, or more necessary to the establishment of our faith . . . for the reducing of Christ's people unto one perfect unity and concord in religion, than by the having of general councils, so that the same be lawfully had, and congregated in *Spiritu Sancto.* . . .[27]

In the meantime Cranmer, presupposing that national kingdom and visible church were coterminous and convinced that the royal sovereignty had been usurped by the sovereign of a foreign principality—who happened also to be the Bishop of Rome—, was quite confident that the Holy Spirit could speak truly through the proper organs of the church-nation.[28] Moreover, since upon the "residue of Christian princes" devolved, according to Cranmer and other "moderate" Anglicans, the responsibility for properly calling a General Council, and for providing that the Pope also be subject to its decisions like any other, and since the princes of Christendom could not for the foreseeable future agree on the time, place, and agenda of such a council, the Parliamentary "Council" of England became the national-ecclesiastical organ invested with (provisional) authority in spiritual matters:

> It symythe expedient that suche thynge as be nowe of late confessed to be abused in tyme past be playnly confermyd by parliament or hooly

prohibite so that it be prohibite that no man within this Realm shall hereafter hold any oppynyon or mayntayne any reasonyng therin contrary to the mynd and determynacion of the parliament in that behalfe.[29]

By the time England had consolidated her conciliar-parliamentary reformation, the Council of Trent appeared remote and irrelevant to the English *rex, imperator in regno suo.* "What has it to do with the royal majesty?",[30] Henry asked disparagingly of Trent, when his own synodal diet had achieved so much. But this could not be the final gesture of the reformed *Ecclesia Anglicana.* In James I the idea of summoning a General Council would flicker momentarily.

Neither Thomas Cranmer nor Thomas Cromwell, moreover, who so sought to undergird the authority of Henry that they were prepared to interpret him as emperor in line with Constantine and his Parliament with or without qualification as a synod of the imperial realm of England in line with that of Nicaea, could ever have anticipated that that supposedly unerring Parliament, under the leadership of another Cromwell, would put to death both a king and an archbishop, and radically alter the polity and confession of the re-reformed *Ecclesia Anglicana* through its creature, the Westminster Assembly of Divines.

## B. *From Anglican Cavalier and Puritan Roundhead to Tory and Whig*

It is not here the place to trace the evolution of parliamentary theory and practice in the seventeenth century, from the Civil Wars, involving the three realms of Anglican-Presbyterian England, Presbyterian Scotland, and Catholic-Protestant Ireland, to the Restoration of the Stuart dynasty in the person of Charles II in 1660, and the Glorious (Whig) Revolution of 1688. In this turmoil of the Second Reformation of England, the *Ecclesia Anglicana,* still preoccupied with polity, broke up into religio-political parties ranging from Catholics, High Church Anglicans, Puritan "anglicans," Presbyterian "anglicans," and, as it were, Independent "anglicans" (called by modern scholarship, nonseparating Congregationalists), not to mention all of the parties still further to the left: Baptists, Fifth Monarchy Men, Levellers, Diggers, Familists, and Quakers. English Christendom unraveled into as many churches and sects as did Christendom as a whole in the sixteenth-century upheaval; but in England the process of division, though it led to civil wars, never led, except in the case of a few extremists, to the abandonment of the idea that insular England should be somehow a religio-political unity. What might be called a lower-case "anglicanism" was the nationalist-theocratic presupposition of all the middle parties of that revolutionary age, from the episcopal Anglicans to the Congregational anglicans[31] (while the extreme right, the Catholics, and the extreme left, the separatists, met in their rejection of this basic "anglican" postulate that Church and society be one).

Nor is this the place to rehearse the evolution of parliamentary theory and the struggle for sovereignty in the seventeenth century;[32] but we can remark in passing that as in the period of the Reformation Parliament the house of Convocation was also sometimes regarded as a competing claimant to the role of representing the English body politic and ecclesiastic, so it was in the reign of Charles I, who, when his Parliament proved recalcitrant, tried to use Convocation for quasi-political ratifications and ecclesiastical measures. But more to our point now is the fact that some of the experience and practice of what would eventually emerge as the institution of a loyal opposition *within* Parliament in the eighteenth century was, in the period of Cromwellian ascendancy, in part worked through in the New Model Army with permanent residues for the development of English parliamentary dialectic.[33]

In the growing tension between a Presbyterianizing Parliament and the Army which it had commissioned, made up of officers with Independent sympathies like Oliver Cromwell and Henry Ireton and of troopers with Leveller convictions, there suddenly took form a quasi-parliamentary body, which, with representative "Agitators" from the common soldiery, formed with their officers a General Council of the Army. The whole Army, modeled on that of Gideon (Judges 6-8), came close to regarding itself as representative of the true British Israel. When Parliament sought to disband the Army of "saints" as a threat to Presbyterian parliamentary supremacy, the General Council of the Army, notably at Putney in the fall of 1647, engaged in a series of debates on matters ranging from immediate political strategy to ecclesiastical settlement, with liberty of conscience a major theme. As the Henrician Parliament once regarded itself as a National Reformation *synod,* so now the Army, primarily made up of Independents and of parties further to the left, regarded itself as a *parliament;* and the antagonists within the radical Puritan Council of the Army polarized into (a) the defenders of property and a franchise based thereon along with government by representation (Cromwell and Ireton) and (b) the more radical defenders of the principle of direct and continuous consent of the governed in universal manhood suffrage: "The poorest he hath a life to live in England as well as the richest he" (Thomas Rainborough and the Levellers).

The profound religious and tactical disagreements within the Council became painfully evident in the course of the intense and forthright debate, all the more poignant for the basic agreement between the In-

dependents and the Levellers—roughly the officers and the troopers—
that, though antagonists, they were together sincerely seeking "the
guidance of God" and the recovery of "that presence of God that seems
to withdraw from us."

At just such a point in the debate Cromwell in fact suggested an ad-
journment, awaiting a different mood "to see what God will direct you
to say to us, that whilst we are going one way, and you another, we be
not both destroyed. This requires [guidance from the] Spirit."[34] Elsewhere he calls for additional representatives from the regiments "that
so there may be a liberal and free debate had amongst us, that we may
understand really, as before God, the bottom of our desires, and that we
may seek God together, and see if God will give us an *uniting spirit*."[35]
Cromwell with his antagonists deplored the palpable contradictions in
the utterance of earnest debaters alike concerned to give expression to
the Spirit, all purposing to be of one mind in Christ (I Corinthians
2:16). He wished to think that these "contradictions are not so much in
the end as in the way."[36] Concerned for unity, yet never willing to cut
off debate, and troubled by the contradictions among equally zealous
exegetes of Scripture and hearkeners to the guidance of the Holy
Spirit, yet confident that "God is not the author of contradictions,"
Cromwell in a reflective and irenic passage in the Putney exchange
finally declared:

> As to the dispensations of God, it was more particular [i.e., specific]
> in the time of the Law [of Moses than in the time of the law] written
> in our hearts, that word within us, the mind of Christ [Hebrews 8:10; I
> Corinthians 2:16]; and truly when we have no other more particular im-
> pression of the power of God going forth with us, I think that this law
> and this [word] speaking [within us], which truly is in every man who
> hath the Spirit of God, *we are to have regard to.* . . . When it [a given
> utterance of such a man] doth not carry its evidence with it, of the
> power of God to convince us clearly, our best way is to judge the con-
> formity or disformity of [it with] the law written within us, which is
> the law of the Spirit of God, the mind of God, the mind of Christ. . . .
> [F]or my part I do not know any outward evidence of what proceeds
> from the Spirit of God more clear than this: the appearance of meek-
> ness and gentleness and mercy and patience and forbearance and love,
> and a desire to do good to all and to destroy none that can be saved.[37]

Cromwell's religio-political meditation around a bivouac fire is a strand
of thought destined to be rewoven into the parliamentary tradition of
debate.

Eventually the passions of the main-line religious parties and social
classes in Army, Convocation, and Rump Parliament found sublimated
expression in the emergence of parliamentary parties of Whig and Tory

after the Glorious Revolution of 1688. The very names of these parties were, originally, slanderous religious epithets or labels, evocative of the bitterness of fratricide and interfaith conflict.

The name Tory was derived from the Erse of Ireland, *tóraidhe,* meaning originally a robber, applied in the seventeenth century to the High Anglican and Catholic lord or retainer who refused to be pushed back into Oliver Cromwell's Irish Reserve, the County of Connaught, to make way for the Scottish and English colonists. The Tory was, so to speak, an outlaw Catholic; and the label was affixed to the most ardent of the royalists who even after the Glorious Revolution would secretly (or avowedly: the Nonjurors) persist in their religio-political conviction about the divine right of James II Stuart to be, by royal prerogative, as it were, the Catholic governor of the Anglican establishment.

The name Whig had likewise a quasi-religious connotation. In its longer form, Whiggamore, it was the night cry of the outlawed Presbyterians in Scotland, who, instead of enjoying the re-establishment of the old Kirk of Scotland after the Cromwellian *interregnum,* found that the restored Charles II, to whom they had been so loyal, allowed the restored English Anglicans and native Episcopalians to impose episcopacy also on the independent Kingdom of Scotland. When, after the Glorious Revolution of 1688, which brought in William III Orange from Holland to replace Catholic James II, Presbyterianism was belatedly re-established in Scotland, the Covenanter nickname Whig was applied to the party of the more fervent and consequent revolutionists against divine-right kingship. By this, High Anglicans (especially, of course, the superseded Jacobites) implied that Whigs were no better than outlawed, upstart Presbyterians (and Commonwealthsmen).

The traditional party names of the English Parliament, perpetuated in the joint or new Parliament of the United Kingdom of Britain after Presbyterian Scotland and Anglican England joined in 1707, were thus partly religious labels, evocative of the turmoil of a century of struggle between Episcopalians and Presbyterians, Conformists and Nonconformists, Anglicans and Free Churchmen. It was in the aftermath of religio-political turmoil that Britain evolved the practice and a doctrine of a *loyal* opposition within Parliament! It drew the name "opposition" from the vocabulary of astronomy, which had also supplied British politics with other terms such as "revolution," "Glorious" Revolution, "rotation" in office, "conjunction," and "influence,"[38] and suggested thereby a cosmic sanction, as it were, for orderly change. The older conception of Parliament as a council suffused with the Spirit was attenuated in the age of enlightenment.

The formative years of the development of a self-conscious theory of parliamentary opposition were those of the first Hanoverians. On the death of William III (married to Catholic James Stuart's elder daughter, Mary) the succession passed, it will be recalled, to James's younger daughter, Anne Stuart. As Queen Anne's death approached, many of the Tory party looked to the Stuart pretender (her half-brother). Another constitutional crisis faced Britain. The Whigs, imitating the Glorious Revolution, sought this time George I, elector of Hanover. In the crisis, Anne's compromised Tory minister, Henry St. John Viscount Bolingbroke, was exiled; and Prime Minister Robert Walpole, virtually supreme in Britain because of George's want of English and his want also of close interest in all but Hanoverian affairs, developed a new Whig party on a rampant system of patronage.

To the Tory party, during the long Whig monopoly, 1714-60, fell the task of advancing the practice and theory of parliamentary opposition. Whereas before the advent of George, the principle of political opposition expressed itself in the tension between Parliament and King, in the age of Walpole and the first Georges the new polarization was that between the opposition party and the parliamentary party of the King and his prime minister. Two groups—the "*Real* Whigs" or Commonwealthsmen largely outside Parliament, with their canon of nonconformist literature from the seventeenth century (including Leveller tracts and the Grand Army Remonstrance and Agreement of the People of 1649),[39] and, as it happened, especially the out-of-office Tories—groped in the Georgian period toward the first articulation of the nature and function of *intra-parliamentary opposition*. Led in the Commons by Sir Thomas Hammer and Sir William Wyndham, in the Lords by Simon Viscount Harcourt, outside Parliament their party found its great theorist in Viscount Bolingbroke,[40] who after nine unsatisfactory years at the court of the Stuart pretender was called back to England in 1723 to be restored to his estates, though excluded from the Lords.

In *A Dissertation on Parties*, a series of letters in 1733, mordantly dedicated to the Whig leader Robert Walpole, Bolingbroke called for a new conception of parliamentary behavior. He defined the meaning of Whig and Tory as current before and after the Glorious Revolution and looked to new definitions. The platform of the old Tory, like himself under Queen Anne, could be characterized thus:

> Divine, hereditary, indefeasible right, lineal succession, passive-obedience, [royal] prerogative, non-resistance, slavery, nay and sometimes popery, too, were associated in many minds to the idea of a tory, and deemed incommunicable and inconsistent in the same manner, with the idea of a whig.[41]

The Whig was defined with special reference to the Glorious Revolution of 1688 and John Locke's interpretation of it in his contract theory:

> The power and majesty of the people, an original contract, the authority and independency of parliament, liberty, resistance, exclusion, abdication, deposition; these were the ideas associated, at that time, to the idea of a whig, and supposed by every whig to be incommunicable and inconsistent with the idea of a tory.[42]

Bolingbroke in his Letters then proceeded to show how flexibility and change could alter the character of party conduct and bring a larger liberty of debate for the common good, without each party's having permanently fixed positions; to show that the bulk of both parties were already "really united; united on principles of liberty, in opposition to an obscure remnant of one party, who disown those principles [the Jacobite Tories, still loyal to the Stuart pretender], and a mercenary detachment of the other, who betray them [the bribed Whigs in service of Walpole]." He noted that the Whigs still found support among the Nonconformists and the Tories among the Churchmen, but he looked forward to the time when current issues and not old positions would determine the character of party alignment and debate.[43]

In the writing of the Deistic[44] Anglican Bolingbroke, with his cosmic and anthropological theories of the meaning of true parliamentary dialogue, opposition, and debate, we can perceive the final secularization of the idea of the presence of the Holy Spirit at the Reformation Council of Henry VIII in "the public spirit," "the spirit of the constitution," "the spirit of the general welfare," in the Parliament of George I, as Bolingbroke traced the relationship of social factions and religious sects in and out of parliamentary party history.

It was in his letter in 1736 to Henry Hyde Viscount Cornbury, *On the Spirit of Patriotism*, that we see the first clear outlines of an emerging concept of an intra-parliamentary, constitutionally constructive, loyal opposition. In this letter of exhortation, distinguishing a false notion of irresponsible opposition from that inherent in the long history of Britain, Bolingbroke called for the same care in forming an opposition party as in running the government:

> [T]hey who engage in opposition are under as great obligations to prepare themselves to control, as they who serve the crown are under to prepare themselves to carry on the administration: and . . . a party, formed for this purpose, do not act like good citizens, nor honest men, unless they propose true, as well as oppose false measures of government.[45]

Elsewhere in the same letter he writes in the same vein:

> They who affect to head an opposition, or to make any considerable

figure in it, must be equal, at least, to those whom they oppose; I do not say, in parts only, but in application and industry, and the fruits of both, information, knowledge, and a certain constant preparedness for all the events that may arise. Every administration is a system of conduct; opposition, therefore, should be a system of conduct likewise; an opposite, but not a dependent system.[46]

Bolingbroke chided the practitioners of an indifferent or false opposition who embrace a cause "faintly, pursue it irresolutely, grow tired of it when they have much to hope, and give up when they have nothing to fear."[47] He noted that the Constitution could not well survive without the *common spirit* of patriotism holding together the two parties bound in committed debate; and he deplored the current want of such spirit:

[T]hough we have preserved the armour, we have lost the spirit, of our constitution: and therefore we bear, from little engrossers of delegated power, what our fathers would not have suffered from true proprietors of the royal authority.[48]

Yet by 1826 the two-party system had so evolved in the direction of legitimizing differences of judgment and policy, that Hobhouse and Canning could, as already noted by way of introduction, speak humorously of *His Majesty's* Opposition and advance still further the parliamentary recognition of the role of criticism and diversity within the unity of national solidarity.

The British Parliament, with its basically two-party system, developed in its own political way to become the mother and model of many parliaments and congresses throughout the democratic world. These parliaments in non-monarchical states, when they adopted "the Opposition" as part of their parliamentary system, added the adjective "loyal" to the phrase, thus replacing the idea of the crown by an intimation of the common body politic. In Britain itself, Tories became Conservatives, Whigs became Liberals, and the latter in turn were at the opening of the twentieth century replaced as the second major party by the Labourites.[49]

The religious carapaces of party origin have now been shed and the cosmic-conciliar sanctions of the idea of loyal parliamentary opposition are no longer in view. And while Parliament in the United Kingdom still has some control over the Establishment in England, though not in Scotland (and the Anglican Church is disestablished in Wales), it has, of course, nothing to say about the emerging structure of the World Anglican Communion. As of today, the idea of a loyal opposition is entirely political, and it is being appreciatively studied by political theorists outside of Britain, notably in Federal Germany.[50]

We turn now to an anticipated relocation of the idea and practice of a loyal opposition in the realm of the ecumenical dialogue and conciliar deliberation.

### III.  THE IDEA OF A LOYAL OPPOSITION IN THE ECUMENICAL DIALOGUE

The political conceptions of government by consensus and government in the face of a watchful but loyal opposition both have their ecclesiastical analogues and antecedents. In the history of Christianity one may observe, for example, that in Greek Orthodoxy, development in doctrine and morals has proceeded slowly over the centuries by way of a largely unstructured *consensus fidelium.* In Roman Catholicism, in contrast, the Pope with the help of his theological advisers or conciliar fathers authoritatively transcribes the current *consensus patrum una cum papa,* whether speaking infallibly or provisionally on matters of faith and morals. Within Protestantism there is a larger measure of evangelical liberty, traceable in part to the asseveration of faith and Scripture as alone determinative at the time of the classical Protestant Reformation. Anglo-American Protestantism shared this principle of solafideism and biblicism; but, far more than Continental Protestantism, working through parliaments, synods, assemblies, and ecclesiastical courts, it at length refined another principle, that of the *assensus dissidentium,* which, though it has never been formally elevated into a Christian proposition, has been a powerful factor in differentiating the thought and behavior of the members of the Anglo-American body politic and ecclesiastic from that of Protestants in other sectors of Christendom.

As in Anglo-American constitutional law a dissenting judicial opinion becomes a permanent part of the court record because at some future deliberation it may indeed come to serve as a precious precedent for a new majority decision, so in Anglo-American politics a respected place has been assigned to every *loyal* opposition which may one day form the government of the nation; and in somewhat the same way Anglo-American Christianity has discovered the uses of confessional diversity in the strengthening of the whole community of faith and the civil order through indirect invigoration by voluntary associations. Accordingly, a distinctively Anglo-American contribution to the ecumenical dialogue is a latter-day conciliarism as modified by long parliamentary usage and especially by the clarification of the proper role of the loyal opposition, issuing in irenic pluralism and in the various kinds of covenantal alliance and ecclesiastical federalism which manage to preserve a mutually corrective diversity for the spiritual good of all.

As the great churches converge, this *assensus dissidentium* constitutes an indispensable supplement to the Orthodox *consensus fidelium* and the Roman Catholic *consensus patrum una cum papa*. For involved in the Anglo-American tradition of respect for loyal diversity is not only the idea of fair play in religious polity but also a dynamic or dialectic understanding of truth and order.

In the foregoing section the development of the distinctively British institution of the loyal parliamentary opposition has been traced with just enough detail to enable us now to identify and clarify the *assensus dissidentium* as its analogue for the ecumenical realm. In ecumenicity this counterpart of the respect which has come to be reserved for a conscientious loyal opposition in politics is the acknowledgment that despite the general Christian longing for oneness and conformity, in the progressive mergers of churches and in their successive renewals, the Christian community is well advised to safeguard the plenitude of its Christian life and order by being ever willing to proceed with its redemptive ministry in the midst even of diversification that may seem at times to border on contradiction or contrariety.

This built-in respect for diversity in even fairly important aspects of Christian life and thought already characterizes a number of the church mergers in the countries of the Commonwealth and in the United States. One thinks of the constitution of the United Church of Canada, of the Church of South India, and particularly of the American Consultation on Church Union, "truly catholic, truly evangelical, and truly reformed" (San Francisco, 1960), and of the British call for One Church Renewed for Mission (Nottingham, 1964).

It is of special interest in the light of our historical survey of "parliamentary" Christianity, that in the Nottingham Conference under the British Council of Churches "the covenanting for union" presupposed that the unions anticipated for Easter Day 1980 would be along "national" lines; that is, for example, that Anglicans in (Northern) Ireland, Wales, Scotland, and England will be uniting with non-Anglicans in each of the four "national" or regional churches. Such is the abiding formative thrust of the original national-parliamentary-conciliar reformation in the once separate kingdoms of England and Scotland!

In reworking the parliamentary dialectic in the ecumenical context, it is recognized at the outset that there are certain incongruities in this analogical transfer. For one thing, parliamentary opposition belongs to the legislative and not to the administrative realm; and in any theory of ecumenical conciliarism the administrative must be seen as pre-eminent over the "legislative." Moreover, even in the "legislative" realm proper to an ecclesiastical council the very center of debate, apart from domestic issues eventuating in canons of discipline, concerns truth and polity, faith and order. Religious truth and divine order surely cannot be maintained or attained by merely political means!

The main purpose, accordingly, of drawing upon parliamentary development and theory of a loyal opposition—after having traced how in fact it grew out of the conviction as to the presence of the Holy Spirit in a national reforming diet—is to set the theory of an ecumenically conceived loyal opposition as an alternative conception of the ecumenical dialogue alongside the even more venerable principle of conciliar consensus. Ecumenical consensus and unreserved compliance after debate presuppose that a deliberative council of representative or magisterial churchmen, sustained and illumined by the Holy Spirit, can in the end conform to a fixed traditional standard and may oblige the overwhelmed minority to *assent inwardly* to the majority decision as consentaneous truth and right. An ecumenical application of the parliamentary principle of conscientious opposition and critical loyalty could help legitimize the persistence of clearly conceived and stoutly affirmed Christian divergencies. As a strong resource of collective and self-corrective Christian life (and not as a regrettable blemish to be glossed over), a forthrightly acknowledged dialectic in the realm of both faith and order (as is surely now the case among most Orthodox, Catholics, and Protestants) brings to the realm of practical and theoretical ecclesiology that sense of interdependence and mutual concern for the common and the higher goal which in political life has given rise to the respected role of the loyal opposition. *Mutatis mutandis* what was said of the political opposition by its first clear formulator could also be said of the conscientious nonconformists (whether catholic, protestant, or perfectionist) in the ecumenical dialogue, that "[t]hey who affect . . . an opposition . . . must be equal, at least, to those whom they oppose . . . not . . . in part only but in application and industry and the fruits of both, information, knowledge, and a certain constant preparedness for all the events that may arise."[51]

It needs to be said at this point to avoid misconception that the analogical transfer of parliamentary dialectic to ecumenics is not primarily intended as a sketch of a possible role of Protestants and the Orthodox within the accepted framework of a reformed papal monarchy. Nor is it *at the moment* of primary use in characterizing the role of the two groupings in what amounts to an almost revolutionary restoration in the Roman Catholic Church of the ecumenical council as a pre-eminent organ or function of the renewed Catholic body politic and ecclesiastical. The main values of contemplating the genesis and the process of His Majesty's Loyal Opposition in the ecumenical context are (1) to help us accept seemingly unbridgeable diversity in formalized theologies and sociologized polities as no insurmountable obstacle to the working out of a more profound unity which is already a fact on one level because of a common loyalty to Christ as Priest, Prophet, and King, and (2) to alert ourselves to the historical anomaly that the roles and goals of conscientious and spirited opposition have several times shifted in history despite the deceptive persistence of traditional formulas, a phenomenon familiar in the much briefer history of parties in a parliament. On the principle of the separation of Church and State, the inviolability of conscience in the religious and the civic realms, on war and peace, on the relation of Christianity to other world religions, on the priesthood of the faithful and the apostolate in the world, on the religious meaning of Scripture in the literal sense, on the dimensions of nature and history in the structure of formal theology, it is increasingly evident that the Orthodox, Catholics, and Protestants have historically shifted their roles more than once in their fresh insight or in their valiant safeguard of a neglected testimony in loyal opposition to the prevailing trends among other Christians.

As we turn to practical churchmanship, we find that there are five kinds of ecumenical disposition towards the historic and present role of councils and a considerable range of judgment as to their significance as ecclesial organs. Of special interest in this connection is the sixteenth-century and late medieval problem of who had competence to call a truly ecumenical council. The *jus convocandi,* of course, exists in every church for its own body politic, but there remains the problem of calling a pan-Christian ecumenical council, a problem all the more insistent for the reason that the communion out of which Anglo-American denominationalism emerged at one time acknowledged the overriding authority of a truly ecumenical council. Needless to say, an "imperial"—i.e., a governmental—convocation would be not only historically anachronistic but also now theologically quite untenable.

## A. *Established, Free, and Orthodox Churches*

As of today, not only the World Anglican Communion but also all the English-speaking denominations that came out of a united Western Christendom with the Established Church of England must recall that the original expectation of the majority of divines in the Henrician Church was that its constitution and doctrine would remain conditional upon the decisions of a future General Council whenever the heads of the Catholic and Protestant states of Christendom could agree to convoke it. Since the national Reformation of England in the sixteenth century, however, all that has imperceptibly changed; for today most churches, communions, and denominations are agreed that the chief magistrate or even the representative political assembly of the several states with Christian majorities (or more likely minorities) has no *jus convocandi*—to use the old conciliar phrase, in order to underscore a constitutional anomaly of almost all Anglo-American Protestant Christianity. For one thing, the English religious parties of the seventeenth century to the left of the non-separating Congregationalist anglicans— for example, the separatist Congregationalists, Baptists, and Quakers— had as *their* formative principle precisely the separation of the Church from the State; and thus, with all the stronger reason, these latter-day English Free Churches have reinforced the general sense of English-speaking Protestantism as to the reversion of the *jus convocandi* to the Church or to the churches. But if the original English Reformation postulate that Christian heads of state together have the *jus convocandi* has long since been tacitly rejected, English-speaking Protestant ecclesiology is still deficient until some new theory of the General Council can be agreed upon by Anglicans and Free Churchmen alike. For the atrophy or truncation of ecclesiology in departure from the original conciliar-parliamentary basis of reformed English Christianity is to be held up not alone against the Anglicans, who at least still speak readily of their *branch* theory of the universal visible Church, though they have largely forgotten the original conciliar presuppositions of the parliamentary establishment of their church under Henry. The anomaly, in fact, is to be held up also against all those denominations which arose out of the episcopal Anglican, royal establishment with its nationalist presupposition that the *whole* of the nation should be embraced in the ministries of one church. Today we are ready to acknowledge that insistence upon national unity represented an historically conditioned misplacement of the proper concern of Christians for universal unity. And the anomaly is felt all the more keenly for the reason that even that national religious unity has long since ceased to prevail and indeed appears today no longer even desirable, when politically coerced or sociologically induced. Accordingly, upon Presbyterians, Congregationalists, and Methodists it is no less incumbent than upon Anglicans to work through the post-Henrician ecclesiological problematic involved in their joint assumption of the *jus convocandi* of councils of reunion in several *nations*.

Besides these four groups, all Protestants in Britain and their innumerable derivatives overseas are in one way or another implicated in the problem because, even though only derivatively, they moved into the modern world as independent denominations out of the distinctively English-British *via media* resolution of the problem of the Reformation Era. The status of the nonconformist bodies as *"Free*

Churches" does not free them very much more than the Anglicans from a responsibility to work out in ecumenical terms the modern implications of the original nationalist-conciliarist character of British Protestantism, the more so for the reason that the doctrine of the invisible church of the elect, which once allowed all Reformed Christians to keep in contact with the article on the One [invisible] Holy Catholic Church, has in modern Protestant theology undergone considerable modification.

A word about the origin of the term "Free Church" is appropriate at this point. It goes back no farther than to the Disruption, led by Thomas Chalmers, in the established Church of Scotland over the issue of patronage in 1843. By 1900 the Free [Presbyterian] Church joined the United Presbyterian Church (itself a merger of several earlier secession groups) to form the United Free Church of Scotland (destined to rejoin the main body in 1929). The importance of the Scottish origin of the term "Free Church" is that only in Scotland was it natural to designate a Presbyterian body, though disestablished, a *church*. In England that term was reserved, of course, for the Anglican establishment and its local parish; the Nonconformists or Dissenters held their meetings in a *chapel*.[52] It was in 1892 that the Nonconformists in England boldly appropriated for themselves the dignity of churches, following Scottish usage, when they grouped themselves in a National *Free Church* Council (later uniting with the Federal Council to form in 1940 the Free Church Federal Council). C. S. Horne gave currency to the term in his *A Popular History of the Free Churches* (1903). The Free Churches embraced, in England, the three dissenting groups of the Stuart period: Presbyterians, Congregationalists (Independents), and Baptists; and the Methodists of eighteenth-century origin. The term has been further broadened in England, Wales, and Scotland, to include also the Quakers from the seventeenth century, the Unitarians growing largely out of the English and Irish Presbyterians, and the Salvation Army growing out of the Methodists. In general, one may say that the terms Puritans, Dissenters, Nonconformists, Free Churchmen, have succeeded each other, though not without much overlapping.

Free Churchmen have their counterpart in the New World and in Britain's overseas dominions and the Commonwealth states; but the term should not be expanded to include all "Protestant" sects. What Henry Pitney Van Dusen called the "Third Force"[53] has had connections with the Free Churches; but the latter, mostly Calvinist in origin, have been, in contrast to many sectarians within the Third Force, residually concerned with state and society at large, even though they have, in latter days, opposed state control and establishment.

The phrase "nonconformist conscience" goes back specifically to 1890 when Hugh Price Hughes, a leading Methodist in the founding of the Free Church Council, called upon Irish parliamentarian Charles Stewart Parnell to resign, because of adultery, if the Nonconformists were to continue to support Irish [Catholic] Home Rule. All through the nineteenth century Nonconformism was a laissez-faire, middle-class, sabbatarian, moral creed, sometimes oppressive of working-class pastimes. Though the nonconformist conscience was originally confined to matters of sex, drink, and social pleasures, by the end of the century other aspects of personal and social justice came within the nonconformist purview.[54]

But to return to our main thought: Anglo-American Christianity, whether of the Free Churches or of the Scottish or English establishment, is inveterately concerned with piety, polity, and politics. In contrast, Protestant denominations deriving from the Continental establishments, Lutheran or Reformed, have in the past been much less interested in polity and in the self-discipline of quasi-political or voluntary associations, and have been largely wanting, both for good and ill, in the vestiges or reflexes of conciliarism with respect to unity, reform, and liberty. The Lutherans have been especially apprehensive about putting order (polity) on a level with faith. All the classical Reformers of Continental Protestantism accepted Scripture and faith as the only basis of reformation and hence on principle refused to the end to cover the ecclesiological nakedness of their territorial establishments with the tattered remnants of conciliarism.

It has already been suggested that what seemed to be the guileless openness and optimism of the representatives of the Anglo-American churches at Pope John's Council could be explained by the pragmatic character of these churches. But it is no less plausible that precisely the Observers from the churches of the "parliamentary-conciliar" tradition should have felt especially the potentially ecumenical character of the Johannine-Pauline Council. It will be recalled that Observers of the English-speaking heritage without exception chose to be present at the second session of Vatican II on that day devoted to the commemoration of the four-hundredth anniversary of the Council of Trent, not necessarily because of a greater pragmatism or a lesser theological precision than their Continental confreres, not merely even because of a supposedly congenital Anglo-American idea of fair play or good sportsmanship, but rather, more profoundly though obscurely, because of the residual, historical feeling about a "General Council."

In contrast, the Continentals, in the moment of recollection during the episode of the Tridentine commemoration, were powerfully reminded that their fathers of the Reformation had on principle (*sola scriptura*) rejected any final arbitrament by a General Council, whether imperial or papal; and therefore on the day commemorating Trent they found themselves unable by their presence to seem to condone ancient anathemas and to give sanction to the principle of conciliar consensus coordinate with Scripture.

Though the forebears of the Anglo-American Observers—Anglican, Presbyterian, Congregationalist, Methodist, and Quaker—had, to be sure, once set aside the unachievable goal of a "General Council" to rely upon a temporary, independent national reform of English and Scottish Christendom, an expectancy has subliminally survived of an eventual call to a truly universal or General Council even in those Britishers, Americans, and others theologically much influenced by the Continent. For English-speaking Christianity has had an increasingly uneasy conscience about a purely national solution of reformation and renewal and has for a long time made various efforts towards reviving the conciliar program.[55]

When we turn from Anglo-American and Continental Protestant Christianity with their historic divergency on the ecclesial significance of a General Council, we find that the Orthodox and the Lesser Eastern Churches function more like the Continental Reformation Churches than like Anglo-American communions and denominations. The Orthodox, of course, also live in a post-Constantinian era and have no imperial figure to exercise the *jus convocandi*. The king of the Hellenes and the archiepiscopal president of the Republic of Cyprus are the only Orthodox sovereigns in the world today, and the most ardent Greek Orthodox patriot-churchman would never argue that the *jus convocandi* has passed from Constantine to the king of the Hellenes. The fact is that the Orthodox world, bereft of both Byzantine Emperor and Orthodox Tsar, has, like Anglo-American conciliar-parliamentary national Christianity, no acknowledged organ for *summoning* a council from the confines of Orthodoxy and almost no theory about such a council whether Orthodox or mixed. There is not even the precedent of an ancient ecumenical council convoked jointly by the five historic patriarchs, the patriarchal pentarchy within the later Roman Empire of the patristic age. The deep Orthodox dread of an imperial-papal church and the appeal alternatively to apostolicity and to the non-synodal consensus of the patriarchal pentarchy and the first seven ecumenical councils is not new. Since the Orthodox participated only marginally and with deep frustration in late medieval Latin conciliarism —a legacy in contrast, bequeathed to both Protestants and Catholics— they are today basically suspicious of any consentaneous conciliarism that might set itself above the dogmatic formulations of the patristic councils and are opposed to any *unitive* ecumenism that would transmute the Council of Churches into a super-Church. In fact, Orthodoxy today is indisposed to think of any modern ecumenical council as "ecclesial." It is at best an "event," not essential to the clarification of tradition and perhaps, under purely human, political, accommodationist pressures, even a *hazard* for Orthodoxy.[56] Lacking thus a viable precedent and suspicious of ecclesiastical bureaucracy, the Orthodox and with them most of the Lesser Eastern Churches are largely content with what seems to many other Christians, particularly to Roman Catholics, to be an anachronistic, national or provincial or ethnic autocephaly with the liturgical memory but without the effectual might of an ecumenical imperial authority.

The fear on the part of the Orthodox of what they themselves might call "Caesarean Christianity,"[57] meaning thereby not imperial but papal Christendom, even when Roman Catholicism is devoted to bringing about world order and peace in the tradition of both pagan and apostolic Rome, was memorably set forth by Ivan in *The Brothers Karamazov,* through whom Feodor Dostoievsky gave expression to the deepest dread of Orthodox Christianity when he had the Cardinal of Seville characterize man's quest for the secure organization of a "worldwide union of men" in faith or for peace as "the third and last" temptation of mankind, as it was of Jesus himself in the wilderness.[58]

The fear of Ivan about a world Christianity that fights in the name of Caesar and commends itself to the world as a means of establishing peace and unity among mankind was expressed *mutatis mutandis* by the Orthodox representatives at the Faith and Order meeting at Montreal in the summer of 1963, when they vigorously opposed an Anglo-American disposition to ascribe ecclesial significance to the World Council of Churches. At most, said Father Georges Florovsky, the plenary assembly or council of the World Council of Churches is "a spiritual event, not an ecclesial institution."[59]

We have thus far characterized as to their attitude toward conciliarism and ecumenical encounter only the Orthodox and the Protestants. But there are altogether five kinds of ecumenical disposition ranged side by side or over against each other in today's world: (1) the pan-Orthodox ecumenism in time, apostolic, consentaneous, but apprehensive of both Roman and Protestant "conciliarism," "triumphalism," and "organizationalism"; (2) the new, but still *Roman,* Catholic ecumenism;[60] (3) the crypto-conciliarism of Anglo-American Protestantism (Anglicanism and the Free Churches); (4) the scriptural fideism of Continental Protestantism distrustful of synodal consensus; and (5) the primitively eschatological "ecumenism" of sectarian "Protestant-ism" (the Third Force,[61] not here discussed). These five ecclesial dispositions ignore or confront or try to work alongside each other without always being fully aware of the deep divergencies with respect to the ecumenical dialogue.

At the present juncture in the reassembly of the majority of the Christian people in ecumencial deliberation, the Orthodox and the other Easterners bring to bear the consensus of the ages, but they are only in the first phases of the "planimetrical"[62] trialogue. The Roman Catholic Church, with its vocation for visible unity and ordered liberty, is perhaps further advanced in the ways of the trialogue, prepared to recognize a considerable range of catholic diversity but still largely wanting even in an ecclesiological or more specifically a constitutional theory that can bridge the historic gap between the post-Tridentine Papacy and the ancient patriarchal pentarchy of the Orthodox. The Reformed and Lutheran state churches of the Continent, once wracked by Nazism and the partisanship engendered by racist tyranny and foreign occupation and more recently sobered by the steady inroads of secularism from within and without, are now open to a new appreciation of visible unity among Christians, as they reappraise, in the light of cumulative biblical criticism, the inherited Protestant position on the relationship of Scripture, faith, and tradition. The true sects or separatists, looking askance at ecclesiastical bureaucracy, still hold that the Holy Spirit has largely departed from the main denominational tribes of Israel, and, as religious remnants, are commonly unwilling to become fully associated with the supra-denominational efforts of the main-line Christian bodies. But even their separatist testimony —with its profound implications as to class alienation, to the atrophy of the processes of spiritual healing, to emotional exhaustion, to spiritual evaporation, and to the neglect of group self-discipline within the Great Church—must be heeded even though, as it were, from a distance.

At this stage in the intrafaith deliberations the conciliar-parliamentary tradition of Anglo-American Protestantism can make a great contribution with its rationale for an ongoing, structured *auseinandersetzung* of ever changing expressions of Christ's loyal opposition within the emerging Great Church of ecumenical aspiration. Furthermore, much more licitly than in the "conciliar" parliaments of the Reformation Era, the contemporary "parliamentary" councils can, because of their ecumenical or supra-national intention, be more plausibly assured of the purifying, illuminating, and confirming presence of the Holy Spirit. Since they are also being increasingly freed from the coercive powers of the civil community and its political assignments, the reuniting churches can in their representative councils give freer voice to conscientious, loyal opposition and more attention to the uses of diversity[63] within unity, to the end that truth, faith, and order may be progressively extricated in debate and deliberation from merely personal, ecclesiastical, nationalist, or sociological limitations and restraints, as the New Testament People renew their mission in the global *Oikoumenē*.

## B. *The Role of a Loyal Opposition Within and Among the Churches*

The parliamentary concept and institution of His Majesty's loyal opposition—the precious political legacy of the successive reformations of the *Ecclesia Anglicana* after the conciliar-parliamentary establishment of the sixteenth century—may be, in the fullness of time, taken back, as it were, into the larger Church and hence into the processes of the councils of the churches.

Yearning for ever greater unity, ordered liberty, and global persuasiveness in their Christian witness, these diverse and still dismembered communions in space and time do not intend to lose or imperil any of the treasured rights, convictions, and institutions which they have severally found good in the genesis and evolution of their separate traditions of Christian stewardship and testimony. But they are converging toward the same parliament of ecumenical deliberation, having long since given up their holy warfare one against the other.

The basic principle of parliamentary opposition is, as we have seen, that it is admittedly partial and tentative, but earnest and resourceful. In politics, once the opposition has passed over to become the governing party and thereby assumes responsibility for the whole, it usually modifies its program; for the role of critic and that of responsible and accountable legislator or executive are essentially different (as are also the respective roles of judge, jury, and attorneys for the defense and prosecution). Parliamentary opposition is thus essentially contextual. This being so, and in view of the fact that a political parliament is concerned with public policy whereas an ecclesiastical council is concerned primarily with truth, polity, and conscience, one may still wonder whether it is after all helpful to try to transpose from the realm of pragmatic politics to the realm of the spirit and of revealed religion the idea of a loyal opposition among the acceptable procedures for advancing ecclesiastical affairs. Granted—one may go on—that a given historic parliament did act like an emergency synod of the nation, approving of prayer books and articles or confessions of faith,[64] still no churchmen are today happy with this compounded "Constantinian" and "Henrician" legacy. Besides, while the idea of a loyal opposition is a proven political institution, it has not thus far been demonstrated that religious truth can be clarified or that spiritual liberty can be secured by the application of the same "parliamentary" dialectic merely because of the rough analogy between a parliament and a council even though a particular parliament did once assume the prerogatives of a council.

In answer one would first wish to insist that just as the martial metaphors of the Church as the "militia of Christ" generally presuppose a profound transmutation and redirection of energies and methods normal in physical warfare, so the transposition of the procedures of parliament to the realm of theological colloquium and ecclesiastical council may likewise be understood to entail alterations and in this case specifically to turn *debate* into *deliberation*—beating (*battere*) into pondering (*liberare*). We should relieve *conscientious* opposition to any given regnant trend in the larger *Oikoumenē* of any obloquy for obstructionism and for a want of charity or of hope and undergird it, instead, with a constitutional and procedural safeguard. The testimony of the theological and ethical conscience in opposition, massive or that of a remnant—for in the Kingdom the first may be last and the last first—is another kind of reasonable service (cf. Romans 12:1 f.) in the renewal and transformation of the commonwealth of faith. Secure in the sense of natural respect for the vigorous prosecution of regnant principles and for loyal opposition, Christians can with increasing confidence come to ponder together the mighty things of God.

A second answer to those who might doubt the validity of the transposition of loyal opposition from politics to ecumenics is that the idea of a spirited, evolving, and respectful opposition is not egalitarian and not necessarily relativistic; and yet it does give full theological, institutional, and specifically procedural recognition to the Protestant insight into and concern for the many disguises, evasions, minimizations, routinizations, and pretensions of all human bearers and defenders of truth.

The presupposition of the concept and the political institution of a loyal opposition is that both the governing party and the opposition respect each other to the extent that both sides acknowledge that the concern of each is for the good of the whole and, more than that, that the good of the whole requires the balancing of powers and considerations; for opposition is the function of being the alert and accountable critic. In the universal Church, of course, in contrast to a parliament, the opposition is *required* to persevere in its disparate witness until such time as a "rectification" has been made, as for example, when the Catholic Church moves towards a vernacular liturgy, a major concern of the first-generation Protestant "opposition," or when Protestantism in its turn completes its reassessment of natural law and natural theology minimized by the Classical Reformers.

The ecclesiological sense of loyal opposition is at first glance a role more congenial to the tradition of the Protestant, especially in the radical Protestant succession with its expectation that more truth is yet to break forth from Scripture; but, in transposing the concept and institution of the loyal opposition to the ecumenical realm, can we not, in our professed loyalty to Christ as Lord and King and in our readiness to heed the drawing and the directing of the Holy Spirit in all deliberations, be prepared to understand, now the sectarian, now the Catholic, now the Orthodox, now the Protestant testimony to be the providentially inspired corrective?

Although it has been critically remarked that "the basic presupposition of Protestant ecumenism is the *parity* of existing denominations . . . against the background of a certain [alleged] 'given unity,' "[65] the ecclesiological theory and practice of loyal opposition does not in truth place all denominations and communions on the same level, as are states or cantons in most forms of federalism and confederation, be it the states in the Senate of the United States, the nations in the Assembly of the United Nations, or indeed the member churches of the World Council of Churches.[66] The concept and the institution of loyal opposition and with it, of course, the overarching concept of the universal Church presuppose the value of diversity—cultural, cultual, and constitutional—and at the same time—with an organic view of the whole Church in historical perspective—postulate, without being invidiously specific, the inequalities of the various participants in the clarification of theological truth and ethical standards.

As already noted, Vatican Council II, much more conspicuously than previous councils like Trent and Vatican I, acknowledged the role of the loyal opposition in the course of its own conciliar debate. Council Fathers, their *periti* and *consultores,* no less than the Observers and Lay Auditors were surprised and enheartened at the extraordinary forthrightness of conciliar deliberation even as they were frustrated or dismayed by what seemed akin to the boldness of quasi-parliamentary factionalism. Then, once the requisite majority of the Council Fathers had registered by their *placets* the guidance and the illumination of the Holy Spirit, invoked in prayer at each congregation and commission sitting, and once the elaborated *schemata* had been confirmed as conciliar decree or constitution by the Pope *una cum episcopis,* the provisional or workaday opposition theoretically dissolved as a constitutional phantom in the formal consensus and in the inward assent of each Council Father already pledged by oath to obedience to the Pope.

But despite the formal and internal dissolution of any provisional "opposition," the morphology of the prelatical parliament is still not without several of the characteristic features of a political parliament. Moreover, since there is in Catholicism today not the slightest uncertainty about the loyalty of all the bishops to the Bishop of Rome, it is not inconceivable in the future that something like His Holiness' loyal opposition may be accorded the fuller constitutional and theological recognition which it now has in practice only up to the promulgation of any particular decree or constitution.[67]

However, the Catholic Church cannot think of its visible sovereign as solely a constitutional symbol of unity, finding itself rather at that stage in its diffusion of the powers of the Pope and Curia in the collegiality of all bishops comparable to the stage in English constitutional evolution when the opposition was between King and Parliament rather than between parties within Parliament.

It is all the more notable, therefore, that as to interconfessional dialogue, Catholicism has clearly come to recognize the claims of a scripturally loyal opposition outside its fold. The presence of fully involved and hospitably heeded Observers under the Secretariat for Christian Unity sufficiently attested to the recognition.

It was, moreover, in recognition of the Protestant concern for the freedom in conscientious testimony that Augustin Cardinal Bea, in his notable *Pro Deo* allocution of January 13, 1963, spoke of a non-relativistic role for creative diversity in the loving quest of unity, speaking in effect for all ecumenists in whatever communion, even though he was exhorting for the moment only his own:

> Obviously it is . . . not a question of making truth a relative and undetermined thing. It is, rather, a question of a real and *binding* love of truth, and it is precisely this love that admonishes us [Catholics] to bear in mind the limitations of our knowledge and recognize also *that side of truth which others see*, without denying, however, that which we ourselves really know about the truth.[68]

Leon-Josef Cardinal Suenens came even closer to the problem of "parliamentary" dialectic when he expressed an openness similar to Cardinal Bea's in the magnificent Hiram W. Thomas Lecture on Unity at the University of Chicago on May 4, 1964. Precisely in discussing the methodology of ecumenism, Cardinal Suenens, even though he was warning against the negative features of debate and parliamentary procedure, was pointing to the role of a truly loyal opposition:

> The debate approach, taken by itself, fosters opposition and emphasizes differences. "Every error," it has been said, "is nothing but the abuse of some truth." We must seek this germ of truth, this aspect of

the real which is obscured by the opposite thesis. Only after we have found it and fully accepted it can we propose a complementary truth which will help us *to discover the truth in all its integrity*.[69]

If great Catholic ecumenists like Suenens and Bea still generally eschew the terminology of parliamentary debate—because in the realm of religion to win an argument is often to lose a soul—and are specifically ill at ease with the imagery of a parliamentary majority and an opposition, many of them nevertheless fully acknowledge the validity of "parliamentary" dialectic in its ecclesiastically sublimated form. Perhaps the most impressive indication, therefore, of a new concern in the Catholic Church for dialectic was the full recognition by Pope Pius XII (in 1950) of the propriety and utility of "public opinion" *in the Church*.[70] More notable still is Karl Rahner's exposition of this papal *locus*.

Rahner (a major *peritus* of the Council who has contributed incomparably to the new conciliar ethos of forthrightness and obedient freedom), after calling for "Free Speech in the Church" on all levels, from theologians to concerned laymen, advocates, *mutatis mutandis,* the recognition of theological free speech:

> If [the clergy] do not allow the people to speak their minds, do not, in more dignified language, encourage or even tolerate, with courage and forbearance and even a certain optimism free from anxiety, the growth of public opinion within the Church, they run the risk of directing [i.e., governing] her from a soundproof ivory tower, instead of straining their ears to catch the voice of God, which can also be audible within the clamor of the times.[71]

In the same context, further along, Rahner writes:

> They [young clerics and laymen] must learn that even in the Church there can be a body something like *Her* Majesty's Opposition, which in the course of Church history has always had its own kind of saints in its ranks—the ranks of genuine, divinely-willed opposition to all that is merely human in the Church and her official representatives.[72]

The most notable episodes expressive of a loyal opposition in St. Peter's and of evangelical freedom within the hierarchy at large were the dramatic effort of American and other bishops under Albert Cardinal Meyer of Chicago to petition the Pope at the end of the third session not to postpone the vote on the Declaration on Religious Liberty, amassing signatures to that end, and the less well publicized defense of his Dutch clergy by Bernard Cardinal Alfrink at a news conference right after the opening of the fourth and final session.

The occasion of Cardinal Alfrink's intervention was the encyclical *Mysterium fidei,* published without any warning on the very eve of the fourth session. Dealing with purported vagaries in contemporary Catholic eucharistic theology, Paul's encyclical was at once interpreted in the Italian press and elsewhere as directed against liberal tendencies in Holland which might even lead to a Dutch schism. In the course of his spirited defense Cardinal Alfrink declared:

> . . . the idea of a Dutch schism can only be entertained outside Holland. But is it not true . . . that the Dutch Catholic community is infected by an anti-Roman spirit? If one interprets the word "anti-Roman" as "anti-Papal," then I categorically deny this assertion with a tranquil heart. On the contrary! If, however, one understands by the word "anti-Roman" that certain persons in the Dutch Catholic community have their objections—which they sometimes formulate sharply— against certain methods of the Roman governing body and against the way in which certain persons employ these methods, in that case I could not and would not want to deny it.[73]

Further evidence of the permeation of the idea of evangelical liberty, loyal opposition, and conscientious voluntarism in Catholicism is the constitution *On the Church in the Modern World,* promulgated at the end of the fourth session, which amply indicates Catholic recognition of the importance of voluntary associations in the evolution of the modern open society of most Western states and gives strong encouragement to participation by Catholics in these national and international organizations and agencies. Full participation in these bodies will increasingly accustom Catholics everywhere to procedures modeled on those familiar in the parliamentary tradition.

In the meantime, it is not primarily within the Roman Catholic Church that the transposition of the parliamentary concept and institution of His Majesty's loyal opposition would have most significance for the present, but rather in the inter-confessional ecumenical colloquies[74] among Continental Protestants, Anglicans, Free Churchmen, and the Eastern Orthodox with the Catholics.

## Conclusion

We have not wished to argue that in the clarification of Christian truth and right, the Church can act wholly on the parliamentary analogy. But one thrust of the historical survey of the English constitutional development has been to indicate that the parliamentary-synodal character of Anglo-American Christianity has been to make the dynamic evolvement of truth through the dialectic of "opposition" congenial to ecumenists in this tradition in the present ecumenical dialogue.

To justify the predilection theologically and ecclesiologically, it would, admittedly, not be quite to the point to appeal to the role of "opposition" in Corinth as it was fleetingly and sarcastically commented

on by Paul in I Corinthians 11:18 f.: "[W]hen you assemble as a
church, . . . there are divisions (*schismata*) among you; and I partly
believe it, for there must be factions (*haireseis*)[75] among you in order
that those who are genuine among you may be recognized." Nor is it
enough to recall that Paul opposed even the prince of the apostles to his
face when they encountered each other in Antioch (Galatians 2:11).
Nor would it be enough to say that the emergence of one-sided theological opinion and extremist practice within the ancient Christian community did actually further, in provincial synod and ecumenical council, the
clarification of dogmatic truth and moral and constitutional canon.[76]
Nor, again, would it be enough to point to the precedent of the *sic et
non* procedure of the scholastic canonists and summists in reconciling
seemingly contradictory elements in Scripture and tradition. For, in all
these examples from ancient and medieval ecclesiastical history, earnest dissent was at best only grudgingly accorded a role in the clarification of absolute truth and right. And the earnest dissenter himself or the
dissenting group, once a consensus of the *major et sanior pars*[77] had
been formulated, too often, alas, fared worse than the schism or heretical tenet itself, for at least the latter could not be done to death. Finally,
even John Henry Newman's conception of the "prophetical office of
the Church [of England]" (1837) between "divisive Protestant Nonconformity" and "despotic Popery" was but his desperate, penultimate
effort, before being received by Rome, to make sense of the Anglican
concept of the *via media* and branch theory in contrast to what we are
calling the British idea of a loyal opposition transposed to the ecumenical realm. In Newman's day there was nothing like the comprehensive ecumenical dialectic now in progress.

It has not been our role to trace the emergence of the ecumenical
yearning, notably in the very Church and world Communion from
which Newman departed in 1845 and in the more radically Protestant
offspring of the *Ecclesia Anglicana*. It must suffice in conclusion to remark, without further documentation, that in the fullness of Christian
time, the sociology of even Christian knowledge has come to be
recognized (the "non-theological factors"), while the dynamics of Christian behavior in ever reassessing the treasures new and old of the community of faith in time and in space have brought us to the point where
a constructive role can now be forthrightly assigned to fraternal, though
formally schismatic observers in the deliberations of the councils and
commissions of almost all churches still separated from each other. And
in these deliberations the loyalty in opposition is at once loyalty to
the abidingly valid in each tradition and loyalty to the Greater Church
of which all may aspire to be a part. In this kind of ecumenical or

conciliar dialogue, Protestantism no longer, as in the sixteenth-century Catholic-Protestant encounters, appeals solely to Scripture, for it has come to recognize the place also of (critically examined) tradition and of (non-coercive) consensus. Accordingly, acknowledging with Johannine-Pauline Catholicism, with updated Tudor-Stuart parliamentary-conciliar Anglicanism, and with perfectionist Sectarianism the purifying and moving presence of the Holy Spirit in council (Acts 15:28), contemporary world Protestantism can safeguard the classical Protestant and biblical-prophetic principle of an ultimate appeal of the moral or theological conscience to the Transcendent in the idea and practice of loyal opposition and evangelical liberty in the name of the divine Sovereign.

# IV / THE MEANING OF "CHURCH"
# IN ANABAPTISM AND ROMAN CATHOLICISM:
# PAST AND PRESENT

*Michael Novak*

This study attempts to encourage Roman Catholics to reflect upon the lessons of doctrine and practice to be learned from the traditions of the Anabaptist or Free Church movement. It begins by noting the original and long-lived misjudgment which Catholic historians have passed upon that tradition, especially in its sixteenth-century beginnings. It next notes similarities between the inspiration of the Anabaptist conception of the church and the inspiration of the Roman Catholic conception of the special religious community. It then discusses the great Anabaptist contribution to Christian—and world—history: the break from the Constantinian order. It concludes by noting how, in our day, the Free Churches have become less like Catholic religious orders and more like "a church"; and how the Roman Catholic Church is at last following the Free Churches in the rejection of the Constantinian order, in the vision of the church as the covenanted people of God, and in the use of the methods of open discussion, lay participation, and consensus as important in her daily life.

The goal of this study is not a facile ecumenism; its purpose is to draw attention to inner demands and trends in Roman Catholicism and in Anabaptism from which each might learn from the other. The study is based on the assumption that the fundamental problem of the Christian churches is not theological but philosophical. For that problem seems to be: which choices of human polity for the structure of a community and for individual life contribute most, over the long run, to fidelity to the revelation of Jesus Christ?

### A NEW JUDGMENT REQUIRED

The Anabaptists of the sixteenth century are probably best known to Roman Catholics in America through their portrait by Ronald Knox in

*Enthusiasm.* Knox portrays the Anabaptists as eccentric people, immature and unwise—swept up by an undercurrent of wild and fantastic emotion beneath the mainstream of European culture. Yet Msgr. Knox has been fascinated by "these enthusiasts." On the last page of his book, he confesses that all through its writing he had been haunted by a refrain from *La Princesse Lointaine:*

> *Frère Trophime:* Inertia is the only vice, Master Erasmus;
> And the only virtue is . . .
>
> *Erasmus:*                                        Which?
>
> *Frère Trophime:*                                        Enthusiasm!

Earlier, Msgr. Knox confesses a more tangible fear: "More than all the other Christianities, the Catholic Church is institutional. Her enemies too easily conclude that she is thereby incapacitated from all spiritual initiative. . . ."[1] Surely readers of the fiction of Evelyn Waugh would guess that a deep spiritual malaise gripped the Roman Catholic Church, and that spiritual initiative had long ago been lost. Perhaps there is a general longing, then, among Roman Catholics for what the Free Churches of the Anabaptist movement have to teach. Perhaps, in this era of the Second Vatican Council, such lessons are being learned.

Catholics are often inwardly constrained from learning from the Anabaptists, however—first by prejudice; next by ignorance; and thirdly by condescension. Prejudice has arisen against the Free Churches because of their supposed reliance upon the emotions and subjective experience. The Catholic distrusts such reliance for both good motives and bad: good because, narrowly construed, the emotions do not suffice for self-criticism or for perseverance; bad because the Catholic receives little instruction in personal, spiritual initiative, usually taking his cues from the institution to which he belongs; Catholic piety is much objectified, and the "excesses" of private devotion are looked upon with much suspicion. Ignorance is operative, because Catholics ordinarily know little of the tradition of the Free Churches, their theology, their heroes, their favored doctrines. The proliferation of sects and, above all, their emphasis on the emotions suffice to dissuade the Catholic from taking the sects with seriousness. Condescension arises from the Roman Catholic belief that Roman Catholicism is "the one true Church" and that this church alone truly knows who Christ is and what he wills.[2] The sects do themselves little justice (in the eyes of Catholics) by stressing in their own rhetoric the elements of feeling, experience, and subjectivity. Such rhetoric seems unfortunate, since it is clear from their doctrines and their lives that intelligence and persevering will are also involved in their living of the Gospels, and to these qualities Catholics are more inclined to pay respect.

Who were the Anabaptists? They were the "full-way" reformers, the radical reformers.[3] Their characters, their intentions, and their doctrines have long been misunderstood. They aroused the fears, hatred, and wrath of Luther and Calvin. Catholic authorities joined the classical reformers in putting them to death: by the sword, by fire, by torture with heated tongs, and—in parody of their own belief in adult baptism—by drowning. Hunted and imprisoned in life, they were blackened also in death by historians among their enemies. Only in recent years[4] have their writings and deeds come to be taken without ulterior purpose, by neutral scholars, by scholars of their own, or by scholars of antipathetic beliefs who are able, now, to be objective. Thus confronted, on their own merits, the men and women of the radical reformation command respect. The theory and practice of religious liberty so much cherished by Christians today is largely of their earning. Their standards of belief, practice, and prayer encourage emulation. The courage and calmness with which they went to death, and their long-meditated, explicit doctrine of martyrdom and the cross challenge all who think of themselves as representatives of the Gospels. The missionary impulse which has motivated and sustained their worldwide efforts for many generations proves the depth of their convictions.

The Anabaptist movement is difficult to characterize. It did not emerge behind one leader solely, nor according to a program worked out in advance. It emerged from dissatisfaction with the "compromises" of the classical Reformation, and from other conditions of the time as well. First of all, the movement was widespread: it arose in Spain and Italy in the south, and in England and Scandinavia in the north, but its most vital center appears to have been in Switzerland and Southern Germany, in Moravia, Holland, and the northern Rhineland.[5] The movement was not primarily theoretical; it seems to have grown according to various pressures of time and place and only gradually to have become conscious of itself.[6] Social and political factors were of high importance in the original impetus of the movement; socialists and Marxists claim it as an early version of their revolution.[7] At certain places and times, the movement erupted into violent revolution: in the Peasants' Revolt and at Muenster; for the most part, it was peaceable and even pacifist. Fears and social scars held over from preceding generations—fears resulting from the frequent, terrifying plagues, from ignorance, from a changing legal and social order—contributed to the credibility of wild eschatological expectations among the peoples.[8] In many respects, the times seem in retrospect like a nightmare, whose dislocations the paintings of Hieronymus Bosch suggest only too vividly.

In their conception of the church, the radical reformers struck to the heart of the crisis of their times. An older social order and an older relationship of church and state were giving way. Where Luther and Calvin tried to carry out their reformation as nearly as possible on theological and ecclesiastical grounds, leaving intact the relationship of church and world, the radical reformers labored for a new cultural order. Important elements in the future of world history lay in their hands. Catholic, Lutheran, and Calvinist authorities were not wrong to see in them a threat to the social order inherited from the time of Constantine; the radical reformers thought of that order as a "fall" and labored for the "restitution" of an older conception of the church and a new order of the world. In view of the subsequent desacralization of the state, the emerging value of religious liberty, and the future pluralism of nearly all world civilizations, we may see in the labors of the radical reformers one of the decisive moments of modern history.

These labors were not accidental but deliberate; they were not generated by the mood of a moment, but sufficed to inspire men to endure years of persecution and flight before the authorities; and they very often cost blood. One of the most vivid images that remains after studies in this area is of martyrdoms like that of Michael Sattler. Sattler was thirty-seven in 1527, the year of his execution; he had been a Benedictine for many years, and had risen to the rank of prior. He became a Lutheran and, in 1525, an Anabaptist. Forced to flee from city to city with his wife, Sattler was arrested and tried in Ensisheim, where he was executed on a beautiful May 20, 1527. There in the marketplace, a piece was cut from his tongue. Twice, pieces of flesh were torn from his body with hot tongs. He was forged to a cart, and five times on the way to the stake the tongs were again applied to his body. Sattler was then bound with ropes to a ladder; a sack of powder was mercifully tied to his neck to hasten his death, and he was thrust into a fire. "Almighty, eternal God," he prayed aloud before he died, "thou art the way and the truth; because I have not been shown to be in error, I will with thy help this day testify to the truth and seal it with my blood." When the ropes on his hands had burned through, he raised his two forefingers and repeated Christ's words: "Father, into thy hands I commend my spirit."[9]

The idea that such martyrs were fanatics was made to take root in historiography; the new order to which they gave witness was in fact disorder in the eyes of Constantinian Catholics and classical reformers. The times were unsettled enough, and some from among the Anabaptists were indeed maccabean revolutionaries who preached fire and the sword. But even in vilifying the mainstream of the Anabaptists, which was by no means maccabean, an early Catholic historian tells us between the lines what peaceable, devoted lives they led—as their Moravian, Mennonite, and Hutterite descendants have continued to exemplify. In a history called *Of the Cursed Beginnings of the Anabaptists,* about the year 1600, the Jesuit Fischer wrote:

> Among all the heresies and sects which have their origin from Luther, . . . not a one has a better appearance and greater external holiness than the Anabaptists. Other sects are for the most part riotous, bloodthirsty and given over to carnal lusts; not so the Anabaptists. They call each other brothers and sisters; they use no profanity nor unkind language; they use no weapons of defense . . . They own nothing in private but have everything in common. They do not go to law before judicial courts but bear everything patiently, as they say, in the Holy Spirit. Who should suppose that under this sheep's clothing only ravening wolves are hidden?[10]

The heart of Anabaptist witness is their notion of the church. That notion, capable of inspiring great Christians, deserves study. Moreover, if it is true that the Roman Catholic Church now embraces the doctrine of religious liberty, gradually instructed in this doctrine by history, then face to face with the Free Churches, Roman Catholicism can no longer be seen as the Constantinian Church. It is no longer accurate, in most countries, to refer to Roman Catholicism as one of Troeltsch's "church type."[11]

What do the Free Churches mean by the idea of the church, and what do Roman Catholics mean? When old prejudices have fallen by their own invalidity, what separates the Roman Church from the Free Church?

### THE ANABAPTIST IDEA OF THE CHURCH

"It was a great step forward," Robert Friedmann tells us, "when Ernst Troeltsch first so clearly distinguished church and sect—although primarily from a sociological point of view. Church is the institution of salvation for all baptized members; sect is the brotherhood of the regenerate, the congregation of saints, a gathered church of true Christians either for the celebration of the Lord's Supper alone or for a collective life according to the Sermon on the Mount."[12] Disappointed because the classical reformers did not sufficiently preach the Sermon on the Mount, the evangelical Anabaptists necessarily broke with them as with Catholicism. Friedmann continues his résumé of Troeltsch's findings: "While the Middle Ages had monasteries for those who strove toward a pure and holy life, the modern times engendered the Protestant sect, with discipline, aloofness from the world, general priesthood of believers, separation from the state—a congregation of volunteers on the basis of a strong biblicism."[13] Friedmann criticizes Troeltsch's division of church and sect as too broad; not all Protestant sects pursue the highly moral course Troeltsch describes. "Nevertheless, it was a great advance to recognize Pietism as the sect-type within the church . . . It is a very significant fact that as soon as Anabaptism became settled or established, it changed from the sect type to the church type. But as it continued to cherish its old heritage, this little church developed a pietistic pattern."[14]

Later in his study, Friedmann reinforces these points by citing the work of Ritschl: "Surprisingly, he found a striking likeness between the Franciscan tertiaries, the (evangelical) Anabaptists, and the Pietists of the seventeenth century. He starts with a glimpse of what he calls the Franciscan idea of church reform: restitution of the early form of Christianity by renunciation of the world, personal purity, poverty and, finally, expectation of the Kingdom of God. Asceticism within the world and a prevailing religious emotionalism in practicing brotherly love are said to be the main features of this group."[15] Anabaptism, in short, appears to Ritschl as "a revival of the Franciscan reformation, a worldly monasticism."[16] Friedmann offers two criticisms: the Anabaptists are more related to the Spiritual Franciscans than to the third orders; the Pietists are more related to the mystical or spiritual Anabaptists like Casper Schwenckfeld than to the Anabaptists proper.[17]

It is this analogy between the evangelical Anabaptists and the Franciscans which is, initially, most interesting to observe. If, for a moment, we conceive of "the Roman Catholic Church" only as a generic name like "the Protestant Church," and look upon the different modes of Catholic life as sects or denominations within the larger whole, the relationships between evangelical Anabaptist piety and Franciscan piety seem more striking. If, for example, one were to visit a Franciscan or Capuchin monastery in Pennsylvania, and to observe the sandaled friars in their traditional robes and see the brothers working on the farm, and then to visit a Mennonite community nearby and observe the traditional clothing and the men working in the fields, one would wonder about the relationship between the books of piety which animate the lives of both groups. One would wonder also about their mutual doctrines on the relationship of Christianity to the world: about retreat, about the Sermon on the Mount, about community of goods, about the relationship between those committed to this special life and others not of the brethren. (It might well be discernible that the Franciscans had made more adaptation to the twentieth century than the Mennonites had, at least in externals; but not so much as the American Quakers, who are, as H. Richard Niebuhr has said, "the Anglo-Saxon parallel to Anabaptism."[18])

Friedmann's discussion of Anabaptist spirituality leads back in many ways to the spirituality of Catholic religious orders. He notes that the Anabaptist ordinance of baptism—the rite, after all, from which their name was drawn—was not looked upon so much as a sacrament, a bringing of grace, as the seal of a free, personal commitment to a new life. "In character such baptism might perhaps best be compared with a monastic vow."[19] Let us pursue this comparison.

Roland H. Bainton made current the name "Left-Wing Protestantism" for the Anabaptist movement.[20] His principle of division was separation of church and state: the right wing accepted the land church; the left wing insisted upon separation, tolerance, religious liberty.[21] Franklin H. Littell—in studies to which we must return—goes farther; he finds the heart of the Anabaptist movement in its conception of the church.[22] Harold S. Bender and after him Robert Friedmann object: the idea of the church is important, but derivative; it is not of the essence. "We have not yet arrived at the heart of the matter when we stop with the idea of the 'church'; at the heart we discover one idea only, and that is the idea of faithful and free voluntary discipleship which the Anabaptist is resolved to accept without faltering."[23] "Such discipleship means that the commandment of Jesus Christ, 'Take up thy cross and follow me,' be taken absolutely seriously. That it implies separation from the world, nonconformity and consequently the narrow path which might end in martyrdom, is only too obvious."[24]

The new brotherhood will not admit members who are only nominally or partially Christian; it is a state of perfection, to borrow the technical phrase used of Catholic religious communities. While Luther decided for a *Volkskirche* to include both saints and sinners, the Anabaptists decided for the opposite way, "for the 'church holy' rather than for the 'church universal.' "[25] "That such a 'church holy' is not only a distant ideal but a distinct possibility for man was demonstrated by the Anabaptists, at least in their first period (to 1560), with much dedication and vigor. It meant, of course, complete separation from the world and nonconformity to it . . ."[26] The Anabaptists made the counsels of the Gospels the rule of their lives.

Because Anabaptism is a lay movement, it cannot well include celibacy among the defining features of its life, but the number of its early and greatest leaders who were originally priests, and even monks, is very high and includes Sattler and Menno Simons. That the spirituality of the monastery should have continued through their sermons and writings to influence their flocks is hardly surprising; neither is it surprising that the persons most zealous for a life of perfection should have been among those protesting abuses in the monasteries and those reacting most strongly against the practice of celibacy. Again and again among these early priest converts one notes their marriage occurring within the year, and most often, it appears, to a wife devout enough to share the hunted life, and perhaps martyr's life, of her husband. One is forced to conclude that the discipline of celibacy, both because of the otherwise nonexistent scandals which it made possible, and because of the emotional burden it placed upon an already turbulent age, played a larger role in the Reformation than is usually discussed.

But the other two cornerstones of Catholic religious life, particularly obedience, are central in the Anabaptist view of Christian life. Discipleship is the core of the Anabaptist view. "Obedience . . . is the Anabaptist term for 'discipleship.' "[27] "Repentance, rebirth, baptism on faith, and a full dedication to a life of discipleship and obedience—this sequence will be experienced henceforth in innumerable cases throughout the sixteenth century."[28] It is important to note that this experience of regeneration is not merely emotional; it is based on resolution, a willingness to endure a lifetime of hardship, routine, or martyrdom. Friedmann is careful to draw a distinction between evangelical Anabaptism and later Pietism. "Pietism is principally characterized by the subjective experience of the fact that the sinner, though incapable of doing anything good, is yet saved through the atoning death of Christ, and the subsequent joy which goes with such an experience. The pietist knows of his sinfulness, but in a struggle of repentance he overcomes it and now rejoices in his feeling of being saved and accepted by the Lord."[29] "With the Anabaptist things seem to be quite different. The rebirth is a radical one, and with it the resolution to a new way in obedience to the 'law of Christ.' "[30]

The Anabaptists appear to spend little reflection on the fact of salvation; they do not seem to meditate long on their own inherent sinfulness. Their theology seems much more hardy and straightforward; they seem simply to take the Lord at his word, and begin to try to do his will as they perceive it. "It was only about one century later, when the basic attitude of the Brethren became weakened or almost lost, that pietistic emotionalism took the place of the former *Nachfolge* or discipleship motive, and with this change (hardly ever noticed) the genuine Anabaptist spirit faded away."[31]

At this point, Friedmann is willing even to raise the question whether Anabaptism can be considered as a part of "the great Protestant family" at all. "Apparently . . . Anabaptism represents a new type of Christianity, different from the traditional patterns of Protestantism in general. It is certainly not a creedal (i.e., theological) church in which the idea of salvation takes the center of concern, nor is it a pietistic church in which the fruits of salvation may be enjoyed."[32] What Friedmann does not suggest, and what seems very fruitful as an hypothesis, is that Anabaptism represents a laicizing of the Catholic monastic spirituality; it is a transferral of the focus of the "state of perfection" from a monastic brotherhood, bound by vow and cloistered by walls, to a lay, married brotherhood bound by believers' baptism and separated from the world by the ban. Its root is not a sense of sin, trust in personal justification, and aggressive social reform (classical reformers); its root is the desire to follow God completely, to withdraw from the world, and to respond to a call to a new and higher form of Christian life (Catholic religious vocation).

Friedmann borrows a contemporary term in trying to elucidate his interpretation of Anabaptism; the connotations of the term are not felicitous, but what he is getting at is clear. He calls Anabaptism an "outstanding example of *existential Christianity*. . . . The term 'existential' means here above all an extreme concreteness of the Christian experience. Such an experience is neither of an intellectual nature (doctrinal understanding) nor is it emotional. For lack of a better description we will call it 'total,' something most typical with all conversion experiences. In this total or concrete Christianity the distinctions between doctrine and ethics, belief and practice, no longer exist. Life becomes here a great 'yes' to the call, something which goes far beyond both mere speculation and mere moralism. Spirituality and obedience become one and the same in such a Christian existence, an unreserved surrender and dedication to the divine will. That such Christian existence has also very little in common with emotionalism becomes likewise clear by now and should make us alert. . . ."[33] This passage asserts quite clearly the sense of vocation, response, and total, concrete giving which characterize the life of the professed Catholic religious, though it does not, of course, specify the three traditional vows. Moreover, it emphasizes an individualistic sense of reality, neglecting the "existential" factors in social life—which Catholic religious are sometimes led to do.

However, the Anabaptist view, like the view of Roman Catholic religious, does imply the common life. "Brotherly love is the most conspicuous sign of such an existential type of Christianity: where it is practiced we might also speak of a work at the Kingdom of God. It is obvious, moreover, that the Kingdom cannot exist for the 'single one' in his isolation but only for those who have united in the *koinonia,* the

*Gemeinschaft* or *Gemeinde.* Earlier we called it the fellowship of committed disciples."[34]

Even the eschatology that arises among the Anabaptists recalls the eschatology of the cloister. "The Brethren are deeply aware of the co-existence of two worlds: this world and the world of the Kingdom. . . . Absolute separation from the world and nonconformity to it easily follow as corollaries. Occasionally we read in Anabaptist tracts phrases like this, 'In these latter and dangerous days . . .' but almost nowhere do we find apocalyptic speculations. Their eschatology is strictly evangelical: the Christian has 'to fight the good fight' (I Tim. 6:12) . . . he has to resist sin with all his strength."[35] The postulant who, after due inquiry, finally asks and receives baptism in faith "will no longer deviate from his new path"; he will "resist sin in all its subtle temptations." It is presupposed that he will have a "genuinely felt self-surrender unto God (in German, *Gelassenheit,* i.e., self-abandoning, yieldedness). . . ."[36] In short, the Anabaptist, much like the Catholic professed religious, does not live a life like others in the world, but sets for his norm the teachings of the Gospels, binding himself under communal discipline to live according to them. He lives now "as if the world were not."

One crucial difference between the Catholic religious and the Anabaptist, of course, is that the former sees himself as living a special form of life within a larger religious community; the latter sees the church as bounded by his own brotherhood. For the former, the Kingdom of God is like a net, gathering in good fish and bad; or like a field in which tares grow together with the wheat. His temptation, of course, and that of the Catholic people, is to think that the "really committed" Catholic is, or ought to be, a religious, while those who do not offer themselves so totally or concretely remain in the lay state. (Theoretically, all agree, a layman can be just as holy as a monk, or holier; but, psychologically, both monk and layman tend to believe that the monk has a better chance at it.) The temptation of the Anabaptist is somewhat similar; it is to mark off "the world" as "out there," as sinful. It must be said that there does not seem to be much spiritual pride in the early Anabaptist communities; the reader of their sermons and tracts is aware rather of their personal seriousness, humility, and dedication, than of vain comparisons with others.[37] Nevertheless, separation from "the others" is the other side of the emphasis upon discipleship.

The Catholic religious cannot by right believe that he is a member of a true, pure community, over against the vast numbers of Catholics; his community is part of the larger church, *all* whose members are called to salvation, though many be as tares, bad fish, or goats among those who will in fact be saved. The dynamism of living faithful to a freely taken religious vow, however, appears to be very like the dynamism of living faithful to believers' baptism. Like religious orders, so also the Anabaptist movement seems to have cycles of fervor and relaxation; but perhaps the more elaborate organizational pattern of the religious order and its more extensive attention to theology offer more footholds for later reformers within the order than would be possible if entire reliance were placed upon fellowship of spirit maintained from generation to generation. That is to say, the structure of religious orders appears to favor a fruitful (as well as a possibly obstructionist) conservatism, with institutionally accessible forces of renewal. Moreover, new candidates for a religious community must come from without, by free choice; the Anabaptist communions face the difficulty of having their children growing up habituated to the community and unable quite so strikingly to "choose" it as its original founders had.

Finally, it should be noted that the ordinary lay Catholic is not merely "born into" Catholicism. In countries like the United States, it has become increasingly easy socially and psychologically to leave the church or to change one's church; it must correspondingly be presumed that ordinarily those who remain Catholic choose to do so. Moreover, at the Easter Vigil ceremony, the liturgy leads the people to reaffirm, and thus to appropriate, the baptismal vows made in their name, while they were infants, by their sponsors. The *Mennonite Encyclopedia* quotes with approval the following reflections by a Catholic writer: ". . . The church wants to make up for the missing experience [of baptism]. So on Saturday before Easter she places us around the baptismal font, fills it with water, consecrates it as a sacred source of supernatural life, sprinkles us with it in memory of our first washing, gives us some to take home, that we may use it in the morning and evening. Do you think of this when the priest carries it through the church every Sunday before High Mass, when you bless yourself upon entering and leaving the church, upon leaving and returning to your home?"[38]

To sum up: the Anabaptist view of the church is rooted in the conception of discipleship. And this conception of discipleship seems very similar to the conception of a professed religious life among Catholics, in at least a few important respects. Such a life is a free, voluntary commitment; it forms a band of the "more perfect"; it has discipline; it encourages the piety of abandonment to God's will; it is undertaken as a living martyrdom, founded on renunciation of the world and on the doctrine of the cross. As a program for Christians living in the world, however, the Anabaptist movement is special; it is for the few; and its most serious internal problem seems to be that of maintaining its early levels of fervor. Meanwhile, the many, too, have to hear the Gospels. What has Anabaptism to say to the world?

### ANABAPTISM AND THE WORLD

Ironically, it is the manner in which Anabaptism separated itself from the world that has had the greatest effect upon the world. For the Anabaptist separation, as Littell points out, was not physical so much as spiritual.[39] For this separation the Anabaptist communities relied, not upon a cloister wall, but upon internal social discipline within their midst. This discipline was accepted as a free choice; the Anabaptist churches are Free Churches, in the sense that one cannot be born into them but must choose to enter them. As a consequence, the radical significance of Anabaptism was its sundering of the Constantinian order of Christian society. For many of the Anabaptists, the era of Constantine marked the fall of the Christian church (for others, the fall came earlier).[40] Anabaptism recovered the sense of faith as a free act; it restored the sense of personal seriousness and commitment, even to the point of martyrdom, involved in choosing to become a Christian. Specifically, it recovered the sense of faith as a free act, not metaphysically (which had never been denied) but *socially*. It denied that the church ought to be coterminous with profane society, to "baptize" profane society, to turn Christianity into Christendom.

The protest of the Free Churches against the established churches did not, in the sixteenth century, succeed in the lands where it arose. The Constantinian era was to be prolonged in the established churches of continental Europe. In England and in America, however, the conception of religious liberty was able to take root in the institutional structure of society.

But if the first contribution of the Free Churches to world history is the break with the Constantinian social order, the second is the method of internal polity adopted in these churches. The first struggle waged by the evangelical Anabaptists was against the landed churches of Roman Catholicism and the classical Reformation. The second was against the maccabean revolutionaries like Thomas Müntzer on the one hand, who would bind the church to the world in new and terrible ways, and against the spiritualizers like Casper Schwenckfeld and Sebastian Franck on the other, who would deprive the church of any community discipline whatever.[41] The original complaint of the Anabaptists, against both Roman Catholics and classical reformers, was the lack of discipline within the established churches; sinners and virtual pagans were included indiscriminately in the community.[42] The Anabaptists saw the main task of the true church as that of maintaining discipline over its members. Littell defines that task in contemporary terms: "The basic task before the churches is precisely one of Christian discipline: to create within the congregation of new Christians that quality of consecrated thinking and obedience which is appropriate to a Biblical people."[43] The Free Churches, therefore, are not internally free: not, that is, free from their own stringent form of discipline. Their originality lies in the method by which they exercise this discipline.

In the classical Christian communities of the sixteenth century, discipline was exercised pastorally, from above, hierarchically. "The locus of authority in Free Churches is different. It is not, as sometimes argued, in the individual conscience apart, which has a constant tendency to warp along the lines of individual self-interest. The locus is in the authority of the Holy Spirit in the midst of the covenantal people."[44] The important elements here are threefold: the covenant; belief in the Holy Spirit who teaches through consensus; and the discipline of the discussion which leads to consensus. "The early Free Churchmen did not favor internal freedom in the Church. Every member was not only free but obligated to participate in the 'talking up' of discipline; and the discipline itself was binding."[45] Let us examine these elements in turn.

In attempting to restore the pure church of the New Testament, the Anabaptists aimed first of all to restore "a vigorous congregational life."[46] They desired personal and communal seriousness, and therefore insisted on an explicit *covenant* or pledge. As Christ was baptized at the age of thirty, so they thought that all who would "walk in His way of submission and martyrdom might thereby know that the Christian life requires mature dedication and discipline."[47] It requires a "degree of understanding (*Vernunft*) which only mature persons can possess."[48] Such dedication begins "in a thoroughgoing repentance,"[49] and issues in the decision "to make personal absolution and to covenant a new life with God and the community of believers."[50] "In Anabaptist teaching, the new birth has Christ alone as foundation and must occur radically in the history of both the individual believer and the True Church."[51] In Littell's view, then—perhaps somewhat overstated at this point— the idea of the covenant, individual and communal, became the constitutive idea of the Free Churches, the foundation of Free Church life.

Secondly, the idea of *the Holy Spirit who teaches through consensus* —i.e., through the conscience of the individual *and* of the community— follows upon the idea of the covenant. The "responsibility of a good conscience toward God" requires "brotherly admonition and exhortation, the practice of intentional fellowship."[52] "By baptism the believer came under the discipline of a Biblical people—a discipline which he himself helped make and enforce."[53] "Group consciousness became a dominant force in baptized life."[54] To unlock the meaning of Scriptures (by "the Key of David"), the individual had the obligation to test his findings against those of others in the fellowship.[55] To have his sins forgiven (by "the Keys of Peter"), the individual again had to have recourse to the community.[56] The center of authority in the movement "shifted from the protesting individual conscience"—even from the inspired, charismatic leader—"to the newly gathered congregations governed by the Holy Spirit in the midst."[57] Quite strictly, the Anabaptists opposed a salaried hierarchy.[58] They believed the Holy Spirit could teach through a responsible community as well as through a professional clergy. "In the matter of spiritual government in its various forms the presence and sovereignty of the Holy Spirit was accented."[59] Two quotations may help us understand this faith. First, from Menno Simons, probably the greatest leader of the early Anabaptists:

> Then if I err in some things, which by the grace of God I hope is not the case, I pray everyone for the Lord's sake, lest I be put to shame, that if anyone has stronger and more convincing truth he through brotherly exhortation and instruction might assist me. I desire with my heart to accept it if he is right. Deal with me according to the intention of the Spirit and Word of Christ.[60]

The second is from Karl Barth:

> Against the papal, but also against the episcopal and presbyterian-synodal concept stands the fundamental fact that they do not serve but actually hinder the readiness, the openness, the freedom of the congregation for the Word of God and the reformation of the church.[61]

The third element, then, in the fundamental principle of authority in the Anabaptist communions, is *the discipline of free and honest discussion*. Each member is obligated to take part. Any member may feel free to contradict any other, even an elder. "This highlights the essential point: not personal prestige, but the achievement of a consensus under the guidance of the Holy Spirit."[62] The apparatus of parliamentary procedure may be very simple. "Sometimes the decision takes years of discussion and seeking for guidance. . . ."[63] "The preparation is more important than the actual vote."[64] "The Free Churches are not, it is clear, 'free' in structure or opinion; theirs is a real discipline and order which emerges among the members, and is not dictated from above either by prince or by hierarchy."[65] This method of consensus is only a method; but it is founded upon a deep faith. "Our fathers, who were not too struck with their own genius to admit dependence upon One far greater and wiser, were accustomed to refer to Him matters of political import as readily as ecclesiastical. They believed that if a people called on His name with abandon, He would not leave them without guidance. The answer would not be an absolute one—i.e., sufficient for all times and places—but it would be enough to live by."[66]

### THE FREE CHURCHES AND ROMAN CATHOLICISM

In the first three sections we have wished to make three points. First, from the point of view of the Roman Catholic, the Anabaptist or Free Church tradition is eminently worthy of study, doubly so because prejudged in the past. Secondly, the thirst for Christian perfection in the Anabaptist community is very like the motivating force of the Catholic religious communities. Thirdly, Anabaptist emphasis upon the free act of faith, the covenant, and the consensus, introduce into Christian polity an admirable way of living out the freedom of the Gospels under communal discipline. It is time to draw pointed lessons from both the Roman Catholic and the Free Church traditions, in the light of the contemporary situation.

In the first place, such lessons must be concrete rather than ideological; we do well not to argue from what Free Churchmen or Catholics are "supposed to be," but from what they are. Good and admirable men live in both communities. Both communities have learned much in the many generations of history which have been lived since the Reformation. Without suggesting a larger body of shared experience than yet exists, we may then point out several ways in which the two traditions are closer to each other now, and will be more so in the future, than they have been since the sixteenth century.

Our first remarks about the Free Church tradition as it is living at present will be critical, but no more so than those of one of its own spokesmen. "Candor compels the admission that, by classical standards, our American churches have taken on the character of establishments. They may still flatter themselves that they have escaped any large measure of political control (the *negative* phase of Free Churchmanship), but in terms of theological and ethical discipline (i.e., the disciplined community witness to the working of the Holy Spirit—the *positive* phase of Free Church life), the larger denominations, at least, are establishments. . . . In the long view, acceptance of status as *social establishments* can be as fatal as *political establishments*."[67] The Free Church tradition, in other words, has so far been better able to cope with the Constantinian establishment than with the secular, democratic establishment.

In the second place, it seems to the observer that the original Free Church idea depended more than it knew upon smallness of numbers, and perhaps upon persecution from without. So long as the communities were small, the method of consensus was manageable. So long as persecution endured, the tension of fervor had to be high. As the numbers of members grew, as the churches became prosperous, older methods did not seem to work as well. As decisions about when to adapt to the changing times resulted sometimes in surrender to worldly values and sometimes to fixation in cultural or technological primitivism,[68] new instruments of renewal and reform seemed called for. As missionary effort expanded, a larger organization of moneys and personnel at home was required. Thus, gradually, the Anabaptist communities appear to have become increasingly indistinguishable from other Christian communities. Seminaries have been founded, pastors are paid salaries, theology becomes more complex, involvement in social ethics demands ever more expertise, national and international church organizations are founded, moneys need to be raised, and many subtle forms of authority other than consensus in the Holy Spirit begin, in actual fact, to be operative both in individual and in communal faith and practice. The original Free Church insight, it seems—useful, admirable, and historically significant as it is—does not move upon a wide enough base to support the weight of a religious community of men in history. Many complementary insights, practices, and methods must in actual fact be brought into operation to maintain the historical life of the Free Church. "The issue between Protestantism and Roman Catholicism is not, therefore, individualism vs. discipline: *the issue is how that discipline is to be attained.*"[69] As the Free Churches, of human necessity, become more professional and bureaucratic, the question of method becomes wider in base, more sophisticated, and more complex.

From the other direction, Roman Catholicism is shedding many of the impedimenta of the Constantinian era. If we are to look at Roman Catholicism as historical development presents it, we must conclude that it is beginning to appropriate Free Church ideals. Those in the Free Church tradition may, of course, look on this progress with skepticism, with condescension, or with hope, as they choose; just as many Catholics look askance at the polity and practice of the Free Churches. But what will be significant for the future of Christianity will be the degree to which all the Christian churches come to grips with the exigencies of communal and individual fidelity to the revelation of Christ—and that may well require learning from each other's strengths and weaknesses.

It would be irksome to go into great detail here about the tentative, gradual movement of Roman Catholicism toward some Free Church ideals. Let us content ourselves with listing several of these developments. (1) The Second Vatican Council has at long last produced a strong statement of religious liberty, consonant with the understanding of religious liberty in the Anabaptist tradition. We may therefore project that, increasingly, moral pressure will be brought upon Constantinian arrangements like those of Spain. (2) The first and second chapters in the constitution on the church discuss the church, not as a bureaucratic organization, but as a mystery and as the people of God, a covenanted community.[70] The traditional hierarchical principle of Roman Catholicism will be retained, but the role of the pastors will be understood primarily as a service to the gathered people and only secondarily as an administrative, juridical rule. Emphasis is laid upon the importance of lay participation in ecclesiastical decisions. (3) According to the widely hailed discourse of Cardinal Suenens at the second session,[71] the constitution will also reflect concern with the doctrine of the Holy Spirit speaking through all members of the church. (4) Although laymen did not really speak in the Council—except on rare occasions[72]—the method of consensus was used regularly at the Council. (5) In preparation for the Council, and in the wake of its first two sessions, many "little councils" were held in individual dioceses or parishes, in which laymen participated. The idea of discussion and consensus appears to be taking root.

Roman Catholic theologians are working in each of these directions. Bishops and Cardinals at the Council supported such directions. Many Catholics already believe and attempt to practice them. That such developments are painstaking and slow is not to be despised; solid historical progress is often slow. In any case, the Constantinian, monarchical, juridical conception of polity which has characterized Roman Catholicism for many centuries is not necessary to her life; and the evolution away from this conception has been well begun. We may employ the maxim that a Council of the Church works behind its times by a generation or two, and suggest that theological and programmatic developments among Roman Catholics are already far in advance of the Second Vatican Council. The Council has clearly approved the general orientation.

How far the evolution will go in dissolving the excessive *Romanità* of Roman Catholic polity is not yet clear. Nor is it clear to what extent the Free Churches will come to grips with their own problems of renewal and reform, particularly in the question of discipline. The Free Churches appear to be no longer small, disciplined, fervent, but complex, embracing both "saints" and "sinners," and ambiguous about questions of authority and decision; they cherish, however, their admirable traditions.

Perhaps God foresees—men do not—how these separate traditions, moving from opposite directions as it were, may one day make one fold.

# V / HOBBES'S THEORY OF ASSOCIATIONS IN THE SEVENTEENTH-CENTURY MILIEU

## D. B. Robertson

### THE HISTORICAL CONTEXT

Recently the *New York Times*[1] published an article with the caption "Eccentric Clubs Abound in Britain." Some of the clubs noted were indeed "eccentric"! England, however, or more broadly the Anglo-Saxon world,[2] has been the spawning ground for voluntary groups which have characterized modern, Western democratic societies. It is not that non-Anglo-Saxon countries have not had voluntary associations in impressive numbers;[3] it is the function that these groups have performed in the societies which has been the most significant point, and this point has been determinative for the type of society which has developed. It is fateful for the health of democratic life in our own society now and in the future.

England in the seventeenth century, especially in the Revolutionary period, and even on through the Restoration, was a land of burgeoning groups, clubs, and organizations of all kinds[4]—or configurations of social power which Edmond Cahn[5] calls "unofficial government" or "powerful magic."[6] Thomas Hobbes, in his better moods, called them "lesser commonwealths,"[7] but in his considered opinion they were dangerous elements in the state.

In seventeenth-century England old patterns of social, religious, and economic power were tumbling, and the forms and patterns of the new age to come were not yet firmly settled. In this creative period, however, English imagination and ingenuity turned to the vast domain of nature and to social institutions. They forced their prying fingers into the secrets of nature. This was an age of phenomenal advance in the fields of science and mathematics. In this period the Royal Society was organized and set on its notable history to make science, the "new philosophy," a corporate venture. Meetings of the group began in 1645, the group organized formally in 1660, and they were granted a Royal Charter in 1662. Englishmen turned with equal interest and with more passionate involvement to the domain of social institutions. They talked, wrote, and fought about questions of what kinds of institutions would be appropriate for religious life and activity, for managing economic realities newly emerging, for using and hedging political power, and for multiple other purposes. They organized and talked and wrote about everything from church and political government to the circulation of the blood to the question of how to improve Dutch windmills! For these and similar purposes they formed a multitude of organizations. This is not to say that there were not some types of clubs or voluntary associations long before the organizational explosion of the seventeenth century.[8] One of the major functions, however, of many of the seventeenth-century groups, and in modern democratic societies in general, was typically new—to cushion the space (and all that can happen in it) between the individual or the family and the powerful modern state or monarch. The high-handed actions of monarchs like Henry the VIII and later "arbitrary" kings like James I and Charles I underscored the need for such mediating institutions.

Out of the decentralized political configurations of the feudal system appeared the powerful modern, national state, in England and on the Continent. Signs of this social and political development were already evident in the later medieval period, particularly in the French struggle with the papacy. The modern national state, in its struggle to bring unity to the community, tended to be absolutist, to seek to dominate all aspects of the life of the citizen. Dominant power justified itself sometimes by "divine right," sometimes on secular grounds, and sometimes did not pretend at all to justify its actions.

In some nations of the West, however, various interest groups—religious, economic, political, "cultural," and scientific—managed (by laborious and painful devices well known) to qualify and regulate very definitely the centralization of power by the multiplication of subgroups that aimed at the dispersion of power. They aimed at the same time to recover something of the medieval sense of community.[9] The church and the world changed and "reformed" together, a fact that, in retrospect, is not surprising. However, in the period following the Reformation there was on all sides a wide range of confusing problems that presented themselves for all persons and groups in society. Rudolph Sohm has observed that "the new-born Gospel meant the reformation of the Church; and the reformation of the Church meant the reformation of the whole world."[10]

#### HOBBES AS CHIEF INTELLECTUAL ENEMY OF ASSOCIATIONS

While it is obvious that the England of the seventeenth century produced great numbers and great varieties of "voluntary associations," it is also true that this age produced the greatest and most formidable enemy of such groups in modern times, namely, Thomas Hobbes.

Hobbes's defenders and apologists have been historically for the most part apologists for monarchy and even totalitarianism. Hobbes has been an eminently popular figure in Germany, though he has had his critics there too, particularly of his interpretation of the natural law. In the Nazi period in Germany he especially was popular as an advocate of "Real-politik." If we go back to his own period in history, following the Restoration (in 1660), we find that Hobbes was a favorite at Court, at least at that of Charles II (Charles II called him "the bear"), though his enemies were numerous, and he enjoyed a rather precarious popularity because Charles II, though his protector, was also sensitive to the social and political trends of his reign.

The tensions indeed were uncommonly severe. Political attempts were made to suppress various groups; some English kings, as is well known, were ruthless and vigorous in repressive measures. This oppression was perhaps more often directed against religious groups, but it was certainly not limited to these groups, and, of course, Cromwell finally suppressed one of the most notable voluntary associations, the Leveller Party. The rulers who pursued a hostile policy toward various groups claimed to do so in the interest of the unity of the state and the crushing of treason, or to maintain some royal prerogative. Group life, then, encountered powerful enemies.

Thomas Hobbes was the most able intellectual enemy of groups within the state—the great enemy, therefore, of democracy in Anglo-Saxon terms.[11] Hobbes flourished in the middle of the century and had had, as he thought, ample opportunity to observe the evil which the proliferation of groups could bring to the state. Hobbes had some not unkind tentative words to say about democracy.[12] He stated that *theoretically* democracy (or "an assembly") may meet his prescribed needs for a strong *de facto* government. In the mature development of his thought, however, democracy, as the Levellers and Locke projected it, and as it has actually developed in the Anglo-Saxon world, stood contrary to Hobbes's sober judgment.[13] His first published work was a translation of Thucydides' *History*. Thucydides was Hobbes's favorite ancient author. Too many of the other ancient authors, popular reading in his day, were, to Hobbes, clearly threats to social order. These "subversive" ancient authors were being read and quoted in the universities, by Anglican divines, and by Puritans of all types. Hobbes, then, though theoretically permitting "an assembly" legitimate status, obviously favored monarchy as a form of government, if not tyranny, in actual practice. In his introduction to Thucydides' *History,* Hobbes says: "For his [Thucydides'] opinion touching the government of the state, it is manifest that he least of all liked the democracy."[14] By the time he published his mature work, *Leviathan* (full title: *Leviathan, or, The Matter, Form, and Power of A Commonwealth, Ecclesiastical and Civil*), in April of 1651, he had clearly arrived at a totalitarian position. This position allowed for no single, legitimate qualification of the power of the ruler. Hobbes and Plato are agreed about the nature of "democracy." Plato, however, has sometimes been cited as a supporter of democracy in various aspects of his ideal state. Hobbes could hardly be claimed by "democrats" in any sense!

*Leviathan* covers a wide spectrum of subjects, including science, religion, natural law, civil law, human nature, and the nature of sovereign power in the state. Of particular concern here, however, are Hobbes's conception of human nature, of contract, of sovereignty (the relationship of subgroups within the state to the sovereign), and the particular attention Hobbes pays to religion. All who share a positive view of the creative possibilities of "voluntary associations" or subgroups within a democratic society must come to terms with Hobbes, the great enemy of group function and of multiplication, the condemner of all gatherings of any type not under the strictest subservience to the state. To understand what Hobbes finally says specifically about "voluntary associations," however, it is necessary to see his judgments in the context of other crucial elements in his thought.

### HUMAN NATURE

Hobbes gives much space in his writings to human nature. It has been argued[15] that Hobbes as a political philosopher was not much interested in human nature as such. It may be that he was more concerned to establish support for his naturalistic politics and ethics with a logical—or, more appropriately, psychological—foundation. But a state, an artificial construct, cannot be understood without some understanding of the state-creating animal. As Hood says, "The cause of the commonwealth must be discovered in the nature of man."[16] Hobbes even draws an analogy between God as creator and man as creator.[17]

Hobbes, it must be noted, was candid enough and objective enough in his approach to human nature to work from himself as subject and from persons he knew well.[18] He purports to do otherwise in places, but in any case he never worked from a stance of "theory" or from a doctrinaire position, though he believed that what he saw in particular men applied to mankind. He thought he knew what motivates man. This approach from "experience" (running through many facets of English life at the time, including much religious interest) is oddly at variance with his "rationalism" elsewhere (in parts of his political works), and it was ostensibly at the center of his quarrel with the members of the "experimenting" Royal Society. At one point he sees these "truths about man" as self-evident truths which anyone may observe by introspection.[19] But who is to say just what is the relative importance of "experience" and "rational" presuppositions that went into the making of Hobbes's philosophy of human nature and political philosophy?

Hobbes elaborates what are to him three main causes for man's perpetual posture of conflict: (1) Competition, "which makes men invade for gain"; (2) what he calls "diffidence," meaning the concern for one's safety; and (3) glory, honor, and reputation.[20]

The fact is that Hobbes chopped off somewhat over half of the Christian doctrine of man.[21] He was overly conscious of "the evil that men do." He was impressed especially with man's capacity for doing whatever served his own vital interests. He saw no sign of any "capacity for justice" on the part of man, except as it was forced on him by the sovereign. Man's other-regarding qualities—necessary ingredients for any serious assessment of democratic possibilities—was hardly a theme of interest to Hobbes. "This man's will to hurt ariseth from vain glory, and the false esteem he hath of his own strength; the other's from the necessity of defending himself, his liberty and his goods, against this man's violence."[22] Man had to be understood essentially in terms of will or "passions." Man's capacities, intellectual and physical, Hobbes assumed to be essentially equal, for where physical superiority failed, man is able by imaginable and unimaginable devices to level the actual engagement of man with man. But man's capacities at the same time make him superior to and more dangerous than any other creature. "Man to man is an arrant wolf . . ."[23] Man shows his nature also, Hobbes noted, by his tendency to play God to other people.[24] Perhaps the most notable and familiar of Hobbes's statements about man and his condition in the "state of nature" is to be found in chapter 13 of *Leviathan:*

> Whatsoever, therefore, is consequent to a time of war where every man is enemy to every man, the same is consequent to the time wherein men live without other security than what their own strength and their own invention shall furnish them withal. In such condition there is no place for industry, because the fruit thereof is uncertain: and consequently no culture of the earth; no navigation nor use of the commodities that may be imported by sea; no commodious building; no instruments of moving and removing such things as require much force; no knowledge of the face of the earth; no account of time; no arts; no letters; no society; and, *which is worst of all, continual fear and danger of violent death; and the life of man solitary, poor, nasty, brutish, and short.*[25]

As already noted, Hobbes's conclusions about human nature were no doubt influenced by his observations of men and events of his own age—a fractious, rakehelly generation, as he saw it, given to faction and passionate behavior. Some have suggested that Hobbes's own personal timidity should be considered as a source of his views of man and politics. But whatever part this may have played, it is hardly sufficient basis for judging his philosophy. In any case, if fear of violent death is a chief factor in the human creation and sustenance of the commonwealth, Hobbes claims to regard man not simply as wicked! "Neither by the word right is anything else signified, than that liberty which every man hath to make use of his natural faculties according to *right reason.* Therefore the first foundation of natural right is this, that every man as much as in him lies endeavour to protect his life."[26] Whatever the weaknesses of reason in the face of and under the dominance of passion, reason at least served the positive function of allowing man to see that order *per se* is more desirable than anarchy or the "state of nature."[27] Thus reason plays some tentative, tenuous, and precarious part in the positive achievements within the commonwealth that man creates. However, to be "sociable" requires sovereign sanctions. Hobbes believed that man can manage a precarious social order, but the hope was based upon the ruler's ability to rule and man's fear of the alternative, and not ultimately upon man's social nature, his capacity for justice to his fellow men. To misuse Reinhold Niebuhr's well-known formulation about human nature and democracy, Hobbes might have said that "man's tendency to do violence makes democracy impossible; man's incapacity to do justice makes centralized power necessary."

Hobbes had no doubt that he had an answer to those who may boggle at his somber view of human nature and possibility. He thought he could point to evidence that, he felt, was obvious and should be convincing to everyone. He cited the reputed life of "savages," particularly in America. He twitted his fellow Englishmen about their habit of traveling armed and with company where possible, of locking their doors at night, and of securing their valuables in chests within their own households against their servants and their children. Further, he saw the warfare of nation against nation as a continuation on a group basis of the struggle of man against man in the state of nature. So that, the state of nature, even within man's created order, is always peeping out and threatening more dangerous forays. Passion and self-interest are the aspects of man to be carefully regarded by the one who would be sovereign and maintain order.

Sheldon Wolin makes a point of stressing the "hopeful" element in Hobbes's political thought.[28] "Machiavelli, Luther, and Calvin might pray to different gods, and Hobbes pray to none at all, yet all four were at one in their response to chaos: chaos was the material of creativity, not a cause of resignation. They were all Platonists in the spirit of their assumption about the plasticity of human arrangements and the efficacy of the human will, and despite (or perhaps even because of) the dark view each had of human nature."[29] Trevor-Roper chooses to emphasize what he calls "The General Crisis of the 17th Century."[30] "Ever since 1618 at least there had been talk of the dissolution of society, or of the world."[31] It is clear to anyone who takes even a cursory look at the literature of seventeenth-century England that a case can be made out either way. "Hopefulness," or at least expectancy of better things to come, finds many expressions. The belief that the "crisis" presented opportunities for really creative solutions for Englishmen was expressed widely.[32] As for Hobbes, one can say that his "hopefulness" centered on one of the necessities for society and on one of the aspects of traditional natural law doctrine, too (though never before with such emphasis!)—that is, on "order." His "hopefulness," then, tended to neglect other values, or at least the form they take, namely, equality and justice. Hobbes's "hopefulness" was finally based on fear and not hope as we ordinarily use the word.

### SOVEREIGNTY

Government, or order, depends for Hobbes on mutual trust—mutual trust, it must be noted, with a special Hobbesian twist. Hobbes's view of sovereignty dates, as Christopher Hill reminds us, "from the actual period of armed conflict in England."[33] But we may rightly ask this question: if a man is the selfish, low creature that Hobbes pictures him to be, how does "mutual trust" make sense as a basis of order? The fact is, says Hobbes, that man's antisocial tendency makes it senseless to expect him to respect other men's rights without coercion. So, mutual trust is *coerced* mutual trust. Agreements or covenants are kept only where *de facto* government is powerful enough to enforce compliance.[34] If sovereignty breaks down, Hobbes would seem to have nothing left as an alternative but chaos. This point led one of his sharpest critics, the Earl of Clarendon, to conclude that Hobbes left the sovereign "on such a Precipice from which the least Invasion from a neighbor, or, from Rebellion by his subjects, may throw him headlong to irrecoverable ruine."[35]

This sovereign power had its use of force based upon a contract or covenant relationship,[36] a very old political concept and one common to the many and various groups of the seventeenth century. For example, Leveller literature is full of reference to it, and it was, of course, central to Locke's thinking later in the century. The idea of contract or of cove-

nant is in this century intertwined with views of the "state of nature"
and the "law of nature."[37] Hobbes's view of contract is peculiar to himself. It is a device for escaping the miseries of his "state of nature." It
is a covenant between individuals, with three essential provisions: (1)
that the individuals mutually submit themselves to a sovereign, (2) who
will forcefully protect each from the other, (3) and the whole from any
other threat. It is, says Hobbes,

> . . . as if every man should say to every man, I authorize and give up
> my right of governing myself to this man, or to this assembly of men,
> on this condition, that you give up your right to him and authorize all
> his actions in like manner.[38]

It is clear that Hobbes's understanding of natural law, and hence of the
covenant relationship, is very different from the traditional view (Hook-
er's, for example) and the view held by many in his own day. Hobbes's
development of natural law conceptions, as of other aspects of his
thought, are intended, for one thing, to deny the Aristotelian notion of
man's natural sociability. Hobbes is more akin to the Sophists here,
but this is true only where convention supports unqualified central
power. Natural law, as generally conceived,[39] involved several very specific emphases: it was *universal,* it was *immutable,* it held out *order* (or
"peace") as a social goal, it declared *justice* to be an ideal for man, and
it held *equality* as a central value in implementing human relationships. Hobbes's natural law was universal all right; however, he ultimately reduced natural law and the meaning of covenant to self-preser-
vation. Natural law is defined as a "precept or general rule, found out
by reason, by which a man is forbidden to do that which is destructive
of his life, or takes away the means of preserving the same and to omit
that by which he thinks it may be best preserved."[40] The first specific law
of nature which lies at the foundation of social life follows from that:
"That every man ought to endeavor peace, as far as he has hope of obtaining it; and when he cannot obtain it, that he may seek and use all
helps and advantages of war."[41] Order becomes, then, the essence of
natural law for Hobbes; for only through this social value can man assure his safety. And although Hobbes enumerates several other "natural laws," they ultimately anchor on the first, and may be finally reduced to "one easy sum: do not that to another which you would not
have done to yourself."[42]

Hobbes's preoccupation with order requires further elaboration.
W. W. Kulski is right in his emphasis on the point that we cannot simply "write off all thinkers who placed other values [besides individual
liberty] higher," and he refers to Hobbes among others as an example.[43]
It is, of course, a truism to say that without order all other social values

may become precarious or non-existent. Obviously overemphasis on order, on the political spectrum, however, builds a foundation for tyranny. Norton E. Long[44] emphasizes the merit of Hobbes's recognition that "the existence of order is problematic,"[45] that "order" should be seen in a broader framework than "the emphasis on force as the *ultima ratio*."[46] Agreed. But when Long defines "anarchy," there is a missing link in connection with Hobbes's concern and in terms of one of the chief struggles in Hobbes's period. "The essence of anarchy is the existence of incompatible and incongruous definitions of the situation among the actors. The essence of order is the reverse."[47] The point is that the struggle between king and Parliament, the context of Hobbes's emerging political philosophy, was not over "definitions." The common law was clear enough in its definitions of the particular prerogatives of king and Parliament. Sir Edward Coke had seen to that! It was a question of "cases," particular issues, which kept coming to the forefront of controversy, and how, if at all, these "cases" squared with the "definitions." Over particular issues communication and cooperation began to break down. Hobbes fled to France when he saw that Charles I could not muster the necessary force to maintain order.

A very significant recent article by Leonard Krieger permits an evaluation of Hobbes's emphasis on order from another approach. Krieger argues that the "historian" is always on a "quest for distortions," and he sees Hobbes as one example of a victim. "A distortion may be defined in this context as a significant discrepancy of a representation from the thing represented. . . . inadequacy or error becomes distortion when the deviation harbors a meaning. Where the philosopher and scientist seek truth and account for error, the historian, on the level of distortion, seeks error and accounts for truth."[48] If to interpret Hobbes as an advocate of totalitarian political views is a "distortion," a plea of "guilty" is duly entered! One can build a case that Hobbes's significant attack (or "qualification," depending on your degree of "distortion") upon freedom, equality, and justice as known in democratic thought and experience was itself a notable case of "distortion." If a description of Hobbes's estimate of the "concession" theory is indeed a "distortion," then let history be written to err on that side of the political spectrum which says "nay" to his "solution"!

Perhaps a crucial aspect of the whole question of Hobbes's preoccupation with order is that he (addressing "the people" as vs. Machiavelli's word to the "prince") puts his greatest emphasis upon control and pays too little attention to other social values. He wants things to "stay put." A question which no one has sufficiently explored is this: does Hobbes's political philosophy make any constructive provisions for social change? There appears to be no such provision. Perhaps

Hobbes's revolutionary age presented to him built-in limitations here. There was, in fact, a fragmenting, sectarian development in his time which was something new in history in both degree and kind. The situation did not, perhaps, at least in Hobbes's mind, allow much levity for exploring the question of orderly change. In any case, his preoccupation with order seems to contain no viable context within which orderly social and political change may occur. Any positive view of the function and power and maneuverability of groups in society therefore remains undeveloped in Hobbes's thinking.

In traditional natural law doctrine, *justice* had usually been considered more basic as the foundation of society (and it was so considered by many in Hobbes's day) than order. Justice involves not just some presumed initial "consent of the governed" but a continuous maintenance of support for government by consensus, by a continuous sense of fairness of treatment and of needs being served. "Consent" in Hobbes comes prior to "justice," for it is the sovereign, having received the individuals' consent, who then defines "justice" and "injustice." None of the elements of resistance to tyranny is implicit; these elements are, in fact, explicitly ruled out. Justice is no revolutionary instrument; it is a human convention, determined by the sovereign. It is not something founded in nature, in human nature, or in "reality." Hobbes argues, and finally states dogmatically, that covenant, and hence the meaning and determination of justice, is a one-sided affair. Says Hobbes: "Nothing the sovereign representative can do to a subject, on what pretense soever, can properly be called injustice or injury, for every subject is author of every act that the sovereign does."[49] Christopher Hill underlines the Hobbesian position in this manner: "Justice is the keeping of contracts: no more."[50] This view is predicated on the notion that the initial contract establishing the sovereign implies respect for and conformity with sovereign fiat, as well as the individual's relationship to any *persona ficta* existing under the sovereign.[51]

Again, to relate Hobbes's concept of *equality* to the democratic tradition is as problematical as it is with other hallmarks of natural-law thinking. Of course, Aristotle's natural inequality he obviously refutes. Hobbes delineates two kinds of equality. One type, already noted, is equality of ability, where intellect and ingenuity can balance off any physical inequalities in men. Also, men are equal in their expectation of satisfying their wants or attaining their ends.[52] In *Leviathan* he presents this latter type as a consequence of the first type of equality: "From this equality of ability arises equality of hope in the attaining of our ends. And therefore if any two men desire the same thing, which nevertheless they cannot enjoy, they become enemies; and in the way to their end, which is principally their own conservation and sometimes their delectation only, endeavor to destroy or subdue one another."[53]

Equality for Hobbes is an observable fact, and he argues no moral basis for it, though moral equality may be implicit from the fact of equality. Macpherson says that Hobbes was the first political philosopher "to be able to dispense with assumptions of outside purpose or will."[54]

One of the bases of friction among men is their seeking after "glory" or "vain conceit"[55]—a sign of their inability to accept the fact of equality. There are no grounds for one man to think of himself as above another. Equality likewise should prevent men from claiming special privileges for themselves.[56]

Hobbes's view of equality had limited implications (if any at all) for the broad range of social-political relationships that were in this period in the fluid state and being broadly debated. But there were some implications he notes. The first one of these is the responsibility of the sovereign to deal equally (equitably) with his subjects.[57] Hobbes makes a special point, too, of equal taxation. "To equal justice [add] also the equal imposition of taxes, the equality whereof depends not on the equality of riches but on the equality of the debt that every man owes to the commonwealth for his defense."[58] However, problems of justice, as confronted, for example, in a democratic context, are not to be settled by the "self-evident truths" for Hobbes. On the other hand, his undercutting of the status of the aristocracy, based on tradition and common law, had implicit in it some dimensions of "levelling," as his critics were sure to point out, placing him in the same category with the "Levellers."[59] This attack on aristocracy was intended to facilitate the sovereign's ability to act. As for obvious economic inequalities in society, these, said Hobbes, are artificial, but he did not draw from the point a radical conclusion. His conservatism here is shown by the fact that only once did he specifically express hostility toward economic inequality. "There is sometimes in a commonwealth a disease which resembles the pleurisy; and that is when the treasure of the commonwealth, flowing out of its due course, is gathered together in too much abundance in one or a few private men by monopolies or by forms of public revenue . . ."[60] Actually, Hobbes wanted to avoid some of the extremes of wealth and poverty, lest either become a threat to peace. Hobbes, interestingly enough, makes special reference to the duty of the government to take care of the unemployed, that is, of those who may become unemployed by "accident inevitable."[61] But Hood is doubtless right in saying that Hobbes's "only concern regarding economic inequality in general was political rather than economic."[62]

In political terms "equality" under natural law conceptions has carried with it, certainly since seventeenth-century England, the notion of

popular government and the right to vote. This conviction was amply developed and fought for, unsuccessfully, by the Leveller Party. Cromwell
simply throttled this principle when he silenced the Party spokesmen.[63]

To return to the relationship of natural law and contract, it is to be
remembered that only the people is bound to the contract. There is
nothing in Hobbes's form of political authority to hide the impotence of
any notion of mutuality in contract. Yes, men are "free" in the state of
nature, but they are free only to opt total obedience to the sovereign—
free, that is, to opt slavery.[64] As Gierke notes,[65] Hobbes demolished
"what had hitherto been the foundation of all natural-law political
systems"; one aspect of the "demolishing" is that the element of
equality was maintained so far as the people are concerned, but there
is no reciprocity on the part of the ruler. Then, too, as Gierke puts it,
"He substituted for two original contracts (the contract of society and
the contract of government) a single contract."[66] The assumption that
the sovereign is no party to the contract ". . . destroyed, in the very germ,
any personality of the People . . . The personality of the People died at
its birth."[67] *Suprema lex*, against many trends and many eloquent
voices of Hobbes's time, was certainly not *vox Populi*! This "politically
deadly" doctrine was the property of numerous groups and individuals
of the period, as the vast literature shows.

A good many pages have been given to arguing whether Hobbes believed there ever was a "state of nature" such as he described or
whether there was ever such a covenant in history. There is no doubt
that it was for him a "logical fiction"—required by his understanding
of human nature and by his observations of man's actual habits. His
view is also to some degree determined by his fear of what could happen
if sovereign power should break down! Hobbes actually had no specific
knowledge of primitive societies, at least not in twentieth-century anthropological terms. His view logically is that man's condition, or
submission to sovereignty, is simply for him the lesser of two evils. In
fact, Hobbes says that his description of man in the "state of nature . . .
was never generally so all over the world." He states, however, that
". . . there are many places where they live that way now. For the
savage people in many places in America . . . have no government at all
and live at this day in that brutish manner as I said before."[68] In any
case, as Norton E. Long says, "Hobbes emphasized the ever present
immanence of anarchy, the latent tendency of society to dissolve into
a warring heap of individuals."[69] Sovereignty, then, must always be
turning back to the notion of power firmly held, if strangely acquired,
by the ruler.

A significant contrast between Hobbes's view of power and that of a
group of his contemporaries may be noted briefly: The Leveller Party,

a group whose existence Hobbes did not acknowledge, developed a very different conception of power. Hobbes purports to derive all power ultimately from God, but if Hobbes really took seriously the derivation of power from God, he very quickly relieved God of any part in its earthly management. In actual practice, power was, for Hobbes, a purely earth-bound affair, shared neither with God or man by the "powers that be." The Levellers, at least the more vocal spokesmen, developed a conception of power as being somehow a shared relationship between God and man. The Levellers were "realistic" enough in their notions of how power, or the exercise of it, looks in actual political affairs. They associated with Cromwell long enough to learn that. Their conception of vocation, however, led to a sense of obligation to share in the exercise of power. If "power tends to corrupt," all right; the law, as the Levellers proposed to establish it, would protect persons against man's "tendency to do injustice." The desired goals of politics are to be left neither to God (as the millenarians and Fifth-Monarchy Men wrongly supposed), nor to a few men who grasp for power, whether they (or he) be king, priest, the Army, or Cromwell! Christians are responsible for making the state responsible and holding it to the purposes of equality, of justice, and of freedom. One might call the peculiar Leveller understanding of vocation—of the relationship of God and man and power—"political synergism," the sharing of redeeming social and political power between God and man. At such a notion Hobbes undoubtedly would have snickered up his sleeve!

## CORPORATION

Without some word about the "corporation" (*universitas*), it is impossible to understand Hobbes's attitude toward the state and the place of groups within the state. Men acting as a body means for Hobbes that someone is acting in the name of the group. The state or sovereign is the only absolute corporation; all others exist by "concession." Groups within the state exist by no right of their own. They find their legitimacy or "personality" only insofar as the state concedes it to them. Thus corporation (or "incorporation") is not, as in our tradition, a device for certain protections within a free society; it is an arm of the state for limiting group rights and activities. In other words, it is a means of control within an absolutist state.[70]

Hobbes quite obviously held to the Roman conception of corporation, along with the consequent suspicion of all types of association. Gibbon records that Roman policy "viewed with utmost jealousy and distrust any association among its subjects . . . and the privileges of private corporation, though formed for the most harmless or beneficial purposes, were bestowed with a sparing hand."[71] The experience of the church in the early part of the second century illustrates the application of this legal stumbling block. Pliny the Younger, writing to Trajan about handling the Christian problem (sometime between A.D. 111 and 113), noted that ". . . by your commands I have forbidden clubs," and this included the "Christian club"![72]

The development of the legal conception of the corporation has a long and complicated history, [73] but Maitland, following Gierke, says that the conception of *persona ficta* did not appear clearly until the time of Innocent IV, who became pope in 1243.[74] Hobbes's conception of political authority is predicated on the absolute right of the sovereign to make or break these artificial persons or associations; here lies the ground of the "concession" theory.

In the light of the English and American experience with voluntary associations, it is surprising to find Maitland making the following statements: "Long ago English lawyers received the Concession Theory from the canonists. Bred in the fellowship of the unchartered Inns, they were the very men to swallow it whole,"[75] though, of course, he was opposed to this supposed "swallowing." Then Maitland proceeds to say that "Nowhere has the Concession Theory been proclaimed more loudly, more frequently, more absolutely, than in America."[76] Maitland records the obvious fact that voluntary associations have flourished in England and America. He argues, however, that groups of all kinds have flourished under the trust concept. Englishmen, he says, have for the last four centuries been able to say, "If Pope Innocent and the Roman forces guard the front stairs, we shall walk up the back."[77] A. B. Keith sees a broader base for associations under English constitutional law. "The right of association is derived from (1) the freedom to contract under common law, (2) the power to form trusts freely, (3) the right to form companies, and (4) the special privileges given to trade unions, taken in conjunction with the laxity of the law of conspiracy."[78]

However one may assess Maitland's treatment of the subject of the status of associations in England, he certainly did not do justice either to American experience or to American law. It is true that the United States Constitution,[79] in its Bill of Rights, contains no specific mention of the "right to associate." When James Madison drafted the Bill of Rights in 1789, he included in the First Amendment simply the citizen's right "to assemble and to petition the Government for redress of grievances." As Edmond Cahn points out,[80] these words are simply repetitions of English usage in the previous century and are highly inappropriate for the American scene. The absence of specific reference to the right to associate, however, no doubt reflects Madison's initial fear of what he called in *The Federalist*[81] "factions." "By faction, I understand a number of citizens, whether amounting to a majority or minority of the whole, who are united and actuated by some common impulse of passion, or of interest, adverse to the rights of other citizens, or to the permanent and aggregate interests of the community."[82] Hobbes would hardly have disagreed. But even in 1787 Madison held that a republic could effectively manage factions. By 1792, he was impressed by the significance of political societies.[83] Madison seems finally to have recognized the values for a democratic society of great varieties of "interest" groups.[84] Whatever Madison's original strictures on "factions," and the way this affected our original Constitutional formulations, Maitland's identification of our view with the "concession" theory of the Romans and of Hobbes is askew!

While we do not have in the Constitution a "documentary given" (to use Edmond Cahn's words) specifying status for "voluntary associations," there has been a growing body of judicial interpretation which finds, in effect and in fact, the right of association solidly based in the Constitution. Briefly, it has been affirmed on the grounds of the First Amendment's "right of assembly," the right of freedom of speech and of the press, and other "rights," though it is well to remember that the right of assembly and the right of association, as we are using the latter expression in this volume, are not necessarily identical.[85] A case involving the "right of assembly" was not acted on by the Supreme Court of the United States until 1876—the case of *United States v. Cruikshank.* While the decision itself speaks only in terms of the right of assembly for purposes of petitioning Congress for redress of grievances, this was the beginning of a series of cases which became more and more specific in stating the right of association, one of the latest cases being decided in early 1963. Justice Arthur J. Goldberg, speaking for the majority, said, ". . . we hold simply that groups which themselves are neither engaged in subversive or other illegal or improper activities nor demonstrated to have any substantial connections with such activities are to be protected in their rights of free and private association."[86] In *De Jonge v. Oregon* (1937), the Court, noting the precedent in *United States v. Cruikshank*, pushed further toward a clear statement of the right of association and indicated the direction of future interpretations.[87]

One other factor related to Maitland's statements and Hobbes's Roman conception of corporation is just as basic. Corporation or "incorporation" does not mean to us what it did to Hobbes and the Romans, except, of course, that there is common notion in terms of the corporation as an "artificial person." But incorporation does not mean subservience to any "mortal god" or absolute corporation. At the same time, to return to Hobbes's overweening concern, democratic governmental recognition of the rights of independent group life has not meant, nor can it mean, that the Federal Government is surrendering its right to maintain order and to prevent certain types of possible abuse.

## HOBBES'S VIEW OF "VOLUNTARY ASSOCIATIONS"

Voluntary associations, in their most creative dimensions, exist in society, as we have noted, in the spaces between the state and the individual and the family. But for Hobbes, the distinction between society and the state quite clearly does not exist. His discussion of voluntary associations will have to be understood with this in mind. It will also be remembered that man is not by nature associational, according to Hobbes, contrary to our whole Hebrew-Christian and democratic tradition. The fundamental association, the state, represents, for him, the lesser of two evils. Said Hobbes: "Men have no pleasure, but on the contrary a great deal of grief, in keeping company where there is no power able to overawe them all."[88] Voluntary associations, therefore, even "legitimate" ones, have the odor of disorder and hostile human relations hovering over and around them.

Hobbes deals with the subject of voluntary associations (or other corporations besides the state . . . and groups not incorporated) in chapter 29 of *Leviathan,* under the caption, "Of Those Things that Weaken or Tend to the Dissolution of a Commonwealth"—a very revealing caption in itself. These groups, referred to as "corporations" or "persons" or "lesser commonwealths," are, he says, "like worms in the entrails of a natural man."[89] This lively analogy sees the human corpus being weakened and finally decimated by those individual little flesh-eaters gnawing away in the human belly, unmanaged, undisciplined, and uncrushed by the willpower, by the head or mind, or by the proper medicine. Death and dissolution are clearly the inevitable end. So, politically speaking, those independent "worms," being a sign of disorder or ill health already resident and ravaging, represent the very nature of disorder and dissolution of the Commonwealth. The fact is that Hobbes looked upon the multiplicity of these groups in his day, whether "legitimate" in his sense or not, as particularly dangerous to the order and peace of the nation. Many of these "lesser commonwealths," to use his most objective term of reference, quite obviously, with plan in hand, wanted to change the old order and to make a new order—thus to subvert the one Hobbes wanted to hold to or the one he projected as an ideal for the future. Hobbes is perhaps a good example of the social-political "conservative" or totalitarian-minded person who always accuses those who want to change anything of wanting to destroy everything. "Democracy," as Hobbes saw it (like Plato, but without Plato's analytical concern with "perfect" and "imperfect" forms of the state, or relative degrees of compromise), is simply chaos. Tyranny is preferable to chaos; to Hobbes you had to be always on the verge of making your choice.[90]

For all of Hobbes's fear of groups, he did nevertheless (in chapter 22 of *Leviathan*) explain conditions under which "lesser common-wealths" or "systems" may exist, always making clear that any legitimate existence is by "concession." The basic difference in the managerial mind of Hobbes between those permitted at all and those grudgingly permitted is between an association thoroughly and firmly created and controlled by the sovereign and a mob.

Associations or "assemblies" come into existence, as does the state, by covenant. All groups, in Hobbes's scheme, may be divided into "regular" and "irregular" or "formal" and "informal" groups, having a definite organization or not having a definite organization. "Regular" groups are those in which one man or assembly of men is constituted representative of the whole number of the membership.[91] The primary difference between various kinds of "regular" associations lies in the real fact of whether or not they are absolute or subordinate. As Hobbes demonstrates in previous chapters in *Leviathan,* up to chapter 29, only the state, "that mortal god," can be absolute or independent. The state is the only "regular," absolute system. Under the category "regular" there are "subordinate" and "dependent" groups—dependent, that is, upon the will of the state. Further, under the classification "subordinate" there are two divisions. The first is "political" or public. Hobbes defines these systems as "bodies politic" or "persons in law" made by the power of the ruler.[92] The second division under subordinate groups he refers to as "private." Private systems are those created for various purposes by citizens themselves, "or by authority of a stranger. For no authority derived from foreign power, within the dominion of another, is public but private."[93]

Under the subordinate groups that can become "persons" under the law and hence legitimate, Hobbes gives a number of illustrations: a town, a university or college, a church, "or for any other government over the persons of men."[94] Added to these are the great merchant companies (whose nature and responsibilities Hobbes elaborates extensively);[95] then there are groups assembled for a limited time, such as may be called by the sovereign as he sees fit. And last of all he mentions families. The family as here interpreted refers to the Roman *paterfamilias,* where the father is lord and master of the household, holding strictly to obedience the children and the servants.[96]

The category, "irregular" systems, refers to those having no representative, or what Hobbes calls a "concourse of people." This type of group is allowed to exist *if* the ruler does not specifically forbid it, or *if* such "concourses" have no "evil design." These groups may include such as are on picnics, in the marketplace, at fairs or shows. People have considerable levity, according to Hobbes, so long as they keep within the prescribed bounds defined by "the mortal god." As for these "ir-regular" groups, "when the intention is evil or (if the number be con-siderable) unknown, they are unlawful."[97] One could speculate, for in-stance, on whether Hobbes would have approved the Putney Debates, an informal gathering of soldiers and officers for a specific purpose and a limited time. The gathering was relatively orderly, so far as we know, but the purpose—to discuss seriously the merits and viability of the Leveller Party's "Agreement of the People"—would likely have been just the sort of political assemblage which would have been offensive. It would have been dangerous even to entertain the notion that gather-ings of this type had any "right" to convene or assemble. The Debates were too "democratic," and to Hobbes would likely have had overtones of a threat to the sovereign power. Hobbes sums up the conditions of legitimacy in these words:

> And as factions for kindred, so also factions for government of religion, as of Papists, Protestants, etc., or of state, as patricians and plebians of old time in Rome, and of aristocraticals and democraticals of old time in Greece, are unjust, as being contrary to the peace and safety of the people, and a taking of the sword out of the hand of the sovereign.[98]

Hobbes places special emphasis on the occasion and purpose of any gathering of people and the number involved.[99]

Private bodies which may be "regular" in Hobbes's definition may also, then, be "unlawful," that is, groups may constitute themselves without having any public authority. He mentions particularly "the corporations of beggars, thieves, and gypsies . . . and the corporation of men that, by authority of any foreign person, unite themselves in another's dominion for the easier propagation of doctrines and for making a party against the power of the commonwealth."[100] He con-cludes his discussion of groups within the state by the use of an analogy between the state and the human body again. The lawful groups are compared with the muscles of the body; the unlawful groups are likened to "wens, biles, and apostemes engendered by the unnatural conflux of evil humors."[101] We may conclude, then, that Hobbes shared none of the democratic views so prominent in his time. He was their most dev-astating critic.

### HOBBES ON RELIGION AND RELIGIOUS GROUPS

Of particular relevance for Hobbes's attitude toward all but the ab-solute association, the state, is the special attention he gave to religion and to religious institutions. Seventeenth-century England was a land of religious consciousness and a land of religious controversy. Politicians as well as theological controversialists used the Bible for their purposes, more naturally and more frequently than we today are wont to call upon the Constitution. Arguments for democracy and for monarchy were couched in religious terms, and bolstered by chapter and verse. Theological and scriptural language was the language of the period, and no one could ignore it. Leo Strauss says that like Spinoza's writings Hobbes's works may be called "theological-political treatises."[102] The Reformation generally, in giving (variously at different places) the king or prince the position of head of the church, underscored more than ever the political and governmental significance of all questions related to religion, and by the same token, all religious questions were understood as legal-political questions.

Hobbes's interpretation of Scripture, according to Strauss, served for him two purposes: first, to use scriptural authority to support his own views, and second, especially to shake the authority of Scripture itself.[103] He wanted to lay his political foundations and bolster sovereign power in such a way that nothing, including Holy Writ, could present a problem. This was especially desirable in a day when that frightful notion of the private right of interpretation was so widely and loudly proclaimed. Hobbes deserves a note, however, and a more thorough study than has yet been made of his interpretation of Scripture. His interpretation is briefly noted in a recent history of Biblical interpretation, but he is really too lightly passed over.[104]

Of all the groups that Hobbes seems to think a danger to the unity and the sovereignty of the state, an independent church could be the most dangerous! The peace-keeping sovereign, having the solitary right to determine what opinions are to be permitted to be expressed in the state, naturally could not permit a free church to exist any more than he could tolerate a free press. In other words, there could be no separation of civil and spiritual powers, no "freedom of religion." A separate, independent church Hobbes refers to as "the kingdom of darkness." Though he refers here more specifically to the Roman Church, the same principle and point would apply even more to "sectarian" religious groups.

Indicative of Hobbes's conviction of the fatefulness of the status of religion in the commonwealth is the increased amount of space he gave to the subject of religion in his three most "political" works: three chapters in *The Elements of Law,* four chapters in *De Cive,* while his most fully developed political work, *Leviathan,* devotes seventeen chapters (fully half of the book) to religion. Hobbes gives special attention to the Church of Rome and demolishes, to his own satisfaction, its claim to authority in the religious realm within any commonwealth. He refers to the papacy as ". . . the Ghost of the deceased Roman Empire, sitting crowned upon the grave thereof."[105] But Hobbes is also especially critical of the Puritans (or Presbyterians),[106] whose preachers claimed some special right to see the truth as they pleased and to use it to attack King or Parliament. The Anglicans he accuses also of having played a seditious role in the civil war. In retrospect, writing *Behemoth: The History of the Causes of the Civil Wars in England,* he traces the corruption of the people to these groups, and he adds a reference to those who "declared themselves for a liberty of religion," and here he mentions the Independents, Anabaptists, the Fifth-Monarchy Men, "besides divers other sects, as Quakers, Adamites, etc., whose names and peculiar doctrine I do not well remember."[107] These people, says he, were the King's enemies, and this enmity was based upon the private interpretation of Scripture, which had been made available to the individual "in his mother tongue."[108]

Two other points must be noted in connection with Hobbes's views on religion. One point is that sovereign "concession" to preach certain doctrines is unrelated altogether to the question of the validity or falsity of the doctrine proposed or preached; sticking always to the question of sovereignty, Hobbes finds his standard on the level of the question of whether the "preaching" supports the sovereign and his peaceful order or whether it subverts it. This conception of "heresy" was prevalent among Protestants and Catholics in the Reformation period. Doctrinal deviation, when propagated, was treated as a criminal act, drawing upon the Roman legal tradition all the way back to Theodosius.[109] Another point is that Hobbes recognized that no one, not even the sovereign, can invade the privacy of a man's conscience. The sovereign, in his view, cares only for the outward performance.

Hobbes suspected and feared religion, then, as a possible divisive force. He definitely wanted to dethrone religion as the ground of or arbiter of political life; but its very potency for social ferment was the basis of his preoccupation with it. The claims of individual conscience to interpret the Bible and Christian doctrine and to preach it spelled chaos. Two aspects of Christianity in its institutional form bothered Hobbes: (1) The Roman Church was a problem because of its presumed long arm reaching into the internal affairs of states afar. (2) The free-church form of organization was a danger because of its divisive implications for the all-important stable order so dear to Hobbes's heart.

Hobbes gave most of his life to advising the citizenry of his native land on their obligations to the sovereign. A goodly portion of this advice dealt with good and bad group relationships. Hobbes spent little time joining or organizing groups. One of the ironies of his personal history is that the one group he had his heart set on joining would not accept him to membership—the Royal Society. The members held that he did not qualify!

# VI / THE VOLUNTARY PRINCIPLE
# IN RELIGION AND RELIGIOUS FREEDOM
# IN AMERICA

*Robert T. Handy*

"In terms of the mysterious symbolism of history," writes a perceptive observer of the American religious scene, "January 20, 1961, may inaugurate the third phase in American Protestantism's understanding of its relation to culture and society."[1] For though a change has been long in the making, the inauguration on that day of the first non-"Protestant" president of the United States may later be seen to have dated an important watershed in American religious history. The first phase can be described as a period of territorialism, in which serious effort was made to transplant the European pattern of established churches in the American colonies. The second phase was that of voluntarism, during which efforts were made to perpetuate a Protestant America under the conditions of religious liberty through the free and voluntary association and cooperation of the Protestant denominations. The third phase moves toward what Martin Marty calls "pluralism in its more fully realized sense," a pluralism in which other than Protestant religious groups have emerged as confident, self-assured bodies, fully at home on the American scene and fast losing minority consciousness. To be sure, religious pluralism has characterized the American religious scene from the beginning, but until recently most of the major and many of the minor elements within that pluralism shared much in common and together worked for a Protestant America. In the third phase, however, the sense of Protestant domination is challenged; the pluralism is no longer predominantly a "Protestant pluralism" but one which shows fairly clear lines of demarcation between the major religious traditions.

This essay focuses on the second phase, which emerged with the triumph of religious freedom. The thesis is that the development of the voluntary principle in religion greatly contributed to the coming of religious liberty and provided ways for churches to survive and flourish under the conditions of religious liberty. The success of voluntarism encouraged the churches to embrace religious liberty as best for them, and allowed them to enjoy it without necessarily examining it theologically or really coming to terms with it in principle. With the coming to a close of the second phase and the opening of the third, both voluntarism and religious liberty need serious and theological re-examination by the churches.

I

The majority of Christians who came to the English colonies of North America in the seventeenth and eighteenth centuries believed in religious uniformity. They accepted uncritically the dominant view that the maintenance of established churches by the state was necessary to civil peace and a prosperous society. Though a few dissenters dared to believe in religious liberty and the separation of church and state, it was only slowly and through the interaction of many forces that religious freedom became accepted and that the churches were fully separated from the states.[2] The voluntary principle in religion, expressed both through concepts of the church as a voluntary association of believers and through the free cooperation of Christian individuals, congregations, and denominations for common causes, was one of the many influences at work which led to the breakdown of the patterns of religious uniformity and establishment. But the coming of religious liberty meant that voluntarism henceforth was to be an inescapable reality on the American scene, and that groups which by history and by theology were otherwise oriented had to come to terms with it.

The sources of the voluntary principle in religion were of course complex. The phrase "the left wing of the Reformation" is a cover-all term which describes a wide range of groups, most of which adopted some form of congregational polity and repudiated any form of established religion. The witness of the Reformation's left wing was borne in America chiefly by the Mennonites. Eventually they came to form a not inconsiderable minority in colonial America, and their insistence on voluntary conceptions of the church and on religious freedom was significant. Historically even more important on the American scene as contributing toward voluntarism were the representatives of "the left wing of Puritanism," especially Baptists and Quakers. They organized their own congregations and meetings on a voluntary basis and kept up a continual pressure against any form of coercion in religious matters. In pressing for religious liberty itself, they used to good effect the methods of voluntary association to work with others for common objectives. But what the left-wing Puritans also contributed was a theory of religious liberty based on broadly orthodox, classical Christian premises. Out of the seventeenth-century debate in England and America among the Puritan groups there developed an understanding of religious freedom consistent with faith and grounded in theological insight. As Professor Winthrop S. Hudson has argued, their commitment to religious liberty was derived in the first instance from the theological doctrines of the sovereignty of God and of human bondage to sin. From these fundamental premises they derived three central convictions. They believed that the visible church must be dependent upon God alone, and hence independent of the state. They affirmed that the church must be made up of the convinced, that is, it must be voluntary in membership. Thirdly, they concluded that inasmuch as unchecked human power leads to rebellion against God it should be limited in both church and state; the tendency of human power to absolutize itself made restrictions upon it necessary. Left-wing Puritan sentiment "was the dynamic religious force in colonial society, and it exerted an increasing influence within all the Protestant churches."[3]

Some Christians of other persuasions than those of the left wing of the Reformation or of the left wing of Puritanism were impressed by the witness of the latter for freedom, and many came to look on the voluntary way with growing approval. In colonies in which Mennonite, Baptist, and Quaker influences were strong—Rhode Island, New Jersey, and Pennsylvania (including Delaware)—there were no state churches. These experiments in freedom proved that it was possible to have peaceful civil states without establishments of religion, and possible to maintain churches by persuasion only. These examples were often noted. For instance, during the contention in the early eighteenth century between Anglicans and Dissenters on Long Island over the right interpretation of the New York Ministry Act of 1693, an Anglican layman, Colonel Lewis Morris, argued that it would be better for his church not to have any connection with the state and its funds at all. He affirmed that the church would be ". . . in much better condition had there been no Act in her favor; for in the Jersies and Pennsylvania where there is no Act in her favor, there is four times the number of Churchmen than there is in this province of New York, and they are so most of them upon principle."[4] Thus emphasized by some whose history and tradition was one of establishment, voluntarism was all the more stressed by those whose position committed them to freedom. So later in the century Baptist John Leland could explain in one of his most forceful arguments for religious liberty:

> The state of Rhode Island has stood above one hundred and sixty years without any religious establishment. . . . New Jersey claims the same. Pennsylvania has also stood from its first settlement until now

upon a liberal foundation; and if agriculture, the mechanical arts and commerce, have not flourished in these states, equal to any of the others, I judge wrong.[5]

These examples were even cited abroad, as when the French people in 1789 were urged to "imitate the Pennsylvanians" in matters of religion.[6]

Acceptance of the voluntary way by churches originally otherwise disposed was also stimulated by the spread of evangelicalism and pietism in the eighteenth century. In the Great Awakening, pietistic and evangelistic ways of interpreting Christian faith set their mark on such traditions as the Congregationalist and the Presbyterian, which historically, either in this country or abroad, had been committed to the way of uniformity. In her study of the New England clergy, Dr. Alice M. Baldwin has observed that the Awakening "brought with it much intolerance, yet out of it had grown a passionate conviction in man's right to freedom of conscience and a struggle, partially successful, to obtain it. It had brought independent judgment and a revulsion against undemocratic methods of ecclesiastical control and state interference . . ."[7]

The voluntary way in religion was also supported vigorously by those who were deeply influenced by the thought of the Enlightenment. Among the most tireless advocates of the Enlightenment view that religion should be entirely voluntary and without any civil support were such leaders as Thomas Jefferson and James Madison. One of the most lucid and influential expressions of the Enlightenment position was in the Virginia Declaration of Rights of 1776: "That religion, or the duty which we owe to our Creator, and the manner of discharging it, can be directed only by reason and conviction, not by force or violence; and therefore all men are equally entitled to the free exercise of religion according to the dictates of conscience . . ."[8]

Voluntarism in religion was only one of the forces contributing to the victory of religious liberty in America, of course. But once religious freedom did become a fact, then voluntarism did indeed become the order of the day everywhere. The familiar distinction between "church" and "sect" largely loses its force and clarity in the American scene, for the "denomination," a voluntary association of men united by common general beliefs for the purposes of accomplishing certain specified purposes, an association combining both churchly and sectarian motifs, quickly became the dominant church form under the new conditions.[9]

## II

Voluntarism not only contributed to the coming of religious liberty, and then became the necessary order of the day when it arrived, but it also provided a means for the churches to survive and flourish in the atmosphere of religious freedom. Especially under the conditions prevailing in nineteenth-century America, with steadily expanding resources of land, population, and wealth, the voluntary way worked well. It worked well not only in religion but also in many other areas of life. William Ellery Channing underlined the growth and importance of the voluntary societies in his "Remarks on Associations":

> In truth, one of the most remarkable circumstances or features of our age, is the energy with which the principle of combination, or of action by joint forces, by associated numbers, is manifesting itself. It may be said, without much exaggeration, that every thing is done now by societies. Men have learned what wonders can be accomplished in certain cases by union, and seem to think that union is competent to every thing. You can scarcely name an object for which some institution has not been formed. Would men spread one set of opinions, or crush another? They make a society. Would they improve the penal code, or relieve poor debtors? They make societies. Would they encourage agriculture, or manufactures, or science? They make societies. Would one class encourage horse-racing, and another discourage travelling on Sunday? They form societies. We have immense institutions spreading over the country, combining hosts for particular objects. We have minute ramifications of these societies, penetrating everywhere except through the poor-house, and conveying resources from the domestic, the laborer, and even the child, to the central treasury. This principle of association is worthy the attention of the philosopher, who simply aims to understand society, and its most powerful springs. To the philanthropist and the Christian it is exceedingly interesting, for it is a mighty engine, and must act either for good or for evil, to an extent which no man can foresee or comprehend.[10]

Orestes Brownson put it in a less philosophical and in a less even-tempered way when he exclaimed that "matters have come to such a pass, that a peaceable man can hardly venture to eat or drink, to go to bed or get up, to correct his children or kiss his wife, without obtaining the permission and direction of some . . . society."[11] In this atmosphere, it was difficult for the churches to avoid becoming like voluntary societies—in many cases willingly and deliberately. Because voluntarism worked so well, it was possible for churches and churchmen of various backgrounds to make the transition to religious liberty without ever going through theological searchings of heart, without ever examining the theoretical foundations for freedom or deliberately repudiating previous positions. The classic and oft-quoted example is, of course, the indefatigable Lyman Beecher, who battled against the disestablishment of Congregationalism in Connecticut tooth and claw, suffering "what no tongue can tell" for what he soon found to be *"the best thing that ever happened to the state of Connecticut."* He found in the interval that voluntarism worked, that it meant not death but life for the church of God: "They say that ministers have lost their influence; the fact is, they have gained. By voluntary efforts, societies, missions, and revivals, they exert a deeper influence than ever they could by queues, and shoe-buckles, and cocked hats, and gold-headed canes" —symbols of the old establishment.[12] Thanks to the effectiveness of voluntary techniques, religious liberty could be accepted without the anguish of theological re-examination, without having to accept the theological arguments for liberty that had been developed. It was enough to accept the fact, enough to repeat the Enlightenment clichés. In his usual provocative way, Perry Miller has thus been able to say,

> The point is, to put it baldly, that both in education and in religion, we didn't aspire to freedom, we didn't march steadily toward it, we didn't unfold the inevitable propulsion of our hidden nature: we stumbled into it. We got a variety of sects as we got a college catalogue: the denominations and the sciences multiplied until there was nothing anybody could do about them. Wherefore we gave them permission to exist, and called the result freedom of the mind. Then we found, to our vast delight, that by thus negatively surrendering we could congratulate ourselves on a positive and heroic victory. So we stuck the feather in our cap and called it Yankee Doodle.[13]

The attractions and the success of voluntarism covered up the theological failure in a way long convincing to most American Protestants.

One of the reasons it did serve so well was because it seemed to the leading denominations to provide a way to ensure the continuing Protestant nature of the nation. For in the early nineteenth century, the nation was in essence Protestant. Denominational leaders hoped to maintain and extend the Protestant domination through voluntary efforts. Though Protestantism was denominationally divided, by mutual efforts and by cooperative participation in common causes it was anticipated that the Protestant tone and influence could be maintained. Professor James F. Maclear has shown in some detail how the former proponents of establishment in New England hoped to extend their sway under the new conditions. He writes that

> coincident with the fall of the New England Establishments, an expansion of interdenominational voluntary societies was undertaken. The Connecticut Moral Society of 1813 was the beginning of many such foundations, spreading from New England to New York and the Middle West. These moral societies were seconded by organizations for allied purposes—tract societies, missionary societies, Sabbath School societies—all striving to extend "that influence which the law could no longer apply."[14]

There was wide general agreement among the Protestant leaders as to what that influence, practically considered, should be. De Tocqueville saw this with great clarity. He noted that the "sects" that existed in the United States were "innumerable," and that they differed in respect to the worship of God. But, he added, "they all agree in respect to the duties which are due from man to man. Each sect adores the Deity in its own peculiar manner, but all sects preach the same moral law in the name of God. . . . Moreover, all the sects of the United States are comprised within the great unity of Christianity, and Christian morality is everywhere the same." Thus the Protestant bodies by voluntary efforts were able to maintain their common influence in a vigorous way. "In the United States the sovereign authority is religious, and consequently hypocrisy must be common," he continued; "but there is no country in the world where the Christian religion retains a greater influence over the souls of men than in America . . ."[15] And in a Thanksgiving sermon at mid-century, Professor Bela Bates Edwards of Andover illustrated a similar point in saying that

> perfect religious liberty does not imply that the government of the country is not a Christian government. The Christian Sabbath is here recognized by the civil authorities in a great variety of forms. Most, if not all, of our constitutions of government proceed on the basis of the truth of the Christian religion. Christianity has been affirmed to be part and parcel of the law of the land. The Bible is practically, however much opposition there may be theoretically, *read* daily, in one form or another, in a large proportion of the common schools supported by the State. There is convincing evidence to show that this real, though indirect, connection between the State and Christianity is every year acquiring additional strength, is attended with less and less of exception and remonstrance.[16]

So voluntarism and religious liberty went hand in hand; the success of the former made the latter particularly attractive, for it seemed to point the way to Protestantism's victory. When David Schaff attempted to sum up the mission of American Christianity early in the twentieth century, quite naturally he began by saying,

> Its mission seems plainly to be to demonstrate that the complete separation of church and state, as we have practiced it, is the principle most favorable for the development of the Christian religion. The self-government of the American church stands for a voluntary return to the condition in which the church found herself placed prior to the conversion of Constantine. . . . The voluntary system is here on trial. It is for the American church to show that the claim made for it is true, that it is the Scriptural method and is best adapted to develop Christian manhood, and to permeate society with the leaven of the Christian religion.[17]

The position held by most Protestants in the nineteenth century thus conjoined a belief in religious liberty with the assurance that by voluntary efforts the nation could be made still more deeply Protestant.

What the exponents of this position failed to see was that, while they intended to hold their dominance by indirect means, they were also in certain respects denying full freedom by indirect means. The observers from abroad often saw this with considerable lucidity. So de Tocqueville could write eloquently of the power of the majority, which he saw powerfully at work in America, and conclude:

> I know of no country in which there is so little independence of mind and real freedom of discussion as in America. . . .
>
> In America the majority raises formidable barriers around the liberty of opinion; within these barriers an author may write what he pleases, but woe to him if he goes beyond them. Not that he is in danger of an auto-da-fé, but he is exposed to continued obloquy and persecution. His political career is closed forever, since he has offended the only authority that is able to open it. Every sort of compensation, even that of celebrity, is refused to him.[18]

And Francis J. Grund, Bohemian-born American publicist, could write:

> Although the most perfect tolerance exists with regard to particular creeds, yet it is absolutely necessary that a man should belong to some persuasion or other, lest his fellow-citizens should consider him an outcast from society. The Jews are tolerated in America with the same liberality as any denomination of Christians; but if a person were to call himself a Deist or an Atheist, it would excite universal execration. Yet there are religious denominations, in the United States, whose creeds are very nearly verging on Deism; but taking their arguments from the Bible, and calling themselves followers of Christ, they and their doctrines are tolerated, together with their form of worship.[19]

And occasionally a "native" exponent of full religious liberty inadvertently revealed where the limits were. Thus Charles G. Finney, leading figure of the "new measures" revivalism, in discussing the temperance movement, finally came to the point of what to do with those who did not yield to the "glorious reform" and give up alcohol entirely. The point was sharp enough:

> And multitudes will never yield, until the friends of God and man can form a public sentiment so strong as to crush the character of every man who will not give it up. You will find many doctors of divinity and pillars of the church, who are able to drink their wine, that will stand their ground, and no command of God, no requirement of benevolence, no desire to save souls, no pity for bleeding humanity, will move such persons, until you can form a public sentiment so powerful as to force them to it, on penalty of loss of reputation.[20]

In certain respects, therefore, voluntarism operated to allow Protestants to stand fast for liberty in principle and yet take it away in practice. As long as there was general agreement on the main outlines of Christian morality, voluntarism worked to further Protestant aims—though not without some sharp tensions at times. Meanwhile, the deeper, theological examination of the full meaning of religious liberty could be bypassed. Appeals to expedience or arguments from Enlightenment premises were enough. Thanks to voluntarism, freedom worked, and in a society in which Protestant morality had not been seriously challenged from without nor had yet revealed deep inner cleavages, it looked as though it would go on working to Protestant advantage. The deeper meaning of religious freedom and its many attendant problems could be evaded.

### III

For a host of reasons, Protestantism could not maintain in the later nineteenth century and in the early twentieth century the dominance in the culture which had been enjoyed in the days of Lyman Beecher and Charles Finney. The swift development of modern science and technology, the rapid increase in population mobility, and the unprecedented growth of great cities all contributed to a growing secularism in thought and to the spread of doubt and skepticism in the culture. Immigration, reaching new highs of more than a million a year no less than six times in the first part of the present century, brought in millions of non-Protestants. The ranks of Judaism, Orthodoxy, and Roman Catholicism were greatly augmented by the shift in immigration sources to central and southern Europe. Further, these other than Protestant religious bodies learned how to use voluntary techniques to their own advantage; they learned the rules of the American game. Judaism found a way of maintaining a kind of over-all unity despite its major divisions (and many minor ones) by use of voluntary techniques. As Will Herberg has summed it up,

> The Jewish community in the United States presents an anomalous picture . . . It has no over-all organization, and every attempt to give it one so as to eliminate 'overlapping' and 'conflict' has failed. It has, therefore, all along given the appearance of hopeless chaos and confusion. And yet this community without central control is capable of great communal efforts; without over-all organization, it yet embraces the vast majority of American Jews. In the last analysis, it is, as we have had occasion to note, based on a voluntarism that is characteristically American.[21]

Roman Catholicism learned how to use voluntary ways too, but in the interests of her well-defined unity. The growth of "Catholic Action" demonstrates the way in which Catholicism has learned to flourish under the conditions of religious freedom and voluntarism. The Archbishop of San Francisco explained this in pointing to the successes of the "coordinator" of Catholic Action in the United States, the National Catholic Welfare Conference, very early in its life (1921):

> In eight months we have coordinated and united the Catholic power of this country. We feel ourselves powerful because our union has become visible. All our Catholic organizations report an increase of energy and do not doubt that, thanks to the N.C.W.C., we can bring Catholic cooperation to its apogee.[22]

Voluntarism proved to be an open door for any group large enough and vigorous enough to push it open. All this meant that American religious pluralism gradually became something different from the days when Protestantism had dominated the culture and could afford to be tolerant of the minorities which were concerned chiefly with their own survival. It became instead "pluralism in its more fully realized sense." As late as 1927 André Siegfried could say, "The civilization of the United States is essentially Protestant. Those who prefer other systems, such as Catholicism, for example, are considered bad Americans and are sure to be frowned on by the purists. Protestantism is the only national religion, and to ignore that fact is to view the country from a false angle."[23] But this situation was already beginning to change by the time he wrote. The "spiritual depression" of the 1920's and 1930's was especially hard on Protestantism, as I have argued elsewhere.[24] The Episcopal Bishop of Central New York could say in 1928 that he had "evidence of a sad disintegration of American Protestantism."[25] The economic depression fell with great severity on an already weakened Protestantism. Currents of renewal at length began to flow, and a genuine recovery, both material and spiritual, can be demonstrated. But a significant transition had been effected in those stormy years. As Will Herberg has summed it up,

> In net effect, Protestantism today no longer regards itself either as a religious movement sweeping the continent or as a national church representing the religious life of the people; Protestantism understands itself today primarily as one of the three religious communities in which twentieth century America has come to be divided.[26]

Protestant pluralism has given way to "pluralism in its more fully realized sense."

In this third phase of relationship of religion to culture, both voluntarism and religious liberty continue to be the order of the day. But Protestants will need to understand these realities in a sound theological way if they wish to retain them. They can no longer be content with arguments for freedom on the basis that it works to their advantage, because that day is past. Appeals to Enlightenment clichés are no longer satisfying—the conclusions may be sound, but the premises lack depth. In part, the meaning of the current Protestant concern for authority and for the doctrine of the church is that a search for sound biblical, theological, and ecclesiological roots on which to base thought and action in a new historical period is under way. Recent studies into religious liberty by denominational, interdenominational, and ecumenical bodies are very much in order, and need to be continued and deepened.[27] The new surge of interest in religious liberty among Roman Catholics is an important manifestation of the need for a deeper theological understanding of the realities confronting churches in the twentieth-century world.[28] In the period that lies before us, the freedom we have needs to be used to seek out solid theological foundations for religious liberty and the voluntary way in religion in order that churches may be better prepared to defend their freedom in a threatening age.

# VII / THE POLITICAL THEORY OF VOLUNTARY ASSOCIATION IN EARLY NINETEENTH-CENTURY GERMAN LIBERAL THOUGHT

*Georg G. Iggers*

## I

Historians and political scientists both in this country and in Germany were fond in the late nineteenth century of speaking of the common Germanic origin of modern liberty. George Bancroft, Herbert B. Adams, John W. Burgess, even Frederick Turner, sought the origins of the English constitution in the forests of Germany. "Here were planted the seeds of Parliament or Self-Government," Herbert B. Adams wrote. "Here lay the germs of religious reformations and popular revolutions, the ideas which have formed Germany and Holland, England and New England, the United States."[1] What distinguished these institutions from the centralistic democracies of ancient Greece or by implication of modern France was in Heinrich von Treitschke's words "the understanding the Germanic peoples had for personal independence" and "civil, personal, and inner freedom."[2] It had been a characteristic of Germanic peoples, it was claimed, to limit the role of the central government and leave a maximum of political responsibility to non-governmental associations, to local control, and to the participation of citizens in public affairs. This common libertarian tradition sharply separated the Germanic world from the etatism of the Romanic peoples with their political roots in Roman law.

This thesis had little foundation in historical fact. Modern ideas of individual liberty had little space in pre-modern corporate life. According to A. D. Lindsay they "had their origin largely in the democratic principles which found their expression in seventeenth-century England, were put into practice in America, and then exploded into the French Revolution"[3] Scholars today tend to see the origin of modern democratic ideas in the church life of the Puritan sects of the Left who in Britain and America in the seventeenth century struggled for the right to worship as they pleased. Here, according to Ernst Troeltsch, are to be found the roots of the old libertarian theory of the inviolability of the inner personal life by the state. From their own religious societies, voluntary associations consisting of faithful who were all called equally by God and participated in the affairs of the congregation, these sectarians—Anabaptists, Quakers, Puritans of the Left—drew the analogy of a state resting on consent.[4] This conception of a society consisting of voluntary associations was largely lacking in Germany. There was indeed no centralized national state as in France. The map of Germany in the eighteenth century still resembled the patched "jacket of a carnival clown." Nevertheless the princes of Germany had succeeded nearly everywhere in establishing centralized, bureaucratic governments which, even if on a smaller scale, resembled the French rather than the British pattern. Nor did the Anglo-American tradition of nonconformist churches exist. Lutheranism had strengthened the authority of princely power in temporal affairs. Nor did the remnants of corporative life in the political or economic spheres possess the characteristics of voluntary associations. Even where the diets had not been suppressed they did not, with the notable exception of Württemberg, constitute representative bodies. Their members had not been elected by even an ever so select electorate but had generally inherited their seats.[5]

A whole tradition of German thinkers from Justus Möser in the late eighteenth to Otto von Gierke in the late nineteenth century, however, identified medieval corporate liberties with Germanic liberty. But this conception of liberty differed fundamentally from the British-American theory of voluntary association. By voluntary associations as defined in recent sociological theory are meant "those social structures of the community which have very limited but clearly specified purposes (excluding the pursuit of private profit), to which people belong deliberately and from which they may resign."[6] The political theory of voluntary associations assumes that the individual is the fundamental unit of society, that all groups exist merely to fulfill the specific, limited purposes for which they have been organized by individuals, and that the state, although never fully a voluntary association in practice, should to the greatest possible extent possess the characteristics of such an association. Its powers should be defined; it should serve a common purpose; and like other voluntary associations it should be governed by common consent.[7] The corporatist position agreed with the theory of voluntary association in denying the absolute sovereignty of the state and viewing society instead as a multiplicity of institutions among which the state was one. Its advocates, too, insisted on liberty of associations. But the corporate idea of associations views the groups which matter in society not as associations formed or maintained by individuals for common purposes, but as ends in themselves; in Gierke's words, as "living Group-persons" (*lebendige Gesamtperson*).[8] These group-persons, it is argued, rather than the individuals that compose them, are the basic units of society. The individual cannot be conceived independently from these groups, membership in many of which is not voluntary but inherited.

## II

Although Germany, like France, lacked a tradition of voluntary association in her political, religious, and to an extent her economic life, the theory of voluntary association there, as in France, played a role in the theoretical arguments for individual liberty and constitutional government advanced in the eighteenth century.[9] Liberalism, however, was as yet only a state of mind rather than a political force. When it first emerged as a political movement in Germany during the Napoleonic Wars it was unfortunately already closely interwoven with emergent nationalism. It increasingly jettisoned ideas of voluntary association and the natural-law arguments upon which these had been based for corporate and organismic theories of society. In the course of the nineteenth century, German liberal theorists turned more and more to doctrines of national sovereignty, which, however, were not as sharply divorced from corporate ideas as they were in French thought of the time. In this process, German liberal thinkers increasingly subordinated the rights of the individual to those of the community and ultimately to those of the state. We shall briefly discuss four stages in this development.

### 1. *Wilhelm von Humboldt and the Idea of Voluntary Association in the Decade of the French Revolution*

The most extensive and systematic theory of voluntary association in German political thought of this period was presented by a member of the Prussian court nobility, Wilhelm von Humboldt.[10] Humboldt had been born in Potsdam in 1767 within the shadows of the absolutistic court of Frederick the Great. He had hastened to Paris in 1789 and had observed the early months of the French Revolution. Deeply hostile to the bureaucratic despotism of eighteenth-century monarchy but also aware of the threats to individual liberty inherent in the representative state, Humboldt in the *Ideas on an Attempt to Define the*

*Limits of the Activity of the State* (1792), often considered the classic of German liberalism, attempted to formulate the political conditions requisite to a free society. "The true purpose of man . . . the one prescribed by eternal, immutable reason," he wrote, "is the fullest and most proportionate development of his energies." The development of man's individuality, however, he continued, requires a maximum of "freedom of action and variety of situation."[11] Man can develop his individuality only when he is free of external restraint. The highest form of society was therefore one in which "every human being develops only out of his own inner self and for his own sake."[12] To achieve this, he argued, the state must be systematically excluded from all "positive" actions for the welfare of the individuals, whether in the spheres of education, morality, religion, or economic welfare.[13] All such "positive" actions on the part of the state he considered "harmful" because they produced uniformity. The state's activities, he urged, must be limited to the "negative" ones of protecting the individuals from threats to their security from without and from each other. Positive actions for the welfare of the citizens ought to be left to "voluntary cooperative organizations of the citizens" (*freiwillige gemeinschaftliche Veranstaltungen der Bürger*).[14]

Like English and French liberal theorists of the time (e.g., Tom Paine), Humboldt distinguishes sharply between the state (*Staatsverfassung*) and civil society (*Nationalverein,* literally "national association"). The state, he argued, was marked by "superior power, force, custom and law," civil society by "free choice, infinite multiplicity, and frequent change." Much more important than the state in providing the services needed by man within the society was the sector of associations freely entered by man for a limited purpose, the "free activity of the people" (*freie Wirken der Nation*). The state was subordinate to civil society, the multiplicity of associations. Civil society, Humboldt recognized, could not dispense with the state. It needed it to maintain order. Nevertheless the state remained an evil, even if a necessary evil, because "it always involves limitations of freedom."[15] Nor was civil society to be viewed as an organic whole. Neither it nor the multiplicity of associations it contained had any existence for Humboldt apart from the individuals that composed them.[16]

At first sight Humboldt's political theory with its sharp separation of state and society and the restrictions it places on the power of the state appears remarkably similar to classical English liberal thought on voluntary associations, e.g., John Locke. Humboldt's essay has often been misunderstood in Germany as an expression of this type of classical liberalism, from which it differed sharply in its fundamental philosophic assumptions. Most of the British and French theories of the limited state in the seventeenth and eighteenth centuries based their arguments on natural, or, in the case of the Puritan Left, divine law. This law was seen as universal and eternal. It posited the equality of worth of all, either in the Puritan sense that "they were all alike called by God"[17] or in the secular sense that "all men are by nature equally free and independent and have certain inherent rights of which, when they enter into a state of society, they cannot by any compact deprive or divest their posterity."[18] This assumes a basic conflict between natural law which is always the same and always right and positive institutions which as the results of historical growth are non-rational and need to be judged by abstract, rational norms. Humboldt nowhere in the *Ideas* speaks of natural rights or of the equality of men. He views individuality not in terms of the basic similarity of men but in terms of their diversity. The state was harmful for him because it intervened in an essentially mechanical fashion in the natural and free development of men.[19] Thus in an extensive letter on the French Constitution of 1791, he criticized the French legislators for ignoring the historical roots of institutions and attempting to reshape France according to abstract principles. "Constitutions cannot be grafted on men like sprigs on trees." The wise legislator determined the direction of change and then went along with it or attempted to modify it by degrees.[20]

It is difficult, however, to see how Humboldt's defense of individual rights could be reconciled with his denial of a common human morality and his great respect for historical forces. In the place of a minimum ethics binding all men, Humboldt saw a multiplicity of individual ethics. The one ethical principle universal among men was the demand quoted above that all men develop all their energies to the highest. The values of individuals were inherent in them. Like Rousseau, Humboldt was apparently confident that man if he developed what was best in him could do no wrong. Nevertheless, the full development of the personality of one individual might conceivably lead to restrictions on the rights of others. Humboldt did not rule out that society was conflict between stronger and weaker individuals. He wished that the state stay out of the conflicts of society and that nature be permitted to run her own course. Consistent with this affirmation of conflict is his panegyric on war—in the fifth chapter of the *Ideas*—which he praised as "one of the most wholesome occurrences in the development of the human species."[21] But if he argued for respect for the forces of history, it is difficult to see how he could avoid recognizing the great institutions within society as products of historical forces with rights and an existence of their own independent of their members. In the course of the following years Humboldt under the impact of war and of romantic philosophy did indeed come to this conclusion.

In one other important way Humboldt's political ideas differed fundamentally from classical liberal thought. Humboldt nowhere in the *Ideas* spoke of the participation of the citizens in the state. Classical liberal thinkers had always viewed the state itself as a voluntary association. For the French Constituent Assembly it had been the only legitimate voluntary association. There is no mention of representation in the *Ideas,* nor any indication that Humboldt does not consider the monarch as the sole sovereign. His concern was merely that of limiting the sphere of political power. As Leonard Krieger suggested, "His concern was not to liberalize the political life of men but to accept the existing political system as the highest embodiment of the state, and then to exclude it from all the possible spheres of human activity, on the grounds that politics was pernicious to the development of the human spirit."[22]

Nor did Humboldt believe in the possibility of implementing the reforms suggested in the *Ideas*. He did not recognize the right to revolt nor did he foresee reform coming as a result of public pressure on the government. The state in seeking to approach the "right and pure theory" must always, he cautioned, take into account "the real conditions of things" which forbade an all too sudden change that might have catastrophic consequences. Man must first be made sufficiently receptive for change before such change could be brought about.[23] Humboldt had no intention in the 1790's of actively influencing politics. He fully accepted the non-political role of the German *Bürger*. Only extracts of the *Ideas* appeared in Schiller's *Thalia*. The complete text was published only posthumously in 1851. As Humboldt wrote to Schiller, "The content [of this treatise] has no bearing on the present-day situation."[24]

## 2. Stein, Humboldt, and the Idea of Voluntary Association in the Period of Prussian Reforms

The *Ideas* had been written at a time when the upheaval in France had as yet little affected the social and political structure in Germany. The following years saw war, the radicalization of the Revolution, the French invasion of the Rhineland, and finally the humiliation of Austria and Prussia. In the aftermath of the defeat of 1806, the advocates of political and social reform around Baron von Stein were called to political responsibility in Prussia. With Humboldt they shared a basic dislike of bureaucratic centralization as well as of the radicalism of the French Revolution. They wished to abolish the most objectionable remnants of the old regime and yet to preserve the continuity of German institutions with the past. Stein in short order during his brief tenure of office between 1807 and 1808 emancipated the serfs, introduced the free choice of occupation by depriving the guilds of their remaining powers, established legal equality, and promulgated a law for the municipalities which provided for extensive local control and for elections to municipal offices. In essence these reforms were liberal in the classical Western sense. They recognized the basic equality of the individual before the law and the right of popular participation in government. Stein foresaw future reforms that would establish provincial diets, a Prussian national assembly, and ultimately a German federal Reichstag. Stein looked to England as a model for reform. He attempted to introduce into the centralized, bureaucratic state something resembling the British notion of local self-government. In this he saw a return to what he believed to be "old Germanic liberty." He looked back nostalgically at the corporative society of the Middle Ages, which he wished to transform so as to bring it into accord with modern conditions, although his actual reform decrees such as the abolition of serfdom or of the rights of the corporations seemed rather to follow French patterns.[25]

In January 1809, Humboldt was called by the king to assume the position of minister of public worship and education for Prussia. In the year and a half he held office he carried through the famous reforms of the public school and *Gymnasium* curriculum and established the University of Berlin with its tradition of academic freedom. In a sense his acceptance of the position as minister of education was in direct contradiction to his earlier opposition to public education in the *Ideas*. Nevertheless he tried to carry out his conviction that the state should not use the schools for political purposes although he did now believe that it should provide every individual with the possibility of receiving an education. He sought to transfer educational responsibilities from the central government to the communities and unsuccessfully proposed that school funds be administered locally.

Humboldt's acceptance of the ministry of education reflected his changed conception of the relation of the individual to the nation. In one sense he had come much closer to classical liberal political theory in his recognition of the desirability of popular participation in government. Humboldt wished to involve as many individuals as possible in the business of government, something he hoped to achieve through decentralization. As many public functions as possible should be carried out by the population on a local level independently of the central government. Both the memorandum he prepared for the Prussian government in 1813 on a German constitution and one he wrote in 1819 on a corporate (*ständische*) constitution provided for local consultative bodies. Administration might be made more flexible, stable, inexpensive, and just if powers were given to local bodies. Such participation would serve the further purpose of increasing the civic sense of the average citizen and through his participation in "legislation, supervision and administration" of instilling within him a higher sense of morality in his professional and individual life.[26] Moreover, written guarantees of individual rights should be granted, including freedom of the press, which was still denied in the Prussia of the time.[27] Nevertheless, Humboldt now sharply rejected the conception of the individual as the basic unit of society. In the final analysis the nation consisted not of individuals, he now thought, but of estates and corporations. These were no longer voluntary associations. They were primary to the individuals. Like Stein, Humboldt foresaw three levels of deliberative estates—local, provincial, and national (Prussian)—as well as a loose German confederation. But elections were no longer to be held on the basis of geographic constituencies but in terms of economic and socially active corporations. Humboldt did not want to eliminate the freedom of selecting one's profession nor did he wish to reintroduce the restrictive economic practices of the guilds. But "the corporations," he wrote, "are to be a political means of dividing the municipal community in classes of individuals that find themselves similarly situated . . . according to the principle that participation in a small, clearly defined body increases civic responsibility and awareness more than activity in a larger mass."[28] The nobility would continue to be recognized as a separate corporation and be represented in a separate chamber in the provincial and national diets although membership in this corporation would now be functional, resting on the ownership of landed estates rather than on birth.[29] In this way, free popular institutions could evolve in Germany, not artificially imitated from abroad but based on organic ties with the German past.

In a fundamental way, Humboldt had held fast to the philosophical assumptions of the *Ideas*. He continued to believe as he had in 1791 that a constitution could not be based "purely on principles of reason or experience."[30] Change must come naturally from within; it should not be imposed from without. Only he now also recognized that not only persons but also social institutions, states, and nations were individuals. He no longer considered the state a "necessary evil" but now saw it as an end in itself, not merely as a technical device in Locke's sense, established by the citizens for the protection of their rights, but as a metaphysical reality. Every individuality, and particularly every nation, Humboldt wrote, was a manifestation of a metaphysical idea.[31] The states possessed the rights of individuals to grow and assert themselves. Germany was not the sum of its citizens but a whole, he asserted in the Memorandum of 1813. Nation, state, and people are one. In a mysterious way, the individuals are bound to the nation.[32] The corporations were not separate from or opposed to the nation but rather functioned within and together with it. And although Humboldt trusted that individual, corporate, and national rights were somehow in harmony with each other, he recognized the primacy of the power-political interests of the nation. "Germany must be free and strong," he urged, "because only a nation which is also strong against the outside can preserve the spirit from which all domestic blessings flow."[33]

### 3. *F. C. Dahlmann and the Idea of Voluntary Association in the 1830's*

The period after 1815 saw a divergent development in Northern and Southwestern Germany. In Prussia, the murder of the reactionary dramatist August von Kotzebue in 1819 by a radical student led to a period of repression uninterrupted until the 1848 Revolution and to the dismissal or resignation of the last important reformers, including Wilhelm von Humboldt. The same period around 1819 saw the introduction of constitutional government in various of the states of the Southwest, Goethe's Saxe-Weimar, Baden, Württemberg, Bavaria, and Nassau. Consequently historians often spoke of two distinct currents of German liberalism during this time, a French-oriented variety in the Southwest, and a strongly English-oriented one in Prussia and elsewhere in the North. This distinction has doubtless been overstressed.[34] Karl Rotteck (1775-1840), professor at Freiburg, active opposition member in the Baden parliament, editor of the *Staatslexikon,* the encyclopedia of politics which graced many German middle-class shelves in the 1840's, appeared as the main spokesman of the principles of 1789 in the Southwest. But he was isolated, a member of an older generation.[35] Even in the Southwest, political opinion, as typified by the Swabian publicist P. A. Pfizer,[36] became increasingly hostile to France and to French revolutionary ideas as the ideal of national unity increasingly overshadowed that of individual freedom. The myth arose of the Germanic origin of English free institutions. Wilhelm von Humboldt and the Baron von Stein had already earlier seen English liberty built on corporate liberties similar to those which had been swept away or undermined in Germany by eighteenth-century administrative absolutism. French revolutionary thought supposedly had seen the state as a mechanical device created on abstract, nonhistorical principles to protect the rights of the individuals who had become atoms without close ties to society. The British constitution, on the other hand, appeared to Humboldt, Stein, and later to the Anglophile liberals of the 1830's, as the product of centuries of evolution, linking the individual to the community. This view, of course, ignored the obvious fact that in revolutionary France the nation had increasingly asserted its supremacy over the individual, while the British development had led to a state limited in its functions and leaving a previously unknown degree of freedom not only to traditional corporations but to private associations and individuals as well. The line between state and individual was much more clearly defined in the Britain of the 1820's and 1830's which the liberals idealized than in the France of Robespierre and Napoleon which they detested.

Friedrich Christoph Dahlmann has been called the "outstanding representative" of the newer generation of English-oriented liberals, and his *Politics Reduced to the Ground and Measure of Existing Conditions* (1835), which appears very pedestrian when compared to the much more brilliant essays of Humboldt before or the carefully thought out *Historik* of Droysen later, was perhaps the most significant presentation of liberal thought in the 1830's. Dahlmann, descendant from an old Hanseatic family from Wismar (under Swedish control at the time of his birth), secretary for many years to the perpetual deputation of the estates of Schleswig-Holstein, was professor of history at Göttingen at the time the *Politics* appeared. He had participated in the drafting of the Hannover constitution granted in 1833 and was among the famous Göttingen Seven who were expelled from that university in 1837 after they had protested the suspension of that constitution by the new king, Ernst August. Dahlmann later gave further effective expression to his Anglophile views in his histories of the French and English revolutions[37] which appeared almost on the eve of the 1848 Revolution. Nevertheless, despite his admiration of the English constitution, the form of government he outlined in the *Politics* resembled much more closely the conservative constitutional monarchies of Restoration France or the Southwestern German states than the British parliamentary monarchy. Strikingly absent was any extensive discussion of individual rights, due process provisions, habeas corpus, the tradition of an independent judiciary, or other cherished English liberties.[38] Not that Dahlmann conceived of the state as absolute. He stressed that Christianity had taught man that the state was not his highest purpose,[39] but he nowhere attempted to define the rightful limits of the state. He did believe in the undivided sovereignty of the state,[40] but he also thought that the "good" in contrast to the "bad" state respected private rights and interfered as little as possible into the non-political spheres of life.[41] He nevertheless carefully avoided any definition of rights. He not only rejected the theory of natural rights but also had relatively less concern for historical rights than other contemporary writers, although he recognized that political science could not do without history.[42] As the title suggests, Dahlmann was primarily interested in an analysis of the actually "existing conditions." Political science was for him an essentially empirical science which attempted to ascertain the actual balance of power in a given situation. Thus he did not commit himself clearly even on the question of freedom of the press or of religion, traditional cornerstones of liberal theory. He thought that the times tended to call for a high degree of the former but could understand that governments might want to place limits on the discussion of foreign policy.[43] He believed that the state should not dominate religious life and even expressed sympathy for a decentralization of the German Lutheran churches which would have widened the sphere of congregational participation in church affairs through the institutions of presbyteries; but he also recognized the state's interest in curbing sects like the Quakers or the Moravian Brethren who preached conscientious objection to war and refused to take oaths.[44] The extension of rights to the Jews, he argued, would have to be determined in each German state in view of the special political and economic forces operating there.[45] He bitterly criticized John Locke, Jean-Jacques Rousseau, the authors of the American Declaration of Independence and of the French Declaration of the Rights of Man, for their assumption that a people consisted of "individuals possessing equal rights." A state was not an "artifice" (*Kunstwerk*) but an "organic body" (*organischer Körper*) in which each individual had his place.[46] Hence, representative bodies should not be chosen on the basis of population but of professional groupings.[47] In a sense Dahlmann was doubtless much more honest in basing his demands for middle-class representation on the "given circumstances" than were French or English liberals who rested their arguments on the doctrine of popular sovereignty but nonetheless advocated an electorate restricted by property qualifications. The rights of the middle class rested for Dahlmann not on ethics but on the position which this class had gained in modern times. Since they had acquired "the knowledge of the old clergy and the wealth of the old nobility," they should also to an extent take over the political functions once performed by these classes.[48] In retrospect, although Dahlmann saw a multiplicity of organizations possessing a degree of freedom operating within the state, he did not hold to a theory of voluntary association in the classical sense.

### 4. Johann G. Droysen and the Theory of Voluntary Association in the Period of the 1848 Revolution

Dahlmann had still stressed the role of the multiplicity of social institutions within the state, although he himself had recognized the character of the state as a "physically and spiritually united personality."[49] A broad current of German political opinion in the '30's and '40's increasingly stressed the central role of the state in society.

The 1830's and 1840's saw the emergence among university professors and the new commercial and industrial classes of a broad but unorganized movement for moderate political reforms in the direction of constitutionalism and national unification. This movement was relatively free of the racialist and romantic conceptions of the student *Burschenschaften,* but also of the radicalism of the more pronouncedly democratic opposition on the left which had in large part fled into exile. Most of the important historians from the Protestant sections of Germany were in this group, Johann G. Droysen, Karl Welcker, Georg Waitz, Max Duncker, Rudolf Haym, Heinrich Sybel (the conservative Ranke being a notable exception), and all of the above played an important role in the 1848 Revolution as members of a moderately liberal faction in the Frankfurt parliament or in local diets. Within this group of moderate reformers, whom the Germans were later to call their "classical liberals," there were many orientations, from the moderately democratic inclinations of Georg Gervinus and Theodor Mommsen to the aristocratic liberalism of Dahlmann. Nevertheless there was much common ground. All endorsed the political reforms traditionally demanded by liberals, a written constitution, a *Rechtstaat* or government by law, organs of representative government elected by districts in place of the traditional estates, equality before the law, the abolition of the civil disabilities of Jews, religious toleration. They considered freedom of inquiry and of the press to be the cornerstones of a free state and regarded the rights of the individual as important, although it is worth noting that neither Dahlmann nor Droysen had considered a written declaration of rights necessary when they were members of the Constitutional Committee of the Frankfurt Assembly. At the same time they wished to attain the unification of Germany under the leadership of a strong Prussian monarchy. The importance of these professorial liberals should not be underemphasized despite the failure of the 1848 Revolution. With the collapse of radicalism as a political force in the course of the revolution, the "classical liberals" became the major current of German liberalism. The reform movement in Prussia a decade later, centered around the *Preussische Jahrbücher,* found many of these same historians in its ranks supported by a younger generation including Heinrich von Treitschke and Wilhelm Dilthey. From among their ranks came the intellectual leadership which formed the Progress Party in 1862 in opposition to Bismarck. From among their ranks came also many of the men who split from the Progress Party a few years later to form the National Liberal Party which accepted Bismarck's solution of the constitutional problem. Men like Max Weber, Ernst Troeltsch, and Friedrich Meinecke, the liberals of a later generation who attempted to reconcile liberal principles with the new industrial realities and who became the spiritual fathers of the Weimar Republic, in many ways still stood in this tradition.

Perhaps the strongest single intellectual influence on the moderate liberal thinkers was exerted by the political philosophy of a man who neither considered himself nor was considered by them to be a liberal, Georg Wilhelm Hegel, who had died in 1831. This was particularly true of the most important spokesman of the group in the Frankfurt Parliament, Johann Gustav Droysen. Droysen, like other members of the moderate-liberal circle, rejected Hegel as a reactionary philosopher of the Prussian restoration.[50] Nevertheless, he like them was deeply influenced by Hegel's conception of the state. For him as for Hegel the state was the central reality in society.[51] The Hegelian view of the state differed sharply both from classical liberal and from traditionalist conceptions. The classical liberals of the Locke variety, or even the young Wilhelm von Humboldt, had distinguished sharply between the sphere of civil society and the state. The state was a mechanical device for the protection of the interests and rights of the individuals who had created it, a "necessary means" and a "necessary evil," but always an evil. For traditionalist thought the state was a social institution which had grown organically as had other institutions with which it was intertwined; its justification rested in its historical character. But for traditionalist thought the state was by no means absolute in sovereignty. The limits of its powers were set by the historical pattern itself, by the traditional multiplicity of political and social institutions. For Hegel the state was the embodiment of reason as it expressed itself progressively in the world, "the march of God through the World."[52] Although Hegel had defended the Prussian Restoration state as the embodiment of rationality, his conception of state power rested essentially on a democratic assumption. Like Rousseau, he believed that a state was just only when it was based on the free consent of the governed. Man was absolutely free by nature, Rousseau had argued; hence a form of government needed to be found in which he preserved his absolute freedom, one in which in obeying the dictates of the government he yet obeyed his own will. Any other form of the state rested on coercion and had no foundation in right. Rousseau had seen the solution of the dichotomy of individual will and the will of the state in his conception of the general will in which all shared.[53] Hegel recognized Rousseau's contribution in basing the concept of the state not on an idea of law or justice external to the state but on will.[54] Will did not mean, however, for Rousseau any more than it did for Hegel the pursuit of inclinations or instincts. The man guided by passions was a slave; the man guided by his own higher interest was free.[55] But in this sense, there was a basic harmony between individual will and general will. The state guided by the interests of the generality could do no evil.[56] Nor could it be in conflict with the will of the individual. The individual in following the dictates of the state was now merely following his own will. For Rousseau, the state needed no limitations on its power, for the moment it acted counter to the general will, which was to say counter to reason and ethics, it ceased being a state in the true sense and became an instrument of oppression that could be countered by legitimate disobedience and resistance. Hegel basically agreed that the free man acted rationally. "Freedom does not consist in the individual acting as he pleases,"[57] he observed. Rather the free mind wished to "make its freedom objective in the sense that freedom shall be a rational system and that this system become concrete reality."[58] The whole history of the world was the process by which the subjective idea of freedom took on objective form, reaching its highest concrete expression in the true state as the "embodiment of rational freedom, realizing and recognizing itself in an objective form."[59] In this way, Hegel's state was even less capable of doing wrong than Rousseau's. For Rousseau's state, like Plato's republic, represented a nonhistorical ideal; it ceased being a state by definition when it violated the general will. Hegel's state was not merely idea but also the product of a rational process of history. As such it could not relapse into barbarism.

The increasing popularization of the state did not necessarily mean democratization. Hegel had pointed to Rousseau's realization that true freedom was not possible in a democracy in which a minority was forced to accept the will of a majority.[60] The general will for Rousseau was not the sum of individual wills.[61] Similarly Droysen denounced the "vulgar liberalism" that insisted on popular sovereignty and constitutional guarantees,[62] although to an extent he favored both. The important thing was not popular participation but a government which acted in terms of the great trends of history, trends which pointed in the direction of liberty and morality. As he wrote in the late 1850's:

> Whether estates or representatives add their two cents worth is irrelevant. What matters is whether the state consciously increases its

power; whether it rules not autocratically but in terms of its great objective interests. Whether these interests are pursued as the result of
public discussion or because of the action of parliamentary bodies or
through the circumspection of administrators does not really matter.[63]

The Prussian government, Droysen felt, ruled in terms of its great
objective interests. Optimistically he saw the steady moralization of
government, the decline of brute force and its replacement by consent.[64]

This emphasis on the state did not mean a desire to suppress the
many associations and institutions which functioned within society or
even to bring them under the direction of the state. Hegel had recognized the role of estates and corporations. Droysen insisted that the
state was only one of the "moral forces" operating in society and
that the state must leave a maximum of freedom to the other "moral"
institutions, the family, science, the arts, the economy, religion,
etc.[65] But these spheres of society functioned only because the state
assured and secured their existence. Hence, the stronger the state,
the freer and greater the culture and the nongovernmental areas
of life.[66] On these grounds Droysen argued in 1847 against constitutional limitations on the powers of the state. "The true character of a
constitution does not lie in its defending the people against the state,
but rather in the state removing from its competence those areas which
do not belong to it."[67] Like Rousseau and Hegel, Droysen was convinced that the true state could do no wrong, for insofar as the
state was the manifestation of morality, it could not violate its holy
purpose without ceasing to be a state in the true sense. Unlike Rousseau, Droysen was convinced that the monarchy within which he lived
was a rational institution and essentially embodied the true state.

This conception of the central role of the state had other political
implications. It meant that the interests of the state had precedence
over the rights of individuals or of associations. And the interests of the
state were interpreted by Droysen and the other German "classical
liberals" we have mentioned as primarily power political in character. As Humboldt had indicated before, only in the externally strong
state could culture blossom, a note which Droysen pursued in his
Hellenistic history. But not only the interests but also the morality of
the state superseded that of the individuals. The actions of the state
were not to be measured by the standards of private morality. Its
morality was one of power political self-interest. There was no room
for conscientious objection. If the citizen as a soldier "wounds, kills,
and desolates," he need not worry, for he "acts not as an individual . . .
but as part of a higher Ego."[68]

Droysen's formulation was perhaps extreme at some points. Yet it was not entirely uncharacteristic. The moderate liberals in the Frankfurt Parliament, contributors to the *Preussische Jahrbücher* a decade later, the National Liberals who swung to Bismarck's support after 1866, tended to agree on the main points: the central role of the state, the irreversibility of the great historical forces, and the autonomy of political morality, which they all confidently believed were not basically in conflict with individual freedom and morality. But how secure were freedom and morality in a society which left relatively little role to voluntary associations in the realm of the political life and few restrictions on the power of the governors? By seeing in the autocratic Prussian dynasty the expression of the general will, the German "classical liberal" theorists had in a sense helped after 1848 to lessen the demands for democratization of the German government and to dissuade popular participation in and concern with public affairs.

The political doctrines of the "classical liberals" of the Droysen type rather than the democratic ideas derived from the theory of voluntary association were to be decisive for German political thought after 1871. The role of voluntary associations had been a minimal one in German political thought. The end of the Enlightenment and the reaction against the French Revolution had given the deathblow to the idea, never strong in Germany. The counter-ideal to the centralized, bureaucratic state in German political thought had been the corporative idea. But the corporative idea was not a democratic alternative to centralization. It contained a basically different conception of the relation of man to society from that found in the theory of voluntary associations. It assumed basic inequalities among men; hierarchical organization; restricted participation. Even more than in France, theories of democracy tended in the direction of the undivided sovereignty of the state. This was to be true of the reform group around Friedrich Naumann who urged democratization during the Wilhelminian period as well as of social democracy. Largely missing was the individualistic, egalitarian ethos found in French centralistic democratic theories as well as in British and American federalistic conceptions. German political theories, whether conservative, democratic, or socialist, rested for the most part on organismic assumptions. Also generally missing was that element of belief in natural law so central in the political theory of voluntary association which held that the state itself was an organization with a limited purpose which could always be judged in terms of this purpose. Luther had already recognized the state as a divinely appointed authority freed in the fulfillment of its tasks from the canons of private morality.[69] Post-Hegelian political thought had radicalized this idea by its conception of the state as itself the embodiment of the moral idea and the general will. *Raison d'état* thus became the highest political principle. And although it would be foolish to draw a line from Luther, Hegel, and Droysen to Hitler, it is difficult to escape the thought that the radical repudiation of natural law and of the theory of voluntary association left Germany more prone than the Western democracies to political nihilism and totalitarianism.

This is not to say that ideas of voluntary association were entirely lacking in post-1848 German thought. As a matter of fact, voluntary associations played an increasingly important role in German political, cultural, philanthropic, educational, economic, and athletic life in those years. Gierke welcomed this development. Writing in 1868, he saw in voluntary associations (*freies Vereinswesen, freiwillige Vereinigung*) an important instrument which protected the "individual against the danger of isolation and atomism" inherent in modern society and educated "the citizen to civic consciousness, an understanding of public affairs and self-government."[70] Nevertheless, the existence of voluntary associations in German life does not necessarily speak for the strength of the political theory of voluntary association in German thought. The analysis of Gierke's complex theory of associations as developed in the four volumes of *Das deutsche Genossenschaftsrecht* between 1868 and 1913 and its impact on German political thought is beyond the scope of this paper.[71] But the role which Gierke ascribed to voluntary associations seemed to be a limited one, to fill the vacuum that had appeared in modern society between corporate associations and the state. In sharp contrast to Hegel or to the German "classical-liberals" we discussed above, Gierke saw the state as a complex organism of autonomous corporate bodies (*Genossenschaften*).[72] But the prototypes of these bodies he saw in the medieval corporations, not in private, voluntary associations. He condemned the emphasis on individual rights (*Individualrecht*) as characteristic of the Romanistic tradition of law and alien to the historic, Germanic conception of groups. In the Germanic tradition, he held, rights had always been seen in a social setting and corporate groups had been viewed not as associations of individuals based on contract, but as "real collective persons" (*reale Gesamtpersonen*), each possessing a corporate constitution.[73] He fought on two fronts, against the centralized, bureaucratic state, but also against "liberal individualism."[74] On the one hand, he attempted to limit the powers of the state in which he saw merely one corporate group in the midst of the many autonomous corporate groups which made up society, similar in essence (*Wesensgleich*) to these other societies, and like them limited in its functions. At the same time, he appeared ready to accept the state in an almost Hegelian fashion as the expression of reason, subject to no superior will. To be sure, he thought, as Droysen and to an extent even Hegel had before him, that reason dictated the autonomy of corporate life within the state. But he did not think of the state in democratic terms, but considered the Hohenzollern monarchy to be normative for nineteenth-century Germany. As Wolfgang Friedmann observed: "Gierke was a genuine champion of corporate autonomy as well as a good German patriot of the Second Reich, and his theory is an unsuccessful attempt to reconcile . . . irreconcilables: to have it both ways."[75] The ambiguities in Gierke's system made it possible, according to Carl Schmitt, for "all conceivable political tendencies from right to left, monarchists, Bismarckists, liberals, and democrats" to consider themselves his disciples and to use his theories for their own purposes.[76] Hugo Preuss, who later drafted the Weimar Constitution, thus carried Gierke's ideas in democratic directions which approximated a political theory of voluntary association. Preuss accepted Gierke's key idea of political society as a complex of interrelated autonomous groups in which the state was merely one group equal in essence (*wesensgleich*) among others, but he viewed differently both the nature of the state and the nature of the associations that composed it. For Preuss, the desirable model for Germany was not Gierke's interplay of a liberalized Hohenzollern state and organistic *Genossenschaften* but a centralized parliamentary state elected on the basis of universal suffrage which, as in Great Britain, left ample room for local self-government and initiative.[77]

# VIII / RAUSCHENBUSCH'S VIEW OF THE CHURCH AS A DYNAMIC VOLUNTARY ASSOCIATION

*Donovan E. Smucker*

Rauschenbusch developed a thorough, detailed ecclesiology of the Kingdom, according to which the true church is seen as a disciplined, democratic, voluntary association which has a direct effect on social institutions; in making this impact the church realizes its sole reason for existence—namely, to serve the Kingdom.

In his Yale lectures he suggested the nature of his doctrine of the church:

> The men who stand for the social gospel have been among the most active critics of the churches because they have realized most clearly both the great needs of our social life and the potential capacities of the Church to meet them. Their criticism has been a form of compliment to the Church. I think they may yet turn out to be the apologists whom the Church most needs at present. They are best fitted to see that while the Church influences society, society has always influenced the Church, and that the Church when it has dropped to the level of its environment, has simply yielded to the law of social gravitation.[1]

This is a picture of mutual interpenetration of the church and society—a concept that is basic in Rauschenbusch's thought.

He discovered a new emphasis on the church. This was not due to a renascent Anglican Catholicism, but rather to "a combination of purified Protestantism and modern social insight." Much of this purification of Protestantism he ascribed to the liberal theologians of Germany and America. In any case, its net effect was to overcome the individualism of Protestant theology, which had been an evil influence for many years.

Nowhere did Rauschenbusch set forth a sectarian conception of the church more clearly than in his series of essays, "Why I Am a Baptist," published in 1905-1906. He is humble about his Baptist connections. He declares that he does not want to foster Baptist self-conceit, because thereby he would grieve the spirit of Christ; nor does he want Baptists to shut themselves up in their little clamshells and be indifferent to the ocean outside of them. He admits that Baptist church organization is faulty in many ways, but he believes that it is built on noble Christian lines, and it is dear to him. He is a Baptist, but more than a Baptist: "All things are mine, whether Francis of Assisi, or Luther, or Knox, or Wesley; all are mine because I am Christ's. The old Adam is a strict denominationalist; the new Adam is just a Christian." [2]

Then he outlines the pattern for the church through his Baptist orientation:

First, it tries to create an organization of really Christian people. This is accomplished through discipline and the retention of definite standards of moral and spiritual achievement. "It admits to membership," he declares, "only those who deliberately apply for it and who can assert they have met Christ and love him and want to follow him." [3] This is a voluntary association for those who seek it. But it is not formless; it has definite standards which are enforced by discipline.

Second, our churches are Christian democracies. The people are sovereign. The power of the church is carried out by ministers and officers in the name of the people. All aptitude for leadership is encouraged, but this must serve the people and must be reviewed by the people of the church from time to time. This democracy has both religious and cultural roots. Religiously, it corresponds to primitive Christianity and to the great wave of popular democracy in England, thus permitting the Baptists to embody and perpetuate the democratic ideals of the Puritan revolution. It has cultural roots in the village communities of the Teutonic ancestors, where so many of our popular liberties originated. As over against this lineage, there is the benevolent despotism of the Roman Church, emulating the despotism of ancient Rome. And there is the rule by bishops in England which became a prop against Puritan democracy. Thus the Christian democracy of the Baptist churches—and ideally, of all churches—affects the culture and is influenced by it. Not to have this democracy in the church is to reflect reactionary origins and, in turn, to perpetuate the cult of reaction.

Third, the Baptist churches recognize no priestly class. The minister is not essentially different from the laity. There should not be a sharp line between minister and laity, but there should be a sharp line between the church and the world. Basically, the priesthood is an inheritance from heathenism and should be avoided because Jesus was not a priest nor a creator of priests.

Fourth, there is no hierarchy within the ministry; there is no caste system of vicar, rector, bishop, archbishop, and pope. To be sure, there are inequalities of natural gifts and spiritual insights. But there must be genuine brotherly equality in the ministry.

Fifth, the churches have home rule. Each congregation is sovereign in its own affairs. This follows the principle on which our country is built. It does not preclude joining larger associations, societies, and conventions.

Finally, the Baptists decline all alliances with the state. At this point, however, Rauschenbusch emphasizes his rejection of the view of some Baptists that the spiritual life has nothing to do with the secular life. He considers this assertion calamitous heresy. Separation means that the state will not dictate to the church on spiritual affairs, or hamper the work of the church, and that the church will not introduce ecclesiastical considerations into politics. His precise formula, given elsewhere, is that there must be a division between church and state in organization, but an interpenetration of life between the church and the state.

According to this concept of the church, which Rauschenbusch cherished for Christianity as a whole, the church emerges as a disciplined, democratic, voluntary association.

The second part of his doctrine of the church is already implied in some of the foregoing material: namely, that the church has a very real effect on social institutions. The previous outline of the church as a democratic, voluntary association included a point on the church as a Christian democracy. Here he showed that this democratic Christian church was influenced by its origins in primitive Christianity, the Puritan revolution, and Teutonic culture. At the same time, this kind of church molds, shapes, and influences the culture in the direction of democracy. Thus the church influences society and society influences the church, whether for evil purposes of interpenetration or for the loftiest Kingdom-democratic purposes.

The form of church organization is of the utmost importance to the social institutions of the culture. The church is not static; it is dynamic, forever re-creating itself. In his first great book he makes this point very forcibly:

> A given spirit will create an institution adapted to itself; but in turn an institution will constantly evoke the spirit that fits it. The Catholic Church by its organization tends to keep alive and active the despotic spirit of decadent Roman civilization in which it originated. . . .
>
> The causal influences running back and forth between the civil and the ecclesiastical organization of the people are far more powerful than is generally understood. The monarchical government of the Roman Church originated in the despotic society of ancient Rome and then perpetuated itself by the conservatism of hallowed religious in-

stitutions. The aristocratic republicanism of the Calvinistic churches originated in the Swiss republics, and then perpetuated itself wherever Calvinism went. The democracy of the Congregational Church bodies originated in the democratic passions of the English Revolution and also perpetuated itself. Thus the Church borrows from the State.

But in the same manner the State borrows from the Church. "The action of religion on the minds of men is so profound that they are always led to give to the organization of the State forms which they have borrowed from that of religion." If a people is accustomed to the spirit and practice of self-government in its local churches, it will find self-government in the civil community that much easier, and any government from above will be unpalatable.[4]

And now for the final generalization on this creative conception of the relation of the church to its culture:

> Thus it seems likely that if the Christian churches had remained democratic and self-governing organizations, the spirit of Christian democracy would have been perpetuated, intensified, and practically trained among them, and would have turned with greater vigor and efficiency to all moral and social tasks lying about the Church.[5]

Rauschenbusch clearly located the heart of his ecclesiology in primitive Christianity, together with left-wing Protestant history, both Continental Anabaptism and the Puritan synthesis of Calvinism and sectarianism. In his speech, "The Church and Money Power," he suggested that the farther down we go in the class structure the closer we come to the left-wing forces of the Anabaptists and that together these interpenetrate to give us our closest approximation to a truly Christian church and culture. The lower classes need the sectarian church, and the sectarian church needs the lower classes. Rauschenbusch always correlates polity and politics against the background of class. For example:

> In the English Revolution the political attitude of each section was quite accurately graded according to its ecclesiastical radicalism. The Episcopalians were for the king; the Presbyterians were for a strong Parliament; the Independents were republicans, and *vice versa*.[6]

Rauschenbusch also, quite characteristically, based much of his ecclesiology on the early Christian community, a common sectarian emphasis. "Wherever Christianity came," he wrote, "we see a new society nucleating." He calls this "the society-making force of primitive Christianity." He loved to emphasize the revolutionary impact of the early church.

Here, then, is the society-making potential of the early Christian community: it tore down that which was false and bound together the true in a simple, primitive democracy.

In addition to primitive Christianity, Anabaptism, and Puritanism, Rauschenbusch was influenced by Richard Heath and Émile de Laveleye. At this point we may ask to what extent Richard Heath's book, *The Captive City of God*, influenced Rauschenbusch. It seems highly probable that this background was actually formative in his development.

Richard Heath was a nonconformist minister in the English Baptist Church and a pioneer in Anabaptist research. His *Anabaptism from its Rise at Zwickau to its Fall at Muenster 1521-1536* (London: Alexander and Shepheard) appeared in 1895. In this book he utilized the writings of the Continental scholars known to both August and Walter Rauschenbusch; these included Cornelius, Loserth, Keller, and Müller. In addition to his status as a Baptist minister and authority on Anabaptism, Richard Heath was an ardent advocate of the social message of the gospel in Britain. His *Captive City of God*, published first in 1898 and again in 1905, is in a sense an English equivalent of *Christianity and the Social Crisis*, although its impact was much less than that of Rauschenbusch's book.

C. H. Moehlman, a living eyewitness, has testified to the outstanding influence of this book on Rauschenbusch. He observes that "Rauschenbusch was so influenced by Heath's *Captive City of God* that he distributed copies to his classes."[7] Moehlman was first Rauschenbusch's student, and then his substitute while Rauschenbusch was abroad, and finally his successor to the chair of church history. There is no available evidence that Rauschenbusch ever promoted another book as he did this one by Richard Heath.

Rauschenbusch himself explicitly confirms Moehlman's statement. In his first book he urged the reader to read *The Captive City of God* by "my friend Richard Heath, a book written with searching insight and prophetic power." This quotation implies a personal friendship with Heath. In his second book, *Christianizing the Social Order*, he urged a total re-examination of church history, adding, "The various writings of Richard Heath exemplify the spirit in which the material ought to be approached." This statement commends the writings of Heath as a whole and approves the over-all orientation of his books.

It is possible that *The Captive City of God* was only confirmatory of what Rauschenbusch already believed. No doubt he was prepared to accept this material from a sectarian-minded Baptist with radical social passion. No doubt, too, the emphasis on a radical sectarian church with a sharp impact on the working class was an idea for which he was already conditioned. However, the testimony of his colleague was that this book did not merely reflect what Rauschenbusch believed, but was part of the *originating* process. Beyond this we cannot go except to look at the basic argument of the book to see what specifically might have influenced him.

Written in a polemical style, this book is a radical attack on the alienation of the church from the working classes by materialism, middle-class apathy, and capitalistic injustice. The church is actually portrayed as apostate. Heath offers figures to show that on the Continent, in Great Britain, and in the United States the working classes are basically lost to the church. This is due:

> . . . not so much to doubts of the truth of the Christian religion as to a settled conviction that the Churches do not truly represent it.[8]

At another point he quotes an American minister, and then comments on this observation:

> "I say it without fear or favour, the preacher is just as much a slave to-day as he would be if sold at a public auction to the highest bidder. And I for one am tired of such a damnable state of things." The cause is evident—the Christian people of to-day are so infected with the business spirit that they know of none but its ideals, and cannot imagine any order of things not governed by its rules.[9]

This apostasy is true of both the Anglican church and the nonconformist churches, the former because it is permanently incapable of reaching the people, and the latter because they are temporarily incapable of doing so. The Church of England does not, never has, and never can preach the gospel to the poor, since the church is unified with the state, and the English state is an oligarchy organized for the protection of property and the maintenance of the power of the wealthy few over the poor majority. In addition, the Church of England condones war, penal sadism, and other evil policies.

The nonconformist churches are also ineffective, because they are plagued with mammonistic middle-class prejudices. Rauschenbusch cites with approval a conference between Nonconformity and labor in 1867 where an exponent of labor dropped the following bombshell:

> They emphatically asserted the thorough worldliness both of the State Church and of Dissent; the former, they said, was rotten to the core, the latter a system of religious commercialism. They again insisted that ministers showed no interest in social questions. They objected to class distinctions in a place of worship, to the nature of the sermons preached, to the formality of worship, and to the want of freedom of speech. The Churches they described as a mere reflex of the world, where the classes, similarly divided in rank, barred and bolted and double-locked their doors against all inferior to them; while the man who should most of all have been free from caste feeling—the

minister—was in effect a member of the dominant class, sympathising with it and acting in its interest. Since this plain speaking there have been no more conferences in London between Nonconformity and Labour.[10]

What is the answer to this ghastly captivity?

First, the Free Churches must demonstrate democracy in their own churches and exemplify it to the social order:

> The most effective way . . . for the Free Churches to improve the social condition of the People of this country is to educate their own members in democratic ideas, so as to show the Democratic Ideal *at work in themselves,* producing a truly divine society. This would be an object lesson indeed![11]

Both Rauschenbusch and Heath were pessimistic about the empirical churches and optimistic as to the creative role of a really radical, prophetic, proletarian, democratic church which would become a small-scale working model for the total culture. Both men were sectarians with specific roots in Anabaptist and Puritan life and thought; and both laid great stress on the original normative pattern of the early church. *The Captive City of God* has a chapter on "Early Christianity and the Democratic Ideal" which makes much of the anti-property communism of the early church and the generally dynamic and creative role of primitive Christianity. The following passage shows how the author viewed the relation of communism to later property relationships:

> Communism, it is evident, was regarded by the Fathers as the only natural form of Society, but as long as men had not faith and love enough to adopt it spontaneously, and to maintain it voluntarily, the principle of private property must be endured, and property held in a communistic spirit. And thus the Fathers, notwithstanding their tolerance of property-holding, always argued as if the property-holder . . . only really had a right to what was necessary to his own existence and self-development, and that this right was based on the common right of all men to share in the usufruct of the earth. Of the rest he was simply the steward of goods to be used on behalf of those who had none, and which if he appropriated to his own use the Fathers did not scruple to call him a thief. If that was not communism there never was such a thing.[12]

Although at times Heath makes the church only the more inspired dimension of a democratic society, he returns to the theme of the great role of the church:

> The Church does not exist to do the work of the civil ruler, the philanthropic citizen and the stage manager, nor does it exist simply to be a fold where the sheep may securely feed, but the Church exists to

> be a City in which a divine Society may develop. It has to witness for
> God and the Kingdom of heaven, and so to keep before the world the
> highest standard of life.[13]

This passage introduces the theme of the Kingdom of Heaven,
which is a complete equivalent of the meaning of Rauschenbusch's
Kingdom of God. It is the Reign of God coming to the earth, prefer-
ably in the church first and then into society; but, in any case, per-
meating the whole culture. Heath is perhaps more reluctant than
Rauschenbusch to see human concern coming apart from the church. As
he (Heath) puts it: "Apathy to the Cause of Christ tends to apathy to
the Cause of the People, while apathy to the Cause of the People tends
to apathy to the Cause of Christ."[14] There is a strong emphasis on
justice, but also some ambiguity on its relation to love.

The ecclesiology of Rauschenbusch was no doubt influenced by Richard Heath. Both agreed that the culture had corrupted the church and
that a radical sectarian church could lead the masses in redeeming
the culture. Heath strongly believed that the latter option was forever
closed to the Church of England and similar state churches.

Émile de Laveleye was a Belgian economist, Roman Catholic in
background. He was born in 1822 and died in 1892. His name was
chiefly associated with theories on bimetallism and primitive property,
but Rauschenbusch was particularly influenced by a small book which
the Encyclopaedia Britannica does not even list among his important
works—*Protestantism and Catholicism in their Bearing on the Liberty
and Prosperity of Nations* (London: John Murray, 1875). A cursory
reading of this book will suggest its radically Protestant character
and reveal why Rauschenbusch's *Christianity and the Social Crisis* mentions de Laveleye four different times. It also suggests why de Laveleye is believed to have left the Roman Church later in his career.

Like Heath and Rauschenbusch, de Laveleye believed that religion is
highly creative in the political realm. His book contrasted the pathological impact of the Roman Church on economic and political life
with the creative and healthy interaction of Protestantism, particularly
left-wing Protestantism, with economic and political institutions.

He avers that Catholic countries must rely on renaissance paganism.
On the other hand, Protestant countries do not have such a dichotomy of morals and religion. Regarding England and America, he
observes:

> [There] . . . things are different: the most decided partisans of liberty
> are at the same time those who profess the most severe morality—
> namely, the Puritans and the Quakers. While Bossuet was formulat-
> ing the theory of Absolutism, Milton was writing that of the Republic,

and it was the Puritans who founded liberty in England and in the United States. In one case the writers who are religious and moral preach slavery, whilst those who advocate liberty respect neither religion nor morals; in the other, on the contrary, the same men stand up at once for religion, morals and liberty.[15]

He also emphasizes the difference between the French Revolution and the democratic upheavals in Holland, England, and America:

> For the foundation of a State, the Christianity of Penn and of Washington is a better cement than the philosophy of Vergniaud, of Robespierre, and of Mirabeau.[16]

He has words of praise for Roger Williams, too. "This man," de Laveleye says, "is a name little known on our continent but which deserves to be inscribed amongst those of the benefactors of mankind. In a world which four thousand years of intolerance had bathed in blood, even before Descartes had established free research in philosophy, he was first to sanction religious liberty as a political right."[17]

He also commends the Quakers of Pennsylvania and New Jersey for founding states on similar principles. Over against this he contrasts France, which persecuted, strangled, and banished "those of her children who had become Protestants," and thus failed to develop those germs of liberty and self-government which had survived in the provincial states. In other words, free Protestantism contained the germs of liberty and self-government which had survived in the provincial states, and free Protestantism contained the germs of liberty, while Roman despotism left a legacy of paganism and despotism.

Over and over, de Laveleye repeated his analysis: (1) Free and representative government is the logical consequence of Protestantism, while absolute government is the consequence of Rome; (2) Protestantism unites a nation, whereas Catholicism divides it by dangerous, angry conflict; (3) Protestantism diffuses knowledge, but Rome tends to suppress knowledge; (4) Protestantism initiates education and science, which lead to prosperity, but Catholic nations lack this sequence and are more prey to poverty; (5) to Protestants, the highest ethic is moral duty, while to Rome it is honor; (6) Protestantism tends to attract intellectuals, whereas Rome alienates them; and (7) the Puritan left-wing Protestants are the most creative in the culture.

From de Laveleye, as from Heath, Rauschenbusch received support for his doctrine of the church: political and economic patterns are borrowed from the structure of religious life, and religious institutions are dominant in the culture—whether for good or evil. Free Protestantism is the most effective religious stimulus to the democratic way of life.

By comparison with Heath, one finds in de Laveleye an optimistic reading of the cultural role of Protestantism. But perhaps this is only a surface difference. Both de Laveleye and Heath agree that Free Protestant institutions are crucial to the culture. Heath believes that both Protestantism and Catholicism are sick. The Catholics cannot come back to health, but the sectarian Protestants could return to robust strength.

In connection with his original reference to Richard Heath in *Christianizing the Social Order,* Rauschenbusch also recommends H. C. Vedder's *Socialism and the Ethics of Jesus,* especially Chapter XI, "The Social Failure of the Church." Henry C. Vedder was a fellow Baptist, holding the chair of church history at Crozer Theological Seminary. He dedicated his volume, *The Reformation in Germany,* to Rauschenbusch: "To the prophet of the New Reformation to whom this story of an older struggle for liberty is inscribed with all esteem and affection."[18]

Vedder, too, found the roots of modern socialism among the Anabaptists, although he was careful to point out that not all Anabaptists were collectivists and that they were more inclined to communism in the primitive sense than to socialism. Despite the tragic failure of the Moravian Anabaptist communists (later known as Hutterites) he felt that their history held both negative and positive values for students of church history.

For him, Luther lacked interest in ethics and Calvin's theology tended toward aristocracy and monarchy. He regarded the Anabaptists as having a dynamic view of life which demanded cultural and ethical changes, as is indicated by the following passage:

> The one party during the Reformation struggle that had some apprehension of the gospel of Jesus, that made some attempt to proclaim anew his teachings and to realize his ideals, the Anabaptists, were overwhelmed with obloquy and persecuted to extermination. It is quite true that they were not a homogeneous party, and that some among them gave just cause for offence by their fanaticism, their appeal to the sword, and their immorality. But these were not the real reasons why the Anabaptists were so reprobated by the reformers, so persecuted by all governments—these were merely the plausible excuses for the relentless bitterness with which they were suppressed. The Anabaptists were despised and rejected for the same reason that Jesus was rejected and despised—they announced a gospel that, if accepted, would have required and produced a reorganization of society on the principle of human brotherhood. Sixteenth-century Europe was no more ready for such a gospel than twentieth-century Europe is.[19]

Here we see one more influence on Rauschenbusch's sectarian ecclesiology: the left wing encourages maximum creativity in the culture, because in seeking to re-create itself within society it develops democracy and brotherhood. The left wing and conventional capitalistic cultures exist in radical conflict. Rauschenbusch corroborated Vedder, and Vedder recommended Rauschenbusch, listing *Christianity and the Social Crisis* as one of the basic books on the social question in the last chapter of his own book on socialism.[20]

This, then, is the Rauschenbusch ecclesiology: the true church is a disciplined, democratic, voluntary association which has a direct effect on social institutions—a definition rooted in the history of the sectarian churches and confirmed by the writings of Richard Heath, Anabaptist scholar and Nonconformist of England; Émile de Laveleye, a Roman-nurtured anti-Catholic who saw churches as master blueprints for the culture; and Henry C. Vedder, Baptist scholar of the left wing and proponent of Christian socialism. Few concepts were more important to Rauschenbusch than his doctrine of the church.

The voluntarism of Rauschenbusch poses basic questions in the current dialogue among the churches. Perhaps the most obvious question concerns the assumption that the Catholic churches, Anglican or Roman, are necessarily incompatible with democratic aspirations. Before *Mater et Magistra, Rerum Novarum,* and *Pacem in Terris* the Roman Church did appear hopelessly opposed to the aroused working classes and the throb of democratic political movements of all types. The Anglican church of his day looked upon Maurice and Kingsley as voices crying in the wilderness. To have anticipated an Archbishop like William Temple was asking too much in Rauschenbusch's context.

Meanwhile, the ecumenical movement recovered the Biblical and theological categories of the church as the Body of Christ, the Bride of Christ, the People of God, and, to a lesser extent, the Koinonia. With the exception of Koinonia these doctrines are incompatible with Rauschenbusch's voluntarism. Yet, at the very peak of ecumenical studies and dialogue concerning the church two forces have emerged which reopen the questions Rauschenbusch raised. The first are the devastating blasts from Berger, Marty, Lenski, Herberg, Littell, Lipset, Glock, and Campbell confirming the captivity of the empirical church to American culture. It is not a pretty picture, and it demands that a big question must be raised over a simple identification of our religious institutions with lofty conceptions like the Body and Bride of Christ. The second explosion has come from the Civil Rights movement, revealing the ambivalence of a church which produces a cleavage with captivity to the culture outweighing the prophetic voices in the church. The hostility to the church is deep in the Civil Rights movement despite the leadership of a Martin Luther King or a Eugene Carson Blake.

Thus, the circle is completed again. Rauschenbusch's question is back in circulation. There is a dimension of authenticity to his view that the church is a dynamic voluntary association which ought to provide an analogous pattern for the social institutions with which it lives; and to his view that a moribund bureaucracy is certain to succumb to cultural pressure.

# IX / A NOTE ON CREATIVE FREEDOM AND THE STATE IN THE SOCIAL PHILOSOPHY OF NICOLAS BERDYAEV

*Douglas Sturm*

It has been argued, with some cogency, that there lies deeply embedded within the history of Russia a spirit of independence and liberty. According to Frederick C. Conybeare, in his study of the Russian dissenters,[1] this spirit attained historical force and sociological form in the various groups of Raskolniks (dissidents) that emerged in Russia beginning with the Old Ritualists' reaction to the attempted liturgical reforms of the Patriarch Nikon in the seventeenth century. Among the factors involved in the nonconformists' schisms of the seventeenth and succeeding centuries was the conviction that the only properly moral basis for the actions and associations of men is freedom. Similarly, Serge Bolshakoff, in an analysis of the various "unofficial" religions of Russia, has argued that "in Russian history Nonconformity nearly always stood on the side of democratic ideals and in favor of a free Church in a free state."[2] This spirit of independence and liberty attained intellectual form in much of the literature and philosophy of Russia in the nineteenth century. Khomyakov in philosophy and Dostoyevsky in literature are two instances of Russian thinkers of that period who were champions of the liberty of man.[3]

Nicolas Berdyaev, about whose social philosophy this article is concerned, may be interpreted as a twentieth-century heir of and spokesman for this history of liberty in Russian culture. Although Berdyaev considered his philosophy highly personal and although he has been criticized for being unable to "go beyond the limits of his own self,"[4] one cannot read his works[5] without sensing his identification of himself with that tradition which includes the felt mission to manifest in cultural and associational form the freedom of the human spirit. That all men are meant to be creatively free is the primary principle of Berdyaev's social philosophy.

This tradition of liberty in Russian history has also been a tradition of anarchy. That is, it has involved either strong opposition to the state as the institutional antithesis of freedom or a justification of the establishment of the state only as a means of mitigating the more heinous expressions of evil and sin. Berdyaev carries on this part of the tradition as well, espousing this "negative" doctrine of the state throughout his works.

It is the thesis of this essay that the principle of creative freedom in Berdyaev's thought does not of necessity imply a "negative" doctrine of the state. Indeed, it is more consistent with Berdyaev's social philosophy to maintain that the state may be an institutional expression of man's creative freedom. In order to substantiate this thesis we shall discuss, first, Berdyaev's doctrine of man, which constitutes the ethical basis of his social philosophy; secondly, some of the fundamental motifs and distinctions of his social theory; and, finally, his doctrine of the state.

I

According to Berdyaev, there is a duality that characterizes human existence: on the one hand, man is made in the image of God and is meant to realize that image; on the other hand, man is a sinful being. Most succinctly phrased, to realize the image of God means to Berdyaev freely to engage in the continuous creation of new values. Berdyaev's ethical concepts of personality, spirit, freedom, God-manhood, love, and creativeness are all expressions of this basic affirmation.

Thus, the essential characteristic of *personality* is the act of decision or self-determination. As a center of decision, personality is changeless. But this changelessness implies a permanent process of change, for personality must constantly determine itself ever anew in relation to God and other persons and in relation to the values and possibilities of the world. Man as personality continually transcends himself in communion with other persons and in creative response to the calling and destiny set before him among the possibilities of existence.

The concept of *spirit* in Berdyaev's thought is virtually synonymous with the concept of personality. In characterizing the quality of spirit, Berdyaev lists as its attributes "freedom, meaning, creativity, integrity, love, value, an orientation towards the highest Divine world and union with it."[6] But the primary attribute of spirit is freedom.

Berdyaev presents as the classic definition of *freedom* this proposition: "Freedom is self-determination in the inmost depths of being and is opposed to every kind of external determination which constitutes a compulsion in itself."[7] To explicate the full meaning of this concept, however, Berdyaev finds it desirable to distinguish three kinds or stages of freedom.

The first is initial freedom or meonic freedom, which on the human level of existence is freedom of decision. By virtue of his source in meonic freedom, man may either respond to or rebel against the call of God. The second kind is freedom as an end or aim. This is the freedom that accompanies the actualization of goodness, beauty, truth, and meaning. This kind of freedom, by itself, is enslaving if it results in the tyrannical organization of human life in the effort to force men to submit to defined standards of truth and good.

Creative freedom, the third kind or stage, preserves and fulfills the other two. This is the freedom that God purposes for man. It is the divine will both that man recognize and realize truth and goodness and that man engage freely in the search for, and realization of, these values.

In Berdyaev's view the world of value is not an unchanging ideal realm. It is undergoing constant change and alteration. Thus "man's position is on the road and not at the final attainment, not at the end to which the road leads. Along that path man seeks and explores the truth, and he goes on seeking and exploring even when the primary ray of truth has already entered into his soul."[8] Man's freedom is his cooperation with God in the creation of ever new values.

This third stage of freedom does not eventuate in tyranny because, inasmuch as creative freedom involves the cherishing of that which is of value and creative freedom is itself the supreme value, he who loves creative freedom affirms it for his fellows. This is at least part of what Berdyaev means when he declares that *"love is the content of freedom."*[9]

True *love,* in Berdyaev's conception, is a union of *eros* (a selective love, moving toward some particular value that may conceivably enrich one's life) and *caritas* (an all-inclusive, compassionate love that moves toward the aid and comfort of the suffering), directed above all else (excepting God) to man. The essence of real love is especially the discovery of another's unique personality and the affirmation of its eternal value. Although such love desires, it does not compel, mutuality. Berdyaev asserts that real love relates man not only to personalities, but also to the other values of human existence—truth, righteousness, beauty. Real and total love, in its final expression, is the affirmation of the life and unique value of everything and everybody. Thus, love seeks to overcome all estrangement and separation; love seeks the universal communion of all with all.

However, Berdyaev recognizes that, given the present condition of the world, there is often a tragic conflict among the values that men love and seek to realize. The particular path chosen by love may, without hostility or hatred, lead to the nullification of one value—intellectual, aesthetic, social, or personal—for the sake of another.

Creative freedom is, as observed, the cooperation of man and God in the creation of ever new values. The exercise of the creative freedom is the birth of God in man; it is the achievement of *God-manhood*. This concept of God-manhood is Berdyaev's means of stating most baldly that the attributes properly ascribed to God—spirit, love, creativeness, beauty, righteousness—are likewise the attributes that ought to be displayed in human existence. But, in his imaging of the divine nature, man is called above all else to *creativeness*. Creativeness is the introduction of novelty into the world in the actualization of goodness, truth, and beauty. In his description of human creativeness, Berdyaev refers to a multitude of diverse areas of human life—music, the arts, philosophy, science, technical discovery, social and political organization, personal relationships, economic invention. But creativeness is itself of value—indeed, of supreme value. This means that in the creation of the valuable contents of life, the possibility of continual creative activity, as the supreme good, ought not to be precluded.

There are two stages in the total creative act. The primary stage is the envisioning of possible values. The creative act, in this aspect, is an act of transcendence in which man is face to face with God. Here one "imagines something higher, better and more beautiful than this—than the 'given.' "[10]

The second stage of the creative act is the expression or attempted realization of the creative intuition. Berdyaev claims that there is always a tragic discrepancy between creative imagination and creative production. Creative production ranges from maximal expression of the envisioned ("realization") to mimimal expression ("symbolization") or even perversion of the envisioned ("objectification").

While creativeness properly passes into form, at the same time "the creative fire must be kindled afresh, it must break up the forms which have become stiff and numb and stream out towards the infinite content."[11] Man's proper destiny is perpetual creativeness itself.

Thus, Berdyaev considers creative freedom to be the final purpose, the *summum bonum,* the ultimate goal of human life. It is the norm with reference to which all the actions and associations of men are to be interpreted and evaluated.

However, creativeness occurs within a world that is sinful, and this is an important factor in Berdyaev's social philosophy. Berdyaev describes man's sinfulness most often as *objectification* and *enslavement*.

Perhaps the most succinct statement of his doctrine of sin or objectification is this passage in which he outlines the four marks of objectification:

> (1) The estrangement of the object from the subject; (2) The absorption of the unrepeatably individual and personal in what is common and impersonally universal; (3) The rule of necessity, of determination from without, the crushing of freedom and the concealment of it; (4) Adjustment to the grandiose mien of the world and of history, to the average man, and the socialization of man and his opinions, which destroys distinctive character. In opposition to all this stand communion in sympathy and love, and the overcoming of estrangement; personalism and the expression of the individual and personal character of each existence; a transition to the realm of freedom and determination from within, with victory over enslaving necessity; and the predominance of quality over quantity, of creativeness over adaptation.[12]

*Socialization,* which is one form of objectification, means the subjection of the individual man to the standards and requirements of a group. The individual is enslaved within the routines and patterns that constitute the life of the society of which he is a part. He becomes an actor, assuming roles that are determined by forces external to himself and that fail to reflect his true personality. Although he may find a degree of security in accepting the socialized pattern of activity, he thereby surrenders his freedom of decision and precludes the realization of his proper destiny. His relationships with other men are regularized and defined, and are thus destructive of freedom and love. Collectivism is that extreme form of socialization and objectification in which the social is most dominant over the personal.

In whatever form, however, objectification—that is, the determination of man's actions and judgments from without—obstructs the possibility of creativeness, of the perpetual search for, and realization of, new values.

Berdyaev argues that objectification is man's lot in all areas of human activity—art, religion, education, political and economic life. But he also argues that the image of God is not totally destroyed; no man can be completely evil; creativeness cannot be lacking in all respects. Rather, objectification and creativeness are both expressed in the life of men and of associations in varying proportions. Thus, man's present situation is marked by the ambiguity of the presence of two modes of existence. Berdyaev describes this ambiguity as the coexistence of three epochs: (1) the epoch of sin and the law; (2) the epoch of humility and redemption; and (3) the epoch of creativeness, freedom, and the spirit.[13] Because of the coexistence of these three epochs, Berdyaev sees three types of ethics: (1) the ethics of law, (2) the ethics of redemption, and (3) the ethics of creativeness[14]—each of which has some bearing on the moral life of man and therefore on his associational life.

(1) It may appear strange that Berdyaev would argue that the rule of law has a justifiable role to play in the events of human life. He himself often lists law among the constituents of objectification and socialization.[15] Law, however, has a double character. (a) On the one hand, law has a positive mission to fulfill. The law is meant to place limits on the most openly offensive expressions of sin. As such, law preserves personal life. By establishing order and producing a minimal unity among men, law helps to provide the social conditions necessary for freedom in a world of sin. The highest achievement of law is "justice [which] demands freedom for all men."[16] (b) On the other hand, law enslaves. Because law is the rule of the society over men, it oppresses personality and thwarts creativeness. Further, because the law is abstract and general, it has no concern for the individual person or the unique case. Also, although the law may constrain a man, it is powerless to change him. The laws of human association may preserve life, but they cannot transfigure it. Thus, the law in fact both protects creative freedom and denies it. But it is clear that the positive moral function of law is, within a world of sin, to limit the misuse of freedom of decision for the sake of the possibility of creativeness.[17]

(2) Within Berdyaev's scheme, the ethics of redemption, which plays only a minor role in his analysis and evaluation of associations,[18] is a transitional ethic. (a) It is superior to the ethics of law, for it transcends the legal division of persons into two groups, the good and the evil. It involves the discovery that all men are sinners, although all men also are created in the image of God. Thus it is an ethic of humility and of compassion. Berdyaev's summary of the ethics of redemption is "to be strict to oneself and kind to others."[19] (b) But Berdyaev argues that the ethics of humility is only a moment on the way to the final goal, the creation of new values.[20]

(3) It is the ethics of creativeness that exalts the perpetual creation of new values to the position of supreme value and that is the culmination of the threefold scheme of ethics. The law, humility, and compassion all have as their final end the realization of creative freedom.[21]

## II

At this point, we turn to Berdyaev's social philosophy, which is built upon the foundation of his anthropology. There are three distinctions that are basic in his theory of associations: (1) the distinction between two modes of association, (2) the distinction between two types of authority, and (3) the distinction between two problems of asso-ciational life, the problems of bread and of freedom.

(1) The two modes of human association are (a) society or the col-lective and (b) community.[22]

(a) A society has the character of a reality that is independent of the individual men who participate in it. But the participants are completely dependent on the society, which, in accordance with its own nature and needs, determines the actions and thoughts of its members. This means the relinquishment of self-determination and creativeness by those members. Although man is related to man within a society, the relationship is indirect, determined by the established organiza-tion of the society, for each individual man has his given objective role, which includes the manner in which he must act with reference to other men in other roles.

This mode of association as defined is obviously the antithesis of personality and precludes the possibility of creativeness. Nonetheless, Berdyaev asserts that it may fulfill a positive function in a sinful world, namely, to introduce law and order, to establish a more or less stable form of communication among men. By embodying the ethic of law, a society may help to minimize the more heinous manifestations of sin, so that the possibility of creativeness is not more completely precluded. Thus, paradoxically, a society is an expression of sin, yet may function at the same time to mitigate the consequences of sin.

(b) The second mode of association is community. A community is that mode of association in which the persons involved are, and re-main, self-determinative and creative. Each participant retains the full freedom that is characteristic of personality. Community is thus constituted by love and freedom; it is a conjoining of unity and multi-plicity, union and plurality.

A community therefore does not have the character of an objective entity that exists independently of its members. Berdyaev argues that, *in fact,* "there are no such things as nations, states and societies existing as collective common realities which stand on a higher level than per-sonality," although associations may have that appearance and that ef-fect. But, he states, "there is such a thing as, for instance, 'Russianness' which exists as a qualitative factor uniting like to like among peo-ple."[23] In other words, associations in the mode of community are universals, and universals are realized—that is, attain reality—only in the concrete, in this instance as qualities of personalities. The implica-tion of this position is that the *societal* mode of association is basically a fiction. Berdyaev does indeed argue that the objectivity of associations and thus their ability to determine the actions and thoughts of men are not something they themselves possess. Their objectivity is created "by the beliefs of the people, by the objectification of a state of mind."[24] Berdyaev also writes that:

> The chief evil in the formation of a collective consciousness or a collective conscience, is that it is only a metaphorical expression. But the reality hidden behind these words is something quite other. By means of this collective consciousness and conscience, which here takes on a mystical sense, one group of people begins to lord it over other groups. Collectivism is a means for domination, and behind it is hidden the will to power.[25]

Although, as defined, these two modes of association are antithetical, both are characteristic of all existent associations, given the ambiguous condition of human life. The ethical problem is to establish and to assure the dominance of community over society, because community is an expression of, and the optimal associational condition for, creative freedom. At the same time, given the fact of sin, some type of organization and discipline is desirable in the associations of men. Thus men ought to seek that type of social organization which will minimize tyranny and maximize personal freedom, or the possibility for creativeness. In other words, they ought to seek to establish justice in the organization of society.[26]

(2) According to Berdyaev, an association inevitably involves a structure of differentiation among its members, a form of authority or hierarchy.[27] The two most basic forms of hierarchy are the social and the personal or spiritual.

(a) The social form of hierarchy depends for its principle of differentiation and authority upon such impersonal criteria as inheritance (social aristocracy), wealth, and majority vote (social democracy). However, these criteria have no direct relation to creative freedom. Indeed, taken as principles of designating authority, they elevate to positions of superiority things of little or no value and tend to annul the possibility for creative self-determination.

(b) The spiritual form of hierarchy, on the other hand, is primarily aristocratic in the proper sense of that word, viz., the rule of the best. The true aristocrat is the man whose life is devoted to creativeness. Thus, spiritual aristocracy does not result in exploitation; rather it is an "aristocracy of sacrificial service,"[28] seeking to realize the best interests of men, the interests of creativeness. The man of spiritual authority does not place himself over against other persons, for his life and destiny are linked with the life and destiny of all persons.[29]

Berdyaev argues that the spiritual form of hierarchy is democratic in the sense that every man is meant to devote his life to creativeness.[30] Every man, that is, ought to be an aristocrat. At this point, we may observe Berdyaev's conjoining of the principles of equality and inequality. According to the principle of equality, all men are meant to be creative and no man ought to be compelled to be subservient to another man's purpose. But, according to the principle of inequality, each person is endowed with a particular vocation; there is a qualitative diversity among men with respect to their gifts, qualities, and creative pursuits.

In the final analysis, the only proper authority is a spiritual, charismatic authority without compulsion and without servitude. However, given the ambiguity of human life burdened with the consequences of sin, some form of compulsory authority is desirable and proper in order to suppress the more flagrant expressions of sin and evil.[31] But compulsory authority, which is usually based on an impersonal-societal criterion, must always be judged with reference to its final purpose, that of helping to provide the conditions for creative freedom.

This means that there are boundaries beyond which societal-compulsory authority ought not to extend, and the question of the proper boundary is related to the two problems of associational life that Berdyaev calls the problems of bread and of freedom.

(3) In Berdyaev's conceptualization, bread is a symbol for those things that are necessary simply for the sake of life, whereas freedom, in this context, is a symbol for those things that are more specifically constitutive of the good life, the life of creativeness. The problem of bread is to mitigate or eliminate poverty, to lessen or eradicate the suffering that derives from economic want or exploitation; the problem of freedom as it relates to man's social existence is to provide the best social conditions possible for creativeness. If there is a conflict between the solution of the two problems, one should sacrifice bread for the sake of freedom.[32] Nonetheless, Berdyaev affirms that the functioning and health of the body are a part of man's total personality, and to be deprived of or to lack bread directly affects the possibilities for freedom and creativeness. Further, the realization of material-economic values is itself a form of creativeness, even though these values in themselves are of a lower stature than the values of truth, beauty, and goodness.[33]

Both of these problems ought to be taken into account as men engage in the formation and transformation of social organizations and structures of social authority. Their proper solution requires that "daily bread" be guaranteed to every man and that all opportunity possible be afforded for every man to realize his creative vocation. The society within which these conditions are met would be a just society, for justice demands freedom for all men and an end to all exploitation.

This means, Berdyaev argues, that, given a world of sin, in at least one respect freedom of decision may have to be minimized in man's social life for the sake of the maximization of freedom. That is, freedom of decision may in any activity be used to enslave, but in economic activity, the exploitation and oppression that may result from a high degree of freedom of decision are most crude. Thus, in accordance with the ethic of law, Berdyaev argues that the material-economic dimension of life ought to be organized and controlled in such a way as to make economic exploitation and oppression impossible and to provide daily bread for all men. "Hence in the name of freedom itself, economic freedom must be limited";[34] otherwise, "the strong will oppress the weak and enslave him, and deny him a crust of bread."[35] It is even conceivable that, given certain conditions, "an economic dictatorship may be accepted as necessary" in order to deal with the question of bread.[36]

However, whereas compulsory social authority and law may be appropriate in the economic-material dimension in order to solve the problem of bread, they should be shunned the closer the cultural dimension of life is approached. The realization of the highest of values must be left to free search. This means, conversely, that man ought not to attempt to legislate against all forms of evil, for to do so would be to stifle any possibility of creativeness. Society and its structures of authority cannot assure the realization of creativeness, but they may and ought to be organized and to function in such fashion to assist rather than obstruct that realization.

## III

Here we turn more explicitly to an examination of Berdyaev's doctrine of the state. The *prima facie* function of the state, in Berdyaev's interpretation, is to serve as an institutional counteraction to the more ostensible and violent manifestations of evil in the associations among men, to establish and maintain order and unity within a situation of actual or potential chaos.[37] Compulsion and the force of law are the implements employed by the state in the attempted fulfillment of this function. This means that the political unity effected by the state is always a superficial unity, for while the constraining organization of the state may mitigate and conceal chaos, it cannot overcome it.[38] The state is powerless to create that profound unity of love and freedom that is constitutive of a communal mode of association.[39]

Unity and order are not, however, ends in themselves, even for the state. The specific and proper purpose of the political order itself is to assist in providing the greatest degree of freedom possible for all persons under its jurisdiction. Thus "the state exists for man and not man for the state."[40] The state cannot make man become creative, but it can and should make conditions more amenable to the possibility for creativeness.

There is, furthermore, no single ideal form of state that by its structure can guarantee that this purpose will be fulfilled. Every form of state, even the worst, carries out its proper mission to some extent; and every form of state, even the best, tends toward a perversion of its mission to some extent.[41] Berdyaev does declare, however, that "what must be supported throughout to the end are those forms . . . which provide the greatest possibility of real freedom, of the recognition of the value of personality, and which acknowledge the supremacy of truth and right over the State."[42] In certain extreme circumstances, these requirements might conceivably be met most adequately by a political dictatorship, if that dictatorship were non-totalitarian.[43] Yet in most instances, it is democracy that suits man's fallen condition better than any other form, although it is not the perfect form in all respects. That is, on the one hand, democracy, as the rule of the majority, reduces human existence to a level of mediocrity. The prohibitions and vetoes of public opinion, the pressure to accept the common and the average, place strictures upon the full creative realization of personality.[44] On the other hand, democracy, at its best, means self-government, and involves the incorporation of human rights within the institutions of government.[45] Real democracy guarantees and institutionalizes the political, economic, and personal rights of man. Political rights are realized through universal suffrage and parliamentary representation. Economic rights are realized through what Berdyaev calls "personalist socialism," that is, the organization of the economic dimension of society so as to assure a living for all men, to guarantee every man an opportunity to work, to make the conditions of work less hard and painful, and to eliminate poverty. However, personalist socialism would not, as totalitarian socialism, structure all of man's activity and organize all his associations. Rather, honoring the creative freedom of personality, it would limit its control to those aspects of man's social life most open to economic exploitation.[46] Further, Berdyaev expresses displeasure with any form of democratic socialism that results in a completely centralized bureaucratic control of the political and economic life of the people. He suggests that some form of decentralized control of the economy involving self-government "from below" might more adequately conform to the purpose of the state and preserve the possibility of the realization of creative freedom.[47]

But the economic and political rights that are guaranteed in real democracy are only secondary rights, derived from the primary rights of man as person, which include freedom of conscience and belief, freedom of thought and of religion, freedom in philosophy and science, in art and literature, in social relationships and organization. The affirmation of these rights is meant to reflect the belief that men should be allowed freedom to engage in the search for what is of value.

Therefore the democratic form of state, in Berdyaev's conception, regulates the activities and associations of men in order to institutionalize and to protect the political, economic, and personal rights of the human person. This means that the state is itself meant to be limited by these rights of the human person. But the state easily oversteps its own bounds, debasing life, stifling freedom, perverting its own purpose. There are some situations of such intensely unendurable and intolerable perversion of the state's purpose that revolution may be morally justifiable,[48] even though revolutions, especially those involving bloodshed, are highly ambiguous and generally productive of only minimal, if any, real changes toward a more just political structure.[49]

States overstep their proper limits of authority not only within their own boundaries and in relation to their own members. They tend also to pervert their true purpose in their relations with each other. Berdyaev finds this manifested in nationalism, imperialism, racism, and war. He contends that the idea of state sovereignty is one of the immediate causes of war, nationalism, and the enslavement that results from conflicts among states. Affirming the desirability of some form of social and political unity embracing all humanity, Berdyaev decries the idea of sovereignty as an enslaving fiction and proposes a political federation of the peoples of the world.[50]

Thus on both the world-wide and the national levels, the function of the political association, given the fallen condition of human existence, is to minimize the enslaving effects of sin by establishing a just order and unity among men. A political order is just, as we have indicated, if it preserves and protects those political, economic, and personal rights that derive from the fact that each man is meant to realize his personality, that is, to be self-determinative and freely creative.

IV

Thus far we have examined Berdyaev's doctrine of man, certain motifs of his social philosophy, and his doctrine of the state. At this point, we shall contend that Berdyaev's doctrine of the state is in part inconsistent with his theory of association.

We have observed that there is a duality that characterizes human existence. On the one hand, man is creative, loving, free, personal; on the other hand, man is burdened by the condition of objectification, socialization, enslavement. This is a duality that characterizes both every single person and every human association.

The state is one form of human association. Even though it is of only "functional significance,"[51] serving a governmental role within human relationships, it is nonetheless an association in itself. Thus the duality that is characteristic of all existent associations within a world of sin must enter into the constitution of the state.

At first glance, it would appear that Berdyaev's doctrine of the state takes this into account. He has argued, as indicated in our analysis, that it is the state's primary purpose to establish order in society for the sake of helping to provide appropriate social conditions for creative freedom in a world of sin. In this sense, the state is a guardian of personality, an instrumentality to assist in the realization of the image of God in human affairs. On the other hand, Berdyaev asserts that the state is a form of objectification and socialization.[52] Its role within society requires the use of compulsory means to impose its regulations upon the citizens of the regime. The state may and does oppress and enslave man. It is the enemy of personality and community.

However, upon closer scrutiny, we see that the duality that Berdyaev attaches to the state is not the same as the basic duality that inheres in all associations. The two modes of association are community and society, these two modes being the associational expression of creativeness and objectification. However, both characteristics of the state, as described above, are within the mode of society. That is, in Berdyaev's depiction, even in its positive mission—to safeguard the rights and liberties of men by imposing law and order in society—the state is functioning as a social form of authority. It is on the level of the ethics of law; it is not itself creative or communal. So Berdyaev writes that the state "is, in fact, the very antithesis of communion."[53]

This is further borne out by Berdyaev's doctrine of the kingdom of God, which is that all-inclusive and perfect community, the complete realization of which would mean the vanquishment of all sin and evil. According to his doctrine, the kingdom of God is an association of pure freedom, which means that within the kingdom of God there is no social authority, no imposition of orders, no compulsory power. The kingdom of God is without oppression or arbitrary constraint. Given his definition of sin, all of these propositions follow. But Berdyaev then goes on to assert that the kingdom of God contains no state; the ruler-ruled relationship is absent within it; the kingdom of God is anarchic.[54]

It is here that Berdyaev's inconsistency becomes obvious. An anarchic association is an association without any structure of authority or governmental hierarchy (although this does not mean that the association will necessarily be disorderly, chaotic, or left to utter confusion), and, since the state fulfills an authoritative function or governmental role, an anarchic community would be stateless. But Berdyaev does not really mean to say that the kingdom of God is without a structure of authority of any kind. As we have seen, he distinguishes between two basic forms of authority, social and spiritual. The spiritual form of authority is not incompatible with the full realization of the image of God in man. Indeed, Berdyaev has asserted that the charismatic, personalist, spiritual form of authority is fully established only in the "era of the Spirit," which is the kingdom of God.[55] To be sure, this form of authority is non-compulsory, non-objectifying, non-enslaving; it is an "aristocracy of sacrificial service,"[56] but it is, nonetheless, a hierarchical structure. It involves a differentiation of function according to the several and diverse forms of genius, talent, and vocation that exist among men. If this is true, then Berdyaev cannot also say that the kingdom of God is anarchic.

However, it may be argued that the kingdom of God, the perfect community, even though not anarchic, is stateless, for the state is, by nature, an expression of the social form of authority. This is precisely Berdyaev's argument. "The state . . . cannot be in the least like the Kingdom of God, because it is always based upon compulsion. But compulsory power has its origin in sin and does not belong to the Kingdom of God."[57] Further, he asserts that the "totalitarian state," which exercises determinative and compulsory dominion over all men in all respects, is "a revelation of the true nature of the state."[58] Thus it is of the essence of the state to be compulsory. By compulsory Berdyaev seems to mean acting in such a way as to preclude or to restrict the freedom of decision, and consequently also the creative freedom, of persons and associations that are or will be affected by the action.

But, we may ask, is compulsion the fundamental attribute of the state, or even the only means by which the state operates? It does appear to be true that the state must employ compulsory means in a world of sin. That is, the state is the central authority within the political community and therefore within a given territory. As such, in a world in which there is compulsion, the state properly employs coercive instruments in order to assure the fulfillment of its functions and in order to suppress any threats to its authority. In Berdyaev's terms, of course, such coerciveness is justified only if the state is acting in some way to protect the rights and liberties of the men and associations within the political community.

However, contra Berdyaev, it does seem to be clear that the state does not act at *all* times and in *all* respects in a *compulsory* manner. The freedom of decision of *all* members of the political community cannot be conceived to be thwarted in any single instance of governmental action, for otherwise the state could not act. But while it may and does, at least in some respects, act without compulsion, it is true, on the other hand, that the state cannot act without power, for the actualization of a possibility is by definition the expression of power. This is to say that power (the ability to act or to be acted upon) and compulsion (acting so as to militate to some degree against freedom of decision) ought not to be confused. Berdyaev seems to confuse these two concepts when he writes, "The state and power are bound up with evil and sin: they are not transferable to any state of perfection."[59] Berdyaev certainly does not *mean* to say this, for the state of perfection, which is the state of perfect community and perpetual creativeness, must involve the expression of power. There is no creativeness without power, for there is no creativeness without the freedom to decide and without the inspiration of God.

If what we have said is true, could it not also be true that the state as an association may not be incompatible with the condition of perfection (the kingdom of God)? Observe that the government, as the central authority within the body politic of a given territory, may be considered to function to organize and to govern the several sources of power of the political association in order to achieve a desired result or in order to realize an envisioned value. As such, the state itself is one of the dominant powers within the relevant configuration of power. The state's power is of a compulsory nature *only* (a) if (or to the extent to which) the state is sinful and therefore enslaving and/or (b) if (or to the extent to which) the state is required to employ coercive means to restrict the more heinous manifestations of sin and evil that are present institutionally or individually within the body politic. Otherwise, the state's action is an expression of non-compulsory power. The full implication of this is that the state may itself be, and at its best is, creative and that the state's authority may be, and at its best is, of the spiritual form. In this sense, the government may function as an agency of the political community for the purpose of creation. Thus not only is the state, as an association, not incompatible with the condition of perfection or the kingdom of God; the state may, as well, be of a spiritual, personalist, creative nature within a world that is in part characterized by sin—by objectification and enslavement.[60]

Indeed, Berdyaev gives a hint that this is his position. In a passage in which he is discussing the proper relation between the state and personality, he writes that "in actual fact the state should in the exercise of its true functions remind one of a co-operative association."[61] This affirmation by itself includes the possibility of considering the government as an agency by means of which the members of the political community can cooperatively create or, in other words, can work together to realize some particular value envisioned by them.

With this conception of the creative role of government, Berdyaev's doctrine of the state would be consistent with his theory of association, and the duality that he ascribes to man, in both his personal and associational being, would be considered to enter into the constitution of the state as well. This would mean that the state manifests three faces: (1) It is a communal association, an expression of the spiritual form of authority, a creative agent. (2) It is a societal association, and as such is both (a) an enslaving, objectifying, sinful force, and (b) a legal, policing, protective institution. In its communal, creative role, the state would be conceived to be a functional association of all the people, constituted in some sense by all the people (directly or through some form of representation), and functioning in the realization of their creative mission for all the people.[62]

Now, however, at the conclusion of this section, we must admit that Berdyaev had no great penchant for consistency. He not only admitted "inconsistencies and contradictions" in his thought; he praised inconsistency in philosophy as "all to the good."[63] Further, we may observe again that the history of liberty in Russia with which Berdyaev was associated was also a history of anarchism. Old believers and sectarians considered the state and other forms of human authority at best as only necessary evils; the anarchist position was expressed by a number of the nineteenth-century Russian intellectuals who considered this position as integral to their "love of freedom."[64] So also Berdyaev, in a brief intellectual autobiography, has affirmed that, following from his espousal of the supreme value of personality and creative freedom, "I have had no love for the state, and combined with this were anarchist tendencies."[65] Perhaps this conjoining of the history of liberty and the history of anarchism in Russian thought is understandable, given the manner and mien of the state in that country's past and present. However, it may be suggested that those who "love [creative] freedom above all else"[66] need not be anarchists; it might be more appropriate to seek not the abolition of the state, but the transfiguration of the state. In this sense, the "liberal's" position would be neither that that government is best which governs least, nor that that government is best which governs most. Rather that government is best which governs properly, in a manner conforming to and expressive of man's proper destiny—the realization and exercise of creative freedom.

# THE VOLUNTARY CHURCH
# AND OTHER ASSOCIATIONS
# TODAY

# X / MISSIONARY SOCIETIES AND THE DEVELOPMENT OF OTHER FORMS OF ASSOCIATIONS IN INDIA

*Richard W. Taylor*

This essay is an effort to trace and assess the influence of the Western Christian missionary enterprise on tendencies toward changes in the forms of associations in India, especially toward voluntary associations. It is quite clear that the dominant influence toward change in this direction came from the British connection. The missionary enterprise was both within and without this connection. On the other hand, the connection in its business, military, and civil facets was the bearer of many influences which may not be attributed to the missionary enterprise simply because in some sense they may have had Christian roots. Even in the recent past the Indian church has tended to take credit for all that was good in these Western influences, while some historians, for various reasons, have tended to overlook the part played by the missionary enterprise.

The traditional social structures and values of India are far from compatible with a rise of free voluntary associations. These center in the caste system with its related joint-family and organic economic structures and in values compatible with indirect government involving consensus of elders, status for the man above social conflict (especially as he helps to resolve it), and depreciation of such conflict, including that type of it central to the integration of some cultures having voluntary associations and called by students of government the adversary process. Group membership and most roles are ascriptive. Groups within the caste structure may be seen as natural associations if *natural* has not outlived its usefulness in this context.

This traditional Indian social structure is far from the opposite of the free associational structure of which American society is sometimes taken as typical. Both are associational. The Indian case would seem to be about the grandest possible example of closed pluralism. While voluntary associational and natural associational types are at different ends of a set of pluralistic structures running from open to closed the opposite set is one of non-pluralistic structures. If this second set is taken as running in the same direction, from open to closed, it would seem to run roughly from ideal feudalism to patrimonialism. The latter, being closed non-pluralism, is the direct opposite of voluntary associational open pluralism. This results from the squaring of some aspects of a *gesellschaft-gemeinschaft* typology on the one hand and a *genossenschaft-Herrschaft* typology on the other. Each of these has usually been treated as a linear model.[1]

India's traditional closed pluralism is reinforced at a religious-philosophical normative level by a sort of absolutism which itself permits and expects many sects, ways, and understandings, theistic and non-theistic, below the final level of the Absolute.[2] This undergirding is itself a kind of closed pluralism of many facets of the One, and it also gives specific support to certain social values and attitudes which tend to oppose social change toward voluntary associationalism. One major point of such support is in the understanding of the adversary process as being the equivalent of claiming that one facet represents the Absolute better, more fully, or more adequately and fully than other facets and the contention that each of the first two of these cases is unlikely and that the last is both impossible and egotistical arrogance. From this it is claimed to follow that the adversary process is also egotistical arrogance and that what is wanted, as over against egoism, is some kind of realization of one's self as All which will both impart a measure of unity to differences and make social activity without involvement as possible as it is assumed to be desirable. Additional reinforcement from the realm of values comes from the fact that both village and caste membership and leadership are not merely ascriptive but that this ascription is vested with *dharma*—religious law of the nature of things—the degree of observance of which determines an individual's future state and status.

In the past some students of traditional Indian society have tended to portray it more as a stagnant atomism than a closed pluralism. This seems largely to have been done by non-Indians who had little understanding of the differing values involved and who tended to view the society only from an external, and often very formal, standpoint. That there is a vast amount of give and take, mutual responsibility, and economic interdependence between the units of pluralism has become much clearer within the last decade of studies.

Any attempt to deal with change in Indian society must include an acknowledgment that an historical glance at this society suggests that it has tended to be unusually unyielding to change from outside influences. Immigrations and conquests have taken place, but their people have usually been assimilated into the associational patterns of closed pluralism with little over-all effect on these patterns. The Jews and Christians and Parsis on the West Coast met this fate as did the Mohammedans later—in spite of the fact that the religious values which they brought with them would be expected to tend to oppose radical caste differentiation, at least within Islam itself where it finally did take root. Internal changes, such as new sects, were also relegated to isolation with the pluralism—even those which arose at least in part as revolts against caste. Nor did changes in rulers make much more difference. The government and social structures of the villages tended to carry on in their traditional way and any adjustment tended to be made by the rulers rather than in the social structure.

Tendencies toward the modification of old forms of association and the adoption of new forms of association in India have come from experience with Western forms, especially in government and education, and from Western ideas. Until almost the start of this century very little influence in this direction came from direct experience of Indians in the West—largely because they were restrained from overseas travel by religious taboos. In many other colonial situations such overseas travel and experience has been a major channel for influences leading to change. Missionaries and their undertakings often did much more to bear liberal ideas than officials did.[3] This is not unrelated to the fact that the colonial couldn't *really* encourage voluntary associations for fear of the political implications and overtones which might become involved. This was also true of political forms at anything like the local level. Even those associations which were allowed had to have a kind of permission and oversight from government since they were required to be registered and so "recognized" by government. In the area of the transmission of ideas about society in the earliest years there is an additional factor which makes it difficult to overestimate the role of the missionary. This is that the official and business-related British tended to be adventurers (not in a dyslogistic sense). Only after finally conquering the Maratha and other remoter powers did it become clear that they were really in India to stay. Gradually this led to an immense psychological change and shift in attitude, thought, and practice.[4] This led to a more intimate involvement with India—of a kind which the missionaries had had from the first. Though of course there was also much difference between these two types of involvement for many on both sides.

The missionaries not only helped to bring new ideas. Their attack on some traditions led to social legislation. Even religious reaction to the

Christian mission often adopted certain aspects of missionary methods and organization.[5] The role of social change of British-introduced education has been great indeed—and more of it than is usually realized was initiated in some relationship to Christian missions. Europeans had done very little in educational projects in India prior to 1793, and there was comparatively little education of any sort outside the cities at that time. On this base much of the formative initial effort in education came from missionaries. "The one important project before 1813 which did not originate from the missionaries was the establishment of a college by Marquess Wellesley at Fort William in 1800. . . . Even in this essentially governmental scheme, however, the missionaries and evangelical clergy were called upon to play an important part."[6] Although the work of the missionaries in establishing their own schools was of utmost importance, their participation in "secular" educational enterprises often was determinative of the character of these. The secular situation in Calcutta around 1820 seems not untypical. The Calcutta School-Book Society was created in 1817 and both the Reverend T. Thomason and William Carey took part in its formation, and in 1820 the Church Missionary Society was making a grant of Rs. 1000 a year to this Society.[7] In 1818 the Calcutta School Society was founded and the Reverend H. Townley and William Carey were on its committee. The London Missionary Society contributed Rs. 1000 to this Society, the Serampore missionaries made an annual subscription of Rs. 100, and the Baptists in Calcutta gave Rs. 50 a year.[8] Most of the teachers in private schools were trained in the mission schools. Just as missionary sources contributed to non-missionary schools the government, Europeans, and some Indians (some of whom acted secretly lest their more orthodox friends learn of their action) made contributions to the schools founded by missionaries.[9] This was the start of regular governmental contributions to all schools. These have continued to the present and are often enough to almost completely run the educational side of even the Christian schools. This has, in part, become a policy of government support to voluntary associations engaged in educational projects (and also in certain welfare projects).

Missionaries were the first and for a long time the only ones to attempt the education of Indian women. "They trained the first Indian women as teachers, and these latter, together with the missionaries' wives, made possible the plan of bringing instruction to girls of higher castes. . . . Later Indian movements like the Brahma Samaj have taken up the cause of Indian womanhood . . . But all these movements, whatever the characteristically Indian forms they adopted, had their foundation in the educational work begun among Indian women by the missionaries round about the year 1820 and developed in the years which followed."[10] It is this kind of pervasive formative influence which we suggest for associational forms introduced by missionaries. While far from the sole force, or even a major force in this century, it has also been far from unimportant.

Another side of this picture is that until 1884, when the Indian Social Conference was founded, "Hindu Society" had no common platform for discussion of and instruction in social uplift, and of course it never had any central authority to exert leadership—either liberal or conservative. This gap was in part filled by the missionary societies which had many of the characteristics of voluntary associations—and later by Indian societies patterned very much on them.

During the last two centuries in India there seem to have been three kinds of responses to the confrontation between India and Europe and the changes resulting from this. These are adoption, revision, and reversion. Professor A. R. Desai has best pointed out the relevance of the first two responses. He suggests that the first is characterized by the view that India's society has been corrupted by superstition and is uncivilized and that the so-called glories of Indian history are mere legends. This resulted in looking toward the adoption of British culture and has been called the position of the Anglicists although Desai uses the term *arrogant imperialists*. The second is characterized by the view that India's past was in fact glorious and her society the best. Desai calls this the *national-chauvinist* position, but probably it has more often been called Orientalist.[11] Adoption seems to fit in M. N. Srinivas's category of Westernization, and reversion in his category of Sanskritization; revision fits partly in each.[12] Adoption and revision are the two types most relevant to our discussion. Each was held both by Indians and by Europeans. Among early and influential missionary educators William Carey was an outstanding Orientalist while Alexander Duff was perhaps the leading Anglicist. Historically, in all kinds of Indian education Carey's position was dominated by that of Duff, but since independence a position not unlike Carey's seems to be coming into its own again. For us perhaps the main point is that both of these positions involved the acceptance of many Western ideas and associational forms—sometimes with very different revisionist content.

Both adoptionists and revisionists have taken up some European ideas either explicitly or implicitly. Often the ideas which have been implicit in the thinking of even the most radical revisionists have not been unrelated to forms of association and social activity. In terms of missionary activities this is early seen in the continuum running from churches through the Brahma Samaj to the Arya Samaj and later including the Ramakrishna Mission and other movements. All, in some degree, thought of themselves as missions in the sense introduced by the Christian missionary societies of the West and patterned their organization upon these—as reflected in the Indian situation. Even the Arya Samaj, the most revisionist of the earlier major movements, founded by Swami Dayananda in 1875, owed much to mission structures, largely transmitted through the Brahma Samaj, in both its organization and its social emphases. In the schools of the Aryaists, even though the daily life, spiritual exercises, and dress of the students were modeled upon a revisionist estimate of traditional old Hindu practices, the content and wider form of the education was essentially Western—having been largely introduced by missionaries before 1823. Likewise long before the death of Swami Vivekananda the Ramakrishna Mission movement, which is also revisionist, was frankly imitating the techniques of the Christian missionary enterprise in terms of schools, medical and preaching missionaries, the training of widows, and so on. This is the more remarkable because as revisionists they had before them the Indian techniques of priestly seminaries, monks, wandering holy men, and asceticism.

The influence of the missionary enterprise on the Arya Samaj did not come only via the Brahma Samaj; it came also through direct contact. In fact, while the reformed Brahma Samaj under Keshub Chunder Sen had much to transmit in this way it also lacked much, as it seems to have gotten by after the reform of 1876 without constitution, governing body, or rules. It seems quite clear that Dayananda copied his missionary-like clothes from the Brahma Samaj after his visit to Calcutta but equally clear that his decision to adopt the Christian missionary methods of education came from direct observation of the missionary enterprise.[13] In like manner the Prarthana Samaj which was formed in Bombay under the influence of the Brahma Samaj movement not only took over from the Brahma Samaj certain forms which it had taken from the missionary enterprise but it also was influenced directly both by general example and by specific contact. In the Bombay case a major formative influence was personal contact with Wilson, a Church of Scotland missionary for whom Wilson College is named.[14]

A somewhat different associational pattern was adapted from the missionary enterprise by the Servants of Indian Society founded by Gokhale in 1905 in avowed imitation of the Society of Jesus. No doubt the fact that Gokhale's city of Poona is between Goa and Bombay—both Jesuit centers (indeed Poona has recently become the Jesuit training center for much of Asia) is not unrelated to this particular transmission. This well-known and influential organization aimed at consecrating to the service of the nation those who had utilized to the full the resources of secular education, under rigid discipline and a very modest monetary allowance and with a lifelong vow. This is somewhat different from the traditional Indian requirement of the lifelong submission of the pupil to the teacher, the subjection of the pupil's will and reason to the direction of the master which Mohandas Gandhi did not hestitate to enforce upon his followers.[15]

The Theosophical Society must not be overlooked in detailing some aspects of the transmission of patterns of association. While hardly an orthodox missionary society, it started out as a sort of Western post-Christian church and always had ties with the Liberal Catholic Church. If under Mrs. Annie Besant's leadership this society became neo-Hindu or crypto-Hindu this helped to give it entree where the church had none. The major Indian institution growing out of this influence was the Benares Hindu University. Earlier the transfer of the Theosophical Society itself to an Indian headquarters added a major neo-Hindu voluntary association to the list of those which mediated associational patterns far and wide.

The dispersion of forms of organization from missionary sources is still noticeable. Even in later revisionist movements this is so. The too common Christian claim that there is no such thing as Hindu congregational worship seems untrue. Chanting and other group activity have been an integral part of much *bhakti* Hinduism and are far from unknown outside this strain. Nevertheless, the rise of quasi-congregational meetings for singing and instruction, after the organizational pattern introduced by missions, at a stated time, often on Sunday mornings and often with a special building set aside for this activity, is something new.[16] It is found widely in neo-Hinduism, that is, in many recent sects such as those founded by Shanshah, Ram Tirth, and Sivananda. A striking example of this continued associational influence is seen in the reorganization of the Ram Tirth Ashram in Dehra Dun. There had been party splits in the group and the constitutional structure was not functioning well. One of the young swamis went to the nearby Christian Retreat and Study Centre and spent much time in the library there studying the constitutions and bylaws of various mission-founded and mission-related organizations. Then, on the basis of this study, he wrote up an adapted constitution for the ashram. It was so well received that the inmates and members of the ashram wanted to make him their leader in recognition of his contribution to their organization.

It has sometimes been popularly suggested that any thoroughgoing diffusion of "Western" forms of social organization would be doomed to failure because of the rootlessness of these forms outside of the

"Christian" culture in which they arose—and on which it is assumed they depend. Even Vivekananda seems to have had this fear at least once.[17] While this suggestion may be nonsense for many reasons, it is possible to suggest in a Weberian way that the cultural roots for such forms of association may be less lacking than is often thought—this would suggest that these roots are especially connected with the ethical aspects of culture. It may be that the diffusion of just these "ethical" aspects has been much wider than is often appreciated. This was suggested by the statement attributed to Nehru while he was lecturing to a British university: that he was a "Christian in ethics." While this may be bad theology there is a sense in which it makes very good sense. In India a not uncommon ethical condemnation is that an act or custom is "unchristian"! This has nothing to do with theology, and yet it is clearly descended from an understanding of the gospel ethic. This facet seems also to appear among the Muslim minority in India. The Muslim Principal of Delhi College has said, "I know how moral values were conveyed to me—by Christian missionaries. . . . their individual lives were such that anybody coming into contact with them would know what Christian values and moral values were . . ."[18] In this same sense it may be said that Vivekananda preached a Hinduism which had absorbed ethics from Christianity.[19] While Ram Mohan Roy, the founder of Brahma Samaj, insisted upon calling himself a Hindu he acknowledged his debt to Christianity—and it was largely just in this area of ethics, which he called moral principles.[20] Gandhi's acknowledgment of a similar debt, especially via Tolstoy and Ruskin, is well known.[21] Indeed, at the National Eucharistic Conference in Madras in December of 1937 the Papal Legate went so far as to point out that Gandhi's ideals had many affinities with Christian ethics and to contend that he had assimilated some of the most important moral teaching of Christianity. He went on to say that outside of the Church no one perhaps had echoed more eloquently the Church's appeal to Christian ethics.[22] While we can hardly say that the Protestant ethic is at the root of the changes in Indian associational patterns we may perhaps suggest that something not unrelated to a version of this ethic, introduced in large part through missionary channels, may not be unrelated to the spread of modified associational structures.

While the relationship between diffused Christian ethics and the *Protestant ethic* is perhaps overdrawn merely by mentioning the two of them together, it is not uninteresting to note that among the Bengal neo-Hindu sects—and it was in Bengal that the first samajes started and later the Ramakrishna Mission began—there were many echoes of the Protestant Reformation in their Hindu reformation and that not the least of these was the concurrent acceptance of much of Christian ethics. Indeed, it has been written by one reared within these Bengal movements that the theory of their leaders was only a "duplication of the theory of the Protestant Reformation. Although their claim to be restoring the pure faith of the Upanishads by ridding it of Puranic excrescences was certainly inspired by an unconscious absorption of the idea of the Protestant Reformation that they were reviving the pure faith of the Scriptures, the Apostles, and the early Fathers, the Hindu reformers looked upon Protestantism as the product of a parallel religious movement and were deeply sympathetic to it."[23]

As has been pointed out, Christian missions have played a large part in introducing India to the humanistic side of Western civilization. Even the revisionists were affected by this in many ways. "The first impulse to start orphanages, for instance, came from the desire to prevent famine orphans from being swept into the missionary fold through mission orphanages."[24] On the other hand, the most radical adoptionists, in relation to even the least indigenized missionary enterprises, did not have presented to them exactly the same associational patterns which the mission-introduced forms of association implied whence they came. For instance, the cultural tendency to encapsulate any sect or social movement, so that it becomes patterned on a natural group, becomes in fact a caste, which has been a primary characteristic of Indian culture, has also been reflected from within the Indian church in certain tendencies toward self-isolation (perhaps compounded by missionary teaching about the dangers of backsliding through association with the heathen). These factors have meant that the church was in fact much less a voluntary association than those from which the bulk of the missionaries came. Perhaps an even more important internal modification is that ordinarily free-church patterns abroad have some power structure from the top down, from the bishops or from the synod, for instance. But usually in such cases there is a countervailing power in the other direction. This may best be traced by the flow of money up from the layman through the congregations and beyond. In the Indian mission situation this flow of money was reversed; it became a concurrent power downward from the top. The power structure is also different, in that at least for some years it typically started in New York or London rather than in any sense locally. This means that even an identical copy of the mission structure in India would not have been a typical voluntary association.

The indirect and totally unintentional influence of missionary efforts on Indian social patterns in general and on associational patterns in particular has probably been very great indeed. Much of this has been in terms of what in communications theory might be called *noise* relative to the propagation of the gospel.[25] The general theory may be represented in a simple diagram:

**Source**                    Channel              Noise                    Destination
of ——▸ Encoding ——▸ of ——————————▸ Decoding ——▸ of
Message                    Communication                                            Message

Here *noise* is anything in the environment that tends to twist, distort, or negate the flow of the message to the intended recipient. For the missionaries the *encoding* of the *message* about social and associational change had both negative and positive aspects. There were feelings in the home boards and on the field that the missionary task was solely the spiritual salvation of those to whom they were sent. On the other hand, increasingly the dominant attitude included the charitable uplift of those to whom they went as an acceptable part of the task. The *channel of communication* was the missionaries who despite training, and often despite specific purpose as well, did contribute significantly to the promotion of social change. Those coming from organizations with special concerns for internal democracy and/or the social gospel no doubt bore more than the rest. Often the missionaries brought with them strongly held opinions about what was right in terms of social behavior and organization—along with a depreciation of native social customs, including the Indian caste system and many aspects of the joint family association, as being unsuited to "civilized" and "Christian" man. In North India the caste brotherhood (*biradari*), a basic ascriptive association in social intercourse and social control, was forbidden to their converts by many of the missionaries. They substituted "proper" Western church courts for it. A few other missionaries tried to bring the *biradari* into the church—or at least did not ban it. In the areas where the former policy was followed, converts were cut off from the possibility of customary social control within the Christian community.[26] Often in India, just because all of the traditional associations were ascriptive and conversion included the probability of being excommunicated (outcasted) by one's ascriptive groups, conversion to Christianity brought isolation to the converts from customary family and larger associations. In such cases often the only substitute associational pattern known by the missionaries was a voluntary one—and it became the basis for the new groupings made possible and necessary by the conversions.

The simple proclamation to the heathen was very early, perhaps always, attached to an adoption of various elements of Western civilization—including associational patterns. But in general the most important and lasting *messages* may have been the indirect ones of the example of the missionaries functioning in the voluntary associational settings of "mission" and church committee meetings—and later expecting national Christian leaders to participate with them in the same settings. This led to the inculcation of broad social attitudes in circles far beyond the immediate centers of missionary activity. Eventually the leading Indian church members, and others, could think of the Christian life only in connection with many voluntary associational forms. That this process started and went far before the availability of mass media such as radio and the cinema, and before the ready availability of the newspaper, made it a greater factor than might be imagined today.

Another area in which the influence of the missionary enterprise was felt and was reflected in changed forms of association was among the so-called Syrian Christians of South India. These Christians can trace their history in India back at least to the sixth century—and perhaps long before. However, until their contact with missionaries from the West, first from Portugal and then from England, these Christians formed an ascriptive natural association along caste lines. Within this ascriptive context, prior to the coming of the Portuguese, the parishes seem to have been rather independent of each other with very little church, as opposed to parochial, organization.[27] The contact with the Jesuit archbishops and Carmelite bishops based in Goa introduced a much more highly structured sort of church organization, many aspects of which were eventually adopted and adapted. The later contact with missionaries of the Church of England led to additional modifications in organizational structure. These tended more toward voluntary associational forms than had the modifications resulting from Portuguese influence. This tendency was accompanied with a revived concern for evangelism which had not been found in these churches before. The tendency and the concern are not unrelated, since while the churches fitted into the caste structure by being ascriptive natural associations they had been uninterested in evangelism and when they became interested then the possibility of new converts entering the association made it already something different from a thoroughly natural association. There seem to have been three major types of reactions within the churches at this juncture. One, involving the smallest numbers, was adoptionist. It led to some Syrian Christians joining with the English missionaries and becoming Anglican Syrian Christians with Anglican forms of worship and of association. A second reaction, rejecting at one time even the possibility of having English missionaries preach in its churches, was nearly reversionist and yet it eventually became somewhat evangelistic and voluntary associational in character—particularly after the third group, which was revisionist, had broken away, thereby relieving internal conflict. The second group may best be denoted as Jacobite Orthodox. The last group, the revisionist, was a reform group which starting as a reform movement within the church was eventually forced out, becoming the Mar Thoma Syrian Church. These reformers were attempting to conform their church to newly rediscovered Biblical standards. This was at its center based in a theological reformation. But, as is usually the case, this theological reformation had social implications—both of evangelism and of renouncing certain rather "Hinduish" practices and observances which seemed to have been taken on over the years. Not the least of these social implications was an understanding of the church as being much more than a natural caste-like association. The freedom of the Mar Thomites was enhanced when they lost a series of court cases which left virtually all of the churches in the hands of the Orthodox. They then reformed their liturgy and went about building new churches. While their present churches have much more of a voluntary associational character than Syrian churches seem ever to have had before, this is far from utopian. For instance, very often new converts from outcaste groups are formed into separate congregations. This makes it possible to meet their special needs better, but critics see also in the pattern a temptation to keep the older congregations nearer to caste-like lines than they feel is desirable.

In the latter part of the nineteenth century, and thereafter, the direct impact of missionary enterprise toward changed patterns of association probably decreased. This is in part because the British government took a greater hand in social uplift and reform in several areas. There were internal reasons also for this reduced direct impact. Not the least of these was the almost frightening increase of internal concern—concern within the missionary enterprise for aspects internal to the enterprise, such as organization, method, and theology. Quite early in missionary circles there was much debate around the dilemma of missionaries trying through social service to lift the people to whom they were sent while they were aware that they were sent to preach the gospel. Eventually, partly as a reflection of the social gospel movement, social work, especially that related to education, medicine, widows, and orphans, became a major facet of the enterprise. This called for mission institutions very like the voluntary social work agencies of America and England but under mission-church auspices. These in turn, as has been suggested above, became patterns for other Indian social work, both by communities for their own members and under the guidance of altruistic "social workers," who often devoted their lives to the uplift of the underprivileged. The Nair Service Society is a striking example of such a communal social work organization in Kerala. Organized by and for the Nair caste along the lines of the agencies introduced by the Church Missionary Society, this society runs many schools and other agencies and must be credited with raising the general social and economic level of the Nairs enormously. While those institutions set up by communities were far from completely open and those under "social workers" were often very paternalistic indeed, nevertheless they did tend toward patterns of voluntary association.

The reversal of the direction of financial power in the mission-church which has already been cited may be considered as an internal basis of reduced impact but perhaps its corollaries are even more important. One of these is a complex of difficulties in the way of real lay voluntary associations within the churches. This is partly so because such potential groups must apply to the hierarchy for financial help and so lose some real, and perhaps vital, part of their independence. But this is also partly so because of the pervasiveness of social norms which stress paternalistic mutuality, the consensus of elders, as the basis for government—as this is incompatible with the constitutional forms brought along with a denominational "board of lay activities," a women's society, or a youth fellowship.

In recent years it is not difficult to point to movements related to the churches of America and the United Kingdom which have tended to modify the missionary-introduced forms of voluntary association. In some cases such movements seem to have made it possible for the substance of such associations within the Indian church to more nearly approximate the already adopted forms. This is particularly true of the movements which have tended to bring overseas money into the picture from outside the hierarchy—thus to some limited extent nullifying the curiously *concurrent* nature of financial power in the younger churches. This has usually been done by making grants available to certain types of institutions or for certain types of ministries. In Christian colleges, for instance, this has meant that the principal, the administrative head, and his board might secure a fair amount of their overseas contribution[28] for the college budget (in terms of money, overseas training for their staff, and overseas personnel for their staff) outside of regular denominational channels.[29] Somewhat similar effects have also resulted from the involvement of denominations other than those which founded a particular college, in contributions of one or more of these three kinds. In addition to relieving the principal from encapsulation in a monolithic power structure, both of these kinds of modification have frequently led to a broadening of the base of his college board of management—with representatives of the newly involved foundations or denominations. All of these factors tend to broaden the base of introduced associational patterns in a pluralistic direction.[30] In addition to these sources, sometimes aid from political propaganda agencies or foreign governments has been channeled into mission institutions through various "movements." In one sense this has probably reinforced the possibilities of pluralism, as suggested above. At another level, however, some feel that this mode of channeling money has great dangers for the younger churches.

A different kind of contribution toward pluralism is offered by schismatic groups with overseas sources of economic power—although within these groups themselves the hierarchical-cum-economic power structure may be rather more rigid than within more institutionalized mission boards and societies. Often such groups arise abroad and are reflected by a split, usually missionary-led, in India. The Canadian Presbyterians who refused to go into the United Church of Canada[31] and the McIntire group of Presbyterians are examples of these. Some such groups have originated in India following schismatic missionaries.[32] At best the two kinds of groups mentioned so far offer an alternate possibility to individuals who are uncomfortable in a particular denominational power structure—but then the variety of the traditional denominations also does this to some extent. Beyond these there are indigenous schismatic groups which have found overseas sources of support for themselves. Perhaps the most striking of these are those which have found this from overseas schismatics. Among these is a group of former London Missionary Society churches in the area of Nagercoil which were expected to become a part of the Church of South India when it was formed. For reasons which appear to have been entirely nontheological the dissident groups in each of these churches banded together forming voluntary associational factions. More recently they have been getting considerable financial aid and legal help from the dissident Congregationalists in America who comprise the National Association of Congregational Churches.[33] Before this there had been no ties at all between the American Board (Congregational) and these Nagercoil churches, although many churches related to the American Board did go into the Church of South India. It seems clear that some of the Americans involved in this situation firmly believe that mission boards and societies have been denying initiative to indigenous leadership and feel that they have a duty to encourage it in the tradition of congregational church patterns of voluntary associationalism.[34] It seems possible that by offering an alternative organizational structure this movement may have helped in the direction of their desire, although it is alleged by others familiar with the Nagercoil situation to have led more directly to factionalism.

Over the years there has been quite a bit of feedback from the younger churches which has affected the activity and sometimes even the structure of the so-called sending churches. The bearing of associational patterns and aspects has not, therefore, been all in one direction. Very early, missionaries, through missionary associations, were instrumental in bringing matters of Christian and social concern related to the British administration of India to the attention of their patrons in the United Kingdom—through correspondence and publication channels related to their sending boards and societies. Recent major examples of specific organizational feedback include the Co-ordinating Council of the Methodist Church, which since 1952 has been a key body in the national structure of American Methodism. It seems clear that the idea of such a council was suggested to a group reporting on the structure of Methodism by a somewhat similar body which had already been found most useful in Indian Methodism.[35] So, too, the proposals for American church union put forward by Eugene Carson Blake at the December, 1960, meeting of the National Council of the Churches of Christ in the U.S.A. were frankly based on both the Church of South India experience and the North India church union proposals.

As has been pointed out above, a major area of transition in India from closed pluralism in the direction of open pluralism, away from natural associations and in the direction of voluntary associations, is found in the growth of caste associations.[36] These are associations for the social welfare and political effectiveness, and not infrequently for improved status, of a closely related group of subcastes. Thus, the *possibility* of belonging to such an association is ascriptive, but to actually be a member of a caste association one must also *join* it. In a sense the fact that these caste associations have an ascriptive undergirding is more a formal than a social or functional characteristic. In these latter ways they are not so very different from the many Western voluntary associations which have prerequisites for membership, such as religious experience, ethnic background, or even common descent from participants in the Revolution. But also it must be realized that the deep psychological barriers between castes which are ingrained during the earliest period of a child's socialization are such as to make "voluntariness" between many in different castes uncomfortable or unthinkable. In local and regional politics such associations, some rather informal and some quite highly institutionalized, and groups of such associations, particularly those based on associated castes near to each other in rank, seem to be carrying increasingly important roles. Although it would be impossible to contend that the missionary enterprise had made a major contribution to this pattern, it does appear that there have been several possibly crucial points of contact. The first of these we find in one of the earliest cases of political action based on caste association—the so-called "bosom controversy" of 1858 in Travancore. Here a group of a palm-wine tappers caste contended for, and gained, the right of their women to wear certain clothing above the waist—a social prerogative which was denied them up to that time but which had been taken up by women from their caste who had become Christian. Thus a crucial factor in this early case is that the liberty sought was that which had already been obtained by their peers under the impact of the missionary enterprise. One suspects too that the desire for this may well have been related to missionary-suggested standards of "decency." Later a similar spread of ideas within this caste was noted when the non-Christians followed the example of the Christian converts in giving up tapping the palmyra palm for jaggery and toddy as a profession beneath them.[37]

It has been observed in census reports, and elsewhere, that caste associations seem to have been more common and more lively among the lower castes.[38] This is not surprising since it is just these groups who have the most common disabilities to overcome. It would seem possible that the general influence of the missionary enterprise may be seen here too. It was just in these strata of society that missionaries were bringing about improved status and conditions for those who became Christian—and this was happening at the same time. Studies of the group which finally followed Dr. Ambedkar into Buddhism, which was essentially a caste association of the Mahar caste and a few associated castes, show that the success of Christian ex-Mahars in overcoming disabilities was far from uninfluential in the genesis of that movement.[39]

There is a sense in which the changing pattern of the family in India is a leading edge of changed patterns of association.[40] This change in the family is from a larger organic joint-family pattern toward a smaller nuclear pattern. Of course the nuclear pattern is not exactly that of a voluntary association, but it does involve freedom of decision and mutual responsibility in a way that the joint family does not. Furthermore, as the nuclear family becomes either a goal or a norm the many binding forces of the joint family (which were exactly the organic ties of the traditional natural associations)[41] loosen, making it possible for other forces toward voluntary associational patterns—of which there are so many involved in the processes of monetization, industrialization, and urbanization—to come into fuller play. As locus and bearer of these changes in patterns of association the family has not been uninfluenced by the missionary enterprise. These changes have been borne in many ways, including the examples of family living of the missionaries and their converts; but perhaps the major way has been that of the Christian girls' schools, which when combined with "the influence of the Indian wife and mother in the home, one is led to believe, what cannot be proved, that mission girls' schools have exercised on the Indian home and social structure an influence that for many years no other agency exercised or could have exercised."[42] Within the church this change toward the very important destruction of the extended family of organic pattern was based not merely on the importation of European culture via missions but much more on the religious institutionalization of equality by which every baptized person is seen as the religious equal of every other, which was borne by the missions. This is the same social-theological basis which led in a similar direction in European cities from organic communities toward an autonomous bourgeoisie. In both cases Protestant views have seemed instrumental.

Throughout this study the Y.M.C.A. and Y.W.C.A. have been assumed as a part of the general missionary enterprise. However, in addition to this aspect of these associations they must be noticed especially. Since 1889 the Y.M.C.A. has tended to have a much larger proportion of non-Christians intimately associated with it, as members and participants in its programs, than mission institutions other than service institutions have had. Also these non-Christians have tended to be more influential members of the community than has been the case with most persons connected with mission institutions. Thus the direct influence of the Y.M.C.A., in proportion to its rather small numbers, seems to have been great. Perhaps because of this and because the Y.M.C.A. has been an appealing combination of a jolly social club and a center of religious instruction, its organization and methods have been copied by many modern religious groups throughout India. These copies, on the basis of voluntary associational patterns, include the Brahmo Young Men's Union and the Students Brotherhood, a theistic replica of a Y.M.C.A. loosely associated with the Samaj of days past,[43] as well as contemporary groups. In this connection it may be observed that the Student Christian Movement of India, which has roots in the Y.M.C.A. and the Y.W.C.A., still appears to be the *only* national student association of a voluntary nature with ongoing stability. As such it will likely be a pattern for any future secular student associations which may arise, in much the same way in which the Y.M.C.A. and mission associations have served in the past. In a somewhat similar way the University Teachers Committee of the Student Christian Movement, together with the Christian Institute for the Study of Religion and Society, has been serving as an association for intellectuals, especially younger college teachers, on a scale which however small has been wider than that of any other such association.[44]

There is a psychological sense in which the typology introduced earlier is misleading, since within the organic closed pluralism we get a hint not of close primary relationships but rather of vast friendlessness.[45] This is not to say that there are not groups which are primary in form. Such are common within the subcaste, and as "smoking groups," for instance, they have been noticed by every observer. The hint is that even within these groups this friendless situation exists. When this is coupled with a realization that within family and lineage groups decisions are ordinarily made by the elders, according to custom, so that there is vast choicelessness for the younger members—as well as inexperience in making choices such as Western voluntary associational patterns assume, and when it is realized that Indian courts codified custom and so truncated its development—it appears remarkable that the tendency toward new social patterns has gone so far as it has. As the values underlying these patterns are accepted more thoroughly by a growing elite, and as they are passed down, voluntary associations may become common. On the other hand, a new sort of closed pluralism may instead become the mode.

# XI / THE COMMUNAUTÉ DE TRAVAIL: EXPERIMENTATION IN INTEGRAL ASSOCIATION

*Verne H. Fletcher*

"We are a little wild here with numberless projects of social reform. Not a reading man but has a draft of a new community in his waistcoat pocket." Thus wrote Emerson to Carlyle in 1840 of the communitarian fever in the United States. (23)* On the other side of the Atlantic this was likewise the period of the schemes of the Utopian Socialists and the principles of the Rochdale weavers. A century later in France a certain communitarian "wildness" reappears, some of it extremely dubious but some of it worthy of retaining our attention. Of particular significance for the theory of associations are the experiments grouped under the name *Communauté de Travail*.

In this instance, it was not so much the "reading man" and his "waistcoat" as the working man and his overalls. For these communities were largely the creation of men who had known the frustrations of the worker under a particularly rigid form of capitalism, who had chafed under the hegemony of the bourgeois class, who were impatient for the continually postponed amelioration of conditions promised by the syndicalist movement, and who were determined to liberate themselves from the tyranny of capital and from the misery of the proletarian condition. Moreover, they were not under the illusion that the proletarian condition could be eliminated merely by a change in masters: they had no taste for collectivism, even if under the name of socialism, and sought rather to promote a socialization "on the human scale." Furthermore, this movement was not characterized by any longing to escape the modern world of industrialization nor by any anarchist disdain of machine production but rather by a "confidence in the progress

---

* The figures in parentheses refer to the bibliographical notes on this chapter at the end of the book. In cases where quotations are not followed by references it will be understood that these are taken from the occasional publications of the *Entente Communautaire* and generally from its organ *Communauté*. (15)

of technology" because of the contribution which the machine can make to the liberation of man. If it is true that industrial work tends to brutalize and deaden man, "it is not the machine which must be blamed, but the structure of the enterprise, the organization of work and the climate in which it must be carried out" under the present systems. The desire of these men was to heal the divorce between "the concern for material progress" and the "concern for man"; in other words, they strove "to place the economy in the service of man in order that his eminent dignity might be respected." (28)

Georges Friedmann, France's leading authority on industrial sociology, quite accurately situates the movement when he states: "The contemporary crisis of excessively-centralized socialist experiments has . . . brought to a place of prominence . . . the study of cooperation characterized by institutions which are flexible and decentralized, making room for autonomous communities in which the individual can find a field for the exercise of spontaneity, initiative, responsibility and participation, and all this . . . in dependence on the most modern techniques of organization and of production." (16) Friedmann alludes here to the two main types of socialism which have contended for the field during the last century and a quarter: centralized, collectivist socialism on the one hand, and federalist, communitarian socialism on the other. There is, of course, no greater advocate of the second type than Martin Buber, whose efforts to recover the insights of "utopian" socialism as of contemporary significance have, to a certain extent, been successful, if not in rehabilitating the term, at least in rehabilitating the idea. (5)*

The *Communauté de Travail* definitely belongs to the communitarian type of socialism, although it would be incorrect to deny a strong Marxist influence (as well as a distinctly Christian influence) in the movement. As a matter of fact, Marx himself was somewhat ambivalent in respect to the communitarian alternative and, as Buber points out, became rather enthusiastic at the time of the French Commune. At this point, says Buber, "a federation of communes and cooperatives . . . is . . . acknowledged by Marx as genuine communism." (5) Nevertheless, it is valid to make a definite distinction and historically it is of great importance. We do not of course propose to write that history here but simply to give some indication of the antecedents of the present-day movement.

---

* It is doubtful whether the term "utopian" can be rid of its more or less derogatory connotations. At any rate, in this essay we will reserve the term primarily to refer to pre-Marxian socialism but will also use it to designate the earlier phase of the *Communauté de Travail* movement during which there was entertained the expectation of the rapid universalization of the communitarian idea. See Bestor's excellent discussion of the evolution of the socialist vocabulary. (3)

### COMMUNITARIAN SOCIALISM IN THE NINETEENTH CENTURY

Communitarian socialism took its rise, as we have indicated, in the second quarter of the nineteenth century in England and in France and from thence emigrated to the United States. If one is interested in communitarian experimentation in this early period, it is of course to the latter country that one will turn. The communitarian efforts to reform society, which in Europe struggled against the weight of centuries, found new hope on the endless horizons of the new country, where there was ample room for all kinds of experiments and for all degrees of failure.* For theory, however, we must look to Owen, King, and the Rochdale principles in England and, in France, to Fourier, Buchez, Proudhon, and, to a lesser extent, Saint-Simon.† In France utopian socialism held the center of the stage up to, and somewhat beyond, mid-century: one bit of evidence for this is that in 1844 Marx was unable to find even *one* French collaborator for his proposed "French-German" socialist review. (22) In contrast to the Marxists, the French socialists emphasized, in Buber's words, "the significance of the small social unit for the rebuilding of society." Their great weakness, on the other hand, was their naïve belief in the natural propagating powers of their ideas, as well as in the pliability of the bourgeois State apparatus called upon, in effect, to assent to its own disappearance: ". . . a government representative of a definite State-order cannot very well be urged to call institutions into being which are destined . . . to abolish that order." (5)

It was from its Marxist wing that French socialism learned its lesson on the facts of power: that behind the facade of social calm in capitalist society there lurks a "state of violence" (to use Emmanuel Mounier's terminology) which, if challenged, bursts forth into "acts of violence" and of repression. This being the experience of the French workers under the regime of Louis Napoleon, it was in this period that a proletarian class consciousness began to develop in France. The suppression of the Commune was the last proof needed by the French proletariat that their only hope lay in the direction of large-scale collectivist action, inspired by the conviction expressed in Louis Blanc's famous statement: "Not to seize power as an instrument is to find it in one's path as an obstacle." It was at the Workers Congress in 1879 at Marseille, when the Marxists held the majority hand over the "cooperateurs," that the new balance in favor of the former was definitely in

---

* Apart from Bestor (2), Holloway (23), and Desroche (11), the best works on the American phase are the old sources, Noyes (37) and Nordhoff (36).

† The best sources from the perspective of this essay are (5) and (30). A valuable treatment, though from a different perspective, is (1).

evidence. Marxist formulas were here declared to be the only "sufficiently powerful means for the achievement of the emancipation of the workers." (10) It is undeniable, as Lasserre points out, that in France, Marxist syndicalism has been the principal means of advance for the workers. It was their impatience with communitarian socialism which led the working class after 1870 to place their confidence in Marxism; however, a reverse trend, Lasserre feels, is now to be discerned as workers become disillusioned with "a merely verbal revolution." (27) It would thus appear that the supposedly discredited ideas of the utopians and the communitarians deserve a second look, and that even the cooperative movement, *if we return to its source,* has a latent revolutionary potential.

At the source of the cooperative movement was a vision of the transformation of society by means of the full or integral cooperative, "where people have the real things of their common life in common," in Buber's phrase. (5) "As soon as possible," said the Rochdale pioneers, "our group [a Consumers Cooperative] will proceed to the organization of production, distribution and self-education by our own means: in other words, we will constitute ourselves an autonomous colony where there will be solidarity of all interests." (7) Thus there was envisioned the formation of a Producers Cooperative to follow the Consumers Cooperative and, finally, in a third stage, the Community of Full Cooperative. And though they never reached the third stage, it is nevertheless "amazing," as Buber says, "how the practical intuition of the flannel-weavers of Rochdale grasped the three essential fields of cooperation." (5) The Rochdale group perceived a further element of integral cooperation: the idea of federalism, i.e., cooperation between cooperatives. In addition, a central notion of William King was the modification of human relationships promoted by the transformation of economic relationships, a notion which was to play such an important role within the *Communauté de Travail.* "When a man enters a cooperative society," wrote King, "he enters upon a new relation with his fellowmen, and that relation immediately becomes the subject of every sanction, both moral and religious." (5) Finally, we may mention the influence of Christianity, which is of importance in the whole communitarian movement although it can only claim to be one among several basic influences. King and Buchez were both thus motivated, the latter stating that the time had come "to mould the teachings of Christianity into social institutions."*

---

* The question of the relationship of the communitarian movement to the earlier Protestant sectarian movement is treated in (9) and (12). See also (11, pp. 21-86; 232-269) and (2, pp. 4-6; 20-59).

The cooperative movement never realized the full intentions of its original theoreticians and soon became frankly unifunctional and segmental, a type of cooperation which must be distinguished from multifunctional, comprehensive, integral or full cooperation. "The first type," writes Desroche, "is limited precisely to economic goals; the second is extended to most, if not all social values. The first is confined, in effect, to its work in common, while the second, beginning with and based on this common work, extends to modes of common life. . . ." (13) It is not surprising that the Consumers Cooperative movement, which "brings people together with only a minimal and highly impersonal part of their total being," should rather quickly lose the spirit of human solidarity which marked the Rochdale pioneers, and should become more and more bureaucratic and segmental since it "only combines certain interests of people but not the lives of people themselves. . . ." (5) The Producers Cooperative, centered as it is around the common production of goods, involves its members more profoundly than does the mere acquisition of goods for private consumption. Buchez, who in 1832 founded the first Cooperative of Production in France, announced three of the principles which became important in the *Communauté de Travail*: The principle of inalienable, indivisible capital; the principle of no hired labor except for a limited period; and, finally, the principle of solidarity with the entire working class. (30) Nevertheless, the Producers Cooperative movement was steadily drawn toward the segmental type of cooperation: in place of common ownership, each member becomes the individual owner of his fraction of the total property; the movement has, moreover, tended to isolate itself from the larger currents of the proletarian struggle; and, finally, the founders of a producers cooperative tend to become a sort of "collective capitalist," the majority of the workers in the enterprise being hired labor. As Desroche points out, this has tended to create, in effect, a situation of class conflict within the enterprise itself, and in many instances the cooperative has reverted to private forms of property ownership. (10)

Closely related to the idea of social property in Buchez was the concept of "mutualism" in Proudhon, who is one of the most important theoreticians for the communitarian type of socialism. Under the concept of mutualism, he proposed the common ownership of the means of production, not by the State, but by the workers within each enterprise. These basic cells would then be federated into larger structures which would promote an equilibrium between themselves as territorial-functional federations and the centralized powers of the State. Proudhon considered a mutualist economy to be the economic arrangement demanded by the injustices of capitalism. The capitalist entrepreneur pays each worker as though he worked alone; but for "that immense force which results from the union and the harmony of the workers . . . he does not pay. . . . Consequently, there always remains a right of common ownership . . . of which [the capitalist] unjustly takes advantage." (30) It is necessary then to promote "industrial democracy" by making "the workers co-owners of the industrial machine," through the principle of "propriété associée," i.e., common, or communitarian ownership. "Mutuality, or reciprocity, exists," writes Proudhon, "when all the workers in an industry [read: enterprise], instead of working for an entrepreneur who pays them and keeps their products, work for one another and thus collaborate in the making of a common product whose profits they share amongst themselves." (5) Mutuality, in this formulation, is not dissimilar to what the present-day communitarian movement means by the economic aspect of "communauté."

We should mention briefly the French anarchist colonies—*milieux libres*—at the turn of the century since, with the triumph of syndicalism, they were in that country the only relay of communitarian experimentation to the twentieth century. With the main branch of French socialism moving strongly to an extreme of collectivism and centralization, the heirs of communitarianism moved toward the opposite pole: "The root principle of anarchism," explains Gide, "is individualism carried to its ultimate consequences. . . . Let everyone do what he likes, on the sole condition that he allows the same freedom to others." (19)* The form is preserved, i.e., renewal of society through small-scale settlements of life in common, but the substance is completely eroded. Notice that the term "community" is generally replaced by the term "milieu." Essentially, these colonies represented an effort to escape the restrictions of society by the creation of a milieu where each could be his own egoistic self. Most of these experiments had the following characteristics: property was theoretically held in common; work was regulated entirely by self-discipline; there was no fixed remuneration since "all shall consume freely according to their tastes and needs"; and family relations were generally frowned upon although the colonists were allowed a "woman comrade." It is not surprising that these "Gardens of Eden" were of short duration, usually collapsing because of the indolence of the members or the authoritarianism of the founders: "The champions of freedom became too

---

* For the best brief account of the French anarchist colonies see (19, pp. 155-165). A detailed study of the movement is (31); the colonies are treated on pp. 355-380; anarchist philosophy on pp. 451-509. For a briefer account of the colonies see (32); and for a still briefer account (8).

despotic." (19) Writing in 1928, Gide speaks of his survey of a century of communitarian experimentation as "something after the style of an obituary notice," since "we cannot point at this moment to a single example of a communist [read: communitarian] society which has really succeeded." Of course, in point of fact, even as he was writing this obituary, that which is perhaps the most significant of such experiments was already under way: the Palestinian Kibbutzim, and fifteen years later France was to witness a new soaring of communitarian experimentation in the *Communautés de Travail*.

In discussing this present-day movement we will not be concerned with any chronology of events but rather with the developments in theory and in practice which have taken place over the twenty-year period of its history. We will, however, distinguish three phases, the dating of which is rather arbitrary, especially in respect to the transition from the second to the third phase. First, the "utopian" phase (1941-1946). This period was associated with the name Marcel Barbu, who acted on the assumption that the time was ripe for the idea of community to inundate and refashion the whole of society—immediately. We date the conclusion of this phase as taking place with the departure of Barbu, although "utopian" thinking still persisted to a more limited degree. Second, the "classical" phase (1946-1957). Universalist illusions were renounced in the face of the harsh realities of economic survival. The goal now is to actually bring into being viable communities which will be both economic and human successes. The classical model was "Boimondau" in Valence, the original Barbu community. In the early postwar period at least a hundred attempts were made, more or less on the Boimondau model, with more failures than successes. In 1950, there were 85 groups registered with the *Entente Communautaire*; in 1954, there were approximately 45 groups; in 1957, around 30 (and in 1961, roughly the same). Third, the contemporary period (1957-    ). This date, while convenient, is not in any sense precise: the crises began much earlier; in fact, they accompanied the movement on every step of the way. However, this was the year of the "Meister report" (33) and more or less corresponds to the point at which the movement determined to face frankly the changes which were taking place in its spirit and structure. We will not attempt to characterize further this period of "crisis and evolution" until the groundwork of the earlier phases has been laid.

### THE UTOPIAN PHASE

It will not be necessary to dwell in any great detail on the first period: that which is of value will be more carefully discussed in connection with the subsequent phase. We will treat here the specifically utopian and authoritarian aspects of Barbu's scheme, first, in respect to the local, and secondly, in respect to the national level. First of all, what does Barbu mean by "community of work"?*

> Work means human activity, in whatever form, and that which we call a community of work is a community of activities, a community of families acting together on the human scale. The factory is certainly at the center of our community of work . . . [but] the enterprise represents only the economic function of the community. . . . The community is not identical with the enterprise, it subordinates the enterprise to its total purpose, it extends beyond the enterprise since it is concerned with life in all its dimensions. (28)

Thus the *Communauté de Travail* is conceived of by Barbu as supplying the total needs of its members and as requiring their total effort and allegiance—beyond that which is supplied and demanded by the family. The original *Acte de Fondation* reads, in part, as follows:

> Each companion commits himself to cultivate his spirit, mind and body. . . . The Community, in return, commits itself to assure to each all the means necessary for his cultivation in the direction of his vocation. Each companion commits himself to the reform of his private life, his family life and his public life in the direction of the common moral minimum of the Community. The companions authorize the Community and their fellow companions to apply corrections as necessary. . . .

These statements, already amounting practically to a monastic discipline and a religious commitment, are completed by the following article: "Each companion commits himself to take a religious or philosophical position and to cultivate himself in the direction chosen, and, where applicable, to practice the chosen religion."†

The achievement of such "total" community quite inevitably re-

---

*It should be pointed out that, with the exception of a few agricultural communities associated with the movement in the early days, all the communities are based on small industrial or artisanal enterprises: light metallurgy, machine tools, electric installations, watchcase manufacture, joinery, furniture manufacture, building trades, picture frames, photography, a team of skindivers, etc. This is one major distinction from other integral experiments such as the 19th-century groups and the contemporary Bruderhof and Hutterite groups, as well as the Israeli Kibbutzim, almost all of which had or have an agricultural base. The small-scale industrial and artisan base constitutes a point of convergence with the Cooperative of Production.

†Barbu himself was a communicant Roman Catholic and doubtless considered his social action as a matter of Christian response. Some interpreters of the early days considered the "community" a Christian affair: (14) and (28). It is certainly true that *some* of the most valuable leaders have been products of Catholic Action. There were likewise some outstanding Protestants. But this is only one of the currents. Others of the great leaders of the "classical" period—Mermoz, Régis, for example—were convinced Marxists. On the whole socialism was probably a more formative influence than Christianity.

quires a measure of authoritarianism, although Barbu conceived of this as voluntary social discipline: "Discipline voluntarily accepted is the first condition of social life. Any man who obeys only under constraint is a coward and will be driven from the community." It should be observed that all these statements of position were discussed and "voluntarily" agreed upon by all concerned but, in view of subsequent developments, one is certainly justified in seeing in these "unanimous" principles the product of an exceedingly forceful and overbearing personality. Other ideas of Barbu are even more disturbing. Note the authoritarian atmosphere of this:

> Human beings are equal in nature, but unequal in value. They have not all received the same gifts nor in the same intensity. They should consequently agree that the community classify them according to their total human value. The leader (*chef*) should be the best (that is, he who . . . has the greatest total human value): the one who sets the example, who educates, who loves, who dedicates himself, who serves. To obey a false leader who does not have these qualities constitutes an act of cowardice. (28)

There would be no point in denying the very clear resemblance to the "Vichy" conception of community imported during this period from across the Rhine.* As a matter of fact, if the history of the movement stopped at this point, we may be certain that any objective classification would find the "Communauté Barbu" under the rubric of pseudo-community, authoritarian style. We are reminded of Rousseau's "forced to be free": Barbu, in effect, commanded everyone to be free in the manner prescribed by himself. It was the totally planned community demanding total allegiance. Barbu conceived of it as a family of families with himself as the Patriarch.† The early community was subsequently described as "a collective solitude."

On the national level, Barbu conceived of the community as having a revolutionary mission with himself as prophet. "From January 1, 1944, the members of the Community commit themselves to living as they would live in a Community on the national scale, composed of cells similar to the Community Marcel Barbu." Then comes the rather dubious claim: "The Community is provisionally considered as invested with

---

* The most accessible exposition of the French version of this pseudo-communitarianism (though by no means the most extreme) is to be found in (38). The most forthright opposition to these ideas was the movement "Esprit" (see the review *Esprit* founded in 1932 by Emmanuel Mounier). For a positive statement of the philosophy of community see the works of Mounier and the indispensable introduction to his thought by Moix (35).

† Berneri: (1) "The contradictions inherent in most utopias are due to this authoritarian approach. . . . The majority of the builders of utopias are determined to remain the masters of their . . . commonwealths. While they claim to give freedom, they issue a detailed code which must be strictly followed."

all the duties and rights of the Communities on the superior levels so long as the latter are not in existence. . . ." Above the *Communauté de Travail* in the hierarchy comes the Community of the cité (i.e., grouping of local communities of work), then the communal, regional, departmental communities, and finally, the National Community, "while waiting for the international community for which we all hope."* It would appear that at every level we may refer back to the original cell which, as a living example, will give rise little by little to the expression of community on the higher levels. We recognize here the old illusion of Owen and Fourier, which ignores the force of resistance of the entrenched status quo and places naïve confidence in its own powers of persuasion. Barbu's revolution bypasses the whole proletarian struggle and quite neatly achieves the whole revolution before the main body of the workers has scarcely been able to make a beginning.

Barbu in 1945 succeeded in winning election to the National Assembly, where he sought a larger platform for the propagation of his ideas. He proposed three bills, none of which became law: the first would have given legal status to the communities; the second would have created a National Council entrusted with the responsibility of creating new communities; the third would have made it mandatory for a capitalist owner to have acceded to the demand on the part of 80 percent of the workers in his enterprise to transform the enterprise into a *Communauté de Travail*. (14) Perceiving that "his" community was no longer behind him, Barbu left the same in 1946, devoting himself entirely to the "Révolution Communautaire"; formed the "Ordre Communautaire," an organization for the propagation of his ideas; and created the "Rassemblement Communautaire Française," destined to be the political arm of the revolution. It scarcely needs to be added that this balloon burst before a year was up.

Meanwhile, Boimondau, distrustful of Barbu's messianism and disturbed by the implied rupture with the masses of the proletariat, refused its adherence to the "revolutionary" organizations and, above all, taking the measure of its own economic condition, concluded that its very survival was extremely problematical. It is at this point that the second phase begins, with the realization that if a *Communauté de Travail* cannot succeed economically it cannot succeed. Thus began the determined effort simply to *endure*.

### THE CLASSICAL PHASE

As we continue our discussion it should be re-emphasized that much which is positive in subsequent developments must also be traced back

---

* Whether the last phrase is Barbu's idea or DuTeil's (14) is not clear. For an excellent summary of the universal pretensions of Barbu's scheme see (10).

to basic conceptions which were also held by Barbu. In presenting only the negative aspects of the first phase it has not been our intention to suggest a total condemnation of the conceptions of Barbu, but only to point out the utopian and authoritarian elements which would have brought the movement to total collapse had they not been repudiated by other leaders. In discussing this second phase, we will present, first, the model, and secondly, its modifications in practice, under three heads: common ownership, collective management, and full personal development within community. We will take as the model the "Charte des Communautés de Travail." The *Charte,* adopted by the General Assembly of the *Entente Communautaire* in 1952, was proposed as a set of criteria for self-judgment and as the minimum requirement for membership in the *Entente.* It was never rigidly adhered to in all details by any community but did serve as an expression of intentions, a goal toward which to strive. It will be useful first of all to set down the twelve principles of the *Charte.**

I. Common and indivisible ownership of the means of production such that the property can never become private nor give rise to any privilege in terms of salary or control.

II. A sound economic basis.

III. The General Assembly of all companions is sovereign but may delegate part or all of its authority to its representatives or to an elected Council which, moreover, assists and controls the Head of the Community.

IV. Election of representatives *à la double confiance* [proposed from above, elected from below].

V. The Rules of the Community adopted by unanimous vote.

VI. Such channels of communication as will keep each companion informed of the activities and problems of the Community.

VII. Emphasis on education in the sense of seriously striving for the complete human development of each companion.

VIII. No exclusion whatsoever on political, religious, or philosophical grounds nor distinction on the basis of race, sex, or nationality.

IX. Active solidarity with the outside world, especially with the working class.

X. Remuneration in no way related to the original capital investment. Remuneration not based on professional contribution alone.

XI. A diffusion of responsibilities such that the management and control, though carried out by the Head of the Community or by the Council, is the result of the effort of each and of all.

XII. No employment of hired labor, except that each worker before becoming a full companion must pass through a period of adaptation and initiation.

1. Common ownership (articles I, X, and XII). The rock-bottom

* The text of the charter may be found in (33). There exists a previous English translation in *Cooperative Living,* V (Fall 1953), 13, 14. We acknowledge the assistance of this translation but have differed from it at several points.

*sina qua non* of the *Communauté de Travail* is the provision that the means of production, the goods produced, and, in short, the enterprise in its entirety, belongs to the community as such. The companions do not own each one his part individually, nor may shares be owned by nonparticipating outside investors. The property belongs rather to the whole community not only collectively but also indivisibly. In other words, the community is distinct from the sum total of the members and constitutes concretely a new social whole. This is underlined by the fact that in case of dissolution the capital, once indebtedness is liquidated, is not "shared out" but reverts either to the federation of communities (*Entente Communautaire*), or to another *Communauté de Travail*. Ex-companions are simply reimbursed for their original capital contribution. Such economic arrangements have no precise legal status under French law. (We have noted above the failure of Barbu's bill to become law.) However, the legal existence of the communities was finally more or less normalized by the incorporation under the statutes of the Cooperatives of Production with the additional phrase *à forme communautaire*. That which is not covered under the legal statutes is stipulated by the internal "Rules" of each community.

The third and final consideration under the question of common ownership is that of companions versus non-companions (hired labor). The classical ideal was that everyone who worked in the community should be either a "companion" (i.e., having invested capital, however minimal in amount, and undertaken to share completely in the responsibility for the existence and well-being of the community), or a potential companion, called *stagiaire* or apprentice. In theory, a period of time was set at the end of which a *stagiaire* either became a companion or left the community. Certain of the communities—for example, those connected with the building trades—were obliged to hire considerable seasonal labor. There was, however, a general trend in the mid-50's for the proportion of non-companions to increase, which meant that a growing number of those who worked within the communities assumed no responsibility for the community as such and had no voice in decisions. This was another factor leading to internal differentiation and antagonism.

2. Related to the second problem, that of collective management, are articles III, IV, V, and XI of the charter. Ownership by the community means, in theory, management by the community. The General Assembly of all companions, runs the theory, is the source of authority; responsibility is diffused throughout the length and breadth of the community. The Head of the community is elected by the General Assembly (or by the General Council which has been elected by the Gen-

eral Assembly), for a period of three years, and is eligible for three terms. The positions on the General Council and all other positions of responsibility are filled each year, either by election of the General Assembly with the approval of the Head of the community, or by the appointment of the Head of the community with the assent of the Assembly. This was known as the rule of "double confidence." As for the provision on "unanimity," the charter speaks of it only in respect to the "Rules" of the community, but it was initially conceived of as applying more generally. The way of looking at this principle at Boimondau is worth citing:

> . . . Almost unthinkable in current society . . . the life in community creates a climate of confidence which facilitates unanimous agreement . . . [since] particular interests and common interests coincide. . . . Experience has shown us that, as soon as the major causes of conflict— opposition of interests, ignorance, distrust, and injustice—disappear, unanimity is readily attainable. . . . Its application however demands much patience . . . [but] it is better to proceed more slowly with everyone, than to go more rapidly by thrusting aside those who cannot follow.

As for the dissemination of information, the main channel of communication and foyer for discussion was the weekly "assembly of contact," seconded by the meetings of "neighborhood groups,"* by gatherings of shop personnel, and by newsletter or bulletin.

In summary, the General Assembly is sovereign; the authority delegated by it can be controlled, called into question, or, if desired, revoked; the channels of information and the wide diffusion of responsibility allow each and all to participate effectively in the management and control of the total program of the community. This was the theory. In practice, however, the theory ran into some very hard facts of life. In the first place, there was the low level of education and of professional qualification. Less than one-third of the companions of all communities (in Meister's survey) had gone beyond primary school; among 1000 communitarians were found only three engineers. Many of the problems which arose in the communities were the result of social circumstances which had hindered the workers from obtaining a desirable level of education and formation. "All are victims of a state of things in society before being guilty of a state of things within the

---

* The initial plan at Boimondau was based on groups of 8 to 10 families living in the same general sector of Valence. It was here that the problems and principles of the community were thrashed out in intimate and continual discussion. These were the real "cells" for the creation of the communitarian life. Very few of the communities, however, have used this formula—the members of the Parisian communities, for example, are too scattered—and even at Boimondau the plan has long since been dropped.

community." (7) The additional observation must not be omitted, however, that these same figures on the low educational level also point to a tremendous strength of will and persistent determination which permitted the communitarians to tackle, with very little technical preparation, and to solve the problems of the creation, even on a relatively small scale, of a successful industrial or artisanal enterprise, especially in a hostile and unsympathetic environment.*

This leads to a second "hard fact" which proved to be an obstacle to "collective management": namely, that industrial production, in and of itself, is hierarchical, bureaucratic, rationalized, dependent on the exercise of authority and on obedience to commands. The real content of the concept "industrial democracy" is, it must be admitted, unclear: it may well be a contradiction in terms. It is of course true, as the recent literature has abundantly demonstrated, that there are degrees of authoritarianism in industrial organization. It is certain, however, that this possible spectrum does not reach as far as the notion of collective management as conceived by the 1952 communitarian charter. This suggests a third fact, and this one the most fundamental of all, for it relates to the perennial nature of man and human society. We will only allude to this consideration at this point: Was not the notion of "collective management" and mutual control, *as formulated in this period,* based ultimately on a mistaken theory of community which ignores the dialectical relationship of equality and authority, of freedom and order?

Let us listen as the movement itself becomes conscious of its libertarian and egalitarian misconceptions through the voice of the head of the *Entente Communautaire* in 1956:

> We began with the postulate that collective management . . . was the automatic consequence of common and indivisible ownership of the means of production and would result in the development of each of the members of the community, because its opposite, capitalist or private property, which confers such power on the holder of capital, implies individual management, obsessed as it is with profit and thus scornful of human beings. . . . We found ourselves then in the midst of anarchy. . . . The companions . . . pretended to exercise the authority, which however has necessarily to be delegated; and those to whom it had been delegated encountered the most serious difficulties in exercising it for the simple reason that they did not clearly hold the authority. And everyone shared the bitter sentiment of a great deception. . . . We understood then that we had committed two major mistakes: 1—that of believing that it is possible to administer an enterprise

---

*The capitalist economy, with which the communitarians, by the force of things, had to come to terms, was not so much hostile as unsympathetic, unconvinced, seeing no reason to take the movement seriously. The labor movement was frequently hostile, seeing in this movement a weakening of the class struggle.

without a strong authority, the necessity for which is recognized by all, and 2—that of naming to positions of responsibility men wholly unprepared for its exercise.

The atmosphere of dogmatic libertarianism is well captured in the following description:

> We were in the habit of discussing everything and as on many other points we fell into a kind of communitarian formalism. . . . We used to say for example: "This is a democratic community, the best proof of which is that we get together 7 or 8 times a week to hash over everything." And, unfortunately, this was true in many of the communities. We assembled continually, we discussed everything, and decided very little . . . which, moreover, nobody bothered to put into effect. . . . And the one in charge, . . . as soon as the meeting was finished, simply made the important decisions according to his own personal judgment. . . .

In other instances, the leadership was totally paralyzed: "assisted, counseled, controlled, judged, verified, by various councils and commissions, . . . they were reduced to a solemn immobility or were abandoned as soon as they took any positive step. The fear of exercising power was, in certain cases, pathological, and its exercise . . . inconsistent."

It was not that there was any superfluity of capable leaders, either from a technical or a human point of view. We have indicated above that the contrary situation obtained. A community was fortunate if it had one man who, by obstinate study of the technical problems involved, could develop the capacity to manage successfully a modern industrial or artisanal enterprise, even though only of small or medium size. Thus, while everyone theoretically had his finger in the pie, in practice the manager, with the addition perhaps of the department chiefs in the larger communities, was the only one able to understand all the elements involved in coming to decisions. The authority of the General Assembly then was in fact limited to the election of the leadership (management) and the approval of decisions already taken. The actual "collective management" was thus concentrated in the hands of a few companions.

What happened under these unavoidable circumstances to the principle of the wide diffusion of information? Certainly nothing was done in hiding. The books were open to all. But even if serious effort was made to explain the intricacies involved, few of the companions would have the elements in hand for the comprehension of these technical details. And without this, what meaning was left to the principle of "unanimity" in all things, let us say, for example, in respect to a particular investment to be made, or a particular change in production schedule, or even to the question as to whether there should be an augmentation of remuneration? How are these things to be democratically and unanimously decided? The painful lack of comprehension of a problem on the part of the workers in contrast to the obvious technical competence on the part of the self-educated leaders, constituted a constraint which could "reduce to silence without, however, gaining the genuine adhesion of the companions." (28)

Given these developments, new situations of conflict arose. For the capital-versus-labor cleavage there was substituted a management-versus-personnel cleavage, added to the potential conflict over salary differential, as well as the companion versus non-companion dichotomy. Thus a schism was "concretely re-introduced . . . and even certain . . . class antagonisms, though formally the root of these antagonisms has been cut by the internal democratic structure. . . ." (10) Though in principle transformed by the common interests and common purposes of the community, the militant union man, used to fighting for his demands—as much a habit for him in his "precommunitarian" existence as eating and sleeping—finds his automatic reflexes once again stirred to aggressive action, but at the same time he experiences a bad conscience since he knows that he is supposed to be in a situation calling for complete mutual cooperation. (7) Was it necessary to conclude then that the idea of collective management was a complete fiction, even a farce, which had simply to be abandoned as a total illusion? On this point, the conclusions of Meister's survey are not that radical: "The idea of collective management has cost a great deal of time and patience and has provoked much conflict and vexation; nevertheless, the communitarians are not willing to give up the notion, even though at the moment it is necessary to give almost complete leeway to those elected to posts of responsibility." Subsequent to Meister's study, as we shall see, there arose a new determination to reformulate and give reality to this principle.

3. The third heading under which we are discussing "classical" theory and its practice is "full personal development within community," the primary statement of which is in Article VII of the charter, and implied in Article Xb. We can be quite brief at this point since much has already been said about the notion that the community should meet the total human needs of its members and about the corresponding obligation of each member to make progress at all levels. The initial vision is well expressed in the motto: "Faire des boîtiers de montre pour faire des hommes."* Indeed, the amazing elaboration of "non-professional" activities in the early days of the movement is an indica-

---

* "Make watchcases in order to make men." Boimondau today is the largest maker of watchcases in France.

tion of a profound desire to compensate for the lack of social and cultural formation which society had denied to the majority of the workers. "The great innovation of Boimondau was to bring culture to the place of work, not only by introducing courses of study, library, etc. within the walls of the enterprise, but especially by the dedication of a certain number of hours of the weekly schedule to these activities." The time spent in such pursuits and the hours of productive labor at the machine were remunerated on the same scale. Courses were organized on basic ABC's on subjects of general culture, on technical questions; lecturers and performers were invited from outside; artistic, theatrical, and musical groups were formed; athletic teams and a weekly newspaper were encouraged, in addition to the building of a fairly adequate library. To this were added discussion groups according to basic religious and philosophical commitment, "requiring of each the respect of the conviction of others and the deepening of his own convictions." (10) In these groups the companions also sought the "common moral minimum" to which all could give their allegiance. In the early days, it was thought that, while a capitalist enterprise might demand for its success no more than the combination of a desire for profits on the part of management, coupled with the fear of starvation on the part of labor, a communitarian enterprise surely demanded some common attitudes and a shared ethical basis. It is not surprising that the high enthusiasm of the early days, in respect to this multiplicity of activities, was impossible to maintain. To the normal weariness of the flesh and the insurmountable handicaps of a poor education was added the general deception of the early postwar hopes for the renewal of the political and spiritual condition of the entire nation. As a consequence, "the community tends to become more and more a unifunctional group and to concentrate on the improvement of the productive effort." (33)

We now have the elements of the crisis before us—a crisis which raised serious question as to the future of the movement or indeed whether or not the movement had any future at all. It almost appeared as though the twilight hour had approached; but such, as it turns out, has not been the case. At a minimum, we might say that even the existence of the movement for two decades says something, if we remember the short duration of most communitarian experiments of the nineteenth century, with the exception of course of the more solid religiously based communities. There was, however, not even this much consolation for those whose confidence had been so great. A general sentiment of disillusionment was expressed, a feeling that "la production a bouffé la communauté."* "Community" was no longer a magic

---

* "The exigencies of production have gobbled up the community," i.e., the distinctively communitarian aspects. Cited in (33).

word (which of course was all to the good). And the question arose, "In what way, if any, do we differ from a Cooperative of Production?"*

Nevertheless, though the creation of communitarian property does not of itself solve all problems, it is a basis on which to build. The vital question is whether there have been any real modifications of the injustice embodied in institutions—modifications which are tangible and durable. Certain positive results became apparent in the course of Meister's interviews with the companions, from which he concludes:

> The communities have created a climate of work which is not found elsewhere, the fundamental aspects of which [as felt by the ordinary worker] are liberty—to be able to give advice, to be listened to, not to be constantly under surveillance—and equality in their relationships with the leaders, who are their superiors only in respect to working relationships, but equal in all the rest. . . .

Mermoz, out of his long and creative experience, testifies: "This atmosphere of liberty has fashioned a new type of proletarian, one who reacts, who expresses himself, who seeks to understand himself and his vocation." (7) That these are precious achievements can scarcely be denied.†

However, the movement was obliged to evaluate realistically its limits as well as its positive aspects, to recognize itself as a useful but only minor and fragile experiment in a century-long struggle of the proletariat toward its self-liberation, and as such to strengthen its bonds with the syndicalist movement on the one hand, and with the Producers Cooperative movement on the other. It was important to realize further that it was not possible for the communitarian movement to exist as a sort of "privileged oasis" in the midst of the larger society since it depended directly on the evolution of that society, not only economically but also culturally, even psychologically. (10) Having admitted all this, however, the movement was ready for a new departure. The report of the general secretary of the *Entente* in 1957 concluded with this challenge:

> . . . After having been born in a period in which our idealism was so blinding as to make us believe that it was capable of triumphing alone over everything, the *Communautés de Travail* went through a period in which economic success appeared, momentarily, as sufficient. . . . The

---

* The tendency toward the convergence of the two movements is discussed by Desroche. (10)

† Along this same line Friedmann, speaking of the worker in the ordinary industrial situation, is of the opinion that "the worker is underemployed" humanly speaking, i.e., "as a man he is bigger than his job"; and referring to the *Communautés* he writes that the feeling of accomplishing a collective task, in a common interest which is one with his own interest, is the only way to overcome the injurious effects of "le travail en miettes" (overspecialization). (17)

time has now come to understand that economic success in itself is neither satisfying nor sufficient, and is perhaps not even a success at all. We must make of it a success which is also a human success.

In response to this challenge, there arose a new determination to make concrete that which had been valid in the early vision, to the degree that it was realizable in present society.

### THE CONTEMPORARY PERIOD

This modest determination has marked the efforts of the movement in the last five years, and if the movement has not gained in momentum it has at least maintained its 1957 level. At the end of 1961, there were 28 communities (with 4 others in the process of formation), grouping from 950 to 1000 workers of which slightly better than 50 percent were worker associates. These figures are comparable to those of 1957; some groups have disappeared, others have taken their place. In addition, the "classical" conceptions have undergone a certain reformulation. If their present form is more modest, it may be considered as at least more realistic. In summarizing these developments we will make use of the same divisions which we have used earlier, i.e., common ownership, collective management, human development.

While the desirability of a certain individualization of shares was recognized, it was felt urgent to check too marked an evolution in this direction. The principle of common ownership was thus reaffirmed in terms of the maintenance of a sizable reserve of capital to be held by the community indivisibly and collectively. But beyond this, and of equal importance, was the proposal for the "federalization" of the principle of common ownership by means of the creation of an intercommunity fund for development (the FODEC) to be financed through the contributions of the individual communities. This central organism, administered by delegates from the participating communities, would serve to promote intercommunity solidarity and to strengthen, extend, and reinforce the communitarian network, "although," as it was said, "we can no longer believe, as did Buchez, in its power of unlimited growth." The FODEC was created (although in 1961 only 12 communities were actively participating) and has achieved positive, if limited, results. Certain communities in difficulty, rather than being abandoned to their own resources, have received financial and technical assistance from the central fund. The FODEC has also permitted the securing of the services of an outside technical adviser whose detailed analyses of the financial and industrial organization of individual communities have enabled them to become established on a more solid economic footing. Initially, it was hoped that FODEC would also be used to create new communities, but this has proven to be beyond its resources. In order further to promote the federalization of the movement it has also been proposed that the *Entente* appoint a representative to each local Administrative Council. Whether this representative would or would not have a deliberative voice is still being debated. These developments have, on the whole, strengthened the principle of common ownership.

The principle of collective management was reformulated in terms of "participation in management." The ultimate sovereignty of the General Assembly of companions was not placed in question, but its capacity for ongoing decision-making in respect to technical matters was recognized as limited, indeed nonexistent. It retains the power of election, the power of revision; it sets the over-all goals, and is entitled to raise questions in respect to the progress, or lack of progress, toward these objectives. The sovereignty of the General Assembly is the "moral and juridical foundation" which makes of the enterprise the "human project of a group of workers"—an economic enterprise, yes, but an economic enterprise for the sake of a human enterprise. (33) Participation in management was now conceived in terms of the right to information and full explanation, the freedom for discussion, questioning, and criticism, the obligation to set goals with a view to the common good; but not in terms of the right to challenge technical decisions as to how the common good could best be served, except indirectly through the representatives ultimately chosen by an arising out of the commonality of the workers.

It came to be understood, then, that democratic organization did not mean necessarily "the absence of hierarchy" but rather the provision for the "protection of the collectivity against the abuse of power." The ultimate source of democratic authority was conceived of as "the mutual and total dedication of all to the common good and to the defence of the common interest." "We may still speak of participation in management . . . even if it is one person who makes the actual decisions," providing that these decisions are taken "according to a policy determined collectively and in full respect of that collectivity." However, respect on the part of the leaders for the community as a whole is not sufficient to overcome abstention or indifference on the part of the workers, nor their lack of technical information. Therefore, in order for "collective management" to make any realistic sense, a renewed effort in the direction of increased technical competence was essential. And this leads to the third point.

"Full human development on all levels" tended now to be replaced by an emphasis on professional development. While the movement remained concerned for the total development of the worker as a person, it recognized that such development "exceeds its own competence and its mission as a communitarian industrial enterprise. The *Communauté de Travail* is first of all a professional community." Not that its preoccupation is limited strictly to production for its own sake, for it seeks to initiate within the enterprise of production "new human relationships." But these new relationships will not result merely from the goodwill of agreeable personalities. Given the real modification of structures effected by the common and indivisible ownership of the enterprise, new relationships—embodying a dialectic of authority and freedom, equality and order—demand for their realization the concerted effort to form workers who are able to participate intelligently, according to their several capacities, by means of an awareness and comprehension of the total productive process. One of the principal efforts of the *Entente,* beginning in 1957, was the creation of a permanent program of education centered on *l'homme au travail* ("the man at work"). A scheme with six parts was developed, and revised in the process of use, comprising an "economic cycle" (the internal structure of the enterprise, the external relations of the enterprise, and the economic structure of society), on the one hand, and, on the other hand, a "social cycle" (the social structure of the community, the cooperative and communitarian movement, and the working class movement as a whole). A recent survey indicates that this course of study has been widely followed and is considered by the participants to have been valuable.

Such is the effort to fulfill the particular competence and mission of a communitarian industrial enterprise which has renounced its "totalitarian presumption" of replacing "all other groups in which men should naturally live and develop themselves." As Desroche puts it: ". . . The human development of its members still remains the goal of the community, but it is now realized more and more clearly that the community is not the only means to this end." This end is better realized, at least in the present conjuncture of Western society and culture, by a plurality of group relationships, that is, in addition to the complex of work relations within the community, "several centers of gravity exterior to the work group." Thus "the formula of multiple unifunctional groupings." (10)*

---

\* Another study, based on a parallel though distinct experiment, came to similar conclusions. (34) The collective effort in the construction and the administration of cooperative housing (in this instance, much influenced by communitarian ideas) did not carry over into leisure-time activities. In several cases, housing cooperatives issued directly out of a *Communauté de Travail,* but membership of the two tended to intersect only partially and the social relationships still less.

The modification of the classical ideal which we have been describing led to a reformulation of the *Charte*. If we compare this 1959 version with the 1952 version (quoted at the beginning of the section on the classical phase) we take cognizance of the distance which has been traveled.

### "La Charte des Communautés de Travail"

#### Common Ownership

I. The means of production are the common property of the workers. This principle is assured, on the one hand, by a sizeable common and indivisible capital reserve within each community, and, on the other hand, is extended through participation in the inter-community fund for development.

#### Collective Management

II. The General Assembly of worker-associates is sovereign. It defines the objectives of the community and controls their realization.

III. The Administrative Council elected by the sovereign Assembly appoints and controls the head of the enterprise.

IV. The *Entente Communautaire,* the federation of the *Communautés de Travail,* is responsible for the technical organization of common and general tasks and for the approval of the objectives of each community.

V. In order that the workers may participate actively in management, a permanent, regular, and clear system of information is put into effect.

VI. In the *Communauté de Travail* the statutes relating to the workers, individually and collectively, are established with reference to the dispositions of the "collective conventions" [union-management agreements in force throughout the economy], and to the provisions of cooperative law [legal statutes under which cooperatives are incorporated]. Beyond this basic minimum, the community elaborates those regulations which are appropriate to its worker-associates.

#### Collective Promotion

VII. The communities, in order to accomplish their particular economic and social tasks, contribute to the development of their worker-associates and to their personal formation by means of professional, technical and cultural education.

VIII. The communities work toward the transformation of their wage-laborers into worker-associates, exercising in this regard no discrimination in respect to opinions or race, nor in respect to political, social and religious activity.

IX. The *Communautés de Travail* are one specific expression of the determination on the part of the proletariat to achieve liberation. Consequently, they favor workers control both without as well as within the communities and strive toward the full participation of the workers in the management of industrial enterprises.

## CONCLUSIONS

In the transformation of theory and practice which has taken place we have already noted a rather clear passage from the integral to the segmental type of association. This realization might induce a certain nostalgia were it not for the fact that in terms of social theory we have more to learn from these transformations than from the original classical formulations. The contemporary history of the French communitarian movement can serve as a sort of laboratory experiment for a theory of associations.

At least it has disabused us of a certain "utopianism," in the perjorative sense of the word. In place of the illusion that a tiny experiment, attractive as it may be, can spread until it encompasses the whole of society, we have the present realistic effort on the part of this movement to develop its own valid insights and to find its place and vocation within the "cooperative sector" of a society, at the same time striving to join with others on a broad front for the collective promotion of a constructive transformation of that society in the direction of a pluralistic democratic socialism. (10)* In other words, it is not possible to produce a new form of work relations as a sort of hothouse plant oblivious to the inclement weather in the world without, for, as Gurvitch puts it, "the sociological determination of the global society tends to prevail over the partial determination of groups. . . ." (21) Moreover, it is doubtful, at least in the present stage of Western society, whether the integral form of association is possible, or even desirable. We may hazard the statement that, at least in technically advanced and culturally pluralistic societies, diversities of persons require for their fulfillment diversities of communities which partially supplement, partially diverge from, and may partially oppose each other. We might point out in this connection a certain inadequacy in the "integral-segmental" terminology which we have used in this discussion of the French communities. While the latter are segmental in respect to the fact that they are primarily communities of *work*—that is, unifunctional communities—nevertheless, at least in principle, the worker-associates are not "segmentalized," in the sense of being treated as an item in the cost of production, or as a certain potentiality of labor power, but are treated integrally as whole persons in their own right.

Furthermore, we have learned through this experiment that any

---

* See Buber's (5) distinction between "schematic fiction" and "organic planning."

doctrinaire egalitarianism must be refused since this simply introduces new sources of conflict for old. Freedom and equality must be dialectically related to order and authority. The internal order of community tends to make this possible inasmuch as its structure of authority is not designed to protect the prerogatives of capital or management against the claims of labor but, on the contrary, tends to protect the majority against the abuse of authority and to ensure that authority is exercised for the common good with full respect for the community of worker-associates as a whole. A clear line of authority is thus consistent with a climate of freedom and mutual respect. Freedom within the order of community may be conceived of, not only as freedom to strive for the achievement of full personal potential, but also as freedom to collaborate in the freedom of others. The order of community is designed to promote a differentiated whole in which each one is respected as a person rather than for his productive capacity alone, and in which an atmosphere of free interchange places on each the obligation to choose and work toward goals with a view to the common good centered around the common task.

It was this orientation toward a common task, rather than toward community for community's sake, which, in the final analysis, saved the movement from complete disintegration. Community does not come into existence through the creation of a pure fellowship of disembodied spirits but through the restructuring of the natural human associations in which men inevitably gather for material and social survival. It is only on the foundation of material things and biological necessities— though in themselves these are recalcitrant to humanization—that men may lift themselves to the level of humanness in community. It is necessary to emphasize this in order to keep our feet on solid ground. When "community" as an ideal takes precedence over the real things of our common life we are headed for trouble.

Moreover, we have learned that the substitution of communitarian ownership for private ownership, on the one hand, and for collectivist state ownership, on the other, though essential, does not of itself create the "new human relationships" implied in the concept of community. In other words, the suppression of private ownership of the means of production is not in and of itself equivalent to the elimination of the exploitation of man by man. Marx himself recognized this at one point:

> The reign of liberty begins . . . beyond the sphere of material production. The civilized man, no less than the savage, must struggle against nature in order to satisfy his needs; this is so in all forms of society under no matter what mode of production: . . . the reign of necessity is always in force. It is beyond this reign that there begins the develop-

ment of those human powers which constitute the specifically human
goal and which are the true domain of liberty. . . . (29)

The *Communauté de Travail*, as much by its partial failure as by its
partial success, reminds us of this domain of liberty beyond the necessary effort of material production. It also reminds us that, whatever
the modifications which may be introduced in respect to social structures and property relations, positive though they may be, we must always reckon with the temporary, provisional, and ambiguous nature of
all human achievements. The continual fluctuation in the historical
process, which repeatedly throws every solution open to question, is
permanent within the process.

If we attempt for a moment to situate this movement within its larger
ideological framework, we may point out its affinity with the broader
stream of socialist and existentialist revolt against a culture dominated
for a century by bourgeois capitalism. In agreement with socialism, it
protests against the tyranny of capital and the misery of the proletarian
condition and, in accord with existentialism, it reacts against the de-
personalization of man and his impoverishment by the sterile values of
the bourgeois spirit. But in opposition to centralized, collectivist socialism which would make room for individual spontaneity and responsibility, and in opposition to a purely subjectivistic existentialism,
it proclaims the necessary mediation of social structures for the realization of the authentically human.

To put it in more abstract terms, we are dealing here with one expression of a profound current in contemporary social thought which
strives to liberate the meaning of the person from identification with the
notion of the autonomous individual; to liberate the meaning of community from its confusion with the notion of a collective being, transcendent to persons; and to develop new social forms in the awareness
of the reciprocal relationship of these two dimensions of basic human
nature. For, at its deepest level, a social theory is based on its particular
conception of human nature. In our opinion, the basic cleavage in social
theory is that which separates, on the one hand, the view that a decision
must be made as to the priority either of the individual as over against
the group or of the group as over against the individual from, on the
other hand, the view that the personal and the social are two dialectically related dimensions of human life in history. This latter alternative
is founded on the idea of the reciprocity of the person and the community, conceived of in such a way as to maintain the distinctive and yet
complementary characteristics of the two elements in question: the person as centered self within the community and the community as ordered multiformity of persons. Both the person and the community are

equally authentic and original, and are constituted reciprocally. The social object—by which we mean that form of human life with which we must deal in developing social theory and in constructing society— is neither a transcendent whole nor an aggregate of individuals, but rather the ordered multiformity of responsible persons.

"What is finally the *Communauté de Travail*?" asks one communitarian, and continues: "It must be recognized that this is ultimately a philosophical question. . . . Our moral experience confirms constantly that the community is not perfect nor even a success, but our moral experience confirms likewise that we cannot cease desiring that community *be*. . . ." We would agree with this evaluation of community as a basic element in authentic human life. We would go further and assert that human community is likewise a fundamental intimation of the divine presence among men. This twofold judgment has been expressed by Martin Buber in the moving terms with which we conclude:

> *Religio*, that is the human person's binding of himself to God, can only attain its full reality in the will for a community of the human race . . . *Socialitas*, that is mankind's becoming a fellowship, . . . cannot develop otherwise than out of a common relation to the divine centre, even if this be again and still nameless. Unity with God and community among the creatures belong together. (6)

# XII / "THE POLITICS OF MASS SOCIETY": SIGNIFICANCE FOR THE CHURCHES

## W. Alvin Pitcher

### A SUMMARY OF WILLIAM KORNHAUSER'S ARGUMENT IN "THE POLITICS OF MASS SOCIETY"*

The mess of societies is frequently explained by their mass. Mass in this case does not mean massiveness. It is not the sheer size and complexity that is distinctive of mass society; rather it is primarily the mode of decision-making.

In this essay dealing primarily with William Kornhauser's analysis in *The Politics of Mass Society,* our concern will be political, although social, cultural, and psychological factors are intermingled. In the first part, following a brief delineation of four types of society, we shall consider mass society in detail, describing mass behavior, mass social structure, mass culture, and mass movements. Then we turn to an analysis of the social processes producing mass phenomena. Next we summarize Kornhauser's rejection of mass society both because it is vulnerable to penetration by totalitarian movements and because it prevents a pluralistic society. At this point, having completed the presentation of Kornhauser's views, and assuming their general validity, we indicate their significance for the church in three areas: (1) the political structure of the church itself, (2) the extension of the church in a mass society, and (3) the role of the church in guiding political life. Finally, we shall evaluate Kornhauser's analysis, first generally and then theologically.

## A. *Four Types of Society (Kornhauser)*

Kornhauser distinguishes four types of society (mass, totalitarian, communal, and pluralistic) on the basis of the following characteristics: access to elites, availability of non-elites, intermediate groups, cultural

---

* William Kornhauser, *The Politics of Mass Society* (Glencoe, Ill.: The Free Press, 1959; England: Routledge & Kegan Paul Ltd., 1960). References are to the English edition.

standards, psychological types, and mechanisms by which people regulate their own and others' conduct.

The elites consist of small groups of people who run things because, according to some standards, they are able to run things. Technically the "term 'elite' is used to refer to those *positions* in a social structure which are superordinate, such that the incumbents claim and are granted social superiority. The term also is used to refer to the *functions* attached to such positions, especially the special responsibility to form and defend value-standards in a certain social sphere." (51)* These are the people who set the standards for the whole society. Access to the elites can be measured both by the ease with which people may become members of the elites and by the ease with which the elites may be influenced from the outside. When the non-elites participate in the selection of elites in a process providing alternative choices and open channels of communication, the elite can be said to be quite accessible; that means they must be responsive to the demands of the non-elite or they will not be chosen.

Both in the mass and in the pluralistic society, the people as a whole, the non-elites, tell the elites what to do. But there are differences. In a mass society the public intervene directly and in an unrestrained manner. In a pluralistic society, the people intervene indirectly, through regular channels and by means of constituted spokesmen. Both in the totalitarian and in the communal society the non-elites are neither permitted to develop machinery to exert influence nor given choices in order that their use of existing election machinery is significant.

Both the mass society and the totalitarian society, on the other hand, have atomized non-elites readily available for manipulation. The people do not have sufficient resources to develop group processes that can provide information and support necessary to enable them to form opinions and patterns of response of their own. They are, as it were, available in mind and body to be shaped and used by the elites. On the other hand, both in the communal and in the pluralistic society the non-elites are much less available for mobilization. In the communal society, tradition and status largely determine what a man thinks and does. For a pluralistic society, it is not the elites but the friends and associates who provide a bulwark between him and the elite.

If we consider intermediate organizations to be those in between the family and the national state organization, we find them lacking both in the mass and in the totalitarian society and present both in the communal and in the pluralistic society. Where they are lacking the elites

---

* Identifying figures in parentheses refer to pages in William Kornhauser's volume.

and non-elites are "directly exposed to one another" and "participation in the larger society must be direct rather than filtered through intervening relationships." (76) Where there are intervening groups these may be of two kinds: (1) inclusive, absorbing many aspects of the individual's life, or (2) non-inclusive, each organization related to only a segment of the individual's life. The first type, the inclusive intermediate group, was characteristic in the communal society. The second type, the non-inclusive, is a central feature of the pluralistic society.

Cultural standards are fluid and uniform in the populistic mass society, fixed and uniform in the monistic totalitarian society, fixed and differentiated in the traditionalistic communal society, and fluid and differentiated in the pluralistic society.

Psychologically our four types can also be distinguished. Mass man is self-oriented and self-alienated. "[He] does not experience himself as the active bearer of his own powers and richness, but as an impoverished 'thing' dependent on powers outside of himself, unto whom he has projected his living substance." (108)* The totalitarian man is group-oriented and self-alienated. The traditional man of the communal society is group-oriented and self-related. The autonomous man of the pluralistic society is self-oriented and self-related.

The mechanism by which man regulates his own and others' conduct is, in the case of mass man, suggestibility and diffuse anxiety; for the totalitarian man it is submissiveness and fear; in the case of traditional man it is honor and shame; for autonomous man, guilt and self-reliance are characteristic traits.

## B. *The Characteristics of Mass Society (Kornhauser)*

Mass society, the phenomenon with which we are primarily concerned in this study of politics, is treated as an abstract type; it is "always a question of the *degree* to which an actual society is a 'mass society.' A society is a 'mass society' to the extent that both elites and non-elites are directly accessible to one another by virtue of the weakness of groups capable of mediating between them." (228) Such a society is characterized by mass behavior; a weakness of intermediate relations, with isolation of personal and centralization of national relations; mass standards; and mass movements.

### 1. Mass Behavior

Mass behavior is a form of collective behavior in which individuals,

---

* Quoted by Kornhauser from Erich Fromm, *The Sane Society* (New York: Farrar and Rinehart, 1955), p. 124.

unstable and unpredictable in their social responsibility, alternately blow hot and cold and try to intervene directly in affairs about which they know little and for which they have no responsibility. *First,* "the focus of attention is remote from personal experience and daily life." (43) It is on national and international events or on whatever else can be known through mass media. This concern, leading to "direct and activist modes of response," (43) is the opposite of that which exists when proximate objects are primary and when response can be definite, independent, real, and responsible. That is, the focus is not on family, business dealings, hobbies, friends and enemies, the township or ward, church, trade union, or other group of which one is an active member. *Second,* "the mode of response to remote objects is direct." (44) There is little or no discussion of the matter at hand. Action is not taken "through groups in which they are capable of persuading and being persuaded by their fellows." (45) And force is recognized as a legitimate method for citizens to use privately to attain their ends. Such behavior, in the *third* place, "tends to be highly unstable, readily shifting its focus of attention and intensity of response." (46) Originating in isolation from the existing order, mass behavior may alternate between apathy (no hope in the existing order) and extremist actions to change or to shape it. Finally, in the *fourth* place, "when mass behavior becomes organized around a program and acquires a certain continuity in purpose and effort, it takes on the character of a *mass movement.*" (47)

## 2. Intermediate Relations

This mass behavior is found in a society characterized by weakness in its intermediate relations, with isolation of personal and centralization of national relations. Everywhere there is a movement from meaningful participation in local groups over which the individual has some control to participation in national groups. This can be seen in the growth of large labor unions, for example, where increasingly bargaining takes place on the national level. Hence, except where all sorts and kinds of peripheral social services have developed, the trade union ceases to provide an opportunity for real participation. Similarly, in the community, Kornhauser contends, "Unless a variety of forms of association are open to him, the individual is not likely to take an active interest in civic affairs—particularly in the metropolis, where the size of the population and the specialization of activities place a premium on voluntary associations as bases of political participation." (76-77) As we have already indicated, this lack of intermediate, independent groups "also removes the basis for self-protection on the part of elites, because it permits direct modes of intervention to replace mediated participation in elites." (77)

In a mass society, of course, someone has to perform the functions necessary to keep the society running. If intermediate groups are weak or absent, national groups take over. "This is indicated by the proliferation of governmental functions in previously autonomous spheres of activity, by the growth of national organizations, and by the concomitant shift in power from local to national centers." (93) Thus, mass society does not represent a state of disorganization but of organization around the state and other national organizations. We must make sure, however, that we do not confuse size with mass. An organization is a "mass" organization only when it lacks "intermediate units which have some autonomy from the central leadership." (95) In such organizations the membership as a whole tends to lose interest, the gap between the bottom and the top widens, and the rank and file become apathetic or look around for some way to get in the swim. Consequently, they are ripe for recruitment by those seeking direct access to the top. They seek to manipulate the top and in turn the top seeks to manipulate the bottom.

It is sometimes thought that personal relations are absent in the mass society. According to Kornhauser, it is not their absence but the isolation of individuals from the mainstream of a developing society that characterizes mass society. Family ties may well be present. The individual who for long periods is totally isolated (that is, without even family ties) is not likely to possess the minimum personal organization required by collective activity; the loss of all family life leads to personal deviance—in the extreme case, mental disorders and suicides—rather than to mass behavior.

3. Mass Standards

Now if we look at the culture of the mass society we find, accompanying the lack of variety in local culture, mass standards that are uniform and fluid. If the "masses," i.e., the people as a whole, determine what is valued, the elites are so dependent upon them (the non-elites) that they must adapt to their values; standards are leveled and necessarily become uniform. "The uniformity of opinion among large numbers of people becomes the supreme standard, superordinate to traditional values, professional standards, and institutional autonomy." (103) Belief in the intrinsic and immediate validity of mass opinion (the popular will) thus, when given primacy, becomes internalized and "prepares people for active service in mass movements seeking to determine policies and personnel for all kinds of institutions." (103) Cultural standards are, however, not only uniform but also fluid, changing frequently and unpredictably. Mass standards, thus, are part and parcel of a mass society in which mass organizations need mass audiences for success.

## 4. Mass Man

Finally, in a mass society, individuals divorced from larger social purposes are separated from themselves. Alienated from the social order, a non-participant in the established groups of a society, the individual lacks a positive conception of himself; he lacks confidence and strong control over himself; he is self-alienated and suggestible. It is not surprising, therefore, that the characteristic response of this man, the mass man, is "diffuse anxiety and the search for substitute forms of integration." (109)* Instead of looking for satisfactions that are in line with his particular personality he accepts those suggested and prepared by the manipulators of the mass media, and thus of the masses. He can do so only because he no longer feels able to decide autonomously on what suits him best. No one can avoid asking the question, "Who am I?" The mass man answers, "I am like everyone else." (109)

## C. *Social Processes Producing Mass Phenomena (Kornhauser)*

### 1. Discontinuities in Authority

If popular rule is introduced suddenly in a society in which there is no long-standing tradition of constitutional government, authority is undermined and the way is opened for mass movements. Or if a society with a democratic pattern of authority does not protect and spawn independent groups and classes, the state is unrestrained and unsupported. In either case democratic rule that is stable and limited is weakened. "Where democratization proceeds without adequate safeguards for authority, it leaves the new rule naked before mass movements which would destroy it. Where democratization proceeds without adequate protection for liberty, it leaves individuals naked before mass-oriented elites which would dominate them." (129) Thus, both representative rule and the rule of law must be strong or the society will quickly move toward autocracy (weak representative rule and weak rule of law) or populist democracy (strong representative rule and weak rule of law). The latter is characteristic of the mass society.

---

* Quoted by Kornhauser from Bruno Bettelheim, "Individual Autonomy and Mass Controls" in *Soziologische Aufsatze,* Max Horkheimer, ed. Theodore W. Adams and Walter Dirks (Frankfurt am Main: Europäische Verboganstalt, 1955), pp. 245-262.

"Democratic rule introduced where the state is already constitutional," Kornhauser contends, "tends to develop along liberal [that is, pluralistic] lines, while democratic rule introduced where the state is autocratic tends to develop along populist [that is, mass society] lines." (132) Where there is rapid transition from autocratic to democratic rule, authority is challenged by the revolutionary character of the transition, by the fact that extremist mass movements usually sponsor such popular rule, and by the almost inevitable brevity in the tenure of democratic government under such circumstances. However, in maintaining authority what seems to be equally important alongside of continuity with constitutional tradition and hence the rule of law, is the willingness and the capacity of ruling groups "to accommodate new social elements, and progressively to share political rights and duties with them." (132) And along with this accommodation to new social elements, the development of a stable democratic order has followed or supported "the emergence of new social forces that *constrained* pre-existing ruling groups progressively to share their power and privileges with wider and wider sections of society. In particular, it has been based on the emergence of a plurality of independent groups jealously guarding their autonomy and authority." (135)

In short, where the introduction of democracy is not accompanied by strong, independent groups that fight for their individual rights and interests, within the framework of a state authority supported vigorously, both authority and freedom suffer. Under these conditions we can expect mass behavior, mass society, and a totalitarian movement to develop.

## 2. Discontinuities in Community

Sharp discontinuities in authority, providing the opportunity for elites to seize power in the name of the masses, find the masses ready to be utilized where there have been sharp discontinuities in community. "The transformation of the rural-agrarian community into an urban-industrial community is fraught with peril in this respect, since at best this change involves pervasive disruption in the relations of large numbers of people." (142) But it is not the transformation itself that supports the development of mass phenomena; the determining factors are the rate and mode of urbanization and industrialization. Kornhauser marshals evidence to indicate that it is not the *degree* of urbanization but the process of urbanization that is crucial. Where there are rapid rates of change in the size and composition of the population residing in any area, mass movements are a possibility.

Industrialization produces masses only when it is introduced in such a

manner as to involve "marked *discontinuities* in social organization."
(150) Extremist mass action is most likely to occur in the early stages
of rapid industrialization where there are marked economic differ-
entials and disparity between pre-industrial and industrial social
statuses. This inevitable alienation "cannot be mitigated unless the
movement into industry is a continuous one, thereby providing 'old
hands' with established expectations to socialize new workers, as well as
a progressive one, thereby providing greater achievements over time."
(152) The rootlessness caused by industrialization is indeed a danger,
and when it is accompanied by the weakness of pre-industrial workingmen's associations (as in Norway) or resistance to the formation of
labor unions (as in France, Italy, Russia, and Spain), it "favors the
atomization of the working class and the formation of mass movements."
(157)

## 3. Discontinuities in Society

Short-run mass tendencies, in contrast to the long-run ones deline-
ated thus far, are produced by such major social catastrophes as severe
depression and national defeat. These weaken both authority and community. Discontinuity in economic life produces most discontent when
countries are undergoing rapid economic growth and expectations are
high. Where the economic crisis is most severe, extremist mass movements make the most headway. But it is not the economic condition
per se but its effect on social relations that is significant for participation in mass movements. "Prolonged unemployment prepares people
for mass movements by making multiple social ties inoperative."
(163) Studies indicate that a person's job is crucial in determining his
self-respect as well as his involvement in society. At the same time,
widespread, prolonged, and severe unemployment affects adversely the
functioning of elites. Popular discontent and self-doubt combine to increase the access of non-elites to the elites and thus to make the leaders more responsive to direct pressure. The situation also prepares some
members of the elites to sell out to a mass movement. "In general, the
demoralization of elites due to their ineffectiveness in coping with critical situations invariably appears to precede and summon mass actions
against the social order." (167)

Similarly war crises, particularly humiliating defeats, summon mass
tendencies. "That the German defeat in the First World War prepared
the way for an extraordinary (mass) mobilization is evidenced by the
large number of political murders after the armistice and by the large
number of self-constituted paramilitary bands that persisted long after
'demobilization,' to become the shock-troops of the Nazi movement

in the succeeding years." (168) An open power situation is created when the ruling elite loses legitimacy and its control over coercion in the wake of military defeat.

In order to demonstrate that his theory of mass society is a better explanation for mass movements than is class theory, Kornhauser examines the followers of extremist political activities. He finds that social alienation (a mass phenomenon) is a much more adequate basis for understanding both the political left and the political right than is economic interest (a class phenomenon). Thus, throughout all social strata or classes, people who are "divorced from community, occupation, and association are first and foremost among the supporters of extremism." (73) The more isolated intellectuals (in particular, freelance writers and artists), poorly established and small businessmen, small farmers, workers in mining and maritime industries, and unskilled workers have weaker commitment to democratic values.

In summary, mass phenomena occur (1) when popular rule is introduced suddenly in a country without a constitutional heritage, (2) where independent social groups and classes do not develop along with democratization, (3) when there is a rapid influx of large numbers of people into particular areas or organizations, (4) when areas are depopulated and feel bypassed by the large urban centers, (5) in the early stages of rapid industrialization, particularly when there are noticeable differences in income and between the new and old social statuses of workers, (6) when workingmen's organizations are not available, (7) during severe depressions, and (8) during and following war crises, particularly after humiliating defeats.

## D. *Evaluation of Mass Society (Kornhauser)*

Kornhauser's thesis is that a pluralistic society is the best society—positively because it provides order (authority) and freedom in the greatest measures, and negatively because it is the best defense against totalitarianism.

## 1. A Pluralistic Society Is the Best Society

In the pluralistic society, freedom and diversity are maintained by a social structure that permits access to the elites and that encourages a multiplicity of independent groups through which individuals may express their diverse preferences. Extensive opportunities for education provide channels for entrance into the elites. A free press and a two-party system provide information relative to the competing elites. Hence the non-elite population is able to influence the elites both through those of its number who become members of an elite and

through instituted channels, chiefly voting. At the same time the proliferation of intermediate interest groups representing diverse interests
(because of the cultural variety) protects the elites. Opposition among
these groups provides a check on the power of any one group to
intervene in the functions of the elites. The separate organization of
different interests—for example, of religion and politics—means that
access to the elite of one sector does not mean access to the elite of
another. The leaders of these intermediate groups absorb some of the
pressures from the non-elites and serve as responsible channels for demands. These leaders of intermediate groups are inevitably bound to top
elites in such a way that protest and pressure must be more responsible
and the authority of elites supported.

Social pluralism supports cultural pluralism in a pluralistic society.
The diversity in values is engendered by the multiplicity of interests fostered and defended by a multiplicity of groups. The freedom of interaction of these diverse groups also results in a "high rate of change in
standards." (104) Such cultural pluralism, an accompaniment of
social pluralism, encourages the comparison of models of conduct and
the formation of "differentiated, autonomous individuals." (110)
These products of the integration of elements from several models have
distinctive identities; they are autonomous. "The *autonomous man* respects himself as an individual, experiencing himself as the bearer of
his own power and as having the capacity to determine his life and to
affect the lives of his fellows." (110) With a clear notion of what he
ought to be internalized as his super-ego, the autonomous man strives
vigorously to be what he thinks he ought to be, driven and regulated
by a sense of guilt in his failure.

The pluralistic society is a democratic society in which leadership is
changed by "free competition for the popular vote." (130) Liberty,
the keynote of the pluralistic society, is not guaranteed by this free
competition, but it provides the most likely environment. The restraints required for liberty are provided by constitutional (e.g., separation of powers) and social (conflicting interest groups) checks and balances. "Unless there is democratic rule (in the sense of popular choice
among competing candidates for leadership), there is insufficient control over minorities (aristocratic or otherwise) to protect liberty. But
unless there is constitutional rule, backed by a system of social checks
and balances, minorities are not protected from majorities, nor from the
state." (130-131)

Civil liberty requires, then: (a) "extensive self-government, private
as well as public, and individuals must belong to several self-governing
units"; (b) "extensive opportunities for elites to formulate policies and

to take action without *ad hoc* interference from the outside"; (c) "restriction on the autonomy of elites, especially in politics": first, "by one another in that they will be constrained to compete with one another for leadership"; second, "by non-elites in that they will be constrained to compete for the people's votes." (230) And, Kornhauser argues, "social pluralism is a social arrangement which performs this function." (230)

## 2. A Pluralistic Society Is the Best Defense Against Totalitarianism

The pluralistic society is least likely to develop into a mass society, a society extremely vulnerable to penetration by totalitarianism. The totalitarian society, as the direct opposite of the pluralistic, subverts liberty. In it, as we have seen, there is low access to elites, high availability of the non-elites, weak intermediate organization, fixed and uniform values, a group orientation, and self-alienation. In short, liberty is negligible because self-government is absent, the elites are not responsible to the people, and self-alienation and social isolation are consciously cultivated in order to atomize and to manipulate the masses. Thus, it is really unnecessary to develop in detail the way in which pluralism prevents the development of totalitarianism, since everything that has been said positively needs only to be reversed to indicate its contribution.

### THE SIGNIFICANCE OF KORNHAUSER'S ANALYSIS FOR THE CHURCHES

We turn now to an interpretation of Kornhauser's propositions. In this discussion, assuming the validity of Kornhauser's analysis, we shall point out its significance for the life of the churches. We assume, it should be noted carefully, that this study is of sufficient merit in itself and of such a nature that it provides a way of looking at some problems which cannot be dismissed lightly by the Christian. We shall discuss the significance of Kornhauser's thesis for three aspects of the church's life: (1) for its role in providing a foundation for culture (the church's transformative function); (2) for its extension; and (3) for its organization (the construction of the church politically).

### A. *Significance for the Transformative Role of the Church*

Whatever our theory of the way in which the church should function to influence our common life, we have to face the fact that churches do affect what happens. The intellectual and artistic life, as well as social and political institutions, cannot be understood apart from a consideration of the interaction of religion and culture. In part this interaction of the church and culture is unconscious and hence a result of the political structure of the church organization itself; in part the influence of the church on culture is deliberate: churches help their members find ways to express their faith in and through cultural life.

According to Kornhauser, American society is in danger. Its main problem, social isolation, stems from the loss and threatened disruption of participation in intermediate organizations, those between the family and the national government. The implied defense against such a catastrophe—involving the menace of mass society, mass movements, and totalitarianism—is the preservation and extension of proximate interests and of participation in intermediate organizations. From this perspective the church, or for that matter any responsible citizen, should support the following social policy and take into account the following principles and problems:

1. Social Policy—Internal

(a) Since a man's job is crucial for his personal integration and his social participation (163), widespread, prolonged, and severe unemployment must be avoided; work must be so organized as to lessen the loss of meaning accompanying specialization and bureaucratization, and, where possible, productive operations will be organized so as to give the worker more variety and participation in more of the process (151); the loss of status and meaning associated with technological innovation will be offset by provision for retraining, and the advantages of innovation will be weighed, where possible, against the effect on pride in craft skills and status; control over work processes by workers will be extended where possible.

(b) In the light of the role of trade unions in providing working class leadership as an alternative to radical, extremist leadership, unions will receive more positive support than they have among many. (154)

(c) In view of the fact that extremist political reactions occur when groups are denied recognition by ruling groups, labor leaders as well as representatives of other classes will be invited to participate in government.

(d) Since one of the problems of large-scale organizations is the failure to maintain a significant role for local units, it is important in all organizations to protect local prerogatives. This means decentralization in government as well as in business, in labor, and in other voluntary groups.

(e) Awareness of the correlation between radical political behavior and the socially isolating effects of rapid urbanization will lead to increased efforts (1) to slow down the influx of people to urban centers, (2) to make more provision for their reception and integration into community life, (3) to avoid the destruction of community life now taking place in urban centers, (4) to increase the role of citizen organizations, and (5) to provide special ways for rural areas to maintain function and status in the light of their changing situations.

(f) In the light of the significance of local involvement the implications of recent studies that indicate the lack of power of citizen organizations will be considered carefully. The significance of the alleged fact that in some communities citizen groups and churches are used chiefly to carry out the decisions made by a few key leaders in the community or outside the local community must be examined. If this is so, sooner or later knowledge of the reality will replace the myth that sustains present participation. The immediate problem, as the authors of *Small Town in Mass Society** point out, is to present the personal and social disorganization that would follow knowledge of the true state of affairs.

(g) If the societies that have avoided totalitarian movements are those in which the lower and middle classes have had a chance to increase their status, as Kornhauser contends (140), it is important to maintain an open society. Studies of class indicate that while there is considerable opportunity for advances in class, status, and power, many factors operate to close the doors of opportunity for those who do not begin life with silver spoons. Life expectancy, health, and education all are less available to a person born into a family with a low income, regardless of the sheer biological potentialities of the organism. To the extent that this situation remains unaltered or changes for the worse it will function, at least so far as it is understood, to encourage mass behavior, mass movements, and totalitarianism. Hence, opportunities must be equalized even more than they have been in the United States. Since educational opportunity is the chief means by which individuals rise above the class and status levels of their parents, it must be made available in such a way that individuals do not feel excluded.

(h) If, as Kornhauser indicates, self-estrangement and social isolation are related to each other and to the individual's lack of identification with the established order, the creation of expectations that will not be fulfilled is dangerous. High-pressure, broadside advertising that creates wants in all classes, wants for which there is little hope for actualization, may accelerate tendencies toward alienation. It is one thing to say to people that they should not expect to have what everyone else has when they are led to believe that there are inevitable inequalities and differences in values; it is another matter when they are

---

* A. J. Vidich and Joseph Bensman, *Small Town in Mass Society* (New York: Doubleday & Company, 1961).

led by the mass media to believe that to be American is to possess what only high income families can possess. Either advertising will be more selective, very difficult in an era of mass media of communication, or it will be an instrument working for the downfall of the present political and social order.

## 2. Social Policy—External

(a) Since rapid industrialization and rapid democratization in countries where there has been autocratic government result in a power vacuum and rootless individuals (142-158), we can expect the conditions for mass society to be present almost everywhere in Asia and Africa. Under present conditions it is hard to find an alternative to totalitarianism for these places. Certainly Kornhauser's analysis indicates clearly that we cannot expect liberal democracy and Western industrial society to provide viable institutions for most of these lands.

(b) The effect of war and of military defeat upon the authority of government, the effectiveness of elites, and the availability of non-elites for mobilization by totalitarian elites indicates that policies of unconditional surrender and total destruction of enemy leadership produce a power vacuum. Foreign occupation, odious though it may be to all, does, according to Kornhauser, counteract mass tendencies. Victor nations, therefore, must be prepared to provide occupational forces until new authority can be substituted for what has been destroyed. Whatever in war threatens authority and community in the postwar period complicates the postwar problems for the victor as well as for the vanquished. The extent to which such conclusions are valid may be questioned in the light of new weapons of war, but their relevance to what we have been called upon to do in Germany, Japan, and Korea is clear.

## 3. Strategy of the Church in Influencing Social and Political Life

(a) Many of the leaders of the churches, swept along by the tides of national and international crises, have felt impelled to develop programs of education and action that involve the local church membership. If not pursued with prudence, such programs may well create mass tendencies as Kornhauser describes them. For, with the best of intentions, nation-wide efforts are launched by bodies of the National Council and of denominations to enlist every possible Tom, Dick, and Alice in a study of innumerable foreign policy issues. Fortunately, in all probability only a few of the already concerned and informed are enlisted in the commendable effort. If the average church member actually took up the gauntlet tossed at his feet and tried to be responsible for the scores of complex problems presented, no doubt he would become privatized or "massmenized." Actually, these two tendencies are part of the same process.

(b) A second implication of Kornhauser's analysis for church strategy lies in the area of the structure of community life. Social isolation, apparently an inevitable threat in our society because the processes of urbanization, industrialization, and bureaucratization are irreversible, is best avoided by policies encouraging participation in intermediate groups. But as Kornhauser points out, intermediate groups are significant in offsetting isolation only when local branches have power. Yet increasingly decisions are made at regional or national levels. The question then becomes one of strategy. Perhaps the church could best use its resources to work for the increased power of local voluntary associations and governmental agencies, on the one hand, and for the participation of its members in these intermediate groups on the other hand. In *God's Colony in Man's World,* George Webber describes a church discipline that requires ministers and members alike to participate in at least one community organization working for justice or brotherhood.

## B. *Significance for the Function of Church Extension*

We are all indebted to Will Herberg's attempt to understand why people are joining religious institutions. In his *Protestant, Catholic, Jew* he indicates the role of church membership in the process of providing an identity for individuals. But the role of the church as an instrument of social identity is decried. To belong to a church or synagogue for the sake of belonging is in a real sense a desecration of the religious institutions for Herberg and for many others. Yet, if the church is serving as a haven for the socially isolated, in the light of the alternatives described by Kornhauser we cannot but question any simple rejection of such motivation, conscious or unconscious. The issue, of course, for Protestants, particularly of the well-established churches, involves the character of those who are joining. All our studies indicate that those who belong to our churches are for the most part those who belong to everything. The church is not serving as an "escape" from or as a ministry to social isolation. Those who would profit most from the "fellowship" of the church, from participation in its life through meaningful involvement, are those, then, least likely to be reached by the "respected" churches. Many of them are not reached by our institutions, either because we do not place our institutions where these persons are or because our traditional programs of extension do not reach them. The danger spots, according to Kornhauser, are the rural areas and the inner cities. The persons under most pressure are the free-lance intellectuals, the small businessmen, the unskilled workers, and the small farmers.

Kornhauser's delineation of the danger to any organization of a rapid influx of members ought to be a warning to those churches that are expanding most. In a democratic organization rapid influx of membership at any time, but especially when the organization is new, gives the leadership an opportunity to control the organization by totalitarian methods. Also it provides a setting in which totalitarian leadership may displace an elite less inclined in that direction. Thus the autocrats of the church have a field day.

## C. *Significance for the Constitution of the Church*

Kornhauser's analysis raises some questions also about the political structure of the church itself, that is, about its constitution. The tendency in church polity is toward centralization. On every hand we are reminded that the congregational type of polity with authority focused in the local church, the church on the corner of Second and Everywhere Avenues, is out of date. It is not able to deal with the complex problems and the concentrated power of our modern societies. From Kornhauser's analysis we see that it is necessary to develop institutions that encourage both local and national leadership. National leaders must lead and be free to lead. But equally important is the opportunity for local responsibility. The rank and file need activities in which they know what they are doing and have the power to do something about the issues involved. The discussion of the elite—non-elite relationship in Kornhauser also suggests that churches could well consider the differences in the roles of ministers, lay leadership, and laymen. The priesthood of all believers in its extreme form would be just as dangerous to "democratic government" as would the extreme form of the Episcopacy; i.e., if either one of these conceptions aided and abetted extreme forms of manipulation by elites or excessive efforts of non-elites to determine policy throughout the whole church, it would contribute to the development of mass men, mass society, and totalitarianism.

A CRITIQUE OF KORNHAUSER'S ANALYSIS IN
"THE POLITICS OF MASS SOCIETY"

Now we shall attempt to provide the basis for an evaluation of Kornhauser's analysis. First, we shall pose questions that might be raised by anyone and especially by a social scientist. Second, we shall look at the study through the spectacles of the discipline of theology.

## A. Critique: Social Science

Four questions might be raised in analyzing such a treatise: (1) What methodology is employed? (2) What value presuppositions underlie the argument or provide the background for the study? (3) What use is made of "facts"? (4) What propositions about man's behavior are asserted?

## 1. Methodology

Kornhauser begins his analysis with the explicit intention of separating theoretical matters from value perspectives. In discussing his use of aristocratic and democratic critiques of mass society he writes, "Our interest is in analyzing the theoretical basis of each approach, rather than in examining the value orientation typically associated with each of them." (24) The classification of critiques as "democratic" and "aristocratic" is "based on an *analytical* rather than a value distinction. However, there is an affinity between each of these theoretical positions and each value orientation." (24) That is to say, most of the analyses of mass society which have emphasized the protection of the people (the non-elite) from the leaders (the elites) have advocated democratic values, and those that have focused on the protection of elites from non-elites have supported aristocratic values. Nowhere does Kornhauser make explicit what this distinction means, for in no place does he define either democratic or aristocratic values with sufficient precision and with analytical tools adequate to clarify the issues.

If democratic values emphasize liberty, or liberty plus certain forms of decision-making that protect liberty, it is not clear how the self-determination of people, Kornhauser's theoretical or analytical proposition describing democratic theories, is different from democratic values described by Kornhauser as follows: "Democracy is essentially an institutional procedure for changing leadership by free competition for the popular vote." (130) If freedom or liberty is the decisive democratic value, it is natural that popular decision should be opposed to the decision of elites; it is natural that the problem should be seen as self-determination (democracy) versus other-determination (aristocracy). But if aristocratic values involve ends and goals, that is, the encouragement of "good" men, not just "free" men, then there is indeed a difference between elite determination (Kornhauser's theoretical dimension) and the goals sought by an adequate elite (Kornhauser's value orientation). From the point of view of Kornhauser's understanding of democratic theory the problem is never one of ends and goals other than freedom. What a man does with his freedom is really secondary;

it enters in only when it interferes with another man's freedom. Thus the problem raised by his methodology points to his underlying presuppositions.

To begin with, to eliminate all democratic theory that does not start from a pluralistic premise is to avoid the problem raised many years ago so succinctly by Aristotle. He distinguished forms of rule in terms of (1) whether one, the few, or the many ruled and (2) whether the rule was in the interest of the one, of the few, of the many, or of the whole. In each case the rule for the common good, for the sake of the whole, involves some consideration of what the good of man is in the circumstances under consideration.

## 2. Kornhauser's Presuppositions

As is so often the case, Kornhauser's presuppositions provide a framework for delineating the problem and for appropriating other analyses. In spite of the fact that this treatise appears to be a "scientific" treatise in the modern use of the word—that is, "purely" descriptive—it is difficult to separate his theory from his values. Kornhauser presupposes, we may assume from this treatise, that value is a very personal matter; nothing is of value except thinking makes it so. The sophisticated version of this position speaks of liberty or freedom as the ultimate value. What *is* the autonomous man, the product, according to Kornhauser, of the pluralistic society? "The *autonomous man*," we read, "respects himself as an individual, experiencing himself as the bearer of his own power and as having the capacity to determine his life and to affect the lives of his fellows." (110) In short, autonomous man is self-determining; the principle of motion is internal rather than external. Self-determination, or liberty, then, is the constitutive value.

Alternative views of political life might begin in different places, either with the political process itself as the ultimate value or with some notion of what man and/or society ought to be. In the latter case, writers speak of true freedom as action in accordance with standards of right conduct or true being. Kornhauser recognizes this distinction (22-23) but fails to recognize adequately the significance of it for political theory. For if liberty, ordinarily conceived of as self-determination, is not constitutive of the good society, then the problem is neither self-determination nor other-determination. A prior question to that of the source of motion or the locus of political power (in the many or in the few) is that of the character of the decision-makers; it is, in other words, more a question of the goals and ends pursued by those who have power than it is a question of how decisions are made.

The real problem is in the nature of the elite. By appropriating part of the aristocratic critique of mass society, the necessity of decision-making by elites relatively free from the pressures of non-elites, Kornhauser evades the issue, namely, how to guarantee that the political elite (the rulers) seek good ends. To indicate that the elite in a liberal democratic or pluralistic society (Kornhauser's preferred model for society) are educated is not to face the issue squarely, for as Kornhauser himself reports, one-fourth of Hitler's S. S. elite at one time possessed Ph.D. degrees.

It may be that it is an injustice to Kornhauser's political philosophy to characterize it in this way, but everything in this book points to the fact that in spite of his desire, a particular political philosophy—one in which the efficient cause is constitutive (freedom) and the formal cause is regulative (checks and balances)—conditions the statement of the problem and the appropriation of other writers' analyses. It is true that the character of the decision-makers is positively influenced by their participation in intermediate organizations, but this again is a formal criterion, assuming that the result of this process is "positive." It is also true that there is an oblique reference to a standard other than the form of the decision-making when Kornhauser writes, ". . . the leaders of intermediate groups, irrespective of their particular aims (so long as these aims are not contrary to the integrity of the community), help to shore up the larger system of authority with which their own authority is inextricably bound." (77) But what this means is not clear. One can only conclude therefore that the real concern of some political theorists, such as Ortega y Gasset and Walter Lippmann, is ignored, and their writings are distorted slightly because of Kornhauser's political predilections. The values that he hopes to include, he includes, in principle, in some places and refers to without defining carefully in others.*

3. "Facts"

Under this caption we might consider several aspects of Kornhauser's treatise. First, he reports on what other writers have said or have claimed to be the case, or he makes statements about what has happened in the past without reference to sources. Second, Kornhauser makes a number of statements in propositional form indicating something about the nature of social reality, propositions that describe what we can expect to happen under certain circumstances. We have chosen to deal with this last category of statement in section 4 below.

---

* See pp. 21, 25, 221, and 229 for references to democratic values; pp. 46, 81, 103, 112, 122, 131, 230, and 231 for references to liberal democracy.

In this section on facts, due to my limited acquaintance with much of the literature reporting on empirical studies, the critique will concentrate on Kornhauser's use of critiques of mass society for other authors. Can the criticism of mass society leveled by those who are classified by Kornhauser as aristocratic be adequately described as concern for the freedom of elites from non-elites? Does not the separation between the "theoretical" and the "value" orientation made by Kornhauser require that the "aristocratic" theories be described differently? Assuming that this distinction is valid, is it not necessary in the aristocratic theoretical aspect to include concern for the goal as well as for the elite determination of policy? A careful reading of Ortega y Gasset, *The Revolt of the Masses,* and Walter Lippmann, *The Public Philosophy* (with my spectacles), reveals more of an emphasis on the quality of the elite than on the freedom of the elite. To be sure, the elite are to be protected from undue interference by the masses or the non-elite, but the real issue is elsewhere; it is summed up in the question, How can we produce and enlist men of character or of quality, men of reason, men created by their saturation in the best of Western culture? To be sure, these critics of democratic tendencies question the contemporary dependence upon freedom and process to raise up an elite of quality. They do fear the intervention of the non-elite; they do seek to protect the elite. But above all, they are concerned that there be an elite. And an elite for them is something more than a group of men who happen to have power or status. Thus an adequate description, apart from a particular value orientation (that is, describing in particular what ends should be sought)—if you will, a "theoretical" use of their analyses—requires two principles rather than one. Whereas Kornhauser has made use of their theory by appropriating their concern to protect elite from intervention, he ought to have said that theoretically aristocratic critics of mass society insist upon two considerations: self-determination of elites and elites of quality.

Similarly, if we consider the so-called democratic critiques of mass society, they will be more adequately described theoretically by two principles: self-determination by non-elites and a process by which elites are chosen. This process can be generalized, of course, to all aspects of society. Thus the concept "equality" can be used to indicate equal access to whatever is to be had: income, deference, safety, or power.

In other words, criticisms of mass society like criticisms of any other form of society can neither be understood nor used without concern for a broader range of political problems than Kornhauser admits as valid. In particular, his lack of concern for goals or ends other than freedom, which is not really a goal in the sense used by aristocratic critics, means that he does not indicate the role of goals or ends either in "aristocratic" or in "democratic" theory.

## 4. Propositions

The main thesis with which this section will deal is the correlation between lack of membership in intermediate organizations and the tendency toward mass behavior and availability for mobilization by elites in mass movements. The thesis can be stated in this way:

"People are available for mass behavior when they lack attachments to proximate objects. When people are divorced from their community and work, they are free to reunite in new ways. Furthermore, those who do not possess a variety of relations with their fellows are disposed to seek new and often remote sources of attachment and allegiance. Where proximate concerns are meaningful, people do not spend much time or energy seeking direct gratification from remote symbols. They may try to understand and influence the course of distant events, but they do so by means of and in relation to their face-to-face relations, at home, in the neighborhood, at work, in their club or union, and so forth." (60-61)

Proximate relations are, as we have seen, relations in which the individual has both the knowledge and the power to participate effectively. They tend to be relations directly affecting the basic concerns of the individual. But Kornhauser also contends that one can be available and still have very satisfying relations in the family and in local organizations. "In other words," Kornhauser writes, "it is entirely possible to have a society in which there are family ties but which is still a mass society due to the lack of intermediate relations." (90) It is, then, not adequate to speak, as Kornhauser does in the passage quoted above, of proximate relations in general. Furthermore, in discussing the social isolation of mining workers, he refers again to the distinction between "individual and group isolation." "Mining communities, though they protect workers from personal isolation, do not relate them to the outside world. The miner is isolated and *feels isolated* from centers of power and activity in the society at large—relative to workers located in centers of communication and transportation." (217) Again, a qualification has been made; it is not just the lack of proximate attachments, it is the lack of a certain kind of attachment; in fact, the definition of the condition becomes quite subjective, for it is the "feeling" of being unattached to the larger society which is crucial. The issue thus seems to be social alienation rather than social isolation. Availability is more a matter of a "mental break with the milieu" than of a physical separation from other people in intermediate groups. (177)\* It depends more upon the cause and hence upon the attitude toward the separation than upon the fact of social isolation. Similarly, the significance of participation is to be measured perhaps more by the attitude toward it than by the fact itself. Certainly, there are many persons whose personal interests are sufficient to prevent their feeling the need for participation in intermediate organizations that link them to the larger society. Some may be alienated because of their participation in a society in which activity is a substitute for meaning. These individuals may be just as latently mass man as are the apathetic. Their availability for mass movement may take a different direction from that of the socially isolated; but in Kornhauser's terms, it will be the same, other-directed. Thus the "organization man" or the "marketing-oriented" man also will be available for someone to mobilize. In Kornhauser's own words, the problem is clear at least: "Some social critics of the new middle class argue that far from being nonparticipants, members of this class engage in group activity to such an extent that they lose their autonomy as individuals. . . . The threat to individual autonomy is believed to lie not in the lack of organization but in the inclusiveness of relations to the organization: the hold of the modern corporation over its members begins to resemble that of the medieval corporation over its members. A closely related issue concerns the quality of many community, religious, and other social ties of members of this class: these relations are often alleged to mask an underlying passivity and lack of commitment, and to feed on a widespread disposition to overconform." (233)

So much for the issue, but then Kornhauser concludes: "These issues remain to be settled, but in any case, the evidence does not support the contention that the new middle classes are composed of atomized masses." (233) Indeed, the issues do remain, and precisely because the crucial issue is not whether the middle-class "belongers" are atomized, but whether only atomized persons—that is, individuals without relations to the larger society through intermediate organizations—are available for mobilization. The fact that, according to Kornhauser's standards, the working classes in America are atomized and have been for some time, without really being mobilized even when their organizations did not receive strong legal support (that is, before 1913), may be an indication that factors other than social isolation and social crisis are crucial. The fact that the Negro has been denied participation in the larger society without really being available for mobilization (until recently) also raises a question about the

---

\* Quoted by Kornhauser from Raymond Aron, "Totalitarianism and Freedom," *Confluence*, II (June, 1953), p. 9.

attempt to place so much emphasis on the presence or absence of a certain kind of social relation.

Another issue arises in Kornhauser's attempt to identify group participation with a realistic concern for national and international affairs, and lack of group membership with lack of concern for the same. "That lack of proximate relations is associated with the lack of day-to-day concern for national and international affairs is indicated by a national survey (1947) which shows that members of voluntary organizations are more likely to hold opinions about issues, are more likely to discuss these opinions, and are more likely to seek their implementation than are those who belong to no organizations." (64-65) Kornhauser cites this study, we assume, in order to show that the attachments of the socially isolated man to the affairs of the nation as a whole are less likely to be rational. He has said, of course, that the mass man tends to fasten upon the larger, more abstract issues rather than upon proximate ones, particularly in times of crises. An alternative hypothesis to the one implied by Kornhauser might be this: the interest in national and international affairs engendered by their relations to intermediate groups will create recruits for the mass society, since in reality the average citizen can know little and do little about the larger issues of the national life, except in rare cases or except when there is concentration on a particular issue. As soon as he is aware of the reality of politics, even on the local level, the more disillusioned, the more privatized he will become. The more social scientists make him aware of his lack of power, the more the man who thought he had power will react. Studies such as Floyd Hunter, *Community Power Structure;* C. W. Mills, *The Power Elite;* and *Small Town in Mass Society,* by A. J. Vidich and Joseph Bensman, certainly indicate that the politically oriented members of voluntary associations are in for serious disillusionment. All of these studies suggest at least a footnote to the continued use of the adjective "independent" to describe the intermediate groups upon which society's salvation seems to depend.

We have already raised a question about the autonomy of the modern American in connection with the mobilization of atomized men. There we asked for a consideration of the availability for other-determination of the "organization man." A related issue involves Kornhauser's thesis that a pluralistic society produces autonomous men. "Social and cultural pluralism invites the development of differentiated, autonomous individuals, for variety in institutions and values encourages the individual to compare different models of conduct and to integrate elements from several models into a distinctive identity." (110) This appears to be a statement of the hope of a liberal democrat rather than a fact. Studies of American character certainly raise questions about what is being produced. Studies of social disorganization suggest that cultural heterogeneity along with mobility is a central factor in personal and social disorganization.

Finally, an important consideration in thinking about the meaning of Kornhauser's analysis involves a consideration of the situation for which it has most relevance. That the circumstances condition political possibilities is clear from frequent indication of the importance of this dimension. For example, in discussing the safeguards against mass tendencies, Kornhauser indicates the need to consider the particular historical context. "Those [intermediate structures] are critical which in the given context are, or have been, major bases of cohesion. It is only natural, therefore, that the aristocratic and democratic approaches, which took shape in different centuries, should identify the dissolution of different kinds of social formations as the major potential source of masses. In the nineteenth century European context, given the feudal heritage, status groups were critical, such that the failure to develop new forms of association to replace them was potentially mass-producing. But in the twentieth century, and especially in America (since it never had a feudal past and hence no fixed hierarchy of status groups), interest groups and other kinds of voluntary association have been more important, and the dissolution of this kind of group life a greater source of mass tendencies." (126-127)

Of course, these comments by Kornhauser fail to account for the aristocratic critic Walter Lippmann, a twentieth-century American, and José Ortega y Gasset, a twentieth-century Spanish philosopher. Nevertheless, the important point is the judgment about the importance of context. We have already seen how this limits the possibilities for the newly developing countries in Asia and Africa and wherever there has been aristocratic rule (Part I, Section C; Part II, Section A). The real question before us in the United States is whether or not we have come to a turning point. Are the conditions still present such that a healthy common life is the result of two processes, participation in a variety of intermediate organizations and a system of checks and balances? Does the increasing fact of and necessity for centralization in operation, economic and political, make obsolete the model of liberal democracy? One thinks of the main streets of our towns, once the scenes of innumerable small businesses, now occupied by chain stores controlled from New York and oriented regionally or nationally in spite of all the efforts to make it appear otherwise. The locally oriented, locally controlled shops that remain are like vestigial organs, around but for the most part living in and off the past, barely able to justify their existence. One thinks of the recent political conventions in which all pretense of the choice of the nominee for vice-president, at least, was thrown aside as it was made clear that the presidential nominee would meet with vice-presidential "possibilities" and party leaders to determine for whom the delegates would willingly vote on the morrow. The questions asked are from within the perspective assumed by Kornhauser; that is, one in which self-determination is the constitutive principle and participation is regulative.

Now, if we begin with views that subordinate self-determination to participation, or that make a balance between the two, or that introduce some material qualifications regarding the kind of desirable participation, another question arises. Are we facing a situation in which the underlying character of man as created by twentieth-century culture is such that freedom for self-determination by the kind of selves we find today is actually self-destruction? If this is our condition, the model for society would take a different shape.

Concern for who decides and how the freedom to decide can be protected would at least share the spotlight with an emphasis upon the character of the decision-maker. Thus, taking the situation into account, as Ortega y Gasset does, would mean turning toward the quality of decision rather than toward the quantity of decision-makers.

## B. *The Christian Faith and Kornhauser's Analysis*

Now let us turn to an evaluation of Kornhauser's analysis from the standpoint of the Christian faith. We shall contend that Kornhauser's suggestion—that an increased participation in intermediate organizations is desirable—is inadequate. While Kornhauser's prescription would be acceptable from the standpoint of some Christian interpretations, we would reject such interpretations for theoretical and practical reasons.

The basic question involves the role of process, i.e., of a certain way of making decisions. The question is: Can we hold that a certain kind of participation in organizations and hence in decision-making processes results in the good life?

We are aware of the fact that responsible Christian interpretations hold that a process that encourages wide participation is desirable. The rationale for this view is rooted in a "realistic" or semi-pessimistic view of man. The contention is that man, because of sin, is unable either to know or to do the good. Hence, it is desirable to encourage processes in which one man's "knowledge" is checked by another's "knowledge" and in which one person's (or one group's) power to affect action is checked by another's (or another group's) power. In this view, the assumption is, and is so stated by its advocates, that man has enough knowledge and enough goodwill to prevent a complete breakdown of the process.

One can reject faith in process on several grounds. First, for theoretical reasons, one may contend that there are good ends to be determined and sought and that to depend on the knowledge and action of people in general is to misplace one's confidence. That is to say, we cannot depend upon a process in which truth, of either a theoretical or a practical nature, is determined by counting heads unless the heads are of a very special kind. Likewise we cannot count on the goodwill of individuals or of groups in general to seek the common good or to arrive at the common good by each seeking his or its own good. This is not to say that multiplication of the centers of decision-making and power are not useful. It is only to subordinate this institution or process (participation in intermediate groups, or balance of power) to another one.

A second reason for rejecting Kornhauser's constructive position and those interpretations of the Christian faith which emphasize process depends upon a practical judgment about our historical situation. Our hypothesis is that we are at the end of the Protestant era. The storms of our times and of our souls indicate a basic unsoundness in the spiritual reality that determines our personal existence. If this basic reality is sound and the problems of existence are of a secondary nature, the free play of forces, or balances of self-interests or other guiding images that emphasize process, can be given a dominant role. If, however, the situation is as we suggest, the problem is more basic and requires a focus other than process. In other words, we can have participation in intermediate organizations which represents a sickness of the soul rather than its health. Or, the purposes served by organizations that involve the participation of thousands or millions may be destructive of personal and social health.

A third reason for questioning Kornhauser's constructive position stems from the hidden assumption that political institutions are not responsible for the good. He assumes, as do many, that other institutions will produce an elite that will find its way to the top of the political hierarchy. Others assume that the political institutions, referred to as the state, have no responsibility for the good. They are to carry out the wishes of persons whose wills are shaped by free—i.e., non-state —institutions. This view of matters must be questioned, for practical reasons. For better or for worse, and inevitably, we believe, the state permeates the life of our times. The personnel and programs of an increasing number of institutions are influenced by political institutions.

Increasingly the state influences the substance of our lives. Is it not, therefore, to beg the question, to suggest that the state is neutral, merely an institution to provide a framework in which other institutions determine the substance of life?

What has been outlined in these all-too-brief suggestions is in summary the following propositions:

First, no process as such or no kind of participation in intermediate organizations guarantees the good (order, stability, freedom, etc.). Without a consideration of the ends sought and served, no process can be judged. Hence, no process is absolute. Every process or form has its day.

Second, the present historical situation is such that we must consider the reshaping of the substance of man's life as more important than the freeing of whatever substance is present to express itself. We are at the end of the Protestant era.

Third, our historical situation is also such that we cannot depend upon institutions other than the state to inform culture with the Christian substance. If the state is not informed by and does not become in part responsible for the good, the Christian substance or foundation of culture will wane even more than it has.

The foundation for these judgments, of course, cannot be developed here. If the problems of Kornhauser's analysis and some of the presuppositions of his position have become clear, our purpose here will have been accomplished.

# XIII / A NEW PATTERN OF COMMUNITY

*Franklin H. Littell*

One of the major characteristics of the society in which we live is the rapid increase of power concentration and technical control. The rate of growth of output in production per man-hour, the increase in the speed of transportation vehicles, in the explosive power of chemicals, in the inter-community and inter-societal contracts of peoples, in the expanding areas of bureaucratic control over masses of men— all can be put on graphs which show geometric increase in the speed of change.[1] Of special importance to us today is the fact that the growth of population, and especially the concentration of population in metropolitan areas, must also be graphed by geometric rather than arithmetical symbols. Americans are one of the most rapidly growing of the world's peoples. They are also one of the most mobile—indeed, the most mobile—among major peoples. All of this lays an extraordinary burden upon the leaderships of our cities and upon our city planning agencies.

### THE BACKWARDNESS OF PROTESTANT IMAGERY

Candor requires admission that we have not, in the Protestant churches and seminaries, caught up with the realities of our situation. The imagery of American Protestantism is still predominantly rural and romantic. We are still largely captive to the vision of a neighborly community with a white church at the center of the village green, and the minister the "person" or "parson" about whom a fair section of public opinion coagulated. In fact, much of our teaching of the ministry and of the laity is still aimed at this disappearing scene.

The truth is, of course, that very few of us have caught up with the implications of popular growth and shift for our institutions. With the conservatism so natural to religion, in the "dialogue with the past" in the churches we refer quite casually to problems and events at the time of Charlemagne—without remembering that at that time the population of Sicily was as great as that of the British Isles; at the time of Elizabeth I—without remembering that the total population of England was then about 2,000,000 and that Shakespeare's London was about one-fourth the size of Memphis; at the time of the "Founding Fathers" of the American Republic—without reminding ourselves that at that time the population of the thirteen revolting colonies was a mere 3,600,000. Of this number, about one-twentieth of the present population, 85 percent were then from the British Isles, and only about 20,000 were Catholics and about 6,000 were Jews. Much of our thinking in the Protestant circles, it seems to me, is still oriented toward the Anglo-Saxon, rural, and Protestant America. With American Catholicism numbering over 40,000,000, and on the threshold of a renaissance of cultural, intellectual, and financial initiative, with American Jewry the center of cultural and intellectual and financial initiative within Judaism, those of us who are Protestant sometimes sound remarkably schizophrenic when we address the pluralistic society of which we are a part as though it were the America of 1790 or even the America of 1890.[2]

The major change which has occurred in American society within the lifetime of our older citizens is symbolized by the rise of the Great City. In 1890, the United States was still predominantly rural, with four out of five persons living on an agrarian economy. According to a recent study, 25 percent are concentrated in just 220 out of over 3,000 counties. Four out of five persons today live in, or within twenty-five miles of, cities of at least 25,000 population.[3] Just as important, one out of four Americans has changed his state of residence since World War II. We are the most mobile people on the face of the earth, and consequently more affected by problems of transportation and communication. What this high mobility and rapid agglomeration means to those of our social institutions that cling to established patterns of behavior can scarcely be imagined, let alone described.

None of our institutions has clung more fervently to known ways than the church. This is true in spite of such rapid social change, in defiance of the fact that—as Dr. John Osman has put it—"The logic of America is the city . . . *Religion today is challenged to create an urban civilization.*"[4]

Take, for a moment, *seminary education*—which is my own vocational commitment. As Dean Walter G. Muelder of Boston University School of Theology put it at the last annual meeting of the American Association of Theological Schools (AATS), perhaps 80 percent of our present seminary program is obsolescent. The problem is not primarily that of translating pastoral imagery, although that is acute. What does the verse "The Lord is my shepherd" mean to city people who have never seen "sheep," "shepherd," or "lord"? Although late deciders are entering the ministry in growing number, from business, the military, and other industrialized professions, most of our young men still come to us from the rural churches. They can be counted upon to make a fair translation, but do they correctly understand the situation they and their people are in? The problem arises from a rural and romantic image of the role of the minister, the place of the church, and the style of life to which numbers of congregations are becoming accustomed.

In agricultural society, there were certain educated persons to whom the society looked for leadership: the doctor, the lawyer, the preacher, and sometimes a maverick editor or businessman who had gotten an education or self-education which put him to the fore. In those times the patriarchal image was still respected, and the preachers were trained in verbal facility, in "pulpiteering." Today, in the Great City, many of the laity are as well educated—or even better educated! They may attend on a speaker who puts on a good performance, much as they select Channel 13 instead of Channel 5 if the program is more interesting. But they will only be bound by the word if they have a part in shaping it. This came out very strongly in an International Laymen's Conference held near Geneva in 1948—the first following the war. The churches brought together on that occasion a conference of the most distinguished leaders of economic and political and educational life in Western Europe. And, as was their habit, the clergy started out to lecture the laity on the responsibilities of laymen. After a day and a half, in the middle of the second afternoon, a layman stood up and said, very simply: "Our problems can't be solved by sermons or lectures. We can only get at them by discussion."[5] The ministry's function had shifted, in good part, from that of the leader who issues statements and instructions to that of the chaplain of the laity in their work in the world. As a generalist, he had been able to give orders freely in a society where all were neighbors and living in a stable agrarian community. Now, he must listen as well as speak: he must face the fact that in their own professional and vocational communities the laymen know more than he does about specific problems and possibilities.

The problem of the seminaries is that we are still training men primarily as "pulpiteers" rather than as discussion leaders and interpreters. And when the young man goes out to minister in a society where community is vocational and professional rather than geographical, he often sinks into those limited areas of city life where a maximum of verbal facility and a minimum of specific information will still suffice: individual and familial religion (especially during the "rites of passage":

birth, marriage, death), local politics, admonition to creative use of leisure time. Called to proclaim the Lordship of Jesus Christ over all of
life—what the Baptists used to call "the Crown Rights of the King"—
he understands an ethics and morals grounded in the neighborly virtues,
in the life of people who live for decades and even generations in
geographical propinquity. But in the Great City we rarely know the
names of those who live across the hall in the apartment building or
down the street in the suburb! Of course we may meet once a month
in the church Men's Club, and use first names freely in an effort to re-
capture for a fleeting moment the days when we were boys together
down on the farm. But we don't know the last names—and my impression is that we don't much care. Our experience and our practical
wisdom, you see, have run ahead of our rational analysis.

The church *social welfare* work reveals the same crisis as seminary
education. There is no time to speak of the practical accommodation
to the realities of a highly specialized and sophisticated urban life which
have occurred. The church pioneered nursing, medical care, hospitals,
homes for orphans and the incapacitated and the aged, relief to the
needy, employment referral. She still maintains many institutions, but
she has to draw increasingly on tax monies to do it and upon specialized personnel trained outside her own areas of control. She still
teaches the role of the Good Samaritan—spontaneous charity. The
churchman who started to arrange care or adoption of orphans without
following legislative and administrative channels would land in jail. The
Good Samaritan himself would land in jail in any of our cities. One of
the leaders of a significant inner city mission has related a relevant
incident. He saw an elderly man struck down by a taxi on the street.
The law required that an ambulance be called and common sense
dictated that he not be moved until medically inspected. So the Reverend Don Benedict, now head of the Chicago City Missionary Society,
waited for an hour and thirty-seven minutes for an ambulance to arrive on the scene and take the man—who subsequently died—to
the hospital. Surrounded by law, the case could not be handled according to the rule of the Good Samaritan: it could only be bettered by
improving the ambulance service.

This is a parable for the Big City. Life has become highly organized
and highly specialized. And "community," insofar as our on-the-job
life is concerned, has become vocational and professional rather than
geographical and generalized. Our first necessity, in the churches and
in the Big City which they are to serve, is to face this fact and the
implications of it. The City is not an anonymous, fragmented, atomistic
agglomeration of humanity—a kind of crowded village where personal

contact has been lost and anonymity is the order in personal relationships. It may remain such, of course, to those who have missed its potential. But the City is in fact a highly sophisticated and complex network of communities. And the men of the church—like the men of the university, of business, and of labor—are challenged to develop those instruments of special and plural forms of service by clergy and laity appropriate to the City.

### THE NEW STYLE OF COMMUNITY

The approach taken thus far has been deliberate: to illustrate the way in which the communities of which I am an officer—the church and the university—are related to the problem. Most of us are members of several such communities, and most of the social controls to which we are subject are the product of such intentional groups.

> In the face of the disappearance of the territorial unit as a basis of social solidarity, we create interest units.[6]

I am not only an individual, with a Social Security number; I am also a person who does a certain work. In the open society, in contrast with totalitarian systems which cultivate return to a simple monolithic structure, these associations shape our lives and even share in political sovereignty. In religious terms, the vocation of a doctor is to be a steward of the health of the society; in political terms, the American Medical Association exercises governmental functions. The lawyer is a steward of tradition, law, and order; the Bar Association, to the extent that it maintains educational standards for novices and ethical standards for practitioners, exercises sovereignty which in many societies has belonged to the state. Personnel managers, elementary school teachers, professors, policemen, barbers, taxi drivers, engineers, bankers, steel workers, miners, real estate dealers, insurance salesmen, automobile dealers, automobile workers, carpenters, clergymen, druggists, and dozens more who perform necessary services in a complex society, live in communities which profoundly affect day to day behavior and within which it is in fact determined whether we have order or anarchy, ethics or the law of the jungle. To the degree that our way of life is successful, we maintain the ordered life of free men through discussion and consensus; to the degree that we fail, in our respective vocational and professional communities, action by the state becomes inevitable.

In the first stage of the industrial society, with a few in positions of power—including remnants of the old estates, the nobility and the clergy—and the masses gathered in a shapeless and faceless labor supply, the crowding of populations has often meant dehumanization, "anomie." This was true of early nineteenth century Germany, where Johann Hinrich Wichern tried unsuccessfully to warn church and state of the perils attendant on treating human beings as things. It is true today of Johannesburg, where Alan Paton and Michael Scott and other sensitive observers have decried the dreadful brutality of man's inhumanity to man. But in the great cities of America, today, we see emerging a new pattern of human relations, of essential community, which may bring the dignity of persons and purposeful work to increasing numbers of our citizens. The medieval city and the Renaissance city did that for such elements of the populace as were then thought entitled to meaningful life. The city in America is called to realize that meaning for *every* man who can say, like St. Paul, "I was born free!" (Acts 22:28).

If I may again use a personal report, it will illustrate the transition which many of us have personally experienced. I grew up in a little town in eastern Iowa, with a population of 1156. I knew every person in town, man and child, by name. I knew their cousins, where they had stood in the War (the only War that fundamentally has affected American life), what they did for a living and how well they did it. I also knew their dogs by name, since I ran the newspaper routes. There were two churches, which were geographically and literally in the center of town, the Epworth League numbered practically every young person in town, including one Catholic and one Christian Scientist. The farmers came to town to trade, and every Wednesday and Saturday night there were band concerts and the stores stayed open.

Last spring I went back for a class reunion. The town now lies one mile north of a major highway just fourteen miles from a city that has tripled in population since World War II. Main Street is dotted with empty store fronts; although the over-all population is increased, they now travel to the city to shop and for recreation. A Catholic church has been built, as has a Lutheran church. There are regular Christian Science services. The high school has been consolidated with those of several neighboring villages. Most significant of all: fully one-third of the breadwinners commute to and from the neighboring city daily. We still send young men to such churches to give community leadership, but the role no longer exists in the neighborhood sense; the church no longer centers the rural community; in fact, the community itself no longer exists in the old sense. The Big City, with its satellites, now shapes the life of most Americans.

There are those to whom this marks the end of America's Golden Age, whose minds seem set on the famous lines—

Ill fares the land, to hastening ills a prey,
Where wealth accumulates, and men decay;
Princes and lords may flourish or may fade;
A breath can make them, as a breath has made;
But a bold peasantry, their country's pride,
When once destroyed, can never be supplied.[7]

There are even complexes of buildings within our cities which try to capture the image, although the reality escapes them, of the rural village we have left behind.[8] There are those who would have us think that the high tide of religion in America was the good old days of Protestant hegemony, where it could be said with truth—as one of the greatest constitutional commentators of the nineteenth century, Mr. Justice Story, did say[9]—that America was a Protestant nation and Christianity part of the Common Law of the land. There are those, and they are highly vocal, who believe that a weak leadership and an enfeebled Constitution will suffice to breast the national combines of business, finance, and labor. For my part, I prefer to honor Thomas Jefferson by remembering that his was a bold and powerful intellect, a brilliant imagination, a high morality of political and social responsibility. I do not believe that we were put here, at this time and in this land of incredible wealth and promise, to play the part of "Miniver Cheevy, born too late."[10] For if "the city is, finally, the natural habitat of civilized man,"[11] we are in America on the threshold of one of the high seasons of human culture. Our choice lies between the primitivist motif, which turned Lot's wife to salt, and the joyful acceptance of these very real and very new kinds of community, with the liberty which accompanies the Great City, liberty which a highly specialized and complex society alone affords.

### THE IMPORTANCE OF DIALOGUE

In the nomadic society, "community" was based on family ties. Leadership was often charismatic and always patriarchal in style. In the agrarian society, "community" was based on geographical propinquity. The village was essentially a defensive unit, against marauders and invaders. Leadership was conservative, and based upon familiarity and dependability. In the industrial society, "community" is based primarily on vocation and profession. We accept willingly as leaders those who are familiar with our day to day problems on the job. Such leaders may have personal thrust, and we are naturally happy when a childhood companion comes to the fore. Most of all, however, we look for the person who can listen as well as speak, who is trained in the art of the dialogue. Although we sometimes slip backward—

and a Hitler or a Stalin is such an atavism, a reversion to a tribal priest-king—at our best we prefer the consensus. The style of leadership which is produced in our associations and prized in our public life is the man who is capable of hearing as well as speaking, who is able to sum up the "sense of the meeting" in a succinct and acceptable way.

The expansion of areas of social existence within which decisions are reached by deliberation and discussion marks the transfer of the principles of the Town Meeting to the vocational and professional communities of which we are a part. It is in realizing the potential of these real communities that the "quick-belongingness," which barely masks the anxiety of the isolates who try to restore a vanished principle of community and therefore are blinded to the principle of community which now exists, is turned into genuine integration and identity with persons with whom we share a common destiny. Even some of our urban sociologists have missed this fundamental point, in their desire to re-create the image of the rural village as the standard of local government. One sociologist, reacting against such romantic efforts, has concluded his observations with the gloomy words—

> Against the vision of suburbia as the carrier for the grassroots faith, the tough-minded observer sees only a continuing spread of the influence of the central city, and the net of the metropolis is cast in larger and larger circles, promising ultimately to engulf us all.[12]

The argument of this paper is that if he is genuinely tough-minded the observer will eschew pejorative words such as "spread of the influence," "net," and "engulf," and perhaps come to perceive that new possibilities of discussion and decision and personality integration exist which, if their potential is realized, are just as significant as was ever the Town Meeting or the *viva voce* citizens' rule of the Greek city-states. More than that! It is calculated that during the fifty years of her flowering, Athens numbered between 310,000 and 425,000 warm bodies: women had no political liberty, there were about 100,000 slaves, and about 35,000 were citizens with full freedom and management of the state.[13] At the time of the early Town Meeting, women had no political voice and the considerable majority of men were slaves, bondservants, or lacked property requirements. Approximately one in nine to one in sixteen enjoyed the privilege of voting as late as 1890. It is certainly a significant fact that actual statistics on cities and people —demographic studies—belong to the period of expanding popular sovereignty:

> Demography is essentially the science of the masses of the people rather than of the ruling classes and only when the masses tended to

become the ruling class did the subject of demography become important.[14]

Common people first become important in the highly complex, industrialized, and specialized society of the Great City, where all kinds of people whom we do not know and can never know personally are responsible for decisions and actions which, wrongly made, could kill us all tomorrow. In nomadic and rural societies, trust was based on personal encounter. Today, it depends largely upon whether we have confidence in the basic integrity of the vocational and professional control groups.[15]

The new communities are superior in several respects to earlier forms; not the least of it is the extension of the privileges and responsibilities of liberty to larger numbers of people. The experience of liberty is an ennobling one, and the American experiment, at the beginning looked at askance by all sound Europeans and by many yet, has produced the most stable and the most vital constitutional tradition in the North Atlantic community. Every other nation in NATO has endured at least one major revolution since the American Revolution, and some have gone through the wringer several times. This might, among other things, lead us to the conclusion that our Constitution cannot be as bad as some of the strident voices of the day like to suggest!

The genius of our way of life is the dialogue, the practice of reaching decision by open-faced discussion among those who share a common responsibility and a common destiny. While the discussion is raging, the free society looks somewhat chaotic—especially from the outside. By contrast, the totalitarian society looks much better ordered than it really is. As Bishop Dibelius of Berlin, who has encountered both Nazi and Communist totalitarianism, has put it, relationships within such a society are like those in a bad marriage: even the most obviously necessary and proper actions of the partner are viewed with suspicion. Experts in the study of totalitarianism refer to its facade as "the mask of anarchy." In the open forum of the open society, on the other hand, the very discussion which creates a consensus as to a decision also creates the will to obey the legislation or decree which enacts it into law. It is not parliamentary tactics, not even majority rule, which builds the basis of trust in the self-governing society.

> . . . what matters most in the tiny democratic societies which we feel to be thoroughly satisfactory forms of government is what comes out of the free give and take of discussion.[16]

The enemies of the open society are those systems or movements which would suppress full, free, and informed discussion. The dangerous fronts are those "where faceless troops are landing."[17] The areas of health are those where free men meet with the "open face of truth" and work out their order and discipline together.

The most satisfactory association which many know is within the lawyers' guild, the ministerial association, the American Association of Civil Engineers, the AMA, the UAW, the Realtors' Association, and the many other vocational and professional communities which largely regulate the world's work and provide the norms and personal relations which inform and inspire our daily living. To the degree that these communities are successful centers of the dialogue between free and responsible men, they guarantee stability and security for all of us and also provide imaginative and experimental leadership in triumphing over new problems as they arise.

### THE RESPONSIBILITY OF VOCATION

Freedom is not an end unto itself, but for the sake of truth. Freedom of discussion does not exist for its own sake, but for the building up of an ordered society. When this dimension of responsibility—of stewardship—is lacking, conversation becomes trivial and meaningless. Without the dimension of ultimate responsibility, discussion is ruled by foolishness. There is that which can be discovered by a good discussion which can be found out in no other way. For this to occur, however, those participating must "have faces": that is, they must show themselves to be creatures who sign their names to their concerns and their opinions, who exercise charity and respect to their neighbors. Individuals without faces, secret organizers of anonymous campaigns, members of secret conspiracies—whether CGT or OAS, or NSDP, CP or John Birch Society—do not belong in the dialogue with civilized men.

In classical antiquity, the conflict of Protagoras and Socrates illustrates the point. The former was a pseudo-intellectual, in this case, who refused to deal with the question and abused the stewardship of time. The sophists characteristically attack the speaker, not the problem, and use their own classifications and ideologies to avoid taking the neighbor seriously. As Louis Fischer said after he had left ideological politics:

> I thought, in my Soviet phase, that I was serving humanity. But it is only since then that I have really discovered the human being.[18]

The wise man listens as well as speaks, directs himself to human beings who are mortal like himself, pursues the pedestrian politics which makes real discussion among real people concerned with real issues a concrete reality.

In the rebuilding of Europe since World War II, a vital role has been employed by certain lay institutes which have emphasized work with vocational and professional groups: lawyers, doctors, personnel managers, bankers, directors of companies, civil servants, elementary school teachers, policemen, automobile workers, shop stewards, architects, and the like. There are now more than sixty such adult education centers in twelve European countries, but the main thrust came at first in West Germany.[19] In the Third Reich the Nazi system had so far corrupted the basic communities of industrial society as to demoralize their members and destroy all standards of professional ethics and morals. Led by men active in the Christian resistance to Hitler's totalitarianism, and now in the forefront of the fight against Communist totalitarianism, these conference centers have functioned in the forefront of the rehabilitation of the professional and vocational communities. The crisis was acute. The German doctors were thoroughly demoralized: four out of five of them were Nazi party members; even if they had not taken part in the terrible experiment on human beings at Auschwitz and Belsen, they were witting. The lawyers, four out of five of them party members, had practiced in a society where, as Goering told the German Bar Association in its 1941 annual meeting, there was no such thing as absolute justice or right: there was only that which served the party. The elementary school teachers, the worst of the lot, counted 84 percent party membership: hating culture and the universities, which they had envied from afar off, they had zealously turned over generation after generation of young boys and girls to be the janissaries of Hitler's violent anti-intellectualism. Among these demoralized groups and many others, after the collapse of the Third Reich, the Evangelical Academies held conference after conference in which were openly discussed two questions:[20]

1. Where did we go wrong? At what point should we have drawn the line? (Those who saw the last scene in "Judgment at Nuremberg" will realize that this is not an easy question, but that it draws a line across the pages of personal history when it is faced squarely.)

2. What is our present responsibility? What do we, better educated and better paid than our fellow citizens in the bunkers and in the fields, owe our people now? What is our vocational stewardship in terms of ultimate moral responsibility?

It is not too much to say that these conferences—in some cases leading to the founding of permanent vocational guilds, with regular magazines or newsletters—have contributed substantially to the establishment of health and stability in West Germany since the war.

It would be a mistake to think of such centers in terms of our church conference centers in America. Their programs are much more like a good university extension program—at Nebraska, UCLA, NYU, Southwestern—at which everyone who is prepared to discuss is welcome. Yet there lies back of this development a profound religious perception, as well as the shrewd understanding that the health of modern society is largely a function of the health of vocational and professional communities. This religious perception is a reaffirmation of the teaching of the great Reformers on stewardship. "Stewardship" was not, at the highest of the Reformation, primarily financial: it had to do with *vocatio/Beruf*—the whole of life where one's treasure is. Christian use of money may be part of it, but the discussion does not start there: the real question is the dedication and the orientation of life. As Luther put it, and he was followed by Calvin and others:

> A cobbler, a smith, a peasant . . . All alike are consecrated priests and bishops, and every man in his office may be useful and beneficial to the rest . . . just as the members of the body serve one another.[21]

The Reformers were sure that a teacher, a farmer, a cobbler, a wheelwright, a soldier, who exercised his vocation in the fear of God and love of his fellows was just as truly one of "the religious" as a preacher or professor of theology. It may be worth noting that in the USA to date, in spite of the new efforts by the Lutherans and the Southern Presbyterians, the most persistent and influential program of vocational guilds has been for years in the Catholic communion. Translated into contemporary terms by adult education centers, this directs an arrow at our vocational and professional stewardship.

Although I have conceived my responsibility as primarily conceptual, it may be suggestive to point toward what specific changes are implied for one institution, at least. The most imaginative reorganization of the churches' ministry in America today involves the discovery and glorification of new styles of community ("para-Gemeinde") beyond the usual concentration on purely individual and familial piety. In addition to the development of professional and vocational guilds, we have an astonishing network of prayer cells, fellowship groups, koinonia groups, *Hauskreise,* "house churches," across Christendom—and not infrequently membership in these face-to-face groups is vocationally monochromatic. For the special ministry, at least, this means gradual disappearance of the generalist, in the group ministries in the countryside as well as in the Big City. If the clergyman is to leave his role as a leader figure in agrarian society, which we instinctively recognize to be anachronistic even when we resist it verbally, and again be relevantly related to the common life, he must become a member of a team of chaplains. Each of these chaplains, in the group ministry, will know how to hear what is being said in at least one vocational grouping, so that he can again say something specifically meaningful from time to time instead of merely exegete timeless truths. He will be a member of a team, he will be a specialist, and he will be an "interpreter"—translating on the border between the claims of the religious community and the pressures of the world. The seminary which trains him will also have to scuttle the curricular and other teaching devices which fit him for the clergyman's role in a world which no longer exists, and rally interdisciplinary effort to train him for useful service to at least one area where lives are really shaped and "community" actually exists.

### IN CONCLUSION

The clue to "community" in the Big City is vocational and professional. The churches, particularly the Protestant churches, have inclined all too often to remain attached to the pattern of community in the old agrarian society rather than realize the potential of the new pattern of community integration. Nevertheless, the logic of our highly specialized and industrialized society is conclusive: our stewardship is expressed primarily in vocational communities, and the genius of these communities is free, full, and informed discussion. The City, which seems to the uninitiated impersonal and atomistic, actually affords greater opportunities for "community" than previous levels of society— once the basic principle of social integration has been mastered.

# XIV / THE CRISIS OF THE CONGREGATION:
# A DEBATE

## Gabriel Fackre

If we were to administer what James Luther Adams calls "the temperature test" to the leaders of American Protestantism, we would soon discover that the mercury rises fast and far upon mention of the local congregation. Church executives, pastors, pioneers in new forms of mission, seminary students, and Women's Guild presidents doing their homework for the big summer conference regularly agonize over the question, "Is the local church obsolete?" A spate of literature that ranges from the tracts of Colin Williams and Peter Berger to the weightier deliverances of Gibson Winter and Hans Hoekendijk has quickened pulsebeats by raising serious doubts about the effectiveness of the congregational form. A cluster of "working groups" on several continents exploring "The Missionary Structure of the Congregation" under the auspices of the World Council of Churches has provided a lively forum for the exchange of ideas. A decline in seminary enrollments, signs of vocational uncertainty in theological students, and vocational unrest in the ranks of the clergy have lent particular urgency to the quest for answers about the relevance of that voluntary association which has long been the center of gravity of organized Christianity in this country.

Well, is the local church irrelevant? Is the day coming when the significant forms of Christian gathering and impact will be at the place of work or leisure, or in the midst of secular anguish and ferment? Or perhaps there will be no explicitly "religious" structures at all, but simply the presence of the committed in those movements struggling to make life more human, movements whose life and work together may, in fact, constitute the new shape of the church. Such proposals as these are being actively put forward by a formidable array of new theologians and practitioners in mission dedicated to renewal and disenchanted with present institutional life of the church. The critique has developed its own conceptual apparatus, framing it in a vocabulary of its blessed words ("holy worldliness," "God's mission," "New Humanity," "exciting," "style of life," "morphological fundamentalism," "come and go structures," "new forms," "dialogue"). We shall attempt to trace the contours of this critical perspective and then sketch the lineaments of a rejoinder that is emerging in the conversation. Those interested in following the most recent twists and turns of the debate as they appear in a sampling of current renewal literature are referred to the footnote documentation.

A SEMANTIC NOTE

The ambiguity of terms has plagued the discussion. While "parish" is often used to describe St. John's by-the-Gas-Station in our American pluralistic and voluntary association setting, either the European state-church connotations of the word or the territorial divisions of the Roman Catholic parish system lurk in the background to confuse the issue. Thus a European criticism of "the parish" based on the impossibility of a full-orbed ministry to the fifteen thousand baptized constituents who have paid their church tax, much less to the functional communities of work, leisure, the mass media, etc., of which these constituents are a part, is sometimes smuggled into the American discussion without recognizing the dissimilar sociological context. Because the word "parish" can contribute to this kind of misunderstanding, we avoid using it here.

The word "congregation" is also problematic. While it has been customary to identify the constituency of St. John's with this word, there is a long tradition in Roman Catholicism that uses "congregation" in connection with religious orders, monasteries, and the ecclesiastical housekeeping chores of the Vatican. More important for our immediate purposes, there is a strong current of thought in the debate on the relevance of St. John's which is either seeking "ecclesiological accreditation" for new forms of Christian gathering and therefore increasingly calling these nonresidential groupings "congregations," or is using the word to describe the being of the church in the new geographic region of relationship which has replaced the neighborhood or village, namely, the "zone humaine" or metropolitan area.[1]

To keep somewhere in range of current usage and yet to leave the door open to a larger use of the word "congregation," we shall use here "local congregation" and "local church" to refer to St. John's and its companions.[2]

SOURCES OF DISCONTENT: SOCIOLOGICAL

In striving to communicate with a particular era, the church befriends one or another pursuit of the human spirit. Thus theology may use philosophical tools to interpret a doctrine, pastors may gain insight for their counseling responsibilities from depth psychology, the specialist in church education may find an ally in the contemporary artist or poet. At the moment, sociology is the mistress whose company is most avidly sought by churchmen.[3] The seminarian's bookshelf, the conference roster, the lay center's faculty, the denominational self-study program, are not complete without a sociological presence. It is in the light shed by the sociologist on both the state of the world and the state of the church that the critic has read the demise of the local congregation. Let us examine some threads of thought that recur in the indictment.

1. The critic affirms that the possibility of effective engagement by a local church with the life of a contemporary urbanite, particularly a middle-class working male, has radically decreased. In the more settled communities of an earlier age, the local church, potentially at least, touched a person at many vital points in his life because that life was by and large embedded in the fabric of the neighborhood or town or rural area well within range of the local church's ministrations. In present urban-industrial society, the boundaries of that reachable circle of life have exploded. Our citizen spends large stretches of his time and energy in an office or factory miles away, or in an airplane miles above, or in a train or car traveling between home and office and airport. A bursting leisure matches the work explosion. The same man with his three-day weekend, longer vacation, shorter workday—with more of the same reported to be around the corner—populates the new playgrounds and leisure cities to be found on the ski slopes, waterways, sands, and in the park camping areas and resort centers that dot the landscape. And even while "home" during the working part of the week, he is drawn beyond the perimeter and vision of the local church to the theaters, museums, bowling alleys, night clubs, restaurants, etc., "downtown" or "out of town." Part of the picture also is the movement in the healing arts from the home-calling family physician to the mass medical center, in the merchandising world from the corner store to the distant shopping center, in the increase of college-bound youth and the comparable out-migration of other day-to-day pursuits.[4]

If man's time and energy are now being redistributed over sectors far from home base, how significant is that part of him that shows up in the pew on Sunday morning, if in fact the business trip or weekend cottage commitment does not prevent it from appearing at all? And how can the local church whose circle of contact does not touch directly man-at-office, man-in-flight, man-on-skis, pretend to be ministering to him satisfactorily or even succeed in confronting him?

What further weakens the influence of the local congregation is the current pace of residential mobility. Corporation advancement policies, migrating rural and minority groups, the status panic, and the general restlessness of American feet add up to the yearly address changes of one in five citizens. As it is sometimes described in church extension circles, the local church "ministers to a procession." When people are in transit, the opportunity for developing rootedness in a local congregation is correspondingly decreased, and the chances of any contact at all are reduced.[5]

The local congregation has traditionally been a gathering of households. Its influence on society is related, therefore, to its capacity to shape family life. However, how significant is this local congregation→ family→society route when the middle term has lost much of its significance by yielding up to other institutions its former productive, educational, medical, and recreational functions?[6]

2. While the first basic criticism of the local church has to do with its estrangement from the centers of *people,* the second pertains to its alienation from the centers of *power.* Thus the local congregation is viewed as out of physical and psychological range of the collectivities, and the locus of decision-making in those collectivities, which shape the world in which we live.

As the critic looks at the local church and its residential setting through spectacles supplied by one school of sociological thought, he sees it as a "reactive" institution. It does not form society; it is formed by society. The national and international "macro-structures," the "productive powers," the vast principalities of industry, government, the military establishment, the communications media, and movements for social change (labor unions, civil rights organizations) are the determining forces of the twentieth-century world. The local church has neither access to, nor influence upon, these processes.[7]

3. Distance from *issues,* as well as from people and power, renders the local church sociologically inept.

The critic points to studies which indicate that the values espoused by a church member in the private world of family, home, and church are left behind when he boards the commuter train hurtling toward the harsh realities of the public world. This ethical schizophrenia, manifest in the businessman who is the epitome of "honesty" in paying the paper boy but who manufactures light bulbs with a built-in death date (and justifies this planned obsolescence as proper to the jungle life of competition), is neither understood nor addressed creatively by the ministries of the local church, cut off as it is from the ambiguities of decision-making on the complex worldly terrain of the 1960's.[8]

Awkwardly positioned for confrontation with people and power of a buzzing, blooming new world, divorced from the complex ethical questions of that world, the local church retreats to what seems to be its area of competence—work on the fringes of society with women and children. As the horizons of the larger world fade, the conception of its ministry also shrinks to the point of being carried on "in a hothouse atmosphere of women's emotional difficulties and children's programs."[9] Narrowing its vision to these matters further incapacitates the local church for dealing with the critical public issues that determine society. Out of touch with the rhythms, structures, and value quests of a new world, the local church simply is not "where the action is."[10] At best, therefore, it should confine itself to the limited ministry it may be able to carry on—a "chaplaincy to families" in the "nature-cycle," the conventional "religious" ministrations associated with "hatching, matching, and dispatching."[11] At worst, it should fold its tents and make room for the new forms which are destined to replace it, structures which are born in the places of ferment, where life is truly lived: in the new work-play streams, and in those currents of political, economic, and social life which are shaping our future.

### SOURCES OF DISCONTENT: THEOLOGICAL

Woven into the foregoing sociological criticisms, sometimes hardly separable from them, are the threads of a theological disenchantment. This discontent has to do with both the conceptual apparatus and the life style of the local congregation.

1. The word "privatism" recurs with frequency in the indictment of the local church.[12] At least six different meanings are given to the word in the literature of protest. The umbrella under which they all walk is the accusation that the spirituality of the church member is fundamentally inward-looking. Its focus is "I, me, and mine."

One expression of this privatized style is pietism. Thus the revivalist who censors out the cosmic dimensions of the Christian faith by reducing it to a transaction with a "personal Saviour," and whose stock in trade is the self-centered piety of the gospel song, is captive to an incurved life of the spirit.[13]

The more sedate, middle-class version of egocentric spirituality is Pealism. Here there is preoccupation with "my peace of mind" and "my positive thoughts," all of which is calculated to reap benefits for "my successful living," including, of course, the Golden Rule dividends of a profitable business.

A more sophisticated form of spiritual incurvature is found in existentialism's absorption in the self's subway noises. Concern with the problems of anxiety, despair, dread, self-rejection, and the leap of faith are viewed by the critic as an exercise in navel-staring, and one more evidence of the contemporary apostate flight from involvement in the worldly arena of God's challenge and grace.[14]

Akin to popular existentialism's labored struggle with "depth" questions is the widespread lay conception of the church as a "come structure" designed to help one face personal burdens and perplexities. Thus the church exists to watch over me in "my sickness," "my bereavement," "my marital problems," "my loneliness." In this connection, the critics regularly roast the clergyman who conceives his role to be that of "holding the hands and blowing the noses" of those who cannot cope with life.[15]

Privatism also describes the local church's captivity to the small circle of neighborhood and family concerns which its narrow residential base predisposes it to focus upon, to which allusion was made earlier.

Going under numerous other names, but fitting quite naturally here under the indictment of a privatized style of life, is the critic's blistering attack on the easy adaptation of the Christian faith to the culture around it. What Adams years ago characterized as "smothering the cross in lilies" now comes under fire as "culture-Protestantism," "the religious establishment," "suburban captivity," "religion-in-general," and "public ideology." A church and faith which is designed to be dysfunctional, controversial, and heterogeneous with the culture has become functional, adjustive, and homogenized into it. The church member caught up in his petty self-aggrandizing private world has turned his back upon the needs of the public world and the claim of the Suffering Servant who gave his life for that world.[16]

Such are the faces of privatism.

2. A neighboring target is "ecclesiocentrism."[17] The critics have helped to make "churchiness" a term of reproach in the current theological lexicon.

The institutional ardor of postwar American Protestantism comes under sharp fire. With the mushrooming of suburban churches, the increase of church membership and resources that characterized this period of religious boom, came an overwhelming zeal for facilities, finance and program growth. The successful operation and expansion of the institution became the be-all and end-all of church life in many places. To be a "good layman" meant to be "active" in the internal life of the local congregation, particularly as that activity bore upon increasing the size, grandeur, busyness, and status of the institution.

The recoil from this overweening institutionalism is framed in the critic's battle cries, "Let's get the church out of the real estate business!" "Away with the edifice complex!" "We are not called to be successful but to be faithful!"[18]

Companion to the lay-encouraged institutional aggrandizement, came a more clerical form of ecclesiocentrism, one with an impressive theological pedigree. It provided a convenient ideological smokescreen for the expansionist interests of the burgeoning new congregations of the postwar boom. We are speaking of the popularity of a high doctrine of the church.

One of the fruits of such trends as the deepening interest in biblical studies, the growth of the ecumenical movement and ecumenical scholarship, the increasing contact with Roman Catholic and Eastern Orthodox thought, and the re-examination of such forgotten Protestant traditions as the Mercersburg theology, has been the growing emphasis upon the mystery and uniqueness of the church.

The critic sees this high view of the church as neatly dovetailing with the more mundane lay interest in making St. John's "the biggest church in town." But worse, it "puts God in a box," making him a "Christian Ba'al," denying his sovereignty and the reality of his extra-ecclesiastical movements. Its bring-them-in conception of mission undercuts the outward-looking servant role of the church and thus gives aid and comfort to the momentum of introversion already present in the pietisms, Pealisms, and institutionalisms of the local church.[19]

The sharp thrusts of the critics have marked the 1960's as a decade of discontent with the established forms and perspectives of an American Christendom. The sociological and theological narcissism of the local church has made it a central assault point in the over-all restlessness with inherited patterns. In and through the discontent and the preoccupation with the ills of the local congregation, however, are laced new theological emphases and proposals for structural redirection. These positive notes are also part of the critical position in the debate about the destiny of the local congregation.

### A NEW THEOLOGICAL MOOD

1. Counterposed to the privatisms and ecclesiocentrisms of our time is what students of Adams learned to call a *kampfbegriff*, a "fighting word": world. Written on the banners of a circle of renewers and reformers (one that includes, but is not limited to, the critics of the local church) is the forgotten word in some of the familiar New Testament affirmations: "Go into all the *world*," "You are the light of the *world*," "God so loved the *world*."[20]

The lifting up of "world" is a rebuke to privatized and churchy introversion. It bespeaks a fresh concern with the "public section" and the "secular," understood as that arena of social, economic, and political ferment where men work and play, buy and sell, love and hate, live and die. The call to the world is the call away from the ghetto life of a subway spirituality and inward-looking ecclesiasticism. It is a mandate to spend oneself as a servant to the neighbor.

While the world refrain is regularly heard in all current efforts at renewal, there is a particular turn the critic gives to it. Alongside of, and sometimes displacing, the accent on the Lordship of Christ *over* the world (which accent furnished the ecumenical fathers of the previous generation with their world-mandate) has come "a new vision of the secular activity of God," a fresh emphasis upon the work of God *in* the world. Going beyond the "presecularized theology" of yesterday, and even beyond the more modest references of another time to the extra-covenantal chastening work of God as a "rod of anger" or the work of God in creation in contrast to his labor in redemption, the new theological mood does not hesitate to speak of God's secularity in terms of "the incognito Christ," "the Christ of the Emmaus road," the action of the Word of God in the world, and the work of the Holy Spirit on the landscape of history.[21]

2. What are the signs of the divine presence? One of the clues to the whereabouts of Christ in the world is the servant-style ministry of Jesus and/or the incarnational love of God which declared itself at Bethlehem to be "for man." Thus where there is evidence of rehumanizing power and possibilities at work—in the civil rights movement, in the technological revolution, in the peace movements, in urbanization—there Christ the Man for others is, alive and at work.[22] This worldly Christ is not interested in "religion" or the "beyond," but in man's humanity. Therefore, he cannot be assumed to be where religious words and rituals are plentiful. He is, rather, where there is a commitment to fellow humanity.[23]

3. Another footprint of the world-working Christ may be found at the "strong points," "the vital center" of human life. The new theological perspective seeks to replace the fallen and "bewitched" label affixed to the world by older theologies, by a higher valuation.[24] Seeking to make contact with a generation bursting with vast hopes of technological advance that will improve the human condition, and of great aspirations for freedom, justice, and peace, this perspective points to the creativity manifest in contemporary society and looks for genuine progress in human affairs. It rejects the reflex action of hostility to persons and movements of power that characterized an older theology. It rejoices with men in their virility, as that virility is manifested

in the world of science and politics. It strives to help men see that the God of the Christian faith is not caught in the crevices of men's lives, not the fireman who comes to put out fires, but the craftsman who shares and exults in the building up of those lives.[25]

4. While aware of the utopianisms of a nineteenth-century liberal theology, the new mood does not hesitate to describe in eschatological terms the possibilities in a history animated by secular working of God. Thus some of its proponents can speak about the "New Creation" which is "Metropolis," about the breaking in of "a New Humanity," "New Mankind," or "New Jerusalem" in such humanizing forces of the twentieth century as the civil rights movement and the imaginative renewal of the city.[26]

5. Since the fundamental work of God goes on in the secular flow, a new way of theology is born. Authentic theological reflection rises only from a deep immersion in the secular processes of grace. To discern God at work, one must be where God chooses to offer himself. The ministry of involvement and the listening ministry are the precondition for relevant theology.[27]

NEW FORMS

From the theological premise that the burning point of God's work is the secular present, it is a short step to a new ecclesiological posture. *Ubi Christi, ibi ecclesia* means in this new setting that the church is and/or must be where the incognito Christ is doing his secular work of making men human. Since the local church is positioned awkwardly vis-à-vis the strong humanizing currents of our time, and gives little evidence of being genuinely for man, it must give way to "new forms" which are set in the midst of the worldly flow, which are in touch with streams of grace there (particularly at the strong points), which are marked by a new servant style of life, and which are "go structures" that prepare and propel men as salt, light, and leaven into the arena in which God is at work.[28]

One cannot blueprint or forecast with precision what these new forms will be, for their birth is situational; they emerge when faithful men participate in the secular flow, relating faith and facts in a specific context. At best, one can suggest some "parables" or "paradigmatic clues" as to the direction we must go.[29]

1. Some parables cited (and proposals for redirection rising from them) suggest that the heritage and resources of the church be grafted onto those places and people in the world which show evidence of power and promise, on the one hand, or anguish and need, on the other. The growth of "chaplaincies," "missions," "little congrega-

tions," and "vocational groups" in business, shopping centers, education, government, and the leisure and entertainment world are clues to the former.[30] The hospital chaplain, the lay "lifeline" team, and the chaplain to the city's "night people" are examples of the latter.[31] The explosion of church-sponsored "coffee-houses" is part of this spectrum of ministry, one which often touches men at both the places of creativity (art, literature, films, involvement in social ferment) and the place of loneliness and alienation.[32] The "house church" is another.[33]

The critic sees the value of these new forms not in terms of communicating some "religious" notions to the worldman, and certainly not as a device to "get people in the corrals of institutional religion," but rather as a "Christian presence" ministering to the real needs to be found today on the Jericho roads of the world, struggling to think through the human questions posed on secular terrain, or giving support to the real outpouring of grace at the points of strength in human life.[34]

2. Another parable of relevance is the community of ordered withdrawal. Within sight of the secular stream by way of the concerns uppermost to its constituents, such a community as this is a life together of reflection and healing. In this spectrum we find the European and American evangelical academies which seek to bring together secular men around a burning secular question, under church auspices and with church resources,[35] the lay centers for research and training,[36] disciplined communities of retreat and renewal such as Iona, Kirkridge,[37] and the intentional communities such as Gould Farm in which Adams has been a pioneer.[38]

3. The ad hoc group or task force brought into being around an issue that cries out for Christian ministration is ranked high by new formers. Of limited life-span, tailored to contextual immediacies and capable of traveling with light institutional baggage, it fits in especially well with the flexibility and relevance prized by the critic of older forms.[39]

4. Very recent thought on the restructuring of the church has moved from the specifics of chaplaincies, academies, and task forces to a consideration of total strategy. Taking as a new fundamental unit of human community in an urban world, the "zone humaine" or metropolitan area, reformers are striving to spell out the shape of mission commensurate with it.[40] Designs for this "new parish" speculate about a pluralism of ministries (lay centers, chaplaincies to functional groups, task forces for training and celebration of the great corporate events, nature-cycle structures), with a focus given by a central building and a team of clergy who function as enablers and as cross-fertilizing agents within and among the multiplicity of gathering and action orbits.[41]

5. For one breed of renewer, the foregoing proposals still smack too heavily of "churchiness." To "bring" the church to the world by way of chaplain or academy or over-all planning with the concomitant Bibles, prayers, and religious words represents the "Constantinian turn of mind" bent upon re-ecclesiasticizing the secular arena.

There are two schools of thought on alternative approaches. One declares that the first step in restructuring the church is the act of participation in the places and among the people of ferment and anguish. When preconceived notions about what should be done or brought to people have been stilled, and the honest uncalculating act of "being-there" for others is lived out, then God in his wisdom will give the clue as to what shape mission will take, and what word must be spoken in that situation. The first task is the act of involvement it-self.[42]

A second school of thought finds even this counsel tainted with hidden churchy designs. The logic of a secular God leads rather to an unabashedly religionless Christianity and hence a totally secular conception of mission unencumbered by the grand descent of a "deus ex machina." What this means ecclesiologically is that the secular shapes that God has brought into being for his secular tasks *are* the church. To participate in a movement or event that is in the current of rehumanization is to "join" the church. Thus a new form of the church in our time, one which is a sign of the aborning New Humanity, *is* the freedom movement. The secular church brought to birth by the incognito secular Christ is the purest expression of a radically secularized theology.[43]

6. Implicit in the five preceding designs for restructuring is an emphasis enjoying strong support in recent years throughout the church: the rediscovery of the laity. Set in the midst of the world, the laity become the logical candidate for the cutting edge of secular mission. The critic may, in fact, describe the laity *as* the new form of the church.[44] In contrast to former times when the layman was seen as a marginal man in the church, as assistant to the clergy, now the tables must be turned, with clergy justifying their existence only to the extent that their theological speciality can aid the laity who perform the fundamental ministry today in the new "secular pastorates."[45]

7. There is one other ecclesiological posture allied to the criticism of the local church which is, strictly speaking, not a "new form" but yet is part of the total spectrum of redirection. It, too, is a re-formation of the church in terms of its secular mission. Yet it may look like the local church in that it may gather in residential community, include families, and even have a conventional church building. What marks it

as part of the critical spectrum is the limitation of its membership to
those who have clear secular accreditation. It is a congregation but
is "stripped down to fighting weight," having "cut the fat out," and restored "integrity of membership." It is a "company of the committed,"
including in its ranks only those who are willing to accept the strenuous
demands of a common discipline and the vigor of deep participation in
secular mission.[46]

### A RESPONSE TO THE CRITICS

Somewhere between a docile acceptance of the critical posture here
outlined, and a frenzied attempt to assert the omnicompetence and
vitality of the conventional local church, there is emerging a third
response. This is the position that is set forth below, one that expresses genuine gratitude for the insights of the new theological and
sociological stance, and yet is prepared to challenge vigorously the
attendant oversimplifications and distortions. Let us look first at the
grateful agreements.

*"World"* is indeed the authentic fighting word for our time. It points
both to the arena which should engage the resources and passion
of the church, and also to that secular working of God often neglected
in traditional formulations of the gospel which domesticated the
divine working—yes, Christ himself—to the churchly and private
sectors.

Because the economic, social, and political principalities and powers
occupy the center of the secular stage, the critics are right in underscoring the importance of the discipline of sociology as an ally of
theology and church strategy.

Also, foolish indeed would be the attempt to deny either the awkward positioning of the local church with respect to important seg-
ments of people, power, and issues, or the overwhelming evidence of
ethical and spiritual poverty in the church.

Again, new forms commensurate with the people, power, and issues
out of reach of the local church, and total strategy to integrate the
needed new pluralism of ministries, are an absolute necessity. For opening our eyes to the need for restructuring the church, we owe a special
debt of gratitude to those who have shaken the foundations of the establishment.

As one examines the posture of the critics in the light of "the minutes of the last meeting"—the fate of "fighting words" in other times
of *kairos*—it seems clear that in world-drenched theology and strategy
there is a process at work which befell battle cries of other times. One
of the lessons of Christian history is that a legitimate accent, a motif

that is rightly bold while other themes are called to be bashful, often succumbs to megalomania. An historically ripe, but nonetheless fragmentary, truth may develop imperialistic designs. The part claims to be the whole, and in doing so censors out other vital dimensions of Christian testimony. Reductionism, the collapse of the total Christian message and style into a crucial but not exhaustive theme, is the root problem in the critical position, one that blurs both its sociological and theological vision. Let us examine the outworking of this imperialism in two major areas of inquiry: the sociological-theological boundary line, and the theological circle itself, dealing very tersely with points the elaboration of which may be found in the footnote documentation.

### ALONG THE BOUNDARY OF SOCIOLOGY AND THEOLOGY

1. The kind of sociological resources upon which the critics often rely is not presuppositionless. To the degree that a Comtian positivism or economic determinism are at work, to that degree there is a prior judgment about the significance of the local church-family-neighborhood configuration which influences the "data." The premise that personality is formed by the macro-structures, and ultimately the productive ones, is not an unchallenged assumption, as evidence the insights of psychodynamics.[47] More basically, from a Christian perspective, the biblical doctrine of man as a unity of creatureliness embedded in the natural-social flux, and as spirit transcending it, does not permit of either an angelism that takes no account of the social-economic rootedness of man, or a sociologism that reduces man to natural-social dimensions.[48]

Christian commentary on the local church cannot accept uncritically the perspective or evidence of sociologism. From its own doctrine of man, as well as from an appreciation of insights from other secular disciplines, it entertains the possibility that the family does not have to be simply "reactive" but is in fact "the Christian nursery" that can play a crucial role in the development of personality, and in turn society.[49] It must also affirm that the tiny tower of spirit which thrusts itself above the determinations of natural-social history can be the target of the Word that is heard and celebrated in the local congregation. Because this Word is sharp and full of surprises, it can shake the foundations of society.[50]

Yet another theological motif that militates against any sociological orthodoxy which would preclude the possibility of a local church-person-family-society route of influence is the reality of the divine freedom itself. A sovereign God is free to do his work in micro-structures as well as macro-structures.

2. The effect of sociological imperialism is manifest in the tendency of the critics to view the problem of the renewal of the church in terms of its restructuring. The confidence placed in new forms as the answer to the church's plight is inordinate, and almost humorous. As important as new structures are, this kind of engineering feat will not assure the rebirth of the church. A new man is needed as well as a new form, and the latter will not create the former. Penitence, commitment, new persons, are the necessary companions of new structures.[51]

3. The critics meekly accede with regularity to what E. H. Wickham calls "sociological predestination," and Bonhoeffer describes as "servility toward the factual."[52] It is one thing to translate Christian faith into contemporary idiom and to redesign church structure in terms of the realities discerned by sociological instruments; it is quite another to soften and adapt strenuous and crucial themes of the gospel to what appear to be massive trends in conflict with them. The critic crosses the line from the former to the latter: (a) When he moves from the obvious need to get into dialogue with power elites in a mass society to the uncritical assumption that there is something permanent about power elites, and fails to press for the dispersion of power among those often used as pawns and objects by dehumanizing pyramid apexes. Uncritical elite-principle thinking contributes to the failure of the critic to see the importance of institutions at the base of the modern pyramids, including the local church, which potentially can play a part in the democratizing of power. (b) When he concludes from indisputable social data concerning the reduction of family functions that the church correspondingly must treat the family as of less consequence. Because of the centrality of the family in the Christian ethos (embodied and pointed to in its nurturing processes, theology, liturgical life, and vocabulary), and as a training ground for personhood, the erosion of the family is not an invitation to accommodation but a challenge to creative resistance.[53] The imaginative and crucial role that can be played here by the local church is missed by the critic, the prisoner of an adaptive mentality.

4. The ideological skirts of the critic are showing in the ease with which he assumes entrée can be made into the new dimensions and levels of the public sector that are appearing. Christians behind the Iron Curtain observe that the political and economic spaces of society are not accessible to them for the establishing of vocational groups, missions, and academies.[54] And while rapport with the institutions of secular society is a possibility in the West, how long can this be assumed to be the case? Some say that we can look forward to equivalent resistance and closed doors.[55] Absolutes in strategy which do not take

into account the variety of present conditions and future possibilities, and which dismiss the significance of the gathering points in local churches that we do in fact now have, and may be some day thrust back upon, are sociologically naïve.

5. A related sociological naïveté is apparent in the failure of the critic to see the significance of a point driven home with regularity by Adams: organization is power. As French Catholic experimentation in new forms came to recognize: "the parish is hic et nunc."[56] Serious confrontation with the modern world will surely not bypass that vast resource of manpower, facilities, and finance represented by the network of local churches throughout the land. As supportive of extra-congregational mission, and as participant in the secular realm accessible to it, the local congregation is a potential launching pad for renewal.

On the American scene, with the high proportion of the population still holding some formal allegiance to local congregations, it also would be odd to develop a strategy which ignored the presence of the multitudes associated with local churches. If nothing else (of course, there is something else), the local churches in this country represent a well-populated mission field.[57]

6. There is a cluster of oversimplifications in the critics' commentary on the relation of the local church to the residential community and about the destiny and significance of the home address itself, oversimplifications which obscure the possibilities of ministry by the local congregation:

(a) Given the nonparochial character of American congregational life noted earlier, the spread of its constituency and the circumference of its concern range far beyond, and frequently have nothing to do with, its immediate residential milieu. Sometimes its milieu is not at all residential, as for example, the "downtown church." It is inaccurate, therefore, to generalize about the local congregation on the American scene in terms of a "residential," "home address," or "living quarter" ministry. In fact, the problem may be precisely that, with its far-flung constituency, it is *not* ministering to its immediate residential environs.[58] On the other hand, with its supra-parochial ties, and/or its proximity to industrial, commercial, and political centers, it may be better positioned for engagement with nonresidential culture than it is credited. In smaller metropolitan areas, as well as in the town and country setting which, though disappearing, is still with us, there is evidence of effective engagement by local congregations with powers that shape the community's life.[59] There are also signs of significant confrontation in major metropolitan areas.[60] The fragmentation of Protestantism and the size of the unit of engagement may be the factors which weaken the public impact of congregations in such situations, more so than does the fact that they are "local churches."

(b) Those local congregations which are set in residential communities are in touch with significant aspects of secular existence, as these are found in local expressions of education, politics, labor organization, community organization, business, and the healing arts. In fact, some of the most critical dimensions of a current secular challenge—the problem of integration in housing and public education—are on the doorstep of the local church. The home address is the headquarters of the unemployed and of many of the aged, two sections of the population which promise to be the center of social concern in the immediate future. While the vision for confronting these issues is seriously blurred, there is no intrinsic reason why the local church cannot use its physical proximity to questions and people of great need as a springboard to involvement with them. Moreover, if social change is effected by ferment from the bottomlands of society, as well as by the decisions of power structures or, more accurately, by pressure on the power elites coming from below, then the fact of "being there" in the midst of the unemployed, the aged, and the racially oppressed to be found at the home address is an advantage to be seized rather than a disadvantage to be bewailed.[61]

(c) While it is true that many in the work force, particularly the middle-class "organization man," have the compass point of their lives moved by their work world, the self-image of these persons is often that of husband, father, and home-dweller. If a suburbanite chooses to define himself in these terms, and shapes his behavior accordingly, this also is a piece of sociological data that must be taken into account.[62] As such, it increases the "living" that is done at the home address, and potentially the significance of those institutions, including the local church, that minister in this orbit of life.

(d) Modesty is in order in prognostications about the fate of life at the home address. While those financially and educationally equipped will use increasing spans of their new leisure at playgrounds away from residence, many will choose to spend it in the basement workshop and the backyard. One wonders also, in connection with the drastic shrinking of both the work day and the work force which is forecast in these days of cybernation and leisure explosion, how really significant the work dimension of life will be for the man of tomorrow.[63] Strategies for mission which herald the "vocational group" and the chaplain or mission to the business and industrial community as the new forms needed for tomorrow's world must learn the same modesty about claims to relevance proper to local congregations.

(e) Adding a further question mark to easy generalization about both the fate of the home address and the importance of the urban-industrial configuration is the advent of the communication satellite. Will the "comsat" make possible a world in which "don't commute—communicate" is the byword, in which the factory will be replaced by the businessman-technician who works from a communication console in his home, and in which the city as we know it will disintegrate? Some say so.[64] Thoughtful church planning for the new age will avoid the oversimplification and the easy slogan.

7. Leadership involved in new forms of experimentation are increasingly pointing to the problem of fragmentation in the lives of those touched by, or participating in, new forms. Thus in between the high moments of insight at a periodic academy engagement there is needed some continuing nurture, life together, and witness.[65] Also, the limited scope and personnel of a work or play group or contact can develop its own parochialism. While some look for the day when there will be a central point of worship and ministry in the zone humaine which gives focus and continuity to the multiplicity of people and structure, the utopian character of such a design makes it of little use in meeting the needs of the moment.[66] The cross-section character of the local church (limited though it be) and the continuing life it provides for those needing sustained communal existence (or those in danger of being "detached junior redeemers") makes it a serious option in the total strategy of the church.

8. There is, indeed, massive evidence of privatism, ecclesiocentrism, and unbending structural fundamentalism in the local congregations of Protestantism. A wholesale indictment of the American churches, however, is out of touch with reality. It takes no account of the following things:

(a) The support for the genesis and continuance of new forms has, to date, come in large part from the "religious establishment," and is ultimately traceable to the resources of local congregations.[67]

(b) Discontent with inherited patterns and evidence of reorientation to the world in ministries carried on by local congregations themselves is now too widespread to be dismissed as the exceptional enterprise of an East Harlem Protestant Parish or Washington Church of The Savior.[68]

(c) While the freedom revolution has revealed gaping hypocrises in congregational life, it has also disclosed in many local churches the presence and power of an aroused conscience which has made itself felt in the drive for passage of the civil rights legislation, and other involvement by clergy and laity, Negro and white, in community and national movements.[69]

(d) One of the crowning ironies of current criticism is the wide reading public and lecture circuit clientele it has developed in the religious establishment: the study groups, summer conferences, pastors' institutes, renewal programs, recommended reading lists, etc., that are part and parcel of modern local church life. The evidence of a willingness to be self-critical (by no means universal, of course) says something about the accuracy of any broadside indictment.

## SOME NOTES ON THE NEW THEOLOGY

1. The imperialism of a fighting word takes its heaviest theological toll at the point of the critic's understanding of the church. The underscoring of the work of God in the world at the points of ethical vitality has pressed the new theological mood to identify the being of the church with its doing.

To say that the church has reality only where it is involved in the theater of historical responsibility is a very tempting notion to someone whose passion is social ethics. The price of it, however, is an unbiblical distortion of the covenantmaking agape of a God whose steadfast love persists in the midst of his people, not because of the merits of their responsible life, but in spite of their demerits of irresponsibility. To demand that the congregations living under Word and Sacrament show their moral credit card before being served up with the title "church" is to deny the sovereign power of God to make his presence felt even among a stiffnecked people. It is a kind of Watsonian behaviorism in ecclesiology that severs the Head from the Body.

The critics have rightly pointed to the domestication of God in a church enclave by those who talk much of the mystery and holiness of the church. They have helped us to see his presence and work on a larger landscape and his freedom over the structures of his own making. Further they have rightly criticized an angelism that ignores the sociological embeddedness of the church. These insights surely mean that not only is there a real work of Jesus Christ beyond the church, but also that, on the one hand, God may in his freedom put an end to an expression of churchness when it has exhausted its usefulness in his design, and that, on the other hand, the mystery of the church must not be used to justify and perpetuate the awkward sociological positioning of a given expression of church life.

It is one thing to affirm these things, and quite another to defend a reductionism which sees the church only in terms of its sociological underside. While the recovery of a more biblical and classic conception of the church by the ecumenical fathers has led to "churchy" ideologies, the polarizing of the question by declaring for some such slogan as "If you want to meet God, go out in the world where he is really working" is exceedingly unhelpful. The "other presence of Christ"—in the world—does not preclude his presence in the church.[70] To deny the reality of this latter presence is not only to put in question the divine promise, but it is also to lose sight of a living sign of the unmerited character of God's care. As God keeps the promise of his Self-offering in the midst of that aggregate of sinners which is the typical ethically and spiritually poverty-stricken local church (the Corinths and Laodiceas of the twentieth century), there is dramatized the unconditional divine love.[71] The re-appreciation in our recent theological past of this classic Christian teaching must not be forgotten in our new enthusiasm for the world.

2. Won't we cut the ethical nerve if we speak of the hidden grandeur of the church as well as of its visible misery? Precisely the opposite, if that grandeur is understood in biblical terms.

The Christ who is companion to the church, as Bridegroom to Bride, Head to Body, Vine to Branches, is no easygoing yokefellow. He comes to his people by his love and not by their merit. But *how* he comes, that is another matter. St. Paul speaks of the love that feels like coals of fire. So the love of Christ burns in his church when it meets those who choose to be its enemy. The apostle speaks also of the sacramental confrontation that takes its toll on those who participate without penitence. Whether the relationship to Christ in the church savors of life or of death depends therefore on the response with which the divine love is met. Christian obedience, including passionate worldly obedience, does not materialize or extinguish the presence of Jesus Christ in his church as if he were some sort of genie; it does determine whether that presence comes to burn or to heal.[72]

To take with absolute seriousness the God who is at work in the church is to be propelled into his world. It is a fearful thing to be called into his presence, to be marked by his baptismal waters, for from this confrontation is born a rigorous mandate.

3. How is it possible to do justice theologically to the work of God in both the church and the world? Where these two realities are acknowledged in the contemporary literature on the mission and renewal of the church, there is little other than the affirmation of the fact of duality.[73] In a way this is healthy, for it avoids scholastic dissection and oversubtle speculation about "modes" of the divine presence. However, the discussion must move beyond generalities, for these do in fact obscure the genuinely different dimensions of the divine working. Some theological exploration of images that suggest the present work of Christ in both church and world is needed.

Do we have a lead in the classic symbol of the threefold office of Christ? Is it possible to say that his continuing work is carried on in his priestly ministrations through the sacraments of the church, in his prophetic ministry exercised through the preaching and teaching of the Word in the church, and in his kingly office finding expression in the events and movements of grace and judgment on the terrain of the world? To know him truly is to know him in the fullness of his *munus triplex* manifest in church and world.

Or if it be said that the kingly office cannot be so severed from the work of Christ in the church, is there some light shed by Kraemer's assertion that the concept of the threefold office must be broadened to include the servant role of Christ?[74] Thus, to meet the Christ who turns to us as servant of the world, we must go into the world where he chooses to live out that office, even as he offers himself as prophet, priest, and king in the midst of the covenant community. Perhaps the Buber image offers a clue. Thus it may be said that the divine confrontation that takes place in sacrament and Word is the meeting of an I and a Thou. Here is the personal engagement in which the divine eye turns toward us (Kierkegaard). Yet God shows himself to us also "in profile." He is one who is alongside us in a common work in the world.

A marginal note on the work of God in church and world is the importance of "involvement," stressed by the critics. As it is true that God discloses himself in the world only to those deeply committed to participation in his suffering service there, it is also true that the reality of the Christ who meets us in Word and sacrament comes home only to those who take a decisive leap into this stream of grace.[75]

4. While the new enthusiasm of the work of God in the world has made a dutiful bow to the Christian realism which counsels modesty in claims and expectations about historical progress, there is an uncomfortable similarity between some current formulations of secular possibility and the utopianism and activism so rightly excoriated by another generation of theologians. Thus the prognostications about Metropolis as the New Creation and the appearance of the New Mankind and New Humanity in some current movements for rehumanization sound little different from the secularized eschatologies of "liberal Christianity" which saw the Kingdom of God descending in the new social order under construction.[76]

Let it be said that the willingness to look to the future with hope, to say with Martin Luther King that "I have a dream," to believe in the genuine possibilities of secular history because God is at work in it, is a step forward in Christian thinking from the needle of another theology that was stuck on the "No" God speaks to man's sin and historical pretension. To see God's "Yes" to and in his history, to rejoice in the signs of health on the public landscape, must not blind us, however, to the temptations to megalomania that accompany every genuine advance. Nor should it blind us to the trans-historical nature of the Kingdom which forbids any secular mystique, or romaniticizing of human movements or achievements. Further, the temptations to an activism that interprets Christianity as an enterprise in benevolence which virile men will somehow carry off is very close to the surface in some American commentary on the working of the secular God.[77] Surely we must not forget the lessons learned from a generation of Christian thought that taught us of the dangers of idolatry, fanaticism, self-righteousness, and despair associated with an uncritical relation to the finite.

5. The new theological mood, and derivative church strategy, has reminded us of a sometimes forgotten accent: the presence of, and ministry to, the rich young ruler. God is manifest at the strong points of human life and he calls us to share the gospel with them. Specifically, we must be with and for man in the powerful currents of technological advance and social dynamism. We must get into dialogue with the power elites.

It is instructive to remember, nonetheless, the upshot of Christ's encounter with the rich young man. Sanguine hopes about influencing power structures in dialogical settings may prove to be exceedingly naïve. Here again the theological wisdom of another day that helped us to see the temptations and corruptions attendant to power must not be forgotten, together with the insight that a tolerable justice is often the result of a realistic balance of power.

More important is the examination of concern for "finding God at the strong points of life rather than the weak points" in the light of the biblical testimony about strong and weak things. While God does indeed use Cyrus and Assyria and Pilate, it is instructive to notice how often "the weak things of the world and the despised" are the object of his special attention. In fact, he seems to regularly turn to them as instruments of his mission, particularly in the light of the disappointing performance of the strong.[78] The person and work of Christ is the chief witness to this. Here is a note that must be sounded loud and clear in our great preoccupation with modern man at his virile points and the corresponding demeaning of those ministrations that "blow the noses and hold the hands" of the spiritually crippled. Not only does God care about the invalid, but in the final analysis, we are all cripples.

6. The loud sound of the world-note has drowned out the less dra-

matic but no less real private mission carried on by the local church. The sickness of privatism should not obscure the important private dimension itself. The comforting and strengthening of the bereaved, the sick, the anxious, the perplexed, and the guilty—a service neither measurable by sociological instruments nor directly oriented to the sphere of world-historical responsibility—is an entirely legitimate ministry.[79] Also a ministry to the private sector is the introduction of persons into the identity of the Christian gospel and the setting forth of the personal claim of that faith which goes on in the educational and preaching ministry of local churches.[80] Woven into this is the preservation from generation to generation of this identity of the Christian faith carried out in the stewarding by local congregations of "the means of grace." Nor can we exclude, because of a narrow Protestant understanding of God's dealings with us, the profound private engagement between a man and God which the Roman Catholic describes as *visio Dei* and the Orthodox as deification.[81]

Of potentially great significance to the public sector itself is the style of life to be found in many local congregations. At worst the clubbiness of the likeminded, but at best a genuine life together where burdens are borne and joys are shared, the koinonia of the Protestant congregation is something of a sign that says, "Here John Doe gets back his face and his name. In a world that manipulates and thingifies him, here is a community where personhood is affirmed. Let this world learn something of what it is like to make men human."[82]

More than a sign and judgment to the world, however, it is possible that the repersonalizing graces can ripple out beyond the circle of the congregation. The influence of the congregations of the left wing of the Reformation on the rise of political democracy in the West, about which the Adams student often heard, are proof that the arc can be widened.

7. Thankful though we must be for the new focus on the laity, and the tearing down of walls between first and second class passage on the Christian ship, we cannot be content with the facile blurring of differences between the role of those ordained by the laying on of hands and those ordained by baptism; nor can we accept uncritically clever formulations which declare that as before the laity were assistants to the clergy, now the clergy must be the assistants of the laity. What is missing in these oversimplifications is the contextual principle. It is true that the laity are in the foreground of the ministry to and in the secular arena. As the church scattered in "general ministry," they are the parts of the Body that enable it to walk and work in the world. When the church gathers for worship, study, and life together in order

to prepare for the penetration of the world, the "special ministry"— those parts of the Body that keep open its lifeline as custodians of the means of grace—plays a responsible role as equipper and trainer of lay ministers. Depending on the context, therefore, the words of Luther about the pastor can be spoken of both the clergy and the laity: "a prince in the Kingdom of Christ."[83]

While there are "varieties of service" in the organism which is the church, there are, of course, flexibilities. As in the human body the malfunctioning of one organ is compensated for in part by the work of another, so the void left by faithless laity or clergy may require like substitutionary action. Also, no rigid wall can imprison the clergyman in the church-gathered, for to do the job he is called to do there, he must often, like a Hosea or a Jeremiah, make a visible sign on the streets of the world.[84]

8. We have spoken before of signs of renewal in the contemporary Protestantism that are obscured by hasty generalizations about the depressed state of the church. If one takes seriously the steadfast love of Christ for the church, this should come as no surprise to us. The commitment of Christ to his people is no abstract benevolence. His love is not just favor toward, but power in, his church.[85] Testimony to the resurrecting grace at work in the establishment regularly refutes those who prematurely write its obituary.

### A CONCLUDING OBSERVATION

In sketching contours of the debate on the crisis of the congregation we have said nothing about the theory and practice of renewal in the local church. That question presupposes the conviction that the congregation is renewable, and that it is a form close enough in touch with reality to be worth the effort. In the current conversation on mission, this is the issue which for many must be first resolved.

There is mounting evidence that the heated polarity between those whom we have here called "the critics" and those who have dismissed with hostility any suggestions at restructuring is lessening. Some of the best thinking among the practioners of mission has moved beyond the polemical either-or.[86] The learnings from the proponents of a world-drenched theology are immense. To digest these, yet to do it critically, and to press for a full-orbed understanding of the ways of God, and what ought to be the ways of the church in this time of peril and promise, is the agenda the future writes for us.

# XV / THE VOLUNTARY CHURCH:
# A MORAL APPRAISAL

*James M. Gustafson*

American Protestantism is made up of "voluntary churches." This is true in several senses. The freedom to be religious in the manner of a man's own choice and the freedom to be nonreligious are guaranteed by the basic law of our land. Thus, from a legal point of view all religious groups are noncompulsory; there is no legal means for compelling church affiliation. Church membership is by consent. Even those churches with a "high" doctrine of infant baptism are in effect voluntary churches. Membership is not complete upon baptism; it must be confirmed in more mature years. In some instances, baptism and confirmation are not sufficient for church membership; decision and commitment after conversion are required. American Protestantism is radically "congregationalized." Many churches are of a congregational tradition in polity, and others have been democratized so that the voice of the laity bears more weight than is characteristic in many European Evangelical churches. The congregationalizing is not only political: Protestantism and even Catholicism in America seek to develop a common life among the members of a congregation, either as a whole or through various societies and groups. Finally, American Christianity is voluntary in the sense that it stresses activity and action, an exertion of the will for moral or evangelical purposes.

The contemporary American voluntary churches are rather different from the Puritan conception of the gathered church. The kind of clarity in definition of basis of membership, social control, and common discipline that informed the earlier gathered-church notion exists in only a few sects. The Puritan gathered church had three tests for membership: the experience of regenerating grace, right belief, and upright conduct. With a certainty unknown to their descendants, the Puritans believed that certain human experiences were sure and certain signs of the efficacious work of Divine Grace, that the proper definition of God could be captured in written documents, and that a man's behavior would reveal the quality of his religious faith. Since the seventeenth century, there has been an almost irresistible development of the gathered church into its compromised forms. The "gathered church" has become the "voluntary church." The decisive criterion is now the will to belong. The theological and experiential marks of authority on which the in-group was defined from the out-group have lost their power. The zest for purity in the churches has given way to an acceptance of the impossibility of its achievement, and consequently to a more or less open membership. Now, instead of being gathered out of the body of strangers into the family of saints, the strangers volunteer to join the community of those like themselves, who find something meaningful in religious life for themselves, their children, or their neighborhood. Men admire the saints among them, and perhaps wish to join their small number. If they fail, however, there is no serious disruption of church life.

### THE BASES OF BELONGING

As a result of the acceptance of the "will to belong" as the functioning basis for church membership, the principles that delineate the in-group from the out-group have shifted. The loose way in which the word "parish" is used illustrates the contemporary confusion. At one time a parish was a geographical mark of belonging, as it still is in parts of Europe. Now the word is used to refer to the people who belong to a congregation, together with their families and friends. At an earlier time it made sense to refer to a congregation gathered out of a parish; now the words "parish" and "congregation" are often used interchangeably. (In the national churches of Northern Europe "parish" and "congregation" are coextensive for reasons other than the misuse of the word parish. The "folk-church" idea is expressed in the almost universal baptism and confirmation of children, and thus almost everyone residing in the geographical territory of the parish is a member of the "congregation.") The geographical mark of parish is not very important in the voluntary church, for the place of residence is not decisive in determining the particular congregation that a family joins. The will to belong is more significant than place of residence for a family's "parish" identification. The threefold test of membership in the gathered church is thoroughly compromised, if not completely lost, and thus the religious in-group exercises relatively little theological and moral discrimination about the persons who choose to join it. The net effect is that various social and social-psychological factors become the operating principles in the determination of church membership.

The voluntary church in a secularized society is at the mercy of powerful social forces in the determination of its social boundaries.

Much evidence supports this suggestion. It is common for people to join a church in their "neighborhood." But neighborhoods no longer coincide with the political boundaries of a town, or with the ancient boundaries of a Catholic parish. In metropolitan areas the neighborhood is defined by characteristics of housing, which in a large measure reflect the level of family income. This, in turn, is governed by the achievement of the employed members of the family, often the father alone. His achievement is a product of his education, the marketability of his personality and talent, and his drive toward success. In short, the neighborhood is generally defined by the combination of factors that are used to indicate a family's position in the social stratification of the society, its social class. Thus it is common for the members of churches in a particular neighborhood to be a relatively homogeneous group.

In nonmetropolitan areas the neighborhood cannot always be defined by housing without strained efforts of gerrymandering. But this does not in itself prevent a social selectivity in church membership. With the variety of American denominations, it is usual for the prospective church member to choose among several options. He might find the church in which the liturgy is most meaningful (which may mean whose decorum is congenial to his socially defined tastes), or the church that provides the kind of preaching he likes (which may mean that which least threatens his personal and social defenses), or the church whose members are more like himself than the members of the other available churches are. The evidence from American community studies which indicates the relative social prestige of various congregations and denominations in villages and towns is by now part of the sociological commonplace. It suggests a functional relationship between membership in a particular church and one's present or hoped-for social status. Thus the congregation is at the mercy of the image of cultural and social achievement and aspiration that it represents.

Social class, however, is not the only factor at work. Since the generations of vast immigration, the national loyalties of people have often determined their church membership. Even the Roman Catholic Church, which has had more success than any other group in transplanting the geographical parish principle to a voluntaristic culture and society, bowed to the pressure for national churches. St. Casimir's, St. Stanislaus's, and St. Anthony's parishes are still likely to represent the religious centers of the Lithuanian, Polish, and Italian populations of a middle-sized American city. Among Protestants the Lutheran denominations have been the obvious example of ethnic religious loyalties. Lutherans in one city might be divided among the Norwegians, the Swedes, the Finns, and the Germans. Only now, after a century and more of life on this continent, are most of these Lutheran groups finding a basis of unity that transcends national heritage. (The basis found may be more a generalized Americanization of third and fourth generation than a common loyalty to the objective teachings and liturgies of Lutherdom.) Presbyterianism and the Disciples of Christ have represented "American" churches in the eyes of Protestant immigrants, i.e., churches of the Anglo-Saxon population.

More visible than social class or nationality groupings is the racially selective character of American church life. The racial loyalty and identification of the white community becomes the basis for a voluntary principle of exclusion. The Negro community has, in the main, no option other than to organize religious life on a racial basis. Historically, the picture is more complex, for the church has been the institution in which characteristic expressions of both religious and cultural life have been made. The social situation of the Negro in America, now undergoing rapid change, has been the milieu for a combination of religious and racial identity. The enforced segregation of churches based upon the racial voluntarism of the white population, and the cultural situation of the Negro population that has had its own religious expressions, are both social factors at the base of church life. In contrast to this, a Christian community gathered around the more objective centers of its life—Jesus Christ, the Bible, a creed, or an historic liturgy —would have no place for a racial basis of the right or the will to belong.

### THE PERVASIVENESS OF VOLUNTARISM

Denominational and interdenominational patterns of life, like local congregations, also testify to the voluntary order of participation and organization.

The same socially selective principles that work in local congregations are effective at the denominational level. Tendencies toward domination by a single class in various denominations are significant enough to make possible a rank order of American Protestantism on the basis of social status. In the main the denominations are racially segregated, with at best hardly more than token integration in any of the major ones. Nationality background, while declining in significance, is still the basis of differentiation for a number of denominations.

The patterns of ecclesiastical organization are generally democratic, with variations in form; for examples, the popular democracy of the

Disciples of Christ, and the representational democracy of the Presbyterians. The affairs of the denominations are carried on in the light of the necessity for the consent and support of the laity. Interest groups among the lay membership have significant influence in setting limits to ecclesiastical policy when their points of view are threatened. This has been seen in recent decades among the major Protestant churches in the sphere of social action. The dependence upon voluntary financial support is the agency through which lay dissent can be most powerfully registered.

Interdenominational activity in local Councils of Churches, or at state and national levels, is subject to most of the same mechanisms of government and consent that one sees in denominations. Their effectiveness in part depends upon the broadest possible support for the organization, which in turn requires highly sensitive antennae to register the presence or absence of "grass-roots" support. Like denominations, they are subject to the reluctance of the laity to grant independence of authority to elected and appointed church officials to speak for the church, particularly on moral issues.

### SOCIAL ETHICS AND THE VOLUNTARY CHURCH

The voluntary character of American church life affects the concern for social ethics at three points. First, there are detriments to, and possibilities for, effective social education and action given by the voluntary social character of Protestantism, especially by its tendency toward single-class congregations. Protestantism's participation in American social stratification and cultural values is two-sided: there are sociologically inevitable restrictions on the freedom of the church to speak and to act; and there are sociological possibilities for a lay church with access to some centers of social action in the society.

The voluntary sociological pattern raises the issue of authority in the churches. In the voluntary church, the question of authority takes particular form, namely, who speaks and acts for the churches? Theological principles and sociological structures are not harmonious with each other on this question. The voluntary church is Christ's church; but the "will to belong" does not give a sufficient basis to permit a congregational majority to speak for Christ. A covetous glance at the structure of Roman Catholicism with its views of hierarchy and priesthood cannot be satisfied. Institutional authority of a Catholic sort is both unrealistic on sociological grounds and unacceptable on theological grounds for Protestantism in America. The issue of authority is common to all democratically oriented voluntary associations, namely, the relation of popular support to effective leadership. But it takes unique form in the churches: the church acknowledges and knows a higher authority—God; but the voluntary churches are not sure who speaks and acts for him.

Thus the third point becomes clearer. What theological and socio-theological principles help us to understand what voluntary Protestantism in America can be? What can the great Christian affirmations of the work of the Holy Spirit or the presence of Christ mean in the voluntaristic church? Is the voluntary church theologically and morally viable? The remainder of this essay deals with these three issues.

### MORAL HINDRANCES AND POSSIBILITIES AT THE SOCIAL LEVEL

The social determination of the churches has wide implications for their nature as moral communities. Indeed, if a "moral" community indicates one with distinctive values that are propagated and acted upon within the group, there is evidence to doubt the existence of the church as a unique body. The consensus of values is likely to express the dominant cultural orientation of the church. At least the evidence is highly mixed; on empirical grounds, as many sociological and psychological studies have indicated, grave doubts are raised about the power of distinctively Christian ethics to shape the attitudes and outlooks, as well as the actions, of people. Some of the social factors involved require further delineation.

What factors make for social homogeneity in churches? The reasons why people belong to particular churches appear to be accidental in relation to any differentiating norms that mark the church off from other groups, or mark one Protestant congregation off from another. The urban church ecologists have shown how difficult it is to maintain a socially heterogeneous congregation in a geographical area that tends to be single-class in residential constituency. The wider movements of population, often called the "invasion-succession" patterns, tend to determine the characteristics of members of churches, as well as of other institutions in a neighborhood. Ideological as well as racial and economic factors are involved. That is, persons gather together around certain values that are held in common, or certain symbols of status toward which they aspire. Urbanism, to quote the title of a deservedly famous essay of Louis Wirth's, is "a way of life." So, one might add, are suburbanism, and the romance of the small town. The ways of life that bring people together in given areas, or form the bonds of unity among them, are brought into church life as well. Sometimes the identification with the status symbols of a group seems to require the "transfer" of church membership to another congregation if not another denomination.

Residential patterns and common ways of life are not alone in supporting social homogeneity in churches. The long leadership of a particular pastor may build up a particular "clientele" of those who find his preaching or pastoral work congenial. A local congregation might well become accepted in local tradition as one that appeals to a particular social or intellectual group by virtue of its leadership and program. In a relatively stable community, such a tradition can survive for a long time.

The tendency toward social homogeneity in American congregations presents the great temptation to equate the socially acceptable patterns of life, the approved ways of thinking and acting, with the truth of the gospel itself. An antidote to this temptation would be to create or preserve social heterogeneity within the churches. This would provide diversity of thought and opinion, and thus would temper the tendency to confuse socially conditioned ways of work, thought, and life with Christian ways. If multi-group churches are to be possible, certain social factors usually must be at work.

What factors make for social heterogeneity in churches? One might assume that the relatively stable small community would make possible social diversity in churches. Presumably, here the ethos of democracy exists at the grass-roots, and status lines are of no significance. The empirical evidence from small community studies, however, points in the other direction. In James West, *Plainville, U.S.A.,* a study of a small Missouri town, and in Vidich and Bensman, *Small Town in Mass Society,* a more recent study of a New York State community, ample evidence is given to indicate a sharp differentiation along locally defined status lines even in the small town.

It is clear that the social stratification affects the life of the churches. The unfortunate fact of rabid competition between denominations and sects in America's small towns is well known. Four or five congregations struggling for survival in towns of 500 people is not uncommon across the land. The availability of options for church membership lends itself to choosing the congregation that is most socially congenial, even in hamlets. And in both of the studies mentioned, there is also evidence of a "de-classed" population, which exists outside of the range of any of the sects. In parts of rural New England, where the religious culture is somewhat more stable (that is, where there is clearer domination of two or three Protestant denominations), there is evidence of greater social heterogeneity in congregations, but it does not alter the general picture. The small church in the small town is seldom socially inclusive in membership.

A factor that would make for heterogeneity is a non-class center of loyalty that is stronger than class identification. Perhaps the most common in parts of the United States is the ethnic loyalty. Descendants of the immigrants from a particular nation may have a residual (and sometimes more vital) identification with their ethnic group through the church; for example, the Norwegians of a small Minnesota town. Class inclusiveness has been minimized, however, by sizable migrations out of ethnic churches by the socially mobile members.

Loyalty to a liturgical or creedal tradition might be the most effective religious-social phenomenon to overcome class determination. In the case of many Lutheran congregations, one has the combination of creedal, liturgical, and ethnic components. In the case of the Protestant Episcopal Church, one sees the importance of a more objective and uniform liturgical pattern. In principle, the existence of more objective points of reference for ecclesiastical life should make possible a more inclusive church on the social level. Whether or not this is the case depends in part upon the absence of several congregations within the same creedal or liturgical tradition, each representing a particular class. Where, for example, several Protestant Episcopal churches are available in a middle-sized or large American city, they are often socially stratified within the denomination. The population in the neighborhood is one factor that makes this so; the ease with which persons can travel to a congenial congregation is another. In order for creed and liturgy to function as points transcending class identification, a small and relatively stable population seems to be necessary.

Special efforts to maintain diversity occur in most American denominations. Often the most dramatic examples of multi-class or multi-racial churches, however, are maintained only during a transitional period in the life of a neighborhood. This is especially true in the large cities. A congregation can maintain a multiracial constituency during the period in which the residential pattern of its neighborhood is multiracial. When the white community moves away en masse, as it usually does, the valiant efforts of pastors and laity to form a congregation gathered without reference to race or class often fade away. Our cities are studded with church buildings that once housed white middle or upper-middle class congregations which declined as this group moved toward the periphery of the area, then became interracial as Negroes or other groups "invaded" the area, and after a decade in this laudable inclusive pattern have tended to become almost exclusively Negro congregations.

Another pattern is the deliberate establishment of new congregations on interracial or multi-class lines. Aside from a certain theological artificiality in this procedure, other difficulties are presented. The characteristics of the ministry, reinforced by its pattern of training, often make such congregations acceptable only to persons of certain educational or social achievements. One may simply substitute, for example, multiracial single-class churches for single-racial single-class churches. Dominantly Negro pentecostal movements that seek to be inclusive are limited in their attraction to white persons not only because of racial prejudice, but also because the patterns of church life are alien to the social and intellectual expectations of educated white persons. The same selectivity might operate on other levels; emancipated, educated, socially free whites and Negroes can belong together in a multiracial congregation, but a social principle of selectivity is probably still at work.

The social and cultural conditions that create and sustain inclusive churches seldom occur in American society. The forces that make for status differentiation along economic, racial, and educational lines in the society as a whole are difficult to overcome within the life of the churches. While heterogeneity in congregations would provide a social basis for overcoming the temptation to confuse socially conditioned patterns of life with those that are divinely ordained and approved, the achievement is itself dependent upon the very human stuff of society and church.

Voluntary churches cannot expect the optimum conditions under which to achieve the purposes and mission of a people called to be obedient to Christ any more than ambitious intellectuals can free themselves from the fatigue that is part of their bodily existence. The human social conditions under which the church exists is part of the stuff of its life. The problems and possibilities for a Christian moral community under the given social conditions can be assessed more precisely.

### PROBLEMS OF A SOCIALLY HETEROGENEOUS CHURCH

The socially inclusive congregation may have difficulties in maintaining interaction and communication between persons representing various socially defined groups. The distinctions between the college-educated and those without higher learning, the bankers and the welders, the farmers and the urbane sophisticates, the adolescents from economically affluent families and those from economically marginal families, all make the processes of forming a moral community difficult. The points of social and cultural differentiation are not dropped upon entering the portals of the House of God. The acknowledgment of a universal center of loyalty and common life does not in itself create a common vocabulary, a common definition of human needs, a common outlook on the purpose and mission of the church, or a common basis of interpersonal relationships.

One often finds as a result that clear social differentiations take place *within* a congregation. For example, in the recruitment of lay leadership for the church, there is a tendency to select persons who have achieved positions of leadership in voluntary associations or vocations outside of the church. The reasons for this are complex. In part the experience and talent that make a person conspicuous in the secular world are often precisely those needed for effective organization in a church. Competence in teaching, in financial matters, in public address and parliamentary procedure, and in exerting influence to gain support for various activities all have utility in the church as well as outside. From a critical point of view, one notes that it is not always easy for talented laymen to revise their ways of work in the light of the theologically defined purposes that govern the life of the church. The norms by which effectiveness are judged in church life are not necessarily the same as those used in other organizations. Thus, a redirection, if not a transformation, of the ways of work of the talented might be hoped for but is not always forthcoming.

The selection of leadership, however, is not always made on the grounds of the utility of talents. It is sometimes motivated by the prestige that the high secular status of the laymen might bring to the church. The capturing and borrowing of prestige often takes place apart from any religious-social rationality that might be involved. There is evidence of this in various phases of congregational life. Some ministers take obvious delight when they can claim a socially prominent person to be a leader in their church. Indeed, occasionally one finds a minister who identifies himself as the pastor of "Mr. Corporation President's Church." Another evidence of prestige-borrowing is in the financial campaigns of the churches. This particular gimmick, for example, was an important device in the high-powered, professionally run fund-raising campaigns of the past decade in American church life. The commitment of the high-status man has the effect of initiating a falling row of dominoes for all who seek some social identification with him.

Another instance of social differentiation within inclusive congregations takes place in various organized groups within the church. Age groupings, for example, have commonly divided various women's groups from each other. The level of interest intended in a particular program can become socially selective and inadvertently call attention to sharp diversities. This can be seen in the development of fairly high-level study programs for adults. The nature of the material to be studied acts as a factor of social differentiation. Furthermore, voluntary groups in churches are often divided by the formation of cliques within them. Men's and women's groups are sometimes divided by factors of social congeniality, and by the absorption into church life of friendship groups primarily directed by life in the residential community. The evidence of the adolescent cliques, drawn often along lines of locally defined status, is apparent to most youth workers. The evidence analyzed by August Hollingshead, for example, in *Elmtown's Youth,* presents hypotheses for the activities of young people in churches that are almost immediately confirmed on the basis of both unrefined and more disciplined impressions.

Leadership is difficult in a socially diverse congregation. In most Protestant denominations, promotional and educational material is clearly directed, though probably unintentionally so, to a broad middle class. Stewardship leaflets, church school material, denomination journals, official reports of denominational agencies, and other published literature reflect the cultural and social orientations dominant among the writers and the sponsors. Evidence indicates that for Protestantism as a whole a middle-class target is probably accurate, but it is not always easy for Negroes and Puerto Ricans of the inner city to identify themselves with the literature, nor is it certain that techniques devised in New York to be effective among Protestant suburbanites will work in marginal churches on the plains of North Dakota, in spite of the nationalization of taste and values.

Ministerial leadership is confronted with special problems by social inclusiveness. If not by social origin, then by education and training, a social distance is created between the minister and those groups in his church who are marginal to his own educational, social, and cultural dispositions. Effective communication with those who do not share the minister's own cultural milieu is difficult. There is no evidence that the minister, any more than the layman, is necessarily emancipated from his own social biases by virtue of his religious faith or his theological education. His professional and social aspirations, as well as those of his family, are likely to orient his patterns of life and ways of work in a direction more toward one group than another in the congregation.

The difficulties enumerated indicate that it is by no means a simple step from social diversity to the development of a religious and moral community in which a consensus comes into being. Yet social diversity offers clear possibilities toward this end that do not exist in more homogeneous religious groups.

### POSSIBILITIES OF A SOCIALLY HETEROGENEOUS CHURCH

Social diversity makes more visible the normative and essential inclusiveness of the religious and moral community. Where there are rather obvious marks of differentiation on a very human level, one is likely to become aware that the center of life in this group is in part removed from the human sameness. The existence of people representing different races, economic states of life, educational achievement, and political points of view in one congregation calls more vivid attention to the love, the forgiveness, the life, and the meanings that the church represents on a universal plane. The actual human materials that make up the complexes of races and cultures existing in the world-wide church have to some extent a microcosmic reflection in a heterogeneous local congregation. Thus the drive toward inclusiveness that is present at the heart of the Christian gospel can be manifest, not to demonstrate a kind of tolerance, nor to show that persons of different life-orientations can live together in a given voluntary association, but to testify to the unity that is in Jesus Christ. The acceptance of diversity is then the religious and social implication of the acknowledgment of a common Lord of life.

The richness of the inclusive church is manifest in other ways. The physical presence of heterogeneity makes it more difficult for a congregation to confuse a particular social mode of life with the religiously acceptable and divinely ordained one. For example, if believers in the welfare state who have a clear Christian devotion and articulate Christian convictions are in conversation with those who believe in the sanctity of the free market, the potential idolatry of either pattern might be limited. But this function of a negative check against idolatry can be turned into something more fruitful in the moral community.

Diversity in a congregation ought to make possible the social and intellectual interaction out of which two important things can occur. First, and most likely, persons with different political and social orientations can become better informed about the bases of judgment of those whom they oppose. Their own thinking might come not only to include a new measure of tolerance for other points of view, but also be modified. The congregation, in meeting, might become a place in which, under the common center of faith, the points of view of persons are developed. The common point of community life, the Christian gospel, might be brought to bear upon the judgments and opinions of various persons. They could possibly see new facets or dimensions in the realm of social and political judgments: dimensions of morality, and finally of faith.

Second, and more difficult, would be the development of some significant moral consensus within the congregation. Moral consensus brought into being under the conditions of social and cultural diversity could not be simply the projection of the ideology of a particular interest group on the screen of divine approval. Rather, it would represent the processes of growth toward community based on a common faith and loyalty shared by different groups. In a voluntary church in which lay participation is more than an expression of the will to belong, there might be the study and conversation that could meaningfully lead to the formation of some common expression of opinion. The religious conditions presumably are present in essence, if not in actuality. These, in contemporary parlance, are the members' acceptance of each other as persons, and not as the manifestations of partial interests or partial functions. Such acceptance would be the social counterpart to the common experience of standing under God's judgment, receiving God's forgiveness, and sharing together in the new life in Christ. Under these religious conditions, one might expect candid and informed exchange of opinion and ideas about responsibility in the world. The imperative element is also present, for common loyalty to Jesus Christ requires that thinking and judgment be brought under the discipline of seeking a way of life and action commensurate with the norms of this community.

The realization of the possibilities latent in the socially inclusive church requires a voluntarism of a different sort than that implied in the will to belong. It depends upon a genuine exercise of the will on the part of the leadership of the church, and on the part of the persons who share more passively in its life. Persons, and hopefully congregations together, would have to exercise the capacity to make decisions under reflection and discussion. Such an achievement in church life is not to be expected in any mass movement, but perhaps will be done in those centers where laity and clergy accept in grace the determination of the will to shape personal and corporate life in the image of God's work and will.

### PROBLEMS AND POSSIBILITIES OF A SOCIALLY HOMOGENEOUS CHURCH

In a sense that pricks the conscience of reflective Christians, most congregations are already moral communities. A latent if not explicit consensus already exists on the major things to be desired in life, the major purposes to be achieved in history, and the principles by which judgments are made. The dissatisfaction comes with the impression that the moral consensus reflects social homogeneity, rather than a community that wills to become a center of life in Jesus Christ. Some aspects of this problematic character have been suggested. A rehearsal of these, however, ought not to keep us from accepting such homogeneity as a place of opportunity for moral witness and action. Some aspects of this opportunity can also be specified.

The problems of a socially determined moral consensus in churches have been most noted in suburbia, but they are by no means there exclusively. The same mistaken identification of the divinely approved order with the social style of life that occurs in Park Forest, Illinois, occurs also in Lanyon, Iowa. The actual patterns that are given community approval differ, but principle is the same. This mistake is made in part because of the absence among church members of diversity in experience and perspectives. The parochialism, or provincialism, leads to a limited view of the world; the absence of diverse groups limits the contact with other sub-cultures. The blissful freedom from conflict, or presence of harmony that men desire (and therefore presumably God approves), is more readily achievable by both laity and clergy. The minister can identify himself with the people with less sense of the over-againstness of the gospel by implicitly assuming that his calling is to consent to the consensus that exists, and to be its servant.

There are, however, two possibilities for a critical moral witness that are greater under the conditions of homogeneity. The first lies in a basic simplification of task, due to the relatively uniform culture that is present among the constituency of a congregation. Minister and laity alike can have a more thorough self-understanding of the one culture represented, in part because it is not incumbent upon them to know many cultures represented in the heterogeneous group. In suburbia, for example, there is no reason why a minister cannot study most of the literature on the contemporary American suburb, its social structure, its tastes and values, the occupational orientation that is present among husbands, the particular patterns that marital difficulties take, and the characteristic patterns that idolatry has in this social milieu. The same self-knowledge can be fostered within the church among its members. The understanding, critique, and constructive possibilities of suburban existence in the light of the church's ministry ought to have a sharpness and pertinence that are increased by virtue of the focus on one sub-culture. The same would be true of rural communities.

The second possibility exists in the middle and upper-middle class congregations. This is an access to influence upon persons in positions of social power. The persons who exercise social power through the decisions and policies of governments, voluntary associations, corporations, and universities or colleges, are often members of Protestant congregations. Acceptance of this social fact as an opportunity does not imply surrender to an individualistic orientation in the church's ministry. A Peale, a Samuel Shoemaker, a Billy Graham, seems to isolate the person from the complexities of his involvement in the world on the assumption that a religiously and mentally healthy man can change the structures, or ignore them. Because they do this does not mean that no other way to deal with middle and upper class churches exists. On the contrary, the church can help the person in a position of power to interpret and understand his job, and his exercise of responsibility, as a place for moral action in the society.

The homogeneous congregation need not be accepted simply as the fate of population movements, nor the manifestation of the shallowness of American Christianity, though in part it is both. It can be seen as a gift of mixed value, but nevertheless one in which the task of the moral witness of the Christian faith needs to be made under more seductive circumstances, and with some potential impact upon the wider society.

A sociological framework is only one in which a moral assessment of the voluntary church can be made. Social conditioning is not a uniformly bad influence on Christian moral community. But a study of it raises the further problem of authority and consensus, for the churches live under an authority that cannot be equated with majority rule.

#### AUTHORITY AND CONSENT IN THE VOLUNTARY CHURCH

Voluntary churches have always had grave difficulties with the problem of authority in the church, and much more so when the will to belong replaces the theological principles of the gathered churches. In the earlier periods, and even today in the lively sects, there was and is a consent to objective norms of belief, conduct, and experience. With the absence of clarity about what the contemporary voluntary church is gathered around, or by whom it is gathered, the danger of anarchy in some important spheres of its life is ever present.

It is argued by many that the very idea of a "voluntary" church in a democratic sense is theologically false. P. T. Forsyth, a defender of chastened congregationalism, suggested that the church is an absolute monarchy, with Christ as its King, and thus echoed some of the seventeenth-century fathers of his church. The church is called into being by Jesus Christ, as each of its members is led to it by the divine initiative. The church is ruled over by Jesus Christ; it has no other Lord but Christ, and all earthly church power and authority is derived from him and is under submission to him. This tends to imply that we belong to the church by consent to participate in and be ruled by Christ, and not by our collective judgment achieved through the processes of democratic voluntary societies.

The rather normal tensions in voluntary associations between the responsible participation of the members and the initiative and power of the leaders is quite a more complicated issue in the church. For in the church both the leaders of the congregation and its members consent to a higher authority. This higher authority does not exist by virtue of its authorization by lower authorities, nor is it simply encompassed in some constitutional formula. It is a Person, known through Scripture and tradition, but in a living way never completely reduced to them. In this section our concern is with the more visible and tangible aspects of the issue of authority; in the following section we shall be concerned with the more exclusively theological dimensions.

An interpretation of the church as a moral community requires that three points of attention be kept in mind. One is the objectively given sources of insight and norms for the community—the Bible and the writings of the tradition. Another is the vast body of those who are members by virtue of the will to belong. The third is the position of the "expert," or the person whose function it is to define the purposes of the church at various levels of specificity, and to bring persons into consent to them. How are these three actually related in the American voluntary church? What possibilities are there for the development of a moral community in these relations? The American situation might be seen better if contrasted with a vignette of the far less voluntary national churches of Protestant Europe.

Where there is a creedal and liturgical pattern in a national church, to which the overwhelming portion of the population belong by virtue of baptism and confirmation, the clarity of objective norms exceeds most of the documents and patterns of life available to the voluntary American churches. The American exceptions would be Lutheran and Episcopal churches. In the national churches the liturgy contains an explicit theological pattern, including the confession of faith in one of the historic creeds. The clergy receive their appointments with at most the assent of the congregations, and are not dependent upon the continued personal support of the people to stay in office. The relatively high degree of autonomy of the clergy in relation to the people enables the minister to speak from the framework of Scripture and creeds without any particular concern for the cultivation of explicit consensus on the part of the members of the church on any particularized issue. Behind this is assumed an objective rightness and truth of the word proclaimed in the church. The net effect is an explicit definition of the purpose and mission of the church in traditional terms, a clergy whose responsibility is defined more in relation to this tradition than it is in relation to the people, and a congregation that is passive in its assent to the authority of creeds, liturgy, and clergy. One effect is the absence of those elements of voluntary life that make the American Protestant laity responsible for the definition of particular purposes and activities in the church. The absence of voluntarism minimizes the activity of the laity. It also makes the life of the church less specific in its relevance to the moral actions of the people, and the life of the clergy simpler (unless they are plagued by problems of conscience and theology, as many are) for they need not develop a lay consensus.

The American voluntary church makes for a more complex working arrangement between the communal norms established by the Christian community in history, the role of the interpreting "expert," and the church members who have the will to belong. *In the complexity given us precisely by the voluntary character of the churches lies the vitality of American Christianity.* First, a description of the processes of authority and consensus in voluntary churches is called for; then the assertion that this is a major asset of the American Christian movement can be defended.

Two important factors make *consent,* rather than assent, the characteristic intellectual and personal relationship between the laity on the one hand, and the interpretation of the normative principles on the other. The first is inherent in Protestantism itself, and more so in the more radical Protestantism of the United States. Protestants claim, and rightly have, a direct access to the norms. They have been given the responsibility as individuals and as persons gathered in congregations to have personal faith, personal knowledge of the God represented in the Scripture and the creeds. Casual assent to doctrine, to the objective and external authority of the church, and to the words of theological or ethical experts is foreign to the sense of personal acknowledgment and participation in Christ and his church that is at the heart of Protestantism. Entailed in the expectation of personal faith and responsible participation is the possibility of heterodoxy: of interpretation, understanding, and experience that is somewhat marginal to the traditionally normative proclamations and expectations of the church. For example, out of the serious responsibilities thrust upon the gathered Congregationalists of New England came Unitarianism, partly because of the Protestant expectation of personal experience and reflection upon what is proclaimed by the church and encased in its documents. The expectation of personal response entails the possibility of diversity in the interpretation of the object to which men respond, and requires that the consensus-forming processes go on in order to maintain consistency within the churches. Mere assent to objective truth, dogmatically defined and proclaimed, and inflexibly dramatized in a particular liturgy, would be foreign to the notion of personal response and responsibility that is inherent in Protestantism.

The second factor in the American scene, historically related to the Protestant cultural heritage, is the pervasive democratization of social life in our nation. Responsible participation in the consensus-forming processes is normative in many institutions of American life. Not only in government and voluntary associations, but even in modern business administration, the maximum participation in decision-making is accepted as a basic principle. To be sure, in many organizations assent has displaced consent; the expert professional authorities formulate the policies or the belief-system, and the membership acquiesces, or is simply propagandized into accepting the opinion of others. But the possibility of revolt exists in labor unions, professional associations, and interest groups, as well as at the polls of governmental election. American Christians do not shed this democratic heritage when they stand in the presence of ministers and the Bible, or of church agencies for social action. They expect to register their dissent from the experts, and even from the norms. They expect to have to be brought into a personal conviction of the rightness or truth of the statements being made, the policies being formed, and the actions being counseled.

The religious and cultural conditions of American Protestantism then maximize the participation of the laity in the consensus-forming processes, at least normatively. Particularly where their own interests are most seriously touched by the actions and proclamations of the church, the laity are quick to express dissent, and to claim exemption from obligations to adhere to what is counseled. The leadership of American churches, then, is confronted with a more difficult but equally more significant task than is often required of the leadership of national churches. The norms—Bible, creed, etc.—must be interpreted in a way that is convincing to the laity. No doubts, dissents, or questions can be ruled out simply by recourse to external authority—whether traditional, rational, or personal. The truth and rightness of the norms has to become an inward truth and rightness, in virtually an existential sense, if the norms are to exercise any compelling power in the thinking and actions of laymen. Thus the American churches are organized in ways that normatively (though not always in fact) can create consensus; that is, they are activized in a host of voluntary age, sex, and interest groups.

The interpretation of the norms is one of the media for consensus formation. Even though this is done by experts (whose degree of expertness varies from the careful Biblical scholar to the inspired evangelist or prophet for whom everything is *prima facie* obvious), it is not convincing on the basis of the credentials of the interpreter alone. The points of reference within which the "expert" does his work in part define the acceptability of what he has to say. For example, few laymen would quarrel with a minister's interpretation of St. Paul's view of law relative to the Jewish understanding of *torah,* for few would claim the competence to dispute it. But should the minister choose to interpret the law of love in relation to the problems of international relations, or of social welfare legislation, he is inviting dispute with the laity. The political and social points of reference of the latter are in a sphere in which the layman believes himself to have competence at least as great as that of the clergy, and usually more so; they touch areas in which his personal interest and conviction are involved; and they represent a more particularized moral and social judgment than the issue of St. Paul and the *torah*. The authority of the religious expert is not granted by virtue of his knowledge and ordination, and therefore neither quiet assent nor vigorous obedience is forthcoming. The leader becomes a person whose function it is *to give guidance to a consensus-forming process,* in and through which particular judgments (including his own) can be clarified and be brought to bear on the relevant points of action.

The size of the sphere within which the consensus-forming process takes place is dependent generally on the breadth of the minister's own concerns, or those of his denomination. A minister of a sect that confines itself to rightly dividing the word of truth with reference only to the Scofield Bible or to a legalistic version of the Christian life, might well develop a moral and religious community with a considerable in-group identification. But the minister and church that seek to understand the norms in relation to the rightness of policies concerning man's temporal good in society will have to cope with greater diversity of opinion, and will have greater difficulty in coming to common consent. Congregations expect to be convinced, and expect to share in the process by which convictions are expressed in a corporate way.

The voluntarism (in the sense of requiring a consent of the will and the mind) that characterizes American Christianity is sometimes lamented because it entails all the risks of the voluntary church (in the social sense of the will to belong). Thus suburban culture Christianity, or the idolatries of rural pietism, are all possibilities entailed in this basic principle. But it is this voluntarism (in both senses) that also entails the possibility that American Christianity will continue as a *social movement,* and not merely as an esoteric, grace-dispensing, irrelevant-to-the-modern-world, objectified and ossified institution. The requirements of consensus formation (with varying degrees of diversity within it) provide the conditions under which churches can become moral communities, representing the cares and the possibilities made known in the gospel within the life of the American people. The prophetic and yet responsible participation of the churches in the moral judgments and social policies that are part of life in the world has maximum opportunities within voluntary churches.

The exercise and fructification of these opportunities, of course, is not automatically forthcoming from the existence of these conditions. Consensus is not developed until the norms of the Christian movement are taken with seriousness in relation to life in the world. The training of leadership for voluntary churches requires not only understanding of the group processes, and the effective means of communication, but also of the norms of the church on the one hand, and the issues in the world to be spoken to and acted upon on the other. But there is no stronger reason to despair about the problems of culture Christianity (which exist as strikingly where the norms of Christianity are preserved with a kind of museum-like purity in other parts of the Western world) than there are reasons to view voluntarism as a major asset of American church life. One cannot conjure an easy alternative to the voluntary church that would potentially be as significant in the development of a Christian moral community. Voluntary churches are the agencies in which the more objective norms of the church are interpreted and given consent. In the complexity of the consensus-forming process, given by the voluntary character of the churches, lies the vitality of American Christianity.

### GOD'S PRESENCE AND HUMAN CONSENSUS

Behind the confidence that American Christianity has in the voluntary churches there lie two possible directions of theological assumption. One is that God is so remote, and so silent, that the life of the church is dependent upon the human cogitation and action that take place in the democratic processes. The formation of a moral community in this case is the effort of a socially contracted group who agree to certain basic principles and seek the implications of these in the areas that require moral decision. This assumption is, probably, regnant within American church life, at least in the churches deeply affected by the Enlightenment and its aftermath.

The second theological assumption is that God is present, and is seeking to speak his word in the life of the church. Although one cannot claim full confidence that the moral consensus of the church is the voice of God, nevertheless his Spirit is present in human deliberation and action. The moral community is called into being by its Lord, nurtured by its participation in his life, and guided by its understanding of his present living Word in and through the life of the congregation. He has witnessed in the prophets and in Jesus Christ, in the events of Israel's history, and in the history of the church. Scripture points toward him, what he seeks to do and what he seeks to say. The moral community is a religious community in the sense of a community gathered in faith, trusting in God and loyal to him. Its deliberation and action are expressions of its efforts to discern God's will and way. The voluntary congregation seeks to walk in the way of the Lord. It has a living Lord who leads it.

All the moral and historical realism of our time tends to make us skeptical of (1) assuming that God can speak through the socially conditioned moral community of a congregation, and (2) assuming that if he did, any difference would be made. We have come to view the church as a human community more under the aspect of sin than of grace; its idolatries are clearer than its obedience to God; its institutionalization is more visible than its moral dedication; its human initiative and activity are more obvious than God's creative and redeeming presence. We are drawn further into doubt by the kind of confidence congregations who really believe that God is present and speaking have in the judgments that they make collectively as groups, and personally as members of groups. In the light of these considerations, we are more likely to defend theologically the *critical, limiting* effects of the consensus-forming process. Just as in Reinhold Niebuhr's famous aphorism about political democracy, so with reference to the church, we are likely to see that the capacities for injustice make voluntaristic churches necessary. Critical voices in the consensus process keep the natural dispositions of the psuedo-Christians from being paraded as divinely authorized. Many theologically alert American Christians do not have confidence in the historical presence and the continuity of God's forgiving and renewing activity made evident in his earthly presence in the humanity of Jesus Christ, and witnessed to by the resurrection narrative. What they perceive is God's absence.

The theological viability of the voluntary church can be substantiated only by a new examination of both the doctrine of the church and the life of the church. Persuasive evidence is more difficult to find pertaining to the latter than the former, but affirmations can be made in both respects.

Doctrinally, the voluntary church is a possibility because of the actuality and the *universality* of the presence and power of God. Traditionally, the defense of the voluntary church has been made more in terms of the *particularity* of the presence and power of God among the gathered saints, who have personally experienced and known his judgment and redeeming grace. A Christian was discerned by certain faithful visible signs to be one whom God elected—religious experience, moral rectitude, and correct belief. These signs were his admission ticket to the fellowship of believers, and his church membership was a declaration of obedience and a submission to discipline. The confidence expressed was finally in the Lordship of Christ over all things, but a Lordship exclusively mediated to those who testified to its presence in the visible signs. Thus the confidence in voluntariness was limited to the few, and the temptation to assume a moral and spiritual superiority was often too great to resist. The churches felt they could virtually legislate for the society—witness most recently the prohibition of the production and sale of alcoholic beverages. A strong moral consensus could be developed, but it was generally within such a narrow sphere of reference points that in effect the universality of God's ordering work and redeeming grace was denied.

The stress on the particularity of the presence of God to the gathered community of regenerate believers has led more often to exclusiveness and to narrowness in moral outlook than to responsible openness to the world. As the believers in historical apostolic succession assume that there is a particular channel of special grace running through the history of the church, so the exclusive voluntary church tends to assume that the forms and manifestations of God's ordering and redeeming work are confined to those who have voluntarily submitted themselves to Jesus Christ in a particular way. Implicit in this ecclesiology is the assumption that Christ really did not die for all men, but only for those who have had certain experience of his presence. Implicit also is the failure to realize that the risen Christ is Lord over all things, and not just over the things pertaining to individual life and the salvation of individual souls.

The Puritans were an exception to some of these distortions, for the Christ known in the church and acknowledged by the gathered congregation was Lord over all. Their gathered churches sought to define the import of the God known in experience for the life of the world around them. But within the assumption of a differentiating, virtually visible status given to the saints was the temptation to take a magisterial rather than ministerial attitude toward the world. That is, the community of the elect might well claim too much for itself in defining what is the right and the good for the humanity of which it is a part.

In contrast to the assumptions of the gathered church, the doctrinal possibility of the voluntary church lies in the universality of the presence of God, of his ordering and restoring activity in the realm of the temporal, the spatial, the human. Congregations are gathered around the one Lord, expressing through their participation not only the promptings of his Spirit, but also their will to belong to him. Church members are those who will to participate in the life and knowledge revealed in Jesus Christ, and in his people. Neither their presence nor their absence conditions the ultimate reality of God's presence in the church and the world. They are gathered to One who lives and rules in spite of their cultural conditioning, their waywardness, their organizational activities, and their distortions of his will and his way. They are gathered to him through various sorts of religious experience, and in various states of clarity or confusion about the meaning of God's will and way for man. The basic foundation of their being together is not their own social contract to come together, but the objectivity of God's work, the universality of his reign, the particularities of his proffered forgiveness of each man and of men together, and the promise of participation in the newness of life made known in Jesus Christ.

The *voluntary* character of the church, then, does not have its first importance *theologically*. The first order of theological importance is not attached to the human will to belong, or to the willing acceptance of responsibility as a community to God for other men. The first order of theological importance lies in God—the person, the power, the ordering work, the reconciler. The *acknowledgment* of him is the basis of belonging—an acknowledgment that brings with it the personal dimensions of fidelity and confidence in him. The voluntary principle as manifest in the consensus-forming process is of the second order of importance, and can be seen as one of the ways by which those who acknowledge God are brought together in a common understanding of what God wills *of them* in their situation of responsibility. If one can restore the significance of the word "practical" to the high status it has in the Kantian use of the "practical reason," one can say that the voluntary character of the church is of practical importance. It is the human organization of life through which a Christian moral community can come into existence, and from which influence and action move into the world.

The acceptance of the principle of the voluntary church as a practical principle may help to keep the points of reference open to the world. On the one hand, when the voluntary principle moves toward the first order of theological importance in the definition of the church, the consensus of the community begins to take on a rigid, legalistic, and finally idolatrous character. When *assent* or submission to the consensus becomes the line by which the distinction between the in-group and the out-group is sharply drawn (the saved and the unsaved, the saints and the sinners), the sphere of its references is reduced, and tendencies toward a false exclusivism occur. On the other hand, when the practical principle of voluntariness is *not* taken seriously, the members of the church either (1) simply participate in the objective dispensing of law and gospel, or the means of grace, or (2) bring no sense of obligation to explore the meaning of the gospel for the common life of man, and thus they simply reflect the consensus of their class, ethnic group, or political and economic ideologies.

The consensus-forming processes take place in the human activities of the churches, and if related to the universality of the Lordship of Christ they necessarily include the serious consideration of the spheres of human responsibility outside of the church. They are parts of the media of the mission of God's people, part of the vocation of God's ministry in the world. Their ideological dignity lies in their practical function (for it is not necessary to assume that anything that is practical has no theological dignity!). Just as so mixed a moral character as King David could through his violent and gracious actions become the practical means by which God's will and way were both made known and actualized in the life of Israel, so also so mixed a moral community as the voluntary churches can become a means of God's will and way in our time. Just as so doubting a person as Jeremiah could be sure both that God put his words in his mouth, and that the day he was born was worthy of a curse, so the mixed human community, seeking to come to a common life in our time, can be responsibly prophetic. As the very manhood of Jesus, with the limitations of culture, of body, and of sphere of relationships and responsibilities, could become the means of God's self-disclosure, so the human practical principles of voluntary church, with their own severe limitations, can embody something of God's presence and God's way.

The concerns of those gathered around the universal reign of God are as extensive as that reign. Yet the actions are set by the conditions under which men live, as precise and limited as the spheres of life extending out from the congregation permit—politics, urban problems, civil rights, consumer mentality, disarmament, alcoholism, and business policies. The pertinence of the moral consensus is related to the concreteness of the human involvement of the congregation. This is a part of the dignity of the practicality and limitations of a human Christian community. The particular social situation of a particular congregation puts the teeth into its moral consensus. Dostoyevski indicated that it is easier to profess a universal unbodied love for all men than to love the man in the same room who blows his nose too loudly and sneezes too often. A moral consensus developed with reference to the annoying issues in which self and group interest are involved is prophetic in the great tradition of the prophets.

The practical theological dignity of the voluntary church is no mean one. It provides some of the concrete human materials in which God seeks to speak and make his order known. The voluntary character of the church is important, for apart from the attention that men give to what God is doing and saying, the vineyard God has sowed produces wild grapes. The voluntary American church at its best joins on the one hand the sociologically conditioned character of life with, on the other hand, the divine presence and word of God in a morally significant consensus-forming process.

# XVI / "SANE" AS A VOLUNTARY ORGANIZATION

*Homer A. Jack*

The National Committee for a Sane Nuclear Policy (SANE) was organized in 1957 because of a need felt by some Americans that increased pressure had to be put on the Eisenhower Administration to achieve a nuclear test-ban agreement. Its organizers were chiefly leaders of existing peace groups who realized that they were not sufficiently concentrating on an issue which no longer involved only religious or secular pacifists but a whole new class of advocates of nuclear disarmament. Beginning in May, 1957, exploratory efforts were made on the need and receptivity of an emergency test-ban campaign—at a time when the Campaign for Nuclear Disarmament (CND) was also being established in England. In November, 1957, SANE began by experimentally inserting an advertisement into *The New York Times* which began: "We Are Facing a Danger Unlike Any Danger That Has Ever Existed." As a result of this single advertisement, widely and spontaneously reprinted in many parts of the country, the tiny group of organizers had a burgeoning movement on its hands. SANE groups formed in cities all over the United States and demanded leadership and organizational services from the founders in New York. By the end of 1958, the three nuclear powers had agreed to a moratorium on nuclear tests. It was sufficiently unstable, however, for SANE to realize that a brief campaign was illusory. A more permanent organization had to be built.

Within a few years, SANE became almost a typical, national, social action organization. It now maintains national headquarters in New York City, with three executives—an executive director, a program director, and a fund-raiser—and twice as many clerical employees. In addition, it maintains a U.N. lobby and a Washington office, the latter manned by a political action director. SANE has approximately 125 local committees, mostly in urban or university centers from Massachusetts to California. SANE's mailing list—of active contributors—numbers 18,000 families, and at least 7,000 additional families are on local mailing lists but not contributing to the national office. SANE WORLD, the organization's newsletter, reaches 20,000 homes, and its pamphlets and other literature are widely used in schools, churches, and other institutions. SANE's national budget for several years has reached $200,000 annually, including special projects but not including the budgets of local committees, some of which have full-time executives. Today SANE has all the earmarks of a "cause" organization—including usually an annual deficit and perennial attacks. The attacks consist of those from the right, including *The National Review,* and those from the left, including *The National Guardian.*

Like most voluntary groups, SANE grew so fast that its structure and activities were not well planned, although on its National Board were veteran organizers of dozens of American committees. SANE was initially conceived as a short-duration campaign, not another feature on the American organizational landscape. Yet with its implicit decision in 1958-59 to become at least quasi-permanent, SANE faced many of the organizational problems which its founders somehow hoped to avoid.

## POLICY

The policy of SANE initially was limited to obtaining a nuclear test-ban treaty. Yet increasingly the whole field of disarmament had to be discussed by the National Board to give the test ban a correct political setting. Thus in 1958-59 the policy goal of the organization broadened to include general disarmament and a strengthened U.N. organization. In 1961, during the Berlin crisis, the policy further broadened to include solutions to political crisis situations which could lead to nuclear war. By 1964, the policy had widened even further, to include judgments about numerous military strategies. The National Board still hesitated, however, to turn the organization into a SANE *foreign* policy committee.

SANE's policy was spelled out neither in sentimental nor in absolutist terms. While undeniably there was an emotional basis for policy, efforts were increasingly made for policy statements to have an intellectual and rational appeal. Also while at least a third of the organizers of SANE may have been pacifists, they had sufficient restraint to frame SANE policy in non-pacifist or at least nuclear pacifist terms. Thus the policy statements of SANE appealed to publics in the U.S. which were ripe for peace action and to whom the rhetoric of the existing peace organizations, mostly pacifist, had little or no appeal.

## DEMOCRATIZATION

The control of SANE initially was in the hands of its founders, a small group of concerned leaders living chiefly in New York City and active primarily in other organizations. The interim, campaign nature of the group precluded any initial plans for the democratization of the new organization. Indeed, there was no category of members of the organization for several years. There were only contributors and active participants. Gradually, however, the local committees wanted a greater share in the making of policy. They formed a Council of Chartered Local Committees and this met at the time of the annual national conferences. Increasingly, National Board members were elected by the Council of Chartered Local Committees. By 1964, one-third of the National Board of 45 persons were thus elected from local committees through the Council. In 1960-61, national membership in SANE was established, although national members still do not directly elect members of the National Board.

While the trend has been increasingly toward the democratization of SANE, resistances have remained, especially in terms of time and money. To conduct a thoroughly democratic organization on a nationwide basis is time-consuming and expensive, especially for the travel of representatives from all parts of the country. SANE's sister organization, the United World Federalists, is much more democratically organized; yet the latter's National Council is geographically representative only because its members attend meetings at their own expense.

## IDEOLOGICAL INDEPENDENCE

Another problem facing the National Board of SANE, especially as the organization became permanent, was one of ideological influence. Peace and disarmament, in an environment of some of the coldest years of the cold war, were ideologically sensitive issues. The founders and National Board of SANE may have been "soft" on peace, but they were never soft on Communism. On a local level, however, a few supporters were sympathetic to Communism and saw in the SANE organization one of the few opportunities in post-McCarthy U.S.A. to participate in a sensitive political movement. None of these persons were ever members of the National Board which, in 1959-60, discussed how best to discourage the participation by Communists even on the local level. Some National Board members, such as Norman Thomas, wanted SANE to handle the matter as did the ACLU and the United World Federalists. This would have involved the issuance of a statement indicating that Communists were not wanted (although such a statement would, it was conceded, not necessarily deter a hard-core Communist). Other Board members wished that there might be "some other way" of handling this problem.

Before the Board had time to arrive at its own solution, U.S. Senator Thomas Dodd publicly indicated that there was some Communist infiltration in a few SANE chapters and threatened to denounce a huge rally SANE was planning for Madison Square Garden in New York City featuring Walter Reuther, Eleanor Roosevelt, and Alf Landon. With this prodding, the National Board made a policy statement on May 26, 1960, welcoming only those individuals to the organization who had a single standard in judging foreign policy. This probably did not prevent a few covert Communists from remaining in the organization, or joining it. The action did offend some members as a kind of latter-day McCarthyism. This charge was unfair, since any private organization should be able to set forth its own membership requirements, as Americans for Democratic Action and the American Civil Liberties Union for more than a decade have done. In any case, few Board members are happy, in retrospect, about the handling of this difficult matter.

## FINANCES

Finance has always been a chronic problem with SANE. From the beginning, one of its chief aims was influencing national policy and thus it never even applied for federal tax exemption on contributions to its treasury. Foundation gifts or even large donations from individuals were practically excluded for this reason.

SANE's budget has ranged from about $50,000 in its first 12-month period to almost $200,000 annually in 1963-64. A surprising amount comes from modest—$10.00—contributions. A few financial angels are sane! Those few looking to SANE have given for special projects, especially the newspaper advertisements which have been so much a hallmark of SANE activity. During the Berlin crisis in the summer of 1961, SANE inserted full-page advertisements in a dozen newspapers throughout the U.S. This cost some $35,000, but put SANE's alternative to nuclear war over Berlin before more than ten million readers.

## IMAGE

One of the problems facing any permanent foreign policy organization is that of image—to the American people, the American government, and the people and governments overseas. SANE has tried to develop an independent image. SANE has become a non-aligned peace organization working in a nation aligned in the cold war.

Initially, SANE advocated a nuclear policy which was not that of the U.S. Government and indeed was parallel at times to the policy of the Soviet Government. By the autumn of 1958, however, U.S. policy had come around to agreeing in principle to the desirability of a test-ban agreement separated from other collateral disarmament measures, and it had agreed to a test-ban moratorium with the U.S.S.R. and the U.K. When the Soviet Union broke this moratorium in September, 1961, SANE did not hesitate to condemn this action. When, also in 1961-62, the U.S. resumed underground and then atmospheric tests, SANE also condemned these actions. In these and other instances, SANE found itself opposing the nuclear policies of both the U.S. and the U.S.S.R. and basically endorsing those of most of the non-aligned states. Thus SANE's position has been an enigma to those in the U.S. and elsewhere who think that any but a slavish endorsement of U.S. policy borders on subversion. SANE's policy is also enigmatic to the Soviets, who demand consistency in others, if not themselves, and somehow expected the same support from SANE in 1961-62 that they received in 1957-58.

The more sophisticated members of the U.S. Administration and Congress appreciate the role of a voluntary American organization emphasizing an independent foreign policy. This can prod the Administration and yet can engender public support for its long-term goals. One of the achievements of SANE, and other organizations, was the creation in 1961 of the U.S. Arms Control and Disarmament Agency. This Agency cannot displace the private organizations working for disarmament, yet it serves an important function in servicing governmental disarmament negotiations and in sponsoring research. The focus of public opinion on foreign policy issues still lies with the voluntary organizations which can be independent and, when need be, critical of the Administration.

### EFFECTIVE POLITICAL ACTION

SANE was conceived as a "next-step" organization. SANE was never contemplated as being a witness organization. There are several of the latter in the peace field, especially the pacifist groups. More than witness to a new foreign policy, SANE wanted to help make one. Thus from the beginning SANE realized that it had to be political, in that it was dealing with what was politically probable if not always immediately politically possible.

SANE began with a strongly non-partisan emphasis (although, in truth, the number of Republicans in its membership or Board was always small). SANE reflected the longer experience of such sister organizations as the American Civil Liberties Union, which cherished its non-partisan nature. ACLU in the manner of the League of Women Voters sent out information about the answers of candidates to pertinent questions, but it did not endorse candidates for public office. Not only were members of all political parties, or none, amongst the members of ACLU, but it had to do business with the winners of political contests—and this would be more difficult if the winner happened to be a candidate not endorsed by ACLU. SANE followed this course initially, but found that a few local committees felt it useful to endorse certain congressional candidates who were not coy about receiving SANE's public endorsement. Thus in 1962 a procedure was established whereby local SANE committees could abandon the non-partisan character of the organization and, under certain conditions, endorse a congressional candidate. Not many were in fact endorsed, but some who were, especially in California, found themselves elected. By and large SANE remained non-partisan, and worked with friendly congressmen in both parties.

A small organization, with limited finances, always has the temptation to become elitist. If only the elite—the influentials, the men next to the policy-makers—can be won over, the goal can be achieved. SANE established a Washington office to work with Congress, the Administration, non-governmental representatives, and the press. Yet SANE never believed that a Washington office was sufficient. On occasion, but on crucial occasions, the Washington representative had to produce evidence of widespread, grass-roots support. So SANE had to work to maintain a constituency of local chapters across the country. The political action director in Washington repeatedly gave signals on how the grass-roots constituency could be most effective in influencing the policy-makers in Washington. This involved telegram and letter campaigns, consultations with the congressman in his home district, and most significantly the March on Washington for Peace in Vietnam in November, 1965.

### PROLIFERATION OF ORGANIZATIONS

In the Soviet Union there is the one Soviet Peace Committee. In the United States there is no one peace organization. Indeed, there is not yet sociologically a peace movement. There are, however, dozens of national peace organizations and hundreds of local chapters. This multiplicity causes problems, especially after the proliferation of peace organizations which has occurred since 1960.

Although the duplication and often competition among peace organizations is generally wasteful, an uneasy peace has been established with the recognition of a division of labor. Also there have been attempts at coordination. The Consultative Peace Council has been a means for cooperation among most of the pacifist groups and SANE. Turn Toward Peace has only partially succeeded in being a forum where peace organizations and mass organizations can come together. Coordination is difficult, but it is possible with patience.

SANE itself was born out of a need for division of labor and appreciates the eclectic approach to peace in a democratic society. SANE's position in the wide spectrum of peace organizations is at what could be called the non-tax-exempt center. SANE shares this spot with at least the United World Federalists and the Council for a Livable World. SANE and the United World Federalists tried to negotiate a merger, but failed. When possible, mergers are desirable; on the other hand, where necessary, the creation of new peace organizations should be understood and not always resented.

### ALIENATION

A final problem experienced by SANE, but also by other American voluntary organizations, is that of the individual alienation of some of its members. A voluntary organization in the United States attracts people for a multiplicity of reasons. Some join because of the policy objectives of the organization. Others join because of friends. Still others participate for business reasons. Motives are mixed at best. A few persons joined SANE in the early years who were Communists or near-Communists. They felt that SANE was, from its beginning, reflecting their goals more than any other foreign policy organization in the United States. They received their first jolt when SANE passed its resolution not welcoming Communists in May, 1960. Some left at that time. Those who did not received their second jolt when, after September, 1961, SANE strongly criticized the Soviet Union for resuming nuclear tests. The few Communists who may have remained in the organization left SANE at this time—or they left the Communist Party.

Yet another kind of person gravitated to SANE almost from its inception. These were not Communists, although some were undoubtedly ex-Communists. They were separated from the wide mainstream of American political (and social) life. They were critical of almost every aspect of American foreign policy. They tried to find policies about which they could be critical whether in fact they existed or not. They had a psychological need to be estranged from American society. Somehow their joining SANE and protesting against American nuclear policy satisfied this need.

Few of these persons—always a minority within SANE—ever moved into leadership positions of National SANE, although they did become leaders in several local SANE committees. They tended to impinge on national policy, but without success. These persons, whether alienated for psychological or ideological reasons, are a source of difficulty in many voluntary organizations. A study should be made of them, so that a more satisfactory way can be found for their participation—or for group therapy.

## EFFECTIVENESS

This is a brief outline of a few of the problems SANE as a voluntary organization has faced in the first nine years of its existence. Each of these problems merits more careful analysis. Ample materials are available, including the living memory of most of the participants. In addition, abundant files of SANE are continuously being deposited in the peace library of Swarthmore College.

How has SANE lived up to the expectations of its founders—or of its thousands of supporters? Six years after SANE was established, the limited test-ban treaty was signed by some 100 countries. It would be difficult to evaluate the contribution of SANE to the signing of this treaty or to America's role in the negotiations. Many influences were involved. Likewise, lesser achievements have been registered in this period, such as the establishment of the U.S. Arms Control and Disarmament Agency. SANE worked hard on this issue, but so have other organizations, and perhaps international factors were more responsible in establishing this agency than organizational pressures.

The National Board and staff of SANE tend to be modest in their claims of effectiveness. Barring some more objective evaluation of success or failure of a voluntary, non-governmental organization, SANE can at least admit that it was there—in the heat of the constantly changing foreign policy battles, at the U.N., in Washington, in Geneva, at the grass roots, and in the mass media. More than that, SANE cannot responsibly claim.

# JAMES LUTHER ADAMS

# XVII / JAMES LUTHER ADAMS:
# A BIOGRAPHICAL AND INTELLECTUAL SKETCH

*Max L. Stackhouse*

This book is written for several reasons. We write out of apprecia-tion and love for a man who has influenced our thought, our lives, and our careers. But we also write to correct what may be a mistake of his-tory. James Luther Adams may not be recorded in history as an influ-ential theologian. Yet he is one. His influence is indirect and less im-mediately apparent than that of other contemporary thinkers. The contributions that he has made and continues to make are not of the kind that are widely recognized. Unlike those whose peaceful and scholarly retirement leaves a legacy occupying several feet of library shelving, he has published no book (apart from his doctoral dissertation), and has been often embroiled in controversy. Yet it is men like JLA (as he signs his perpetual stream of memos) who serve in every age as consolidators of value, husbanding the fruit of a thousand minds and nourishing the minds of innumerable students, friends, correspondents, and publishers.

We said "husbanding," for indeed he has a cultivating love for the lore of many ages, a love that allows him to participate in wide-ranging sensibilities. In James Luther Adams one finds the curious, and sometimes contradictory, combination of medieval saint, Renais-sance humanist, Marxist critic, Enlightenment encyclopedist, sectarian enthusiast, and bourgeois compulsive. Yet he is, in many ways, a pro-totypical modern man, attempting to find, confess, and, where neces-sary, carve out a sense of meaning large enough to preserve men from the perennial idolatries and aimlessness that flesh is heir to.

It should be clear that any attempt to delineate the many aspects of his character is no simple task, for he is so multifaceted in his interests and abilities that one cannot be sure where the center is. He sometimes appears, like a model of a complex atom in modern physics, to be pri-marily a constellation of energy in motion only momentarily and artificially fixed into a given form for pedagogical purposes. Yet it is this dynamic quality that allows such explosive insights and disallows any description that attempts to trace the relationships of all the orbits through which the constituent particulars of his personality move.

In spite of the difficulties, the purpose of this effort is to attempt the construction of such a model, one that remains necessarily a rough sketch by virture of the subject. The central lines of this sketch will trace the form and development of his thought by means of interlocking analytical and chronological accounts. It will be adorned, as is every conversation with JLA, with anecdotes and impressions.

We begin by characterizing his mode of thinking, for not only must we have some sense of the whole to understand the parts, but it is the quality of his mind and his particular way of approaching problems that is most striking to those who come in contact with him—most striking, that is, besides his sensitivity and personal warmth.

James Luther Adams is a critical and comparative, not a reflective or systematic thinker. He thinks vis-à-vis other minds, external evidence, or objective events. He seldom sets forth a point of view and works through the logical implications thereof, but continually engages one point of view with the historical alternatives. He plays off, so to speak, one set of cultural repositories against another or others. The variety of approaches, the conflicting ways of looking at a problem, the historical settings of various alternatives, and the consequences of dealing with perennial human problems in one way rather than another —these are the issues that are crucial to him.

A paragraph that overdramatizes this point but that is thus representative in an "ideal-typical" way appears in his essay "Basic Causes of Progress and Decay in Civilization," wherein he discusses the relationship of religion to civilization.

> Some people view religion as the enemy of civilization; others think of it as the mother of civilization and culture; still others think of civilization and especially of civility as the enemy of true religion. Because of its tendency to preen itself on man's sophistication and on his cultural achievements, urbanity, Spengler asserted, long ago "killed Christianity." In contrast, Gibbon attributed the fall of Rome to the rise of barbarism and religion. Kierkegaard, on quite different presuppositions from Spengler's, insisted that there is a world of difference between the roots and fruits of Christianity and the roots and fruits of urbanity. For Kierkegaard urbane poise freezes the knees of the "man of the world": being completely self-sufficient, he is not capable of genuine religious humility—he aims to be his own redeemer. With still different presuppositions John Henry Newman contrasted the ideal of the gentleman with the ideal of the Christian, sardonically defining the gentleman as one who refuses to cause pain. Harold Laski believes

that progress in civilization is possible only with the elimination of religion. In contrast to certain of these views we find Hegel asserting that
religion is the womb of culture; Arnold Toynbee believes civilization is
the womb of religion, and indeed religion is the only enduring product
of civilizations in their rise and fall; and Edmund Burke held that
civilization is the result of two things—the spirit of the gentleman and
the spirit of religion.[1]

How does it occur that Adams should come to such a way of thinking,
writing, and teaching? Suggestions for an answer are found in his life's
history.

Of his background we know relatively little in a direct way.[2] James
Luther Adams was born in Ritzville, Washington, in 1901. His father,
James Carey Adams, was a Baptist premillenarian country preacher,
later to become a Plymouth Brother. His mother, Lella Barnett
Adams, was also a "true believer." The details of the name-giving are
not known, except that his given names were of earlier use in the family; but the anomaly of James Luther, in view of Luther's opinion of
James and Adams' opinion of Luther, not only is now the source of
comment in introductions at various functions, but is somehow prophetic of the creative contradictions inherent in the bearer.

The most significant anecdotes of JLA's early history, the ones that
he remembers as being most significant, are spelled out in the autobiographical chapter in *Taking Time Seriously* and partially recapitulated
in D. W. Soper's *Men Who Shape Belief*.[3] But only the barest outlines
are found there, and perhaps the genuine flavor can best be tasted by
reading Sir Edmund Gosse's *Father and Son*,[4] an autobiographical study
of a Plymouth Brethren lay preacher (a zoologist professionally) and
his son whose interest in literature led him into a larger fold, or, as his
father thought, out of the fold altogether.[5]

One finds in Gosse's now almost classic account several themes that
are indeed applicable to James Luther Adams. Gosse characterizes the
type of thinking operant in his household as more that of an attorney
than of a philosopher. Positively, the marshaling of historical witnesses
as well as the importance of obtaining explicit consensus among the
peers and following the rules of justice are precisely the way in which
Adams treats a subject in his writing and lecturing. The fact is supplemented by the interest that Adams has in jurisprudence and the precision he demands in ethical casuistry. His interest in the history and
philosophy of law appeared early in seminars under Roscoe Pound,
William E. Hocking, and Helmut Coing. In his own seminars he has for
years promoted the study of Natural Law. His concern for Althusius
as a pivotal thinker in the history of Protestant political theory ap-

pears full-blown in the work of his former student Frederick Carney. Much of what JLA has presented in the history of Protestant social ethics he has viewed in connection with the work of the jurists, from Althusius through Friedrich Julius Stahl and Otto von Gierke to Rudolf Sohm. Otto von Gierke's *Genossenschaftsrecht* has served as a basis for his own associational philosophy and periodization of Western history. JLA often voices lament for the lack of interest in legal literature and problems among contemporary Protestant theologians. He is fond of speaking of the Three R's—Reformation, Renaissance, and Reception—as the foundation of modern civilization. But his participation in the Civil Liberties Union is perhaps an equally good illustration, for every intellectual concern that is to have reality for Adams must take form in institutional participation. His participation in the Civil Liberties Union has given him occasion repeatedly to become personally involved in the defense of individuals harassed by superpatriots or unjustly snared by the Walters-McCarran Act. Some of his files on these individual cases cover as much as a decade and have entailed an enormous amount of effort. Very often the injustice to be corrected has been the fault of lawmaking or law-enforcement agencies.

But negatively the concern for legal modes of thinking also plays a role in JLA's thinking. The "legalistic" approach to human problems by Gosse's father (and by Adams') leads one continually to have to establish innocence. This need, so dramatically set forth in the modern mode in the writings of Kafka, leads to such a radical demand for proving innocence that inhumanity is the result. Against this JLA rebelled and continues to protest. One must be willing to get his hands dirty at the expense of a manicured soul. This rebellion away from withdrawal and toward participation is one of the chief sources of his concern for voluntary associations.

Another significant factor mentioned by Gosse is the fact that professional interests are spoken of as avocations. Again we see a factor that appears in JLA's life and thought. His service to the Lord, to the church, and to his fellow man is his real vocation, and the various professional abilities that he has developed are means to that end. Since his early days when, carrying his violin to accompany singing, he went from village to country crossroad on horseback with his father, he has traveled and preached, using his secular excursions as a means for "evangelism." The full vocation of the ministry combines scholarly research, administration, cure of souls, social criticism, and citizenship responsibilities as well as preaching the Word and performing the sacraments. Although other institutions must differentiate in our society, the church must maintain an integrative center, and pastors must be capable of leading the flock in many and varied ways. JLA believes in the prophethood as well as in the priesthood of all believers.

The premillenarian expectation of "meeting Jesus," with all the attendant implications, are an aspect of Gosse's account which also shows up in Adams' own memory.

> My earliest recollection goes back to the year 1906 when I was four years old. Our family was kneeling in prayer, each of us burying his head in a pillow. We could scarcely breathe, for our farmhouse was in the path of one of the worst dust storms of a decade in the Pacific Northwest, and we were praying for relief. . . . I was told much later that my father . . . prayed then and there for the Second Coming. . . .
>
> My father was as other-worldly as the head of a family could possibly be. Very often he would tell us after family prayers before retiring at night that we might not see each other again on this earth.[6]

Several themes appear in this passage that are of considerable significance for the understanding of Professor Adams. One is the tension between the necessities of this-worldly living and the professing of other-worldly interests. This theme, treated systematically by Troeltsch and Weber in regard to Calvinistic Puritanism (Adams taught courses on Troeltsch and Weber in alternate years at Chicago, is now editing a translation of Troeltsch's writings and previously edited Weber's *Sociology of Religion*[7]), not only describes a major tension in JLA's life and thought, but also accounts for his fascination with the problem of alienation, which, according to the Marxian definition, means having an ideological theory that obscures rather than reveals the true state of affairs.

On the positive side, however, the tension of eschatology with history, and the continual searching in the events of history for signs of the times, is an unceasing endeavor of his life which perhaps derives from this eschatological watching of his youth. Although he recognizes the mechanical way in which this was done by his father and other adherents of "the whole plan of salvation according to the Scofield Reference Bible," the crucial significance of repeatedly asking the whence and whither of human events remained, and indeed has become a dominant theme of his thinking.

One result of the mentality imbued accidentally in his earlier days, but later accepted in a series of self-critical decisions, is the radical "work ethic" that JLA exemplifies.

An account of his working and moneymaking (he has never had difficulty making money, although he has carried heavy responsibilities in view of his father's fiscal incapacity and although he is radically critical of people who make decisions on a financial basis alone) has been sent to me by J. Bryan Allin, his friend since 1920.

At ten years of age JLA (his family called him Luther) was the janitor of the little country schoolhouse for the pay of one dollar a month.[8] During the summer months he shocked oats and did other farm chores, and for a while he drove a derrick for two dollars a day. He had the constant care of two horses. He was also, part time, a night clerk at a University Club, and sold brushes house to house.

By twelve years of age he was the office boy of Dunham Engineering Company, and sold newspapers on the street during the noon hour. He raised rabbits, besides selling some aluminum goods, knick-knacks, and home furnishings made by other boys. A newspaper article in his home town appeared at this time with his picture, saying, "Luther Adams has banked $100."

At fourteen he worked in a carriage shop and carried two paper routes, netting about $15 a week. On the side he ran errands for a combination collection agency and matrimonial bureau.

At age fifteen, family finances forced him to leave high school. He learned stenography in night school in order to get a job with the prosecuting attorney, at $75 a month. While employed there, he developed his shorthand to the point that his secretaries could still read his script before he recently switched to tape-recorded dictation. By 1918, when he was seventeen years old, he was the private secretary to the superintendent of the Northern Pacific Railroad and was earning $113 a month. He next became Chief Clerk of the Operating Division.

During these several years it appeared that he might succumb to sheer exhaustion and fatigue. Doubtless the question of the meaning of what he was doing crossed his mind several times, but he persisted, returned to high school, and graduated at the top of his class.

He went to college, where his busy schedule continued, as, indeed, it has until today although intellectual, cultural, and human interests began to displace commercial ones. Some of the jobs that he held from 1920 to 1924 while he was attending college full time are:

> Dispatcher's clerk for the Northern Pacific on the midnight eight-hour shift. Worked at the Minnesota Union (where the men ate). Ran a collection agency. Read to a millionaire, Mr. Bean, at night. Organized a printing company. Worked in a cigar store. Was secretary to Rev. Mr. Henderson, a Baptist minister, and Professor van Roosbroeck (professor of French). Sold advertising, automatic typewriters, and mailing lists. Organized a radio sales organization. Typed for Professor Swift. Taught salesmanship and Business English. Invested in a book store.[9]

The significance of this energetic involvement is that a pattern was set, a style of life developed, that demanded the utilization of every available moment. He not only takes time seriously in its theological and philosophical senses, but tries also to fill each moment with some useful effort. One manifestation of this is found in his regular attendance at gatherings where decisions are being made. He once said that history in a democracy is made by those who take the time to go to important committee meetings and to stay to the end. By participating in those political, ecclesiastical, and associational organizations that make decisions, JLA is ever engaged in the business of defining and redefining the changing cultural needs, sensitivities, and perceptions of modern social existence.

However remarkable, it is not this aspect of his life in college that was most notable at the time. Rather it was the germinal process of deprovincialization (as he calls it), accompanied by a rather agonizing shaking of the foundations (as Tillich calls it), that really allowed James Luther Adams to become what he is instead of a tycoon, an organization man, or a religious fanatic (although, as he reports, "I preached on the street and at the Salvation Army during my earlier years in college"). Deprovincialization is a painful exorcism for anyone, the more so for one strongly conditioned to an absolute and explicit faith and by continual success in business. The more one was rooted in faith before, the more he must rebel. As JLA himself puts it:

> I decided that it was my mission to attack religion in season and out. I became a "campus radical" and joined with some other quondam Fundamentalists to publish an undergraduate free-lance sheet which we smugly called the *Angels' Revolt*. My new law was in the scientific humanism of John Dietrich and my new prophecy was in the anti-Rotarianism of H. L. Mencken.
>
> One of the great surprises of my life came at the end of my senior year in college. I had been taking a course in public speaking and all my speeches had been vicious attacks on religion as I knew it—at least, they had been as vicious as I could make them. The shock came one day when on leaving the classroom I happened to say quite casually to the professor that I did not know what I was going to do after graduation. I was already profitably engaged in business, but I was thoroughly discontented. The professor replied in a flash, "You don't know what you are going to do? Why, I have known for months. Come around and talk to me some day." And then, right there in the presence of my enemies, the Fundamentalists, he smote me. "There is no possible doubt about it," he said. "You are going to be a preacher!" Later, I went by night, like Nicodemus, to question this strange counselor. Within six weeks the arrangements were complete. I was to attend Harvard Divinity School.[10]

This Nicodemus indeed arrived at Harvard Divinity School at the start of the following semester. He came as a flaming . . . but he didn't know what noun was to follow. People who knew him during this period remember him as one passionate for learning, drinking in more than several average students, and moving into conversation with professor, janitor, and cook alike, receiving-antennae constantly sensitized. He was assigned field work at All-Souls Church in Lowell, where his own enthusiasm for scholarship and literature, even if unfocused, was transmitted to people previously untouched or unmoved by the world of letters. The picture of a young theolog, sitting on the woodpile reading to and discussing with workers who swore and smoked as well as ate during the noon hour, made several respectable eyebrows rise.

Indicative of the kind of man that JLA is, are reports of his constant efforts to provide acquaintances with something to "stretch their minds." He bought records, books of poetry, or reprints of paintings to give to landladies, bakers, or other friends. He conducted three-hour sessions of listening to symphonic recordings, relating the music to the other arts, the religious movements, and the events of the period. That this love for music did not express a narrowly artistic interest is shown by JLA's interpretation of the role of Johann Sebastian Bach in his own spiritual development.

> Nathan Söderblom has remarked that Bach's St. Matthew's Passion music should be called the Fifth Evangelist. So was Bach for me. One night as I sang, with the Harvard Glee Club, the Mass in B Minor under Koussevitzky at Symphony Hall, Boston, a renewed conviction came over me that here in the Bach Mass, beginning with the *Kyrie* and proceeding through the *Crucifixus* to the *Agnus Dei* and *Dona nobis pacem,* all that was essential in the human and the divine was expressed. My love of the music awakened in me a profound sense of gratitude to Bach for having displayed as through a prism and in a way that was irresistible for me, the essence of Christianity.[11]

From his training at Harvard Divinity School three influences are recorded as being most significant, although the fruit was slow in coming and he was still to pass through the stage of classical humanism. One was the tradition of social responsibility in Unitarianism and of pluralism ("the uses of diversity") coupled with the historical, critical method promoted at Harvard. JLA was inducted into this tradition through his acquaintance with some of the leading young Unitarian ministers of the New England area. It might be said, for those not familiar with old Yankee Unitarianism, that it is much less subject to the charge of theological poverty or to the epithet "non-Christian" than are some of the syncretistic and scientistic strains of Unitarianism. (JLA, his friends, and former students are responsible for the recent journal, *The Unitarian Christian,* an inherent contradiction only for those not familiar with Unitarian history.) The issue of these acquaintanceships has been "The Greenfield Group" and subsequently in the Middle West "The Prairie Group." These groups with their somewhat rigorous disciplines of study have been a main bulwark against atomic individualism in Unitarianism. Similar organizations have formed more recently in New York, Washington, and California. JLA sometimes explicates one aspect of his doctrine of God as "a community-forming power," and further explicates the community as necessarily having some form of explicit faith and discipline. If this definition is correct, the Greenfield and Prairie Groups are evidence of God's working. The participants formed a fellowship, or *koinonia,* and self-consciously assumed a discipline to attempt hammering out a theology of the church, a more adequate hymnology, liturgy, biblical criticism, and conception of history, by intensive engagement with the outstanding theologians of main-line Protestant and Catholic orientations.[12] Following a pattern adopted by von Huegel, they pursued an elaborate program that combined the study of theology (or the Bible) and the study of some other discipline (economics, art, political science)— the dialectic between grace and its medium. Another group of which JLA was a charter member, while related to Harvard, was the "Brothers of the Way." They, too, maintained a discipline, this one requiring every member to adopt devotional disciplines and also to be a participant in a controversial "secular" organization, feeling that only by means of the abrasive clash of important disputes are deep-seated values exposed. These groups and other relationships that JLA has maintained in Unitarian circles have been a theological, intellectual, and social leaven for many in the denomination for over three decades. One long-time associate, Professor John F. Hayward, Associate Professor of Theology at the Meadville Theological School, wrote in his preface to *Existentialism and Religious Liberalism,*[13] "In the background of all my thinking and in the foreground of my affections, stands my former minister, teacher, one-time colleague at the University of Chicago, and continuing compatriot in the liberal ministry, Professor James Luther Adams. He is foremost among those cherished persons who have led me 'to behold the beauty of the Lord and to enquire in his temple.' "

JLA was also influenced by Dean Sperry, especially as he directed Adams' attention to literary studies, to devotional literature, and to the writings of Baron von Huegel. Adams writes:

> Von Huegel's philosophy of critical realism, his emphasis on the role of the body, history and institutions in religion, his attack (along with

Maritain's) on the pure spirituality of unhistorical, non-institutional, non-incarnational religion became determinative for my conception of religion.[14]

Much of this side of von Huegel was the more impressive because of the way in which he showed how James Martineau, a Unitarian theologian, espoused similar views. The issue of these themes was not to come to the fore until several years later.

The third influence, although much less direct since he was no longer at Harvard when JLA arrived, was Francis Greenwood Peabody. "Peabody was not only one of the early proponents of the 'social gospel' but also the first teacher in the United States to demand and create a permanent place for systematic Christian social ethics as a University discipline in a liberal education as well as in professional theological education."[15] Further, Peabody "took into account German theological scholarship; he also attempted to come to terms with Marxist literature and with the thought of the European Christian socialists."[16] JLA, as Peabody's spiritual descendant, now occupies the Mallinckrodt Chair at Harvard.

He graduated from Harvard Divinity School, was ordained a Unitarian minister, assumed the pastorate at Second Church, Salem, Massachusetts, spent the summer in Europe,[17] and returned to marry a student of music and a Unitarian, Margaret Ann Young, all in 1927.

The trip to Europe in 1927, just as Hitler and the Nazis were beginning to flex their political muscles, was highly significant, for during that stay JLA first became acquainted with the philosophy and social criticism of Paul Tillich, an acquaintance and an influence that was to stay with him for some time.

Margaret Young was a member of the First Church (Unitarian) in Salem. JLA's business sensitivities of long standing were undoubtedly touched when he took her on an early, if not first, "date" to hear a Bach *Passion* and she requested that he get inexpensive tickets. Puritan frugality, cultural sensitivity, a liberal outlook in politics, and personal charm claimed his heart.

During his pastorate in Salem, where Mrs. Adams' father was a banker, a major strike occurred. It was one of the bitter, town-splitting affairs that occur when workers become articulate and organized, when management feels its prerogatives threatened, when a small number of industries dominate the economy, and when the first signs of structural instability are blinked away. The issues were muddied by Communist agitation. Resolving that something had to be done, the Reverend Mr. Adams proposed to a group of ministers that they take collective action and look into the matter. Several of the clergymen called members of their churches who were managers of the factories, and were assured that the situation was well in hand and that nothing needed to be done. So they did precisely that. But JLA was not to be so easily dissuaded even though his church, too, had its strong share of managers and of managerial sympathizers. He single-handedly tried to find the facts of the matter. It turned out that the workers (mostly Roman Catholics) had a just grievance, that the managers were distorting the facts in paid advertisements in the newspapers, and that other reporters had not gone beyond the surface. From mill managers in neighboring towns he uncovered the real scandal of the situation, how dishonest the Salem owners were, and decided in the eleventh week of the strike to deliver a sermon on the dispute. The situation became more serious, bitterness increased, and talks between management and labor were on the verge of breakdown. Adams not only preached his sermon at a joint summer service, but went to the newspaper editors and asked them to print his analysis of the situation, at least to let the public look at the other side of the disagreement. When they hesitated, he told them that he had a pulpit and would preach on their reluctance if they would not cooperate. The newspaper hit the streets at 11 a.m., Monday, with the sermon starting on page one and continuing inside. The bargainers were recalled by late afternoon. By 8 p.m. agreement was reached, the strike was over.

The negative reaction was strong on some sides, but JLA maintained that he had not "taken sides" and had only made demand for informed public opinion and open discussion. No one knows, of course, what the many factors playing into this resolution were, but about three thousand workers, wives, and families thought they knew. They started a victory procession that ended on the front lawn of the Reverend and Mrs. J. L. Adams. Further, when he started to speak at their request and was interrupted and almost attacked by one Communist agitator, the latter was physically (and somewhat indelicately) removed from the area by the workers.

The significance of this painful siege in the life of James Luther Adams is twofold: (1) Like his earlier reaction to Nazism, it is empirical evidence that his thought would be shaped by participation in political and economic struggles, and (2) it appears to have been for him an existential confirmation of *Millhands and Preachers*[18] that those churches claiming to have eternal foundations for their faith are also subject to the dangers of culture-religion, justifying the ways of their contributors.

JLA had previously embarked upon a master's program in English and Greek at Harvard, in part to find another vocation since he saw little of significance in the church, in part to pursue his literary concerns, and in part to study under George Lyman Kittredge, John Livingston Lowes, and Irving Babbitt.[19] Much of his time was devoted to philology, but he became, as his friends report, a raving humanist, almost unbearably so. The influence of Irving Babbitt—whose conservative, classical humanism, with accents on the importance of identification and involvement, shaped several generations of Harvard students —appears to have been internalized and radicalized by JLA. The very intensity of his involvement in this literary humanism was highly significant for Adams in the early 1930's; for while many of the young intellectuals, disillusioned with the Social Gospel in its superficial post-World War I form, and disenchanted with the "American Way of Life" after 1929, turned to scientific humanism, or to various types of relativism, the young Adams was able to maintain a critical attitude against these even while having them broaden and deepen his concerns. While he was indeed to become associated with liberal causes in the 1930's, it is only the undiscerning who could not see the radical differences between his position and dogmatic Marxism. Further, with the realistic view of man involved in the literary humanism of Babbitt, he asserted that "the central problem of civilization [is] . . . ethical standards and, without being obscurantist, . . . stressed the necessity of something like conversion, of a change in the will whereby a man would develop inner ethical control and work toward a richly human, universal norm." As he continues, "Through Babbitt's stress on these ideas I came to understand and value Greek and Chinese humanism, the Christian doctrines of sin and grace, and the Christian emphasis on conversion and humility. I also thus acquired a skepticism of the romantic liberal conception of human nature which was later to be so severely scrutinized by 'realistic theology.' "[20] And by the end of the '20's and into the early '30's, JLA was devouring these "realists." Reinhold Niebuhr, Walter Marshall Horton, Alfred North Whitehead, John Bennett, and von Huegel became crucial figures in opening the doors of criticism, even against the humanism that he endorsed.

The question was asked by this generation, In what kind of context is man to be seen? Surely he does not stand alone, divorced from nature and history, and just decide, *metanoia,* without trying to discern where the kingdom is. He is supported, sustained, altered, and influenced by environmental factors of all kinds. The ideational, natural, and temporal settings of man and the influence of these on his decisions became increasingly clear to JLA as he became self-conscious of the provincialized decisions that he himself had made in the past. In short, he began to ask what historical and natural conditions were necessary for mature, self-critical decision-making and for the preservation of a civilization that attempted to have a wide dispersion of decision-making and power.

Suggestions for provisional answers came from several sources, and the style of thinking that we have called comparative-critical began to appear in his scattered essays. Although he was still a pastor (not only in Salem, 1927-33, but later also in the Wellesley Hills First Unitarian Society, 1933-35), his interest in literature found expression in the teaching of English (he still abhors nothing so much as a dangling modifier) at Boston University (1929-32), and in journals such as *Hound and Horn,* whose list of contributors, including T. S. Eliot, Archibald MacLeish, Conrad Aiken, Robert Oppenheimer, Francis Fergusson, and Austen Warren, to name a few, reads like a Who's Who of that period. His personal acquaintance with T. S. Eliot is particularly treasured. JLA saw Eliot once a week at tea for graduate students in English when Eliot was the Charles Eliot Norton Lecturer at Harvard. They had a chance to renew their acquaintance in London in 1935, when Adams went to Europe to do some research on the literary sources of Bishop Hurd's literary criticism and to devote a year in preparation for his new teaching assignment in Chicago. Through Eliot (also a pupil of Babbitt) he became personally acquainted with certain literary and philosophical figures in England and later in France.

To this observer, one *Hound and Horn* article, perhaps only of secondary importance when written, appears to be particularly significant. In the review of *Vigile,* a Paris journal,[21] we see several themes that suggest those percolating concerns that appear repeatedly and increasingly in his writing and lecturing.

One theme is his dialogue with other-worldliness in its more sophisticated expression. Mysticism, in the classical sense and as represented to the modern world in the works of Baron von Huegel and Rudolf Otto, is ever a concern of Adams, for it raises the question of the mediacy or immediacy of revelation and knowledge. He wrote in a commentary on Jacques Maritain's article on St. John of the Cross, "Mysticism, Protestant or Catholic, is always in danger of regarding the means which the church furnishes for uniting God and man as 'intermediary,' as separating God from man. Common sense, as well as tradition, demands that mysticism be always aware of the need for mediators, Christ and the Church."[22] The notion that "nothing but the infinite can save us" just does not fit with *"salus extra ecclesiam non est."* The questions became, therefore, (a) since Christ and his church must mediate, how may these best be understood and structured? Or to put it in quite another way, the movement from spiritual bondage to spiritual freedom demands changing the types of social organization.

Freedom, to stay free, must organize. And (b) how can an adequate hermeneutical principle be devised to discern where in the plethora of God's creation, human action, and man's thought, God's will is to be known?

While protesting repeatedly against the "un-catholic desire for pure spirituality" which he sees variously formulated in St. John of the Cross, Rousseau, and Descartes (and others), he appears nevertheless to be continually troubled by and attracted to the self-validating reality of immediate experience. Rudolf Otto, not only because of his sense of the encounter with the Holy, but also because of his historical and eschatological sensitivities as seen in *Kingdom of God and Son of Man,*[23] was influential.

These themes had been present earlier. After assuming the pastorate in Wellesley, JLA turned to a more systematic reading of theology and began to see a significance, not previously clear to him, in the religious life. Indeed, while studying in Europe several years later (1935-36), he followed the example of von Huegel and secured a spiritual director for a while at the Seminary of St. Sulpice in Paris. He reports of that experience:

> Two hours a week for a period of three months with one of the finest spirits I have known will not be forgotten. Here I came to know a man for whom the devotional life was far more than a discipline. It was a growing in the grace and knowledge of Christ. He did for me what I should have expected from a Protestant: he acquainted me with a living Christ. Yet the Christ he made vivid for me was not the har-binger of the Kingdom, but rather the obedient servant of God in the inner life and in the personal virtues.[24]

This concern with spiritual direction was an analogue to his interest in public worship. The Greenfield Group had given much attention to problems of public worship. They had produced a revision of liturgy which had been adopted in a number of churches; in this connection they had also promoted the adoption of the German chorale in substan-tial measure in the Unitarian hymnal. During this period (1935-36) in Europe JLA studied liturgics for a semester with Robert Will of the Strasbourg Theological Faculty. He then proceeded to study the Liturgi-cal Movement of the Benedictines, especially at the famous monastery of Maria Laach in Germany.[25] (Later on, Ernst Koenker under Adams' stimulus would write the major Protestant work on the Roman Catho-lic Liturgical Movement.) In this period he also spent much time with Rudolf Otto in Marburg, considering "the renewal of liturgy" in Protestantism in its relation to New Testament studies. Liturgy, in Adams' view, is always in danger of becoming a static rite and of inhibiting the prophetic element of Christian faith. Rudolf Otto with his paradoxical "realized eschatology" injected the dynamis of directed time into the space of the sacrament.

The problem of history, of time, plagued him. The content of supposedly pure spirituality was subject to temporal influence. That was empirically and existentially so. One must see the mediate character of the spirit. What are the factors that mediate the spiritual reality? Increasingly he came to the conclusion that language is insufficient. Writing, confessing, speaking, and preaching, even the whole literary heritage he loved, as important as they were, did not finally determine the spiritual destiny of nations. It is concrete historical institutions that shape life most massively. Institutions, indeed, provide the nexus for preservation, transmission, and alteration of language and cultural memory, as well as the conditions for receptivity to alternative choices in conversion. Selection and definition of terms and remembered events are primarily, although not exhaustively, social processes. It thus was not accidental that Adams, during this period, became acquainted personally with the French Protestant religious socialist, André Philip, a professor of law in Lyons and a member of the Chamber of Deputies.[26] In the efforts of the religious socialists Adams found an attempt to link theology and the world in a way that took history and institutions seriously, even if they, like the members of the *Kairos* circle in Germany, were sometimes more theoretical than participating.

The problem of history also began to become clear to him in other ways, for even as he had been aware of the importance of the Radical Reformation through his involvement with the Unitarians and through his reading of Troeltsch, it was during the next decade that he became more systematically concerned with a "third history" of the Reformation. As the Catholics could not be counted on for a full account of the Reformation movement and the Lutheran and Calvinist historians tended to read the data of the Reformation in a way not to the liking of Catholic historians, so neither could be counted on to portray accurately the "Left Wing." The Anabaptists, the Mennonites, the Münsterites, and all the other varieties of wilding growth are not to be dismissed out of hand just because they were successfully suppressed during the sixteenth century. This concern has flowered, as do many of his interests, in Adams' students—in this case most notably in George H. Williams. Even more important to American history are the proto-democratic and quasi-equalitarian sectarian movements in and around the Cromwellian Revolution. The Diggers, the Levellers, the Seekers, the Separatists, and the whole range of such groups represent a variety of social creativity that has shaped the modern world more than it acknowledges. (It was the study of these movements that initially brought Adams and D. B. Robertson into association; Adams read D. B. Robertson's doctoral dissertation, *The Religious Foundations of Leveller Democracy,* before it went to press in 1951.)

Adams came to see that the Marxists and the sectarians themselves, while treating the material in a highly ideological way, had done a service in turning attention to these movements and figures once again. Even more important became the theorists of voluntary associations who recognized the crucial importance, limitations, and perversions of these groups—Figgis, Maitland, Barker, and Channing.

Further, the problem of the relation of nature to immediate history struck James Luther Adams at this time in full vigor. It appeared in two ways: politically and theoretically. Both during the 1935-36 trip to Germany and later in 1938, JLA was inevitably concerned about the emerging power of Hitler and the inability of the church, even where willing and sensitive to the need, to head off the demonic appeal to "the German nature."

The fact that so few effective, free-wheeling, voluntary associations had ever developed in Germany since the assassinations of the leaders of the Left Wing in the Reformation was, according to JLA's perspective, a contributing factor. The limited historical possibilities of human action and association had not been able to contain the laws of tooth and claw inherent in nature in the time of crisis. Indeed, the historical church and the theological tradition in many cases contributed to their own dissolution.

More personally, he began to ask what he was doing to prevent something like that from happening in America. (He had once resisted the organization of an anti-Nazi demonstration on Boston Common.) This reflection and self-examination resulted ultimately in many efforts and actions. Among these are some of the earlier protests against racial segregation.

JLA happened to be chairman of the library committee of the Federated Theological Faculty of the University of Chicago during a WPA project to catalogue a huge stack of some 70,000 pamphlets dating before the Civil War. Adams noticed that no Negroes were among the employed, brought the matter before the committee, and got unanimous agreement that the personnel should be integrated. After carrying on correspondence about the matter for some time, with no results, he went in person to see the director of the projects in that area. He confronted the executive, a prominent businessman weighing some 250 pounds who enjoyed, as Adams tells it, "physically and spiritually throwing his weight around." The executive resisted any recommendations concerning his authority, his policy, or the program in the libraries.

Finally the time came for a showdown session. The administrator invited Adams to his office (in the midst of an enormous outlay of glass-partitioned bureaus) at 5:15 after all other employees had left. For about an hour and a half, the conversation became more and more heated until finally something like the following climax was reached:

"Obviously, you are just a professor; you have never had to meet a payroll, and haven't the slightest notion of the problems of an executive. We're going to have great trouble if we introduce Negroes into the project. The workers won't stand for it!"

"Well, I'm not convinced that they won't stand for it. I am convinced, and I have talked with some of them, that some of them are also displeased. There are others, of course, that won't like it, but after all, the Negroes are American citizens, they pay taxes, WPA is a federal project, and the WPA ought to join the United States. I am speaking to you in the name of a committee that agrees unanimously on this policy. And if you don't want to follow the policy, which is, really, in accord with the United States Constitution, you can just take the project out."

The executive was shocked. He could scarcely believe this, but Adams continued:

"And I think that we ought to take it out right now. We want nothing to do with it."

"You mean you don't want those books, you don't want those thousands of pamphlets catalogued?"

"No! They have not been catalogued for over a century, and they can wait until this becomes a possibility within the framework of the American Constitution."

"But you don't realize the complexity of executive decision-making. There would be pandemonium if I tried to introduce such a policy overnight. You have to realize the problems of being an administrator and an executive."

"I don't have to discuss with you *my* executive abilities. You are the executive, and you are the one who has the executive ability, as I understand it. But I have to tell you that in this instance I have the authority and the power to tell you what to execute. Perhaps you do not often find yourself in a position when others have power over you, but you are in one now. So, if you have such great executive ability, will you show me how? Do your stuff. Now, what are you going to do with me, and what are you going to do with the library committee? I am your 'problem.' They are your 'problem.' Do your stuff."

The executive had to surrender.

"Well, there will be a lot of trouble!"

"I don't think there will be trouble. But if anybody doesn't want to work for the WPA, and if he would rather be unemployed, he is free to leave the job. But, despite my alleged lack of executive ability, I venture to predict that no one will leave just because Negroes are brought in."

So the project was integrated. No one left the project.

But not all efforts were so successful. In one lecture that he gave recurrently to American servicemen (in officers' training) to teach them about the Nazi enemy, he outlined the Nazi racist philosophy in such a way that the audience became thoroughly incensed. Many of them would not recognize, however, that their attitudes about the Negroes were closely allied with the dominant racist motifs of the Axis, nor would they admit that "America First" and "Deutschland über Alles" were close cousins. He was quietly relieved of his duties.

But even while he was still in Germany, his interest turned to those groups actually involved in resistance. By 1938 this interest was more intense, and Adams in the company of Peter Brunner (now on the Heidelberg faculty) spent several months observing underground movements and the behavior of the churches in the face of this "natural nationalism." He interviewed numerous Nazi and anti-Nazi leaders, taking some home movies that would make several leading German theologians, some of whom are still living, quiver in their boots with many a *mea culpa*. "The Cult of Authority," to quote Georg Iggers' book title out of context, was in full reign and was not to be vanquished, as Bonhoeffer (if not many Bonhoefferians of today) learned, by confessional statements alone.

Never one to stand in the wings of a dispute, JLA became so involved that he was apprehended by the Nazis and had his passport withheld for a while. Ostensibly, he was questioned for having been seen on the streets with a Jew, but he has always felt that his involvement with resistance groups was known to them.

Several important events occurred between his visits to Europe. Upon his return from the 1935-36 visit, the Reverend James Luther Adams became Professor James Luther Adams, teaching Psychology and Philosophy of Religion at The Meadville Theological School in Chicago. The impact of this young teacher on the students at Meadville, according to their reports, cannot be overestimated. The excitement of the intellectual enterprise, the expanding of horizons historically, internationally, and socially, and the direct importance of commitment and involvement left its mark on a whole generation of Unitarian pastors and scholars. For Adams himself, it was in this position that he began to deal with the theoretical aspects of the relationship of nature and history.

Since 1927, JLA had been intrigued by the thought of Paul Tillich, eventually writing his doctoral dissertation on "Paul Tillich's Philosophy of Culture, Science, and Religion" (published in 1965 by Harper and Row). Tillich, along with Troeltsch, has been a crucial influence on Adams' thought. And in Chicago, he encountered again "process philosophy," confirming a philosophical interest initially stimulated by courses taken under Whitehead at Harvard. Both Tillich and the "process philosophers" had a sense of the ontological rootage of man in the nature of being and the pertinence of that problem to the human situation in history. Sensitivity to Being, Becoming, and Time were necessarily bound up with discerning "the times." The attempt to relate ontological, historical, and institutional matters, a concern of long standing, was a crucial part of Adams' critical reading of the conflict between Tillich and the process thinkers. While he always pressed the question of what the more theoretical formulations mean in terms of social organizational structure and the distribution of authority, the continuing dialogue on the relationship of history, metaphysics, and politics in which Tillich tends to ontologize history and the process philosophers tend to historicize ontology fed and nurtured Adams' ever-questioning drive. Even while he can say, "There is much in Tillich which still remains for me obscure and where understood unacceptable," and while he can call some process philosophy an ontological evasion of the institutional dimension of existence, the fact remains that this debate strongly influenced his view of the relationship of nature and history, and the theological importance of that relationship. One might say briefly that he has become an historical contextualist, taking the cultural epoch as his context, and always asking what principles are in operation therein and what view of Being or Becoming is implied by making one decision rather than another. The fact that he edited Wieman's *The Directive in History*[27] in 1949, only one year after his translation of Tillich's *The Protestant Era,*[28] is more than coincidental.

This concern for historical context, and especially for the relations between theology and social organization, is reflected in the critique of individualistic existentialism which for years has punctuated JLA's lectures. Thus he has viewed Kierkegaard as a one-sided proponent of Christian faith: he centers attention upon personal and interpersonal aspects of piety to the neglect of institutional implications and responsibilities. The Marxists for their part exhibit indifference to personal virtues. What Kierkegaard lacks Karl Marx has, and what Karl Marx lacks Kierkegaard has. To both of them JLA likes to apply the Sainte-Beuve maxim that nothing is so much like a swelling as a hole. The Kierkegaardian lack of concern for institutional problems and responsibilities appears today in the ontologism of Heidegger and in the *Innerlichkeit* and "pietism" of Bultmann. Warnings against false securities do not provide any substitute for a positive social theology or for political participation. Adams predicts that the inadequacy of Bultmann "pietism" will become evident the moment the Erhardt economic miracle begins to fade. This "pietism" presupposes the stability of the socio-political order; it does little to give shape to that order. In this respect it ignores a basic presupposition of the Bible. This presupposition lies behind the doctrine of the covenant, namely, that God is a community-forming power and that man's response to it entails full social and political participation.

The manner of working through the problems of the world are almost as interesting in JLA's life as the problems themselves. For instance, when he becomes wrapped up with an author or problem he cannot sleep. Many students report that his lights burn late into the night. One evening in Chicago, after going to bed he found he could not sleep and, slipping his robe over his pajamas, crossed over to the nearby library to make use of the wakeful hours. He became so involved that he failed to notice the hour and only belatedly started on his way back home. He arrived at the library door just in time to greet the librarian coming to work. Both he and she were embarrassed.

During this period he began to develop a propensity to answer questions with bibliography. It became part of the lore of the school that if one wanted a complete, cross-indexed, annotated bibliography on almost any topic, he had but to capture JLA at the corner of Woodlawn and 57th Streets, on his way home from classes. At Harvard, the same point is made by graduate students, who tell incoming B.D. candidates that Adams has nightmares that somewhere in Widener Library is a book he has not read.

Adams' academic interests are always supplemented by activity. I shall only report a partial, indeed selected, list of organizations and activities in which Adams has been involved, but these should show how seriously he took his own injunctions regarding the importance of voluntary associational participation.

Member, State Board, Americans for Democratic Action
Editor, *Christian Register*
Member, Unitarian Commission of Appraisal
Editor, *Journal of Liberal Religion*

Assoc. Editor, *The Protestant*

Chairman, Independent Voters of Illinois

Chairman, National Advisory Committee, Department of Social Responsibility, Unitarian Universalist Association

Chairman, Admissions Committee, Albert Schweitzer College

Member, Advisory Board, American Christian Palestine Committee

Member, Unitarian Commission of Planning and Review

Assoc. Editor, *Faith and Freedom* (British)

Co-Editor, *Journal of Religion*

Chairman, Advisory Board, Beacon Press

Member, American Committee for Cultural Freedom

Consultant, Legal Defense and Educational Committee, National Assn. for the Advancement of Colored People

Member, Apollos Club

Member and officer, Christian Action, Chicago Chapter

Vice-President, Chicago Chapter, Protestants and Other Americans United for Separation of Church and State

Member, Religion and Labor Foundation

Member, American Assn. of University Professors

Member, Middle West Theologians Ecumenical Group

Member, National Committee to Repeal McCarran Act

Member, State Board, Civil Liberties Union

Member, Unitarian Fellowship for Social Justice

Member, Hyde Park Community Conference

President, Society for the Scientific Study of Religion

Member, International Council, La Société Européenne de Culture

Member, Congress of Racial Equality

Member, National Advisory Board, Northern Student Movement

Member, State Board, American Assn. for the United Nations

Member, American Society for Political and Legal Philosophy

Member, American Society of Christian Social Ethics

Fellow, American Academy of Arts and Sciences

Member, American Sociological Association

The major trends of JLA's life have been suggested. The dominant, overarching result of his thought has been the development of an associational interpretation of history.[29] The various periods of history and the various philosophies of each epoch are exegeted primarily through, and find much of their importance in, the kinds of social structures characteristic of the period. A typical statement from his lectures is, "If you want to know what a man means by a given set of theological concepts, ask him what his ecclesiology is," although he recognizes that theological meaning is not thereby exhausted. The ways in which power is distributed, authority functions, and institutional requirements are met in the church are the best place to take the pulse of a theology. Further, if a man sets forth a political philosophy or a set of moral principles, ask him how he is to implement this in the community—that will give you some notion of what it actually means.

But this is not merely a theoretical concern for JLA; it is a quite practical matter. While it is true that it is various refinements on this set of fugues that provide the center of his lecturing concern and the substance of his correspondence, these concerns find their embodiment in his own involvement. He is still active and holds office in a variety of organizations, most notably in ADA and Civil Liberties Union, although the move to Harvard did cut him off from certain channels of inside information and some organizations that he had cultivated for two decades in Chicago.

The impression should not be left, however, that it is only political and parapolitical efforts that occupy him. While these are important, two other areas of activity and sensitivity should be mentioned. Both are interests of long standing, but have come to focus especially since Professor and Mrs. Adams came to Harvard and began spending their summers in the Berkshires. Since his youth Adams had an interest in music, nurtured in his youth even though his parents feared that it might turn to jazz, and at Chicago in lunch-break chamber music sessions with some friends. Also for nearly two decades while Adams was in Chicago, students would gather in the Adams' living room once a week to listen to recordings, discuss composers and compositions, and attempt to relate this art form to other aspects of cultural life. (Adams now has one of the finest hi-fi and stereo component rigs I have seen.) Mrs. Adams had studied at the New England Conservatory and was considered an accomplished pianist. Dr. and Mrs. Adams had been also, respectively, members of the Glee Club and of the Radcliffe Choral Society. (Mrs. Adams attended Radcliffe for three and one-half years, although she actually received her degree from the University of Chicago.) The interest in music has persisted; they spend their summers now only seventeen miles from Tanglewood, where the Boston Symphony plays almost daily, and are in regular attendance at these concerts.[30] Also they have become interested in Ted Shawn's School for the ballet at nearby Jacob's Pillow. For Adams, this has, characteristically, become a passion. The expression of ecstasy, creativity, and spirit through disciplined form and the body could not but intrigue one of his persuasions.

But the majority of their time in the Berkshires is taken up by their involvement with Gould Farm,[31] a therapeutic halfway house for those who have emotional disturbances and are on their way back to society. Gould Farm is located near Tanglewood and Jacob's Pillow. Frequent weekends and most summers are spent at Gould Farm in working, talking, and discussing with those trying to break free of bonds that inhibit existence by establishing new associations.

His energies are still not exhausted. In the summer of 1952 he was asked to become a member of a Study Tour of the Middle East under the auspices of the American Christian Palestine Committee. During the course of the extended trip he lectured in England and at the Albert Schweitzer College in Switzerland. In 1953 he delivered the Noble Lectures at Harvard, and it was soon thereafter that he was called to Harvard Divinity School. In Tokyo in the summer of 1958, he was a participant in the Ninth International Congress for the History of Religions, an experience that provided the occasion for the development of many friendships in the Orient as well as in Europe. During that summer he also lectured in Rangoon, Calcutta, and Bangalore. In 1960, he delivered a paper at the Arminius Symposium in Amsterdam and had the opportunity to renew European acquaintances.

More recently, in the school year 1962-63, he traveled in Europe on his sabbatical, being relieved at Harvard by his former student, James Gustafson of Yale. He delivered the Hibbert Lectures in England, lectured widely in Germany and Italy, and was a guest professor at Marburg University. Perhaps the most remarkable thing about these trips is JLA's ability to sustain the contacts and friendships made during his excursions. From all over the world in each day's mail come letters, manuscripts, and reprints. His daily mail is a funnel through which theologians and ethicists from many countries channel their products and from which they derive much sustenance.

One could continue and supplement such a chronicle at nearly every sentence, for if one can prevail upon JLA to "repeal reticence," as he says trying to get others to talk of themselves, the stories flow like an artesian well—and with the artistry of a master bard. But space forbids. One can now only ask briefly what is the significance of such a constellation of concerns in the modern theological scene.

In a day when the harsher shouting of THE WORD by self-conscious Neo-Reformation theology is getting somewhat smaller audiences, when the radical existentialism produced by the *anomie* of the post-World War II period is recognized as insufficient for full understanding of modern man, when the Ecumenical Movement within Protestantism and within Christianity at large is the dominant mood, even if we are not sure why or whither, it is instructive to listen to one who has heard, really heard, many speakers for some time.[32] JLA is a liberal who refused to be intimidated by the attempts of some branches of Neo-Protestantism to shout down a caricatured straw man. At the same time he was sensitive and receptive to the just criticisms against the false securities of a liberalism that was becoming LIBERALISM. While he persisted in unmasking the pretentions of a liberalism that attempted to erect itself into an inverted dogmatism, he continued to demand that the neo-orthodox theologians acknowledge (1) their indebtedness and continuity with certain aspects of the 19th century, and (2) the power that the social situation exerts on their efforts, lest they erect culturally determined temporality into a presumptuous and false eternality.

Hence, he provides some helpful hints for the new generation that must attempt, as each generation must, to construct a theological and associational framework that is adequate to the understanding, fulfillment, and transformation of the life that we now live interpreted by the faith we know. JLA suggests again and again a possible direction for what appears to be an emergent, chastised neo-liberalism.

The critical-comparative approach with which we started our tale is one that is necessary not only for understanding his life nor only for suggesting his significance for theology at large but also for understanding his students. For it is in the theologically sensitive social witness of pastors trained under him and in the theses and books of his graduate students that the seminal, if diffuse and sometimes even fragmented, ideas of Adams are worked out systematically. Yet it must be said that any student who has tried to grasp the depths of these efforts has felt frustrated at the inability to measure up to the standards set by Adams. And while, working under JLA, the student becomes sure that he will never really be a scholar, that he will never be able to box the intellectual compass in a comparable way, he also becomes sure that he will henceforth know a scholar when he sees one.

Again, his style of teaching is as interesting as the subject matter and the results. He strides into his 9:00 a.m. class, having just come from a committee meeting or from two hours of dictating correspondence. He greets the brethren as he takes off his hat and coat, which, after class, he will invariably forget to recover until the next class is about to start in the same room. He opens his briefcase, and hauls forth voluminous notes and often several books that he plans to make reference to. (This practice seems to be in decline, but those who knew him in his first few years of teaching report, perhaps apocryphally, that he had to make several trips to get all the volumes to be used in the classroom.) Then, like an old evangelical who has memorized the Bible, he consults the pages before him only long enough to trigger his mind. Stalking around the room, he then delivers himself of his lecture.

The lectures themselves have been variously characterized, partly, I suspect, because of the variation of the lectures from year to year. While the main concerns remain the same, surrounding these is an ever differing way of painting the picture. The concerns are the perennial efforts of Man to discern the realities of his situation under God and in history, but the treatment is ever changing. If one reads the lecture notes of students ten years ago and compares them with his own, one finds the outline strikingly similar, but the interlinear excursuses are a catalogue of what Professor Adams has been reading or experiencing, a chronological account of man's alternating sensitivities that occur in the literature on the subject under discussion.

But his teaching is not confined to the classroom, nor has it ended. (The difficulty of writing about someone whose career is still in full bloom is that it necessitates an artificial conclusion, stopping where there is no end.) His teaching reaches as far, one is tempted to say, as the mails will carry.

It is not inappropriate that we speak of his correspondence when we speak of his writings. His letters flow with incredible volume and scope to every corner of the globe. For innumerable theologians, philosophers, former students, friends, politicians, and acquaintances, James Luther Adams serves as a one-man clearinghouse of information. He knows where the research on such and such topic is taking place and where one might find a bibliography on a given subject. He also knows the wives and children and private interests of most of the correspondents. Perhaps, thus, it is appropriate to close with a quotation from a letter that could be duplicated a dozen times from as many countries.

Franklin Littell spoke for us all when he wrote, on hearing of the preparation of this biographical sketch:

> The thing I hope you will emphasize is his extraordinary generosity to scholars everywhere. For example, I have never taken any classes with him. Nevertheless, he has sent me reprints, bibliographical notes, etc., for all these years (since 1938) and taken the most direct personal interest in helping me learn. During the years I spent in Germany, nearly a decade, he was my best correspondent and advisor on what was happening in intellectual circles here, what books to read and so on. This generosity of spirit is typical—the most typical thing about Jim besides his encyclopedic knowledge.

# XVIII / VOLUNTARY ASSOCIATIONS
# AS A KEY TO HISTORY*

## James D. Hunt

The faith of a free man is a dependence upon creative powers not of his own making which finds its focus in cooperative effort for the common good. Ultimate meaning and ethical purpose are thereby affirmed, but then James Luther Adams makes his distinctive and characteristic demand:

> The third tenet of the free man's faith is that the achievement of freedom in community requires the power of organization and the organization of power. The free man will be an unfree man, he will be a victim of tyranny from within or from without, if his free faith does not assume *form,* in both word and deed. The commanding, transforming reality is a shaping power; it shapes one's beliefs about that reality, and when it works through men it shapes the community of justice and love.

Effective spirituality requires that power be asserted on behalf of freedom and justice, and above all it requires participation in (or the formation of) associations that can be effective in the face of political realities. "The decisive forms of goodness in society are institutional forms," he asserts.

This article will take associations as the key to Adams' thought, first as a principle for understanding society and history, and secondly as an ethical principle, that is, for shaping society and history.

### AN ASSOCIATIONAL PHILOSOPHY OF HISTORY

By identifying associations as the significant concept for his interpretation of history and society, Adams points to the sociological dimension of his interest in history and to the ethical nature of his theologi-

* An abridgment of a chapter of *James Luther Adams and His Demand for an Effective Religious Liberalism* (unpublished Ph.D. dissertation, Syracuse University, 1965). This section consists largely of direct quotation and close paraphrase of Dr. Adams' published work, supplemented by tape-recordings of conversations between D. B. Robertson and JLA in 1964.

cal concern. History is made by persons and groups in the context of social forces. History is thus understood chiefly in terms of the appearance and interplay of various types of associations and institutions, while ethics is to be understood as demanding participation in history through such associations, and theologies and theories of ethics are to be understood in large measure in terms of the churches that propound them. Man as a historical being is to be understood in terms of the types of association (voluntary and involuntary) under which or in face of which he lives, or in which he participates.

An associational theory of history illuminates the variety of particular situations which have contributed to the development of modern man. Thus it is a type of historical reflection less well suited to talking about man as such than about man as a concrete historical being in a particular context. Such an approach will stress the diversities of human experience and the concrete particularity of each situation. Furthermore, it will stress the interplay between thought and social structures.

One may determine the character of society in part by observing the types of assocation in it and the relations between them. The history of associations and associational theory in the West shows a succession of patterns. The primitive church was a voluntary association in the sense that one became a member in principle by virtue of choice, though the Christians believed the church to be created by God and not by man and though the entire family often joined the church. In effect the church asserted the right of freedom of association. Alfred North Whitehead has observed that the dictum "Render unto Caesar that which is Caesar's and unto God that which is God's" became a novel principle of social organization, differentiating between politics and religion. Subsequently the church became a bureaucratic organization with centralized authority; it entered into junction with the state and became also an involuntary association. In feudal society one may observe a shifting tension between associations of an authoritarian character and those of a consensual nature. Not only the sects and heresies but also the guilds and towns in one way or another asserted free association. In the Reformation, the Right Wing maintained the conception of "Christendom," the theory that both truth and social stability require uniformity of religion, while the Left Wing, despite suppression, maintained the principle of freedom of association. In seventeenth-century England the principle of freedom of association took the form of a demand for separation of church and state, while under neo-Calvinist influence the internal organization of the church was transformed in a manner which has been called protodemocratic. Radical laicism, the right and responsibility of every member to participate in making social decisions, and the protection of the minority were affirmed. Following upon these developments much of this church associational theory was taken over by analogy into the field of politics and applied to the state in theories of constitutionalism, free assembly, and wider suffrage. The liberal society spawned an immense variety of voluntary associations, including of course the voluntary business enterprise, free of state regulation, which later became a gigantic voluntary association with specialized interests and oligarchic patterns of control. In a mass society, patterns of participation in voluntary associations emerge in which social decisions are effectively made by oligarchic groups (pressure groups), while mass participation is chiefly in associations concerned with sociability, hobbies, and prestige or status, and the churches tend to promote a merely personal ethic and to ignore non-ecclesiastical associational responsibilities.

The variety and complexity of these associational patterns may be brought under the control of a typology of associations which may be related to historical periods. While Adams has not developed a particular typology or periodization of history, he has shown a lasting interest in the formulations of a number of early twentieth-century German social theorists. Max Weber adumbrated a philosophy of history in terms of his typology of authority—traditional, rational-legal, and charismatic (relying here in part on Sohm's *Kirchenrecht*). Ernst Troeltsch, Weber's associate, offered a typology of religious associations—church, sect, and mysticism—which becomes the basis of a philosophy of church history. He has also offered a typology of Christian political theory, arranged according to the degree of reliance upon individual spontaneity or upon the external shaping disciplines. But it is in Otto von Gierke, the jurist, that this associational theory of history and its periods may be best seen. In his magnum opus, *Das deutsche Genossenschaftsrecht* (The German Law of Associations), Gierke offers a theory of the periodization of Western history from the time of Charlemagne to the eighteenth century, a theory that characterizes the periods in terms of the dominant types of association. Central to it is the struggle between rival conceptions of community: the "lordly union" (*Herrschaftlicher Verband*) in which authority emanates from the top down, and the grass-roots consensus, in which authority emerges from the people.

This particularizing mentality which tries to interpret history in terms of events and changing social structures has its roots in the Bible. The characteristic literary form of the Bible is narrative, and the narrative concerns the fate of the associations through which God reveals his will in history, the covenant community and the church.

Prophetic religion in particular saw God as active in history, choosing his people, forming the community, liberating it from bondage, holding it under judgment, and promising it fulfillment. The answer George Foot Moore once required of his students, "A prophet is one who foretells doom!" points to their character as epochal thinkers: they think in terms of ages, interpreting a crisis as a crisis of an age, and seeing themselves as called to foretell the coming of a new epoch. In the New Testament the historical interpretation eventuates in eschatology, wherein history points toward a meaning that is not to be realized in history. Adams finds particularly fruitful here Rudolf Otto's conception of the Kingdom as paradoxical: both present power and future possibility, as that great German liberal set it forth in his last book, *The Kingdom of God and the Son of Man*. Recent New Testament studies, on angelology and the doctrine of the Kingship of Christ, have borne out Adams' contention that redemption as conceived in the Gospels included the institutions of society as a whole. Evil was conceived in terms of principalities and powers, and as Jesus suggests in his prayer, "Lead us not into temptation, but deliver us from the evil one," the Kingdom of God carries on a struggle against the invisible powers of darkness which corrupt and distort and even destroy order and justice and peace. In these Biblical studies Adams finds support for his contention that the controlling concepts of the Bible (covenant, Messiah, kingdom of God or of Christ) are drawn from political existence—those aspects of life which concern the total community. God calls a community into existence, and the doctrine of the covenant asserts that each member of the community is responsible for the character of society as well as for his personal character. Alongside the political symbolism in the Bible is domestic symbolism, drawn from the life of the family: lover and beloved, father and child, Israel or the church as a bride. This domestic symbolism underscores the interpersonal relationships and the role of affection; but it is not the controlling symbolism. The Old Testament should be understood as employing political symbolism with domestic symbolism in its arms, for God is King, and that means that the demand for meaningful human existence has to be understood as the responsibility of the whole people for the character of its institutions; and then the domestic symbolism gives still further indication of what the internal relationships should be of those people who make up the political entity, and of the relationship between God and the individual and God and the community.

Parenthetically, it may be observed that a historical interpretation through epochs Biblically articulated has been a part of Adams' experience since his youth in a Fundamentalist group (Plymouth Brethren) which took seriously the periodization of history in the Scofield Reference Bible, although the successive dispensations merely revealed human impotence and heightened the expectation of the Second Coming. Adams has described his own religious development as a transformation of this attitude, from perceiving himself a stranger in time to perceiving time as the essence of both God and man; and from thinking of salvation as an escape of the elect from time, to envisaging it as taking place in community and in time. Thus he entitled his autobiographical essay "Taking Time Seriously," asserting that the significance of events is to be found in the struggle between good and evil, between justice and injustice, and suggesting further that this meaning must be "taken": it must be sought and grasped. It does not come except to those who respond to the divine power by the exercise of power in the flow of events.

The elements of a philosophy of history which appear in Adams' writings show a strong preference for voluntarism, and his major statement on the interpretation of history, *The Changing Reputation of Human Nature,* calls for the adoption of a voluntarist interpretation to supplement and correct rationalism. By voluntarism is asserted that will or creativity is the decisive factor in human nature and that will is the ultimate constituent of reality. In general, a voluntarist view exalts the dynamic aspects of existence, conceiving of man's proper goal as the fulfillment of the life-giving powers inherent in existence. Here the elements of struggle, contradiction, and tragedy rather than the element of harmony are emphasized.

Adams' voluntarism received a major stimulus from Irving Babbitt and literary humanism. As a former sectarian who still thought of religion in terms of commitment, Adams found himself frustrated in the objective, value-neutral atmosphere of the Divinity School, where the emphasis was on historical studies. The frustration became acute at the point of preaching. In this dilemma, Babbitt appeared as a man who was fighting for something, a man who had a programmatic, civilization-saving gospel. He had a notion of the major trends of Western civilization, offering his classically-oriented humanism against the destructive obscurantist trends of romanticism. With Babbitt as a teacher, a survey of ideas or men was not merely a succession of pictures, but a series of positions in face of which one had to take a stance, and Adams found this exhilarating. Certain religious and ethical concepts, especially the Christian doctrines of sin and grace, in a humanistic reinterpretation, became plausible and important within the context of a realistic conception of man that emphasized the central problem of civilization as that of ethical standards and stressed the necessity of something like conversion or change in the will. He also derived from Babbitt a framework for the study of ideas, the conception that ideas come in families and have a morphology which can be identified through various changes, so that a particular point of view might express itself in a variety of forms under varying circumstances. Babbitt, of course, gave the greatest attention to romanticism and its morphology, and when Adams went to Germany in 1927 he found himself able to identify the young Nazi movement as a late form of romanticism, and thus to account in part for the impotence of liberal theology in face of Nazism, for liberalism shared some of its romantic features.

Christian voluntarism finds its rootage in Paul and Augustine, and Adams turned next to a study of Augustine's psychology of the will. One becomes what one loves, and one gives attention to objects by reason of an act of the will, or decision. Adams, in indebtedness to Heinrich Scholz, found Augustine's conception of the Two Cities an application by analogy of his theory of the drama, wherein the former professor of rhetoric applied the Greek dramatic conception of a conflict of wills to history.

The voluntarist view conceives history and human experience in terms of conflict, which thus becomes not a peripheral or merely pathological aspect of existence but a central fact and a concept by means of which both health and pathology must be interpreted. A model of human experience based on reason and equilibrium is inadequate to account for change and the dynamic factors of history. Adams reserves some of his strongest disdain for the doctrine of an automatic harmony of interests as it can be seen in laissez-faire economics or in liberal theology. In each case he wishes to supplement the model with insights drawn from a conflict model of society which employs will and power as central elements. In sociology the outstanding representative of equilibrium-model theory is Talcott Parsons, and Adams has become vividly aware of some of the questionable implications of his position since coming back to Harvard. Most of his students take work with Parsons, and consequently tension is to be observed between the thrust of Adams' courses and the thrust of Parsons' "social system." Adams finds an ambivalence created in his students, who appreciate the comprehensiveness of the "social system" but at the same time exhibit discomfort in the place of the complacency of the system, its disposition to explain problems away by promising they will be taken care of by equilibration, and its relative lack of empirical research on specific problems. On the other side, students respond favorably to Adams' insistence on conflict and on the prophetic dimension of the Bible and Christian faith, and to the focus placed upon specific problems in the social order; at the same time they experience frustration in face of his unwillingness to explain things in terms of "a social system." Adams places little reliance on automatic forces making for equilibrium, but much emphasis on responsibility for participation in the processes that make for social justice. His emphasis on associational theory serves in some measure as a systematic approach, delineating forms of participation in change and in power conflict and in the exercise of constraint.

A voluntaristic interpretation of history places questions of power at the center of interest. Conflict is an expression of vitality, and historical action is expressed in terms of power and requires the analysis of power. Nor is the concept of power alien to religion. It is both the basic category of being and the basic category of social action, and thus may be taken as an integrating concept for both theological and sociological analysis, presenting both descriptive and normative perspectives within the same framework.

The conception of power appears throughout Scripture, where God is presented as "great in power and justice," where the power of the Lord comes upon the prophet, where power went forth from Jesus, and where the disciples were promised that they would be clothed with power from on high. Great deeds are done in the power of the Spirit, in face of the principalities and powers. The gospel itself is called the power of God for salvation to everyone who has faith. Religion cannot be described without the concept, nor can power be properly described without employing religious concepts. Adams understands the fundamental structure of the universe dynamically, as in Tillich's formulation, "The power of being," and in the process philosophy of his former teacher Alfred North Whitehead.

Adams insists first of all that power has always a double character. Theologically stated, it is God's law and love and also man's response to the possibilities of being, the exercise of man's freedom. Power is thus both God's law and man's response, necessity and freedom. Its essential character is fully displayed in a brief passage of Plato, cited by Whitehead:

> My suggestion would be, that anything which possesses any sort of power to affect another, or to be affected by another even for a moment, however trifling the cause and however slight and momentary the effect, has real existence; and I hold that the definition of being is simply power. (*Sophist* 247)

Here being is indentified with power, and power is seen in its duality as the condition and limit of man's social existence. Power is present equally in the capacity to exercise influence and in the capacity to be influenced. Power exhibits duality, but it is one in this duality: There is no adequate conception of power as freedom except as it is simultaneously conceived as law and except as it is viewed in a context of interaction ultimately grounded in the divine power of being.

The dialectic of power operates on many levels. Theologically, there is a dialectic between the two primary terms—God's law and man's freedom—and also a dialectic within each term, as power is seen in both active and passive forms. God is creative and redemptive power, primarily active, in Christian thought, but he takes satisfaction in man's free obedience and in this respect is responsive to man's behavior. Man possesses creative freedom, but he is also influenced by participating in God's power and in the other manifestations of creativity in the human community.

The typical sociological definition of power as the capacity to influence others in accordance with one's own intentions is a truncated definition. Max Weber's definition, for one, makes explicit reference only to this active power as "the probability that one actor within a social relationship will be in a position to carry out his will despite resistance, regardless of the basis on which this probability rests." Power is *Macht,* and the definition makes room for force, for domination, and for manipulation, but it does not explicitly include the power of those who are dominated nor does it comprehend power as responding to influence. Understood only as man's freedom, this power is the basis of Lord Acton's dictum that "Power tends to corrupt, and absolute power corrupts absolutely." In this case power is corruption, and personal piety may be cultivated, like Candide's garden, only by avoiding involvement. Yet if power is conceived as response as well as assertion, as law as well as freedom, then it may be creative rather than destructive.

Weber's definition, or any other that includes only active power, is inadequate for a conception of community, or for a democratic conception of participation, where the mode of power required is better expressed by the term "mutuality," or the capacity to enter into give-and-take, to cooperate without submission, and to participate in discussion toward the formation of consensus. Weber's formulation accounts for "power over" others, but it does not include an adequate conception of "power of," the ability and possession of the group itself, which is signified by the conception of power as response. Adams stresses that the capacity to be influenced is not merely a passive quality, but includes the capacity to make an active response, as in the case of a listener's response to Beethoven. In a similar manner the power of the early church was based on the capacity of the early Christians to recognize and respond to the significance of Jesus, their response including the formation of a new community, whose strength included their power also to resist the world. In all of these instances it should be emphasized that power does not exist *in vacuo;* it exists in some relationship, between nature and man, between men or groups of men, or between God and men. As a relation, it must always be stated in two terms: law and freedom.

The decisive aspect of associations is power, conceived as the capacity to participate in making social decisions. Man as a social being forms groups, and his power to form groups is an aspect of his being. He also participates in groups which he did not directly form, and within groups his power of participation relates to the crucial questions of the structure of the organization, leadership, the assignment of responsibilities, policy decisions, and decisions regarding the implementation of policy. Thus Adams is particularly interested in forms of association which are open to participation and through which men exert power in history, toward the formation of a free and just society. The forms of association which exist in a society in a historical moment are the forms of power in that society, and an effective social ethic requires the organization of power for its purposes and in the forms that permit realization of its purposes.

"Every citizen who thus possesses by law a share of political power, *is* one of the powers that be," William Whewell wrote. The analysis of power leads to a study of the role of the groups in which power is held and lost, for human history is the history of groups. Thus history, sociology, and prophetic theology converge upon the concept of the association, voluntary and involuntary.

### THE VOLUNTARY ASSOCIATION AS AN ETHICAL INSTRUMENT

"The voluntary association concerned with public policy is an indispensable element of the democratic society." This is the central assertion of Adams' social ethics. This section of the article will set forth briefly some major dimensions of his treatment of associations: his conception of religion as associational, his associational conception of ethics, and some critical reflections on associations.

Throughout his career Adams has been insistent on the institutional aspect of religion, following T. S. Eliot in his criticism of Babbitt's humanism, that it called for a religion without a church. Despite Babbitt's welcome attack on atomistic individualism, it was the Roman Catholic lay theologian Baron Friedrich von Hügel to whom Adams turned for a persuasive doctrine of institutions based on a historical sense and on an interest in the devotional life. The church as an inclusive institution and as a vehicle for the transmission of tradition offers a discipline and a corrective to individualism. Purely personal religion tends to be thin, feeding on self-sufficiency. The greatest enemy of religion, von Hügel held, is not materialism but "pure spirituality," the illusion that religion does not involve the body and the senses in specific acts of self-discipline and worship. Although von Hügel ignored the economic aspects of institutions, failing to take contemporary history seriously and thus not developing a prophetic social ethics, he helped Adams become acquainted with Ernst Troeltsch, the greatest Protestant student of institutional Christianity. Adams has become a leading American interpreter of Troeltsch, commending his recognition of the historical nature of Christianity and his appreciation for the variety of Christian manifestations, especially the variety of Christian ethics. Troeltsch holds that an authentic Christianity will stand in tension with the culture in the full-fledged sense of being concerned about the full range of social institutions and problems, and in his idea of Compromise examined the process whereby a universal religion comes to terms creatively by means of mediating elements in political and economic matters to form a unity of civilization. Therefore the history of the Christian ethos is the continually renewed search for this compromise, and of opposition to the compromise, so that the "essence" of Christianity is to be seen only in terms of its multifold manifestations, which never exhaust its vitality, and it is still open. Adams goes beyond Troeltsch in recognizing the historical and associational nature of the Biblical faith as well, stressing the doctrine of the covenant, and in rejecting (with Tillich) Troeltsch's philosophical framework of idealistic theism.

Adams' most distinctive emphasis with respect to the church is on the importance and role of discipline. Discipline in the church is another word for the practical means by which a religious group maintains its character and resists mere accommodation. Disciplines are commonly understood as penal and remedial, but more significantly they represent the process in community whereby charismatic power is engendered and recognized. The disciplines represent the place where the dialogue of spirit and law occurs for the creation and re-creation of community. The process can emerge and be effective only in a primary group of person-to-person relations, a small committed group, an *ecclesiola in ecclesia*. The divine community-forming power works initially and decisively through such groups, and there the vitalities of the sect become manifest: intimate fellowship, explicit faith, the expression of concerns, the identification of adversaries, the achievement of consensus, the protection of the freedom of the spirit, the definition of models, the practice of self-criticism of the group, and the disciplined definition and application of norms to the whole life of the believers. Adams often cites the Whitehead axiom, "Definition is the soul of actuality." It is only through the small committed group that renewal of the church comes, and it is only through the small committed group in face of meaninglessness and suffering that the meaning of history finally manifests itself. Through such groups also, diversity is nourished, and support is given to the efforts of individuals to relate "religion" to reality and develop community. Prophetic religion especially requires institutional form and a historical and associational analysis of culture, as Adams indicated in one of his earliest addresses by contrasting the martyred prophet with "the prophet who keeps his job." Both prophesy to the church, but the latter binds the congregation and himself in a common discipline in the service of sustaining and transforming powers.

The theological dimension of these powers is seen in the doctrine of grace, which Adams identified as the distinctive feature of religion. The doctrine of grace is a recognition of the supporting powers, or the way in which an individual is strengthened. Adams had early in his career found in Babbitt a humanistic reinterpretation of the doctrine of grace, but it was a truncated concept, and what was particularly lacking was the element of "strengthening grace." Babbitt's "higher will" was equivalent to "illuminating grace," or the revelation of standards, but illumination without assistance merely heightens the burden and does not save. The search for a more adequate doctrine of grace is the theological aspect of Adams' quest for an adequate doctrine of institutional religion. The church, as von Hügel indicated, is not merely a burden which the individual is called upon to support; it supports the individual in his effort to relate religion to social and personal realities. To the Unitarian Ministers Institute at Greenfield, Massachusetts in 1934, he set forth (with Andrew Banning and Vivian T. Pomeroy) a report on "The Religious Content of Liberalism" which stressed the doctrine of grace and called for the adoption of disciplined group study and worship. The "Greenfield Group" of Unitarian ministers, formed on the basis of this report, undertook a study program based on von Hügel's practice in *Letters to a Niece* of studying simultaneously two rather different topics, one sacred and one secular. The first year's assignment combined St. Francis de Sales and Karl Marx. Adams' interest in devotional communities, especially among the Benedictines and more recently the Zen Buddhist, also exhibits this conjunction of group discipline and the doctrine of grace.

A nonhistorical and noninstitutional conception of piety may be found in the work of the Lutheran jurist and lay theologian Rudolf Sohm, to which Adams has given much attention. Sohm conceives of Christianity as a purely inward and spontaneous response to the Word. The early church had no law except the authority of the Holy Spirit, but it became corrupted into the Roman Church by the adoption of an alien principle, the principle of law, an authority that belongs to the political order. "The natural man is a born Catholic," Sohm contended, attributing the change to a desire for security. The fall of the church was its transformation from charismatic authority to bureaucratic authority, a conception Weber was to use extensively. This conception of religion has the merit of stressing the divine community-forming power rather than the institutional church as the creative agent, but as a conception of faith it is politically and culturally disastrous. For Sohm, the polity of the visible church is a matter of indifference, and since faith cannot be expressed in polity, social-action programs are limited to charity rather than the quest for justice. Adams points out that Sohm failed to recognize the forms of authority in the early church and the gospel, and that his conception of the Spirit is constricted. In Sohm the Lutheran divorce of religion from history in the Two-Kingdom theory comes to fruition.

Adams' associational conception of religion owes more to Calvin and the Left Wing of the Reformation. Calvin considered the polity of the church to be a central issue, and in subsequent history the Calvinists have shown a genius for establishing associations, as Troeltsch has pointed out. Through Calvinism came also a revival of the doctrine of the covenant. The Left Wing, in the name of the freedom of the Spirit, asserted a new conception of autonomous Christian personality supported by "inner light," the rejection of coercion in belief and in the shaping of public policy, the principle of the consent of the governed, and a pluralistic conception of the churches and society. Such principles of radical laicism, as derived from the Radical Reformation through English Nonconformity, provide the basis for the development of voluntary associations. The congregational form of church government and its separation from the state are the prototype of the voluntary association concerned with public policy.

Voluntary associations serve as a principal means in modern society for the articulation and protection of differences, as did the non-conforming congregation. They provide an instrumentality for the freedom of the individual to associate with others in the promotion of forms of consensus which are not shared by the total community. At least in principle, they resist a monolithic social order: they stand between the individual and the state and provide a means for dispersing power and opportunities for participation. They protect the freedom to criticize, the freedom to express newly felt needs, the freedom to define the situation in a new way, and the freedom to instigate or to implement social change. Thus they become, in a mass society, an indispensable means for dealing with injustice, with strain and conflict, and for shaping public opinion. By engendering the habit of discussion and participation, and training leadership, and providing opportunities for the definition and expression of concerns, they help prevent the appearance of splits that could create revolutionary situations. We may say that voluntary associations institutionalized and gradualized revolution. Mass man may be defined sociologically as the man who is not a participant in the process of decision-making with respect to public policy. Such participation for the citizen and churchman can only be effective through associations, and accordingly any realistic ethical program must include the requirement of participation in the groups which seek to affect policy for the general welfare.

The doctrine of vocation, which has been typically reduced to a doctrine of work on the job, needs to be re-established in a manner that articulates the responsibility of an individual to respond to the power of God by assuming an obligation to participate in the making of group decisions. As Adams spells it out, the obligation is fourfold: first, to help make the general citizenry aware of the decisive importance of voluntary associations in the articulation and implementation of public opinion, contravening in this way the dehumanization brought about by the mass society; second, to give oneself directly to associations that aim directly to overcome social evils, in this way exerting oneself especially for the sake of underprivileged groups; third, to encourage those forces which work against oligarchic tendencies within voluntary associations and within political and economic associations; and fourth, to promote the free discussion of public issues and of fresh possibilities of policy and organization.

Curiously, Protestantism, despite its promotion of voluntary associations in the past, has also contributed to a decline of participation in associations concerned with public policy with its conception that religion has to do with the inner life and the family life of the individual but not with public issues. This pietism may have intensified the piety and inwardness of the individual, but in many quarters it has also removed the social and political order from the religious domain. Protestantism has an almost inexhaustable capacity for neglecting the community element in the divine-human relationship, for which it may appeal with ease for sanction in the Gospels. Thus, Christian ethics reduced to personalism, systematic theology with no reference to institutions, psychotherapy without a sociological framework, and abstract existentialism that talks about concreteness and decision but does not drive toward actualizing concreteness and decision in the social historical situation—these are the forms which the pietistic mentality takes. Playing a variation on Lord Acton, Adams asserts that impotence also corrupts, making one become merely the object or victim of power. True piety is not powerless, he asserts, but is found where the freedom and fulfillment of the individual are inextricably connected with the freedom and fulfillment of the groups to which he belongs.

The vocation of true piety, which includes responsible participation, includes the vocation of guarding against the perversions and the pathology of voluntary associations. There is, for example, the notion that voluntary associations can in all circumstances provide viable forms of integration in the community, a view associated with liberalism and anarchism. But in the face of serious economic maladjustment, or of major structural social needs, the demand for voluntary associational solution of the problem may be motivated by a class ideology. Likewise, voluntary associations may serve special interests rather than the general interest, that is, may function as pressure groups for narrow and particularistic interests. There are internal dangers to guard against also, especially Michels' "iron law of oligarchy," which asserts that the larger the organization the more readily it is subject to the disfunctions of bureaucratization. Such control by a power elite is aggravated in those professional associations where membership is not really voluntary. Further, there is a loss of personal freedom in organizations that repress minority opinion. The opportunities and dangers of associations in a pluralistic society were recognized by William Ellery Channing in his "Remarks on Associations." The pressure group in particular is a conspicuous illustration of the phenomenon that voluntary associations may be the means of concentrating power as well as of dispersing it.

The voluntary association is an indispensable instrument of Christian ethics, though not without its dangers and possibilities of perversion. Here ethical purpose and social structure meet for the disciplined release of power that is ultimately divine. In the small committed group faith becomes explicit and its implications are explored, and countermodels against the models of "the world" can be defined and made effective. Such associations are the means whereby the church and the individual achieve involvement in the world and participate in those processes which determine public policy. Ethical reflection that neglects the associational forms of power will remain impotent, and men who do not participate in groups that work actively for justice and liberty are irresponsible and dominated underlings. Our responsibility in society is to respond to the community-forming power of God by participation in the associations that define and re-define the actual situation, in the associations that give utterance and body to prophetic protest, in the associations that provide the occasion for the Christian and the non-Christian to enter into dialogue and even to achieve a working consensus, in short, in the associations that contribute to the shaping of history.

*Compiled by Ralph Potter, Jean Potter, and James Hunt*

BOOKS AND ARTICLES

### 1923

*The Angels' Revolt*. Minneapolis: University of Minnesota, 1923-24. Student Magazine co-edited by J. L. Adams. Mimeographed.

### 1927

"Service to God First Task of Religious Man," *The Salem Evening News* (Mass.) (February 28, 1927).

### 1931

"The Minister with Two Occupations," *The Christian Register,* CX, No. 38 (September 17, 1931), 713-714.

### 1932

"Humanism and Creation," *Hound and Horn,* VI (1932), 173-196.
"The Tyranny of a Free Minister," *The Christian Register,* CXI, Nos. 29-30 (July 21, 28, 1932), 451-452, and CXI, Nos. 31-32 (August 4, 11, 1932), 469-470.

### 1933

"Liberals and Religion," *The Christian Register,* CXII, No. 8 (February 23, 1933), 118.
"Assailing the Liberal's Defence: Its Symptoms But Not Its Essence," *The Christian Register,* CXII, No. 12 (March 23, 1933), 181, 194.
"Sic et Non," *The Christian Register,* CXII, No. 19 (May 11, 1933), 298.
"Need Well-Informed Public Opinion for Ending Mill Strike," *The Salem Evening News* (July 17, 1933), 1.

### 1934

"By Their Fruits," *The Christian Register,* CXIII, No. 18 (May 3, 1934), 296.

"The Liverpool Controversy," *The Christian Register,* CXIII, No. 30 (August 16, 1934), 496-497.

Editor of Symposium, "Contemporary Thought Around the World," *The Christian Register,* 1933-34. Included is article by James Luther Adams on "Baron Friedrich von Huegel," *The Christian Register,* CXIII, No. 37 (October 11, 1934), 603-606.

"Military Training in Our Colleges," *The Christian Register,* CXIII, No. 46 (December 13, 1934), 760.

## 1935

"Some Unsettled Accounts," *The Christian Register,* CXIV, No. 17 (April 25, 1935), 277.

"To Ask or Not to Ask," *The Christian Register,* CXIV, No. 33 (September 19, 1935), 541.

## 1936

*Unitarians Face a New Age,* Report of Commission of Appraisal of the American Unitarian Association (Boston, 1936), 348 pp. Document issued by Commission of which Dr. Adams was a member. Chapter on "Theological Education," special assignment to J. L. Adams, pp. 99-110.

## 1937

"Kurt Leese and German Liberalism," *The Christian Register,* CXVI, No. 28 (August 5, 1937), 463-465.

Translation of Theodor Siegfried, "Rudolph Otto, Theologian: An Apostle of the Kingdom of God," *The Inquirer* (London), No. 4971 (October 9, 1937), 485-486. Also in *The Christian Register,* CXVI, No. 42 (November 25, 1937), 696-698. Article originally appeared in *Protestantenblatt* (Berlin-Bremen-Köln) (April 4, 1937).

## 1939

Translation of "A Sad Document" (a pro-Nazi comment on Karl Barth's letter to Professor Hromadka), *Protestant Digest,* I, No. 2 (January 1939), 88-89.

"American Churchman Sees Parish Raided by Nazis," *The Hour* (New York: American Council Against Nazi Propaganda, June 30, 1939), 1.

Translation (with J. B. Allin) of "The Protestantism of Rembrandt," by W. A. Visser 't Hooft, *Protestant Digest,* I, No. 5 (April 1939), 79-85.

"Dr. Adams' Letter to a Responsible Official of the National Conference of Christians and Jews," *Protestant Digest,* I, No. 8 (July 1939), 1-7.

Translation of "Christianity and Peace," by André Philip. *Protestant Digest,* I, No. 8 (July 1939), 16-31.

"Why Liberal?" *Journal of Liberal Religion,* I, No. 2 (Autumn 1939), 3-8.

"Taking Time Seriously," *The Christian Century,* LVI, No. 36 (September 6, 1939), 1067-1070.

"Treasures New and Old," *The Christian Register,* CXVIII, No. 40 (November 9, 1939), 653-655.

## 1940

Translation (with Ernst Fraenkel) of "The Religious Symbol" by Paul Tillich. *Journal of Liberal Religion,* II, No. 1 (Summer 1940), 13-33.

"Recent Books on Democracy and Religion: A Survey," *Journal of Liberal Religion,* II, No. 2 (Autumn 1940), 93-100.

"The Liberalism that is Dead," *Journal of Liberal Religion,* I, No. 3 (Winter 1940), 38-42.

*On Being Human—The Liberal Way.* Boston: American Unitarian Association, Tract No. 359, 26 pp.

## 1941

"Emancipation Proclamation—1941," *Protestant Digest,* III, No. 12 (June-July 1941), 14-20.

*Frontiers of Freedom,* pamphlet reprint of a radio broadcast over NBC Blue Network, October 26, 1941. Reprinted in *Congressional Record,* 87, No. 191 (October 28, 1941), A4887-A4889.

"Freud, Mannheim, and the Liberal Doctrine of Man," *Journal of Liberal Religion,* II, No. 3 (Winter 1941), 107-111.

Memoir of Irving Babbitt by James Luther Adams and J. Bryan Allin, in *Irving Babbitt: Man and Teacher,* eds. F. Manchester and Odell Shepard (New York: G. P. Putnam's Sons, 1941), pp. 271-280.

## 1942

"Protestant Principles" (A basic policy for *The Protestant:* a statement of the Executive Council, Paul Tillich, chairman, Wilhelm Pauck, Gerhard Meyer, James L. Adams), *The Protestant,* IV, No. 5 (April-May 1942), 17-19.

"The Axis is Longer Than You Think—The Anti-Negro, Anti-Semitic, Anti-Labor, Anti-Progressive Axis," *The Protestant,* IV, No. 5 (April-May 1942), 23-28.

## 1943

"The Changing Reputation of Human Nature," *Journal of Liberal Religion,* IV, No. 2 (Autumn 1942), 59-72; IV, No. 3 (Winter 1943), 137-160. Reprinted as a brochure.

"Ten Books for Lenten Reading," *The Christian Register,* CXXII, No. 3 (March 1943), 84.

"Putting on the Whole Armour," *The Jaybird Listens* (Lake Geneva, Wis.: Conference Point, Summer 1943), pp. 1-2.

"Man in the Light of the War," *The Christian Century,* LX, No. 9 (March 3, 1943), 257-259.

"The Catholic Crusade," *Journal of Liberal Religion,* V, No. 2 (Autumn 1943), 101-110.

## 1944

"The Religious Problem," in *New Perspectives on Peace,* ed. G. B. de Huszar (Chicago: University of Chicago Press, 1944), pp. 227-264.

"Unity and Freedom in the New Federated Faculty at Chicago," *The Christian Register,* CXXIII, No. 1 (January 1944), 29; and *The Christian Leader,* CXXVI, No. 4 (February 19, 1944), 110-111.

*Policies for Germany,* University of Chicago Radio Round Table, No. 305 (January 23, 1944).

"Liberal Religion in a United World," *The Christian Register,* CXXIII, No. 2 (February 1944), 54-55.

"A Handbook on Postwar Reconstruction, Summary and Discussion with Bibliography," *Journal of Liberal Religion,* VI, No. 1 (Summer 1944), 47-55.

"Protestant Priests of Mammon: Spiritual Mobilization, Incorporated," *The Protestant,* V, No. 12 (October 1944), 14-18.

## 1945

"Peoples' Congress of Applied Religion," *The Protestant,* VI, No. 1 (January 1945), 30-32.

"Sources of Religious Insight," *The Christian Register,* CXXIV, No. 2 (February 1945), 45-48.

"The Evil That Good Men Do," *The Maine Church Exchange* (Saco, Maine), Vol. XI, No. 1 (Spring 1945), 2-8.

"Orthodox Church and Soviet State," *The Protestant,* VI, No. 2 (February 1945), 13-17.

"The Law of Nature in Graeco-Roman Thought," *Journal of Religion,* XXV, No. 2 (April 1945), 97-118.

"The Law of Nature: Some General Considerations," *Journal of Religion,* XXV, No. 2 (April 1945), 88-96.

"Unitarian Philosophies of History," *Journal of Liberal Religion,* VII, No. 2 (Autumn 1945), 90-107.

"What Kind of Religion Has a Place in Higher Education?" *Journal of Bible and Religion,* XIII, No. 4 (November 1945), 184-192.

## 1946

"Monthly Message," *Faith at Work,* I, No. 6 (February 1946), 4. Monthly publication of the Religious Associates of the National Citizens Political Action Committee (CIO).

"A Faith for Free Men" in *Together We Advance,* ed. S. H. Fritchman (Boston: Beacon Press, 1946), pp. 45-65; and in *The Epic of Unitarianism,* ed. David B. Parke (Boston: Starr King Press, 1957), pp. 149-154. Excerpt reprinted in *The Beacon* (Melbourne, Australia), No. 114 (April 1949), 5.

## 1947

"The Prophethood of All Believers," *The Christian Register,* CXXVI, No. 3 (March 1947), 95-96.

*Unitarians, Unite!* (co-author). Boston: American Unitarian Association, 1947. 35 pp.

## 1948

"The Evil That Good Men Do," in *Voices of Liberalism: 2* (Boston: Beacon Press, 1948), pp. 53-64.

Translation of *The Protestant Era* by Paul Tillich, with concluding essay, "Tillich's Concept of the Protestant Era" (Chicago: The University of Chicago Press, 1948). Abridged Edition: Chicago: The University of Chicago Press (Phoenix Books P19), 1957. (Dr. Adams' concluding essay, along with other material in Part 5, omitted from the paperback edition.)

"The Impact of Modern Thought on Unitarianism," *The Christian Register,* CXXVII, No. 5 (May 1948), 21-23. Co-author with Thaddeus B. Clark.

"Affirmative Liberalism. 'Oyster-Shell' and 'Jelly-Fish' Nihilism," *The Christian Register,* CXXVII, No. 6 (June 1948), 22-25.

## 1949

Henry Nelson Wieman, *The Directive in History* (Ayer Lectures), ed. and with an Introduction by J. L. Adams. The Phoenix Series (Boston: Beacon Press, 1949). General Editor, James L. Adams.

## 1950

"Basic Causes of Progress and Decay in Civilization," in *Orientation in Religious Education,* ed. P. H. Lotz (New York: Abingdon-Cokesbury, 1950), pp. 61-74.

Wilhelm Pauck, *The Heritage of the Reformation.* The Phoenix Series (Boston: Beacon Press, 1950). General Editor, James L. Adams.

"Christian Socialism," *Encyclopaedia Britannica,* Vol. X, 639 f.

"Christian Socialism," *Nelson's Loose-Leaf Encyclopedia,* 1950.

"Love and Law and 'The Good Old Cause,'" *The Divinity School News,* XVII, No. 3 (August 1, 1950), 1-8.

"Voters' Protest," *Christian Science Monitor* (Boston), Vol. 42, No. 253 (September 22, 1950), 20.

"Academic Nudism at the University of California," *The Pittsburgh Courier* (September 30, October 11, 1950).

"Social Morality and Medical Care," distributed by the Department of Adult Education and Social Relations, American Unitarian Association (Boston, October 7, 1950). 9 pp.

"Free Church Movement Shows Limited Upsurge in Germany," *Christian Science Monitor,* Vol. 42, No. 270 (October 11, 1950), 11.

"Theological Bases for Social Action," *Journal of Religious Thought,* VIII, No. 1 (Autumn-Winter 1950-51), 6-21.

"Public-Supported Higher Education: A Unitarian View," in *Religion in the State University,* ed. Henry E. Allen, Conference on Religion in the State Universities (University of Minnesota: Burgess Publishing Co., 1950), pp. 68-75.

## 1951

"Inquisitions Old and New," *The Chicago Jewish Forum,* IX (Summer 1951), 229-235.

"Natural Religion and the 'Myth' of the Eighteenth Century," *Harvard Divinity School Bulletin,* XVI (1951), 17-32.

"Why Another Fantastic Dogma in the Twentieth Century?" *Biosophical Review,* IX, No. 4 (1951). Symposium by Julian Huxley, Frederick Kettner, John Haynes Holmes, and James L. Adams. 19 pp.

## 1952

"Tillich's Interpretation of History," in *The Theology of Paul Tillich* (The Library of Living Theology, Vol. I), eds. Charles W. Kegley and Robert W. Bretall (New York: The Macmillan Co., 1952), pp. 294-309. (Macmillan Paperbacks, 1961.)

## 1953

"Our Responsibility in Society," Address at Oxford Congress of International Association for Liberal Christianity and Religious Freedom, 1952, in *Authority and Freedom* (Delft, Holland: W. Gaade, N.V., 1953), pp. 43-62; also in *Faith and Freedom* (Liverpool), VI, Part 2, No. 17 (Spring 1953).

"The Love of God," in *The Meaning of Love,* ed. Ashley Montagu (New York: Julian Press, 1953), pp. 233-248.

"Israel in the Near-East Context," *Land Reborn,* V, No. 2 (March-April-May 1954), 14.

Charles Hartshorne, *Reality as Social Process.* The Phoenix Series (Boston: Beacon Press, 1953). General Editor, James L. Adams.

## 1954

Letter to the Editor (regarding desirability of maintaining dialogue between East and West), *Comprendre* (Venice, Italy), No. 25 (1954), 54-55.

"Francis Greenwood Peabody," Section in *The Harvard Divinity School: Its Place in Harvard University and in American Culture,* ed. George H. Williams (Boston: Beacon Press, 1954), pp. 179-182.

*The Biblical Doctrine of Man and Society.* Ecumenical Studies No. 2. London: Student Christian Movement Press, 1954. (Dr. Adams was a member of the Ecumenical Committee for the World Council of Churches out of whose discussions this book was written by the Chairman, Professor G. Ernest Wright.)

*Who Has Faith in Man?* (with others). *The University of Chicago Round Table,* No. 829 (February 28, 1954).

"The Chief End of Man," *Harvard Divinity School Bulletin,* XIX (1954), 39-47.

## 1955

"Hidden Dangers of Anti-Israelism," *The Christian Register,* CXXXIII, No. 9 (November 1954), 16-18. Reprinted in *The Jewish Advocate* (Boston, Mass.), 116, No. 1 (January 6, 1955), 1, 11.

"Religion and the Ideologies," *Confluence,* IV, No. 1 (April 1, 1955), 72-84.

"The Grace of Staying Together and Growing Together: Comments on the Ecumenical Movement," *Faith and Freedom* (Liverpool), VIII, No. 3 (Summer 1955), 131-134; also in *Forward Together* (IARF Magazine, The Hague, Holland).

"Présence de la culture" (On Professor Harold C. Urey), *Comprendre,* Nos. 13-14 (1955), 203-205.

"Présence de la culture" (On the Scientist and the State), *Comprendre,* No. 15 (1955), 146-147.

"Notes on the [Sociometric] Study of Gould Farm," *Cooperative Living,* VII, No. 1 (Winter 1955-56).

## 1956

"The Political Responsibility of the Man of Culture," *Comprendre,* Société Européenne de Culture, Venice, Italy, No. 16 (1956), 11-25.

"Présence de la culture" (On Professor Malcolm P. Sharp), *Comprendre,* No. 16 (1956), 114-115.

## 1957

*Taking Time Seriously* (Glencoe, Ill.: The Free Press, 1957). (A volume of collected essays, assembled for publication on the occasion of Dr. Adams' completion of twenty years in Chicago, presented to him at a farewell reception when he left Chicago for Harvard Divinity School.) 74 pp.

Translation of "Feuerbach" by Karl Barth (Introduction to *The Essence of Christianity* by Ludwig Feuerbach) (New York: Harper Torchbooks Series, 1957), pp. x-xxxii.

"The Ages of Liberalism," *The Journal of Religious Thought,* XIV, No. 2 (1957), 101-117.

"From the Essenes to the Kibbutzim," *Land Reborn,* VIII, No. 11 (August 25, 1957), 13-16.

*Changing Frontiers: Vanishing and Emerging.* Supplement to *The Unitarian Christian* (Boston, October 1957). 12 pp. Also in *The Unitarian Register,* Vol. CXXXVI, No. 6 (Midsummer 1957), 10-12, 45.

"The Ministry of the Clergy and the Laity," *Teamwork, Journal of the Universalist Ministers Association* (Avon, Ill., December 1957), 3-4.

## 1958

*Religion and Freedom.* New York: Fund for the Republic (privately printed). Remarks as participant in Seminar sponsored by the Fund for the Republic, New York, N. Y., May 5-9, 1958.

"Culture," "Ethics," articles in *A Handbook of Christian Theology,* ed. Marvin Halverson (New York: Meridian Books, 1958).

*The Saint-Simonian Doctrine,* translated from the French by Professor Georg Iggers. *California Cult,* by H. T. Dohrman (Boston: Beacon Press, 1958). First of two volumes in a series, "Sociology of Politics and Religion." General Editor, James L. Adams.

"The Social Import of the Professions," *Bulletin of the American Association of Theological Schools,* No. XXIII (June 1958), 152-168. An address given at the Twenty-First Biennial Meeting of the American Association of Theological Schools. Excerpts reprinted in *Selected Readings on the Legal Profession,* assembled under the auspices of a committee of the Association of American Law Schools (St. Paul, Minn.: West Publishing Company, 1962), pp. 72-76.

"Today's Religions Can Meet the World's Needs Today," *Proceedings of The International Association for Liberal Christianity and Religious Freedom,* 1958. General Resolution adopted by the Congress of the International Association for Liberal Christianity and Religious Freedom (Chicago, August 15, 1958).

"Ordination Prayer," *The Unitarian Christian,* XIV, No. 1 (Fall 1958), 15.

"The Uses of Diversity," *Harvard Divinity School Bulletin,* XXIII (1958), 47-64. Reprinted as brochure.

## 1959

"Rudolph Sohm's Theology of Law and the Spirit," *Religion and Culture: Essays in Honor of Paul Tillich,* ed. W. Leibrecht (New York: Harper & Brothers, 1959), pp. 219-235.

"Willard Uphaus Sentence Protested; New Hampshire's Interpretation of State's Bill of Rights Queried," Letter (with Paul L. Lehmann) to the editor, *New York Times,* December 20, 1959, 6E.

"The Institutional Consequences of Religious Beliefs," Abstract, *Bulletin of the Society for the Scientific Study of Religion,* Spring 1959. Presidential Address, Society for the Scientific Study of Religion, April 11, 1959, Chicago.

"Initiative and Response," *The Unitarian Christian,* XV, No. 1 (October 1959), 3-5, 17.

## 1960

"Présence de la culture" (On Dr. Erik Erikson and James McBride Dabbs at the Gould Farm Institute on Race Relations, Gould Farm, Great Barrington, Mass.), *Comprendre,* Nos. 21-22 (1960), 334-336.

"The Uses of Analogy in Religious Social Thought," *Proceedings of the IXth International Congress for the History of Religions* (Tokyo: Maruzen, 1960), pp. 469-474. Address at the above Congress, September 1958.

"Contributions of Occidental Religion to Cultural Understanding," *Proceedings of the IXth International Congress for the History of Religions* (Tokyo: Maruzen, 1960), pp. 7, 184-185.

Articles "Aberglaube" and "Bruderschaften, geistliche. II. Amerika," *Weltkirchen Lexikon* (Stuttgart: Kreuz Verlag, 1960), pp. 7-8, 184-185.

## 1961

"Ernst Troeltsch," *Encyclopaedia Britannica*, Vol. XXII (1961), 489.

"The Unity of Mankind in Our Divided World," *News Digest*, International Association for Liberal Christianity and Religious Freedom, No. 46 (1961), 8-10.

"Ernst Troeltsch as Analyst of Religion," in *Journal for the Scientific Study of Religion*, I, No. 1 (October 1961), 98-109.

"Bibliographical Focus: Ernst Troeltsch," *Journal for the Scientific Study of Religion*, I, Nos. 1-2 (1961), 114-124, 220-225. Papers from Adams' Seminar on Troeltsch, edited by James Luther Adams.

"E. Troeltsch: *Historismus und seine Probleme*," *Journal for the Scientific Study of Religion*, I, No. 1 (October 1961), 109-114. A review by Paul Tillich from *Theologische Literaturzeitung*, XLIX (1924), 25-30. Translation by James L. Adams.

## 1962

*Samuel Charles Spalding, 1878-1962*. Great Barrington, Mass.: Gould Farm, 1962. Privately published. 3 pp.

"The Study of Christian Social Ethics at the Divinity School," *Harvard Divinity School Bulletin*, XXVI, No. 3 (April 1962), 11-21.

"Evangelism and the Intellectual, Part 1." Symposium with the Reverend Billy Graham: Professor Richard R. Neibuhr, Dr. Harold J. Ockenga, and James L. Adams at Rindge Technical High School Auditorium, Cambridge, Mass., under the auspices of the Harvard University Law Forum, March 26, 1962, *Decision*, III, No. 10 (October 1962), 8-9.

"Arminius and the Structure of Society," in *Man's Faith and Freedom: The Theological Influence of Jacobus Arminius*, ed. G. O. McCulloh (New York: Abingdon Press, 1962), pp. 46-63.

"A Council Observer Tells of Warmth, Splendor," *Boston Globe*, XXII (November 22, 1962), 71.

"Centerstance: An Essay on the Purposes of a Liberal Arts Education," *The Liberal Context*, II (Winter 1962), 9-11.

"Report from the Vatican Council," *The Unitarian Christian*, XVIII, No. 2 (December 1962), 13-14.

"Présence de la culture" (On Leo Szilard), *Comprendre*, No. 25 (1962), 155-158.

Letter to the Editor (regarding proposed congress on relations between East and West), *Comprendre*, No. 25 (1962), 226-227.

### 1963

Translation of *The Dogma of Christ* by Erich Fromm (New York: Holt, Rinehart and Winston, 1963). Title essay of the volume, pp. 3-91, translated by James L. Adams.

"Fresh Air Into the Church?" *Challenge,* Unitarian-Universalist Association, I, No. 3 (January 1963), 8-9.

"Vatican Council II: Pro and Contra," *News Digest.* The Hague: International Association for Liberal Christianity and Religious Freedom, Bulletin No. 51 (1963), 8-12.

"Amerika—Ein Land der Hoffnung: Die Kirchen und die Neger," *Evangelische Verantwortung,* XI, Heft 7 (July 1963), 8-12.

"Présence de la culture," *Comprendre,* Nos. 25-26 (1963), 340-342.

Max Weber, *Sociology of Religion,* translated from the German by Professor Ephraim Fischoff (Boston: Beacon Press, 1963). Third volume in a series, "Sociology of Politics and Religion." General Editor, James L. Adams.

"Der Gebrauch der Analogie in der Sozialphilosophie," *Jahrbuch der Schweizerischen Philosophischen Gesellschaft,* XXIII (1963), 1-17.

### 1964

*The Politics of Johannes Althusius,* translated from the Latin by Professor Frederick S. Carney (Boston: Beacon Press, 1964). Fourth volume in a series, "Sociology of Politics and Religion." General Editor, James L. Adams.

Tribute to William J. Barnes, M.D. *Annual Report* of The William J. Gould Associates, Inc., Great Barrington, Mass. (Spring 1964), p. 1.

"They're a peril, and they're an opportunity." Interview regarding "medical transplants." By Robert Hermann. *The National Observer,* 3, No. 10 (March 9, 1964), 1, 16.

"We Cannot Rest on Reputation: Our Department of Social Responsibility," *Unitarian Universalist Register-Leader,* CXLVI, No. 10 (December 1964), 6-7.

### 1965

"Enlarging Horizons," *Harvard Business School Bulletin,* Vol. XLI, No. 2 (March-April, 1965), 12-14.

*Paul Tillich's Philosophy of Culture, Science, and Religion.* New York: Harper & Row, 1965.

"Interrogation of Paul Tillich," in *Philosophical Interrogations,* Sydney and Beatrice Rome (eds.) (New York: Holt, Rinehart and Winston, 1965), pp. 404-405.

## 1966

"The Indispensable Discipline of Social Responsibility," *Journal of the Liberal Ministry,* VI, No. 2 (Spring 1966), pp. 87-96.

"Paul Johannes Tillich, 1885-1965" (with Erik Erikson, Gordon Kaufman, and Amos N. Wilder), *Harvard University Gazette* (June 1966).

### In Preparation

*By Their Groups.* Hibbert Lectures (1963) now being expanded. To be published by Harper & Row.

Collected Essays of Karl Holl. Translation with Introduction.

Collected Essays of Ernst Troeltsch. Translation with Introduction.

### REVIEWS AND PREFACES

## 1929

Jacques Maritain, *Three Reformers. Hound and Horn,* III (Fall 1929), 114-120.

## 1932

F. R. Barry, *Christianity and the New World. The Christian Register,* CXI, Nos. 27-28 (July 7-14, 1932), 441.

*Vigile.* Quatre cahiers, 1930. *Hound and Horn,* V, No. 4 (July-September 1932), 694-701.

Irving Babbitt, *On Being Creative and Other Essays. Hound and Horn,* VI, No. 1 (October-December 1932), 173-196.

## 1933

George Boas, *Philosophy and Poetry. The Christian Register,* CXII, No. 28 (July 20, 1933), 475.

Lawrence Clare, *Prayer: Its Method and Justification. The Christian Register,* CXII, No. 33 (August 24, 1933), 556.

S. Spencer, *The Meaning and Value of Religion. The Christian Register,* CXII, No. 46 (November 23, 1933), 675.

## 1934

J. Elliott Ross, *John Henry Newman. The Christian Register,* CXIII, No. 3 (January 18, 1934), 43.

Bonamy Dobree, *John Wesley. The Christian Register,* CXIII, No. 11 (March 15, 1934), 179.

Jacques Maritain, *Some Reflections on Culture and Liberty. The Christian Register,* CXIII, No. 19 (May 10, 1934), 315.

G. Coverdale Sharpe, *Liberty at the Crossroads. The Christian Register,* CXIII, No. 40 (November 1, 1934), 662.

## 1935

Clement C. J. Webb, *A Study of Religious Thought in England from 1850. The Christian Register,* CXIV, No. 11 (March 14, 1935), 178.

Willard L. Sperry, *Wordsworth's Anti-Climax. The Christian Register,* CXIV, No. 35 (October 3, 1935), 576.

André Malraux, *Man's Fate. The Christian Register,* CXIV, No. 43 (November 28, 1935), 713.

## 1937

C. A. Beard, *The Discussion of Human Affairs. Unity* (Chicago), CXIX, No. 4 (April 19, 1937), 80-82.

Gerald Heard, *The Source of Civilization* and *The Third Morality. Christendom,* III, No. 4 (Autumn 1937), 645-650.

*Hymns of the Spirit.* A review of the Services of Religion in this volume. *The Christian Register,* CXVI, No. 38 (October 28, 1937), 628-630.

W. E. Hocking, *Thoughts on Death and Life. Unity* (Chicago), CXX, No. 8 (December 20, 1937), 130-132.

## 1938

Rudolf Otto, *The Kingdom of God and the Son of Man. The Alumni Review* (Presbyterian Theological Seminary, Chicago), XIII, No. 4 (April 1938), 236-237.

## 1939

Edwin A. Burtt, *Types of Religious Philosophy. Christendom,* IV, No. 2 (Spring 1939), 282-285.

W. W. Fenn, *The Theological Method of Jesus. Unity* (Chicago), CXXII, No. 10 (July 17, 1939), 158-159.

Peter A. Bertocci, *The Empirical Argument for God in Late British Thought. Christendom,* IV, No. 4 (Autumn 1939), 601-604.

*Services of Religion for Special Occasions* (Boston: Beacon Press, 1938). *The Christian Register,* CXVIII, No. 40 (November 9, 1939), 653-655.

## 1940

K. E. Kirk (ed.), *The Study of Theology. The Christian Century,* LVII, No. 6 (February 7, 1940), 183.

J. S. Bixler, *Religion for Free Minds. The Christian Century,* LVII, No. 18 (May 1, 1940), 578.

Theodor Siegfried, *Das protestantische Prinzip im Kirche und Welt. Journal of Religion,* XX (1940), 192-194.

## 1941

Wilhelm Haubold, *Die Bedeutung der Religionsgeschichte für die Theologie Rudolf Ottos. Journal of Religion,* XXI, No. 1 (January 1941), 69-70.

George P. Conger, *The Ideologies of Religion. Christendom,* VI, No. 3 (Summer 1941), 443-446.

William C. Kernan, *The Ghost of Royal Oak. Journal of Religion,* XXI, No. 1 (January 1941), 106.

D. C. Macintosh, *The Problem of Religious Knowledge. The Christian Century,* LVIII, No. 45 (November 5, 1941), 1373-1374.

Reinhold Niebuhr, *The Nature and Destiny of Man. Christendom,* VI, No. 4 (Autumn 1941), 576-580.

## 1942

William H. Roberts, *The Problem of Choice. Ethics,* LII (1942), 243-245.

Theodore Maynard, *The Story of American Catholicism. New England Quarterly,* XV, No. 3 (September 1942), 534-536, and *The Protestant,* IV, No. 8 (November 1942), 65-67.

G. Vaughan, *Temples and Towers. A Survey of the World's Moral Outlook. American Bar Association Journal,* XXVIII (November 1942), 770.

Susanne K. Langer, *Philosophy in a New Key. The Christian Register,* CXXI, No. 11 (November 1942), 415.

## 1943

Stewart W. Herman, Jr., *It's Your Souls We Want;* William Temple, *Christianity and the Social Order;* N. S. Timasheff, *Religion in Soviet Russia. Free World,* VI, No. 2 (August 1943), 185-186.

Michael Straight, *Make This the Last War. The Christian Century,* LX (September 1, 1943), 989.

*The Second Symposium of the Conference on Science, Philosophy and Religion. Journal of Religion,* XXIII, No. 4 (October 1943), 292-293.

Lynn H. Hough, *The Christian Criticism of Life* and *Patterns of the Mind. Review of Religion,* VII (1943), 193-196.

## 1945

Jacques Maritain, *Christianity and Democracy. Journal of Religion,* XXV, No. 3 (July 1945), 217-218.

Lyman Bryson *et al., Approaches to National Unity. The Fifth Symposium of the Conference on Science, Philosophy and Religion. The Christian Century,* LXII (November 14, 1945), 1257-1258.

Robert E. Fitch, *A Certain Blind Man, and Other Essays on the American Mood. Journal of Religion,* XXV (1945), 152-153.

## 1947

Henry J. Cadbury, *Jesus, What Manner of Man. The Chicago Sun* (December 3, 1947), 14A.

## 1948

Ernst Troeltsch, *The Social Teaching of the Christian Churches.* 2 vols. *The Christian Register,* CXXVII, No. 5 (May 1948), 11-12.

Max Picard, *Hitler in Ourselves. Journal of Religion,* XXVIII (1948), 298-299.

James H. Dunham, *The Religion of Philosophers. Christendom,* XIII (1948), 535-536.

H. A. Rommen, *The Natural Law. Church History,* XVII, No. 4 (1948), 344-346.

Karl Barth, *The Only Way;* Karl Jaspers, *The Question of German Guilt;* Max Picard, *Hitler in Ourselves. Commentary,* IV (December 1948), 588-590.

## 1949

Cecil Northcott, *Religious Liberty. Chicago Theological Seminary Register,* XXXIX, No. 4 (November 1949), 37; also in *The Christian Register,* CXIX, No. 1 (January 1950), 2.

H. D. Lewis, *Morals and the New Theology. Journal of Religion,* XXIX (1949), 305-307; also in *Chicago Theological Seminary Register,* XL, No. 1 (January 1950), 33.

Stuart G. Brown (ed.), *We Hold These Truths: Documents of American Democracy. Chicago Theological Seminary Register,* XXXIX, No. 1 (January 1949), 38.

## 1950

Robert W. Sonen, *A Unitarian States His Case. The Christian Register,* CXIX, No. 10 (December 1950), 3; also in *Chicago Theological Seminary Register,* XL, No. 4 (November 1950), 40-41.

J. Haroutunian, *Lust for Power. Chicago Theological Seminary Register,* XL, No. 1 (January 1950), 33-34.

A. Roy Eckhardt, *Christianity and the Children of Israel. Chicago Theological Seminary Register,* XL, No. 1 (January 1950), 32-33.

### 1951

H. G. Wood, *Frederick Denison Maurice. Chicago Theological Seminary Register,* XLI, No. 1 (January 1951), 33-34.

Gerald Heard, *Morals Since 1900. Chicago Theological Seminary Register,* XLI, No. 4 (November 1951), 31-32.

E. Rosenstock-Huessy, *The Driving Power of Western Civilization. Journal of Religion,* XXXI, No. 2 (April 1951), 150.

Ernst Benz, *Westlicher und Oestlicher Nihilismus;* Karl Jaspers, *The European Spirit. Theology Today,* VII (1951), 540-542.

Malcolm Hay, *The Foot of Pride. Land Reborn,* XII, No. 6 (December 1951).

### 1952

James H. Nichols, *Democracy and the Churches. The University of Chicago Magazine,* XLIV, No. 5 (February 1952), 4.

### 1954

Fritz Buri, *Christlicher Glaube in Dieser Zeit. The Christian Register,* CXXXIII, No. 9 (November 1954), 3-4.

### 1955

William Hordern, *Christianity, Communism and History. Bulletin of Crozer Theological Seminary,* XLVII, No. 4 (April 1955).

### 1957

Benson V. Landis, compiler, *A Rauschenbusch Reader. Harvard Divinity School Bulletin,* XXIII (1957-58), 166-167.

*Cross Currents. A Quarterly Review.* Vols. VI (1956) and VII (1957). *Harvard Divinity School Bulletin,* XXIII (1957-58), 167.

Howard C. Kee, *Making Ethical Decisions. Harvard Divinity School Bulletin,* XXIII (1957-58), 184-185.

Lyman Bryson *et al., Aspects of Human Equality. The Fifteenth Symposium of the Conference on Science, Philosophy and Religion. Harvard Divinity School Bulletin,* XXIII (1957-58), 182-183.

### 1958

"Introduction." Rudolph Sohm, *Outlines of Church History* (Boston: Beacon Press, 1958), pp. ix-xv. Paperback.

## 1959

Jacob Weinstein, *The Place of Understanding. Hyde Park Herald* (Chicago, Ill., August 26, 1959); also in *Jewish Frontier,* XXVI, No. 10 (November 1959), 23-25.

## 1960

"Foreword." William Kimmel and Geoffrey Clive (eds.), *Dimensions of Faith* (New York: Twayne Publishers, 1960), pp. 7-13.

Wilson Smith, *Professors and Public Ethics: Studies of Northern Moral Philosophers Before the Civil War. Proceedings of Unitarian Historical Society,* XII, Part 1 (1960), 104-105.

Franklin H. Littell, *The German Phoenix. Men and Movements in the Church of Germany. Harvard Divinity School Bulletin,* XXV, No. 1 (October 1960), 24-25; also in *The Unitarian Register,* CXL, No. 3 (March 1961), 14.

## 1961

Max Scheler, *Ressentiment. Harvard Divinity School Bulletin,* XXV (April-July 1961), 21-22.

Rudolf Bultmann, *Existence and Faith. Perkins School of Theology Journal,* XV (Fall 1961), 53-54; also in *Journal of the Liberal Ministry,* II, No. 1 (Winter 1962), 45-46.

R. W. Albright, *Focus on Infinity. A Life of Phillips Brooks. The American-German Review,* XXVIII (December 1961-January 1962), 36.

## 1962

"Foreword." Ellis H. Dana, *The Real Meaning of Communism* (Madison, Wis., 1962). Brochure. 54 pp.

Hester Hasting, *William Ellery Channing and L'Academie des sciences morales et politiques 1870: L'Étude sur Channing and the "Lost" Prize Essay. The Unitarian Register and the Universalist Leader,* CXLI, No. 5 (May 1962), 20.

Bernard P. Brennan, *The Ethics of William James. The Unitarian Register and the Universalist Leader,* CXLI, No. 6 (June 1962), 23.

Roland Bainton, *Early and Medieval Christianity. Journal of the Liberal Ministry,* II, No. 3 (Fall 1962), 151-153.

Robert M. Hutchins and Mortimer J. Adler (eds.), *The Great Ideas Today. Harvard Divinity School Bulletin,* XXVI, No. 2 (January 1962), 23-25.

R. M. MacIver (ed.), *Dilemmas of Youth in America Today. Harvard Divinity School Bulletin,* XXVI, No. 3 (April 1962), 25-26.

## 1965

Brooks R. Walker, *The Christian Fright Peddlers. Harvard Divinity School Bulletin,* XXIX, No. 4 (July 1965), 118-123.

### UNPUBLISHED DOCUMENTS

## 1934

"Some Practical Applications." One of three Greenfield Papers presented by the Greenfield Group in Greenfield, Massachusetts, at the annual meeting of the National Unitarian Ministers' Association, 1934. Mimeographed.

"The Religious Content of Liberalism" (The Greenfield Papers), by Vivian T. Pomeroy, Andrew Banning, and James L. Adams. Mimeographed.

## 1937

"Christianity and Humanism." Address delivered at the University of Iowa. 1937. Typewritten.

## 1938

"The Liberal Conception of Religious Experience and Revelation." Address at IARF Congress, Bentveld, Holland, 1938. Mentioned in *The Christian Register,* CXVII, No. 32 (September 15, 1938), 486. Typewritten.

"Anglo-Saxon and Teutonic Methods in Theology." Address at meeting of International Religious Fellowship, Leiden, Holland, 1938. Summary in *The Christian Register,* CXVII, No. 32 (1938), 522-523. Typewritten.

## 1939

"A Faith for Liberals to Live By." Syllabus for a course held under the auspices of the Unitarian Religious Education Institute, Mid-West, June 18-29, 1939, Lake Geneva, Wis. Mimeographed.

## 1940

With E. E. Aubrey and others, "The Ethical Reality and Function of the Church." Memorandum by the Chicago Ecumenical Discussion Group, 1940. Mimeographed.

With James Bissett Pratt, "The Congregational Idea." Prepared for the

Congregational-Unitarian-Universalist group meeting at Yale University at the invitation of Drs. Douglas Horton, F. M. Eliot, and Robert Cummins to work for closer intellectual cooperation between the denominations, 1940. Mimeographed.

## 1942

"Crystallizing Unitarian Beliefs." Outlines of lectures given at Lake Geneva Unitarian Summer Conference, 1942. Mimeographed.

## 1945

With E. E. Aubrey and others, "Preaching as an Expression of the Ethical Reality of the Church." Memorandum by the Chicago Ecumenical Discussion Group, 1945. 14 pp. Mimeographed.

## 1946

"The Angels and the Authorities. Toward the Understanding of Romans 13:1-7." Translation of essay by Günther Dehn, *Theologische Aufsätze. Karl Barth zum 50. Geburtstag* (München: Kaiser Verlag, 1936), pp. 90-109. Andover-Harvard Library, Harvard Divinity School. Typewritten.

## 1948

"The Class Struggle and Religious Socialism." Translation made in 1948 of essay by Paul Tillich from *Religiöse Verwirklichung* (Berlin: Furche-Verlag, 1930), ch. 9. Meadville Theological School Library and Andover-Harvard Library, Harvard Divinity School. Typewritten.

"Sin and Salvation." Paper read at the Chicago Philosophy of Religion Association, 1948. Mimeographed.

## 1950

"Social Morality and Medical Care." Reply to Frank G. Dickinson (American Medical Association), "Social Morality and 'The Cradle-to-the-Grave' Philosophy," M-30, 1-12-50. Issued by The American Unitarian Association. Mimeographed.

## 1951

*Philosophy of Religion* by Paul Tillich. This long essay originally appeared in Max Dessoir (ed.), *Die Philosophie in ihren Einzelgebieten* (Berlin: Ullstein, 1925), pp. 769-835. Typewritten translation.

## 1952

"The Place of Discipline in Christian Ethics." Paper read at the Theological Discussion Group, Washington Cathedral, Washington, D.C., 1952. Mimeographed.

## 1955

"The Arts and Society." Paper prepared for the Theological Discussion Group, Washington, D. C., 1955. Mimeographed.

"The Concept of History." Aphorisms by Walter Benjamin. Translated from the German by James Luther Adams and Olric Prochazka, 1955. Mimeographed.

"The Liberal Christian Looks at Himself." Foundations of Liberal Christianity Lectures, conducted in cooperation with the Comparative Religion Class, All Souls' Unitarian Church, Washington, D. C., 1955. Mimeographed.

"Tillich's Dialectical Method in Social-Structural Analysis." Paper read at the American Theological Society, Midwest Division, April 22, 1955.

## 1959

"Nuclear Energy and Christian Perspectives," in *The Church and the Use of Nuclear Energy for Peaceful Purposes.* Department of the Church and Economic Life, National Council of the Churches of Christ. Report of a Consultation convened at Arden House, Harriman, New York, January 1959. Mimeographed.

Remarks as Participant in Conference of Social Scientists, March 15-16, 1959. Union of American Hebrew Congregations, Committee on Worship Research. Mimeographed.

Condensation of James Luther Adams' Presidential Address at annual meeting of Society for the Scientific Study of Religion. "Summary of Proceedings at Chicago Meeting, April 10-11, 1959." Mimeographed.

## 1960

"Taking Time Seriously: An Approach to the Theology of Political Responsibility." Address at Penn State University, 1960. Typewritten.

## 1961

"The Evolution of My Social Concern." Transcript of address at the annual meeting of the American Association for Teachers of Christian Social Ethics, Louisville, Ky., 1961. Typewritten.

"Archibald Thompson Davison. In Memoriam." Sermon delivered in

Andover Chapel, Harvard Divinity School, February 16, 1961. Typewritten.

## 1963

"Kirche und Gruppe: Aspects of a Christian Doctrine of Vocation." Typescript in German of address at Free University of Berlin, 1963.

"The Voluntary Association as an Indispensable Institution of the Democratic Society." Lecture at University of Padua, 1963. Typewritten.

## 1964

"The Liberal Ministry in a Changing Society." Transcript of an address to Mid-Winter Institute, New England Unitarian Universalist Ministers Association, North Andover, Mass., January 28, 1964.

"We Wrestle Against Principalities and Powers." Sermon preached at ordination of Dr. Hans Rosenwald, New Director of Albert Schweitzer College (Churwalden, Switzerland). First Parish, Cambridge, Mass., June 7, 1964. Mimeographed.

"Broken Cisterns and Earthen Vessels." Sermon preached in Vassar College Chapel, Poughkeepsie, N. Y., February 28, 1964. Mimeographed.

## 1965

"Ideology and Utopia." Translation of Paul Tillich's review of Karl Mannheim's book of that title, from *Gesellschaft,* VI (1929), 348-55. Andover-Harvard Library, Harvard Divinity School. Typewritten.

"Theocracy, Individualism and Associations: A Critique of Max Weber." Address at annual meeting of Society for the Scientific Study of Religion, October 29, 1965. Typewritten. To be published in a *Festschrift* for Prof. Ernst Benz of Marburg University.

## 1966

"Karl Marx from a Protestant Perspective." Address at International Symposium on "Marx and the Western World," University of Notre Dame, April 24, 1966. Typewritten.

# NOTES AND ACKNOWLEDGMENTS

## I. THE NATURE OF VOLUNTARY ASSOCIATIONS

### Karl Hertz

1. Harlan Cleveland and Harold D. Lasswell (eds.), *Ethics and Bigness* (New York: Harper & Brothers, 1962), p. xvi. Used by permission of Conference on Science, Philosophy and Religion.

2. Robert M. MacIver, *Community* (New York: The Macmillan Company, 1928).

3. R. M. MacIver and Charles H. Page, *Society: An Introductory Analysis* (New York: Rinehart and Company, 1949). Used by permission of the author.

4. *Ibid.,* p. 12.

5. *Ibid.,* p. 13.

6. *Ibid.*

7. *Ibid.,* pp. 453-493.

8. *Ibid.,* p. 454.

9. *Ibid.,* p. 455.

10. Ralf Dahrendorf, "Out of Utopia: Towards a Reorientation of Sociological Analysis." *American Journal of Sociology,* 64 (1958), 115-127.

11. Gerhard Lenski, *The Religious Factor* (Garden City: Doubleday and Co., 1961), pp. 324-330.

12. *Society,* p. 9.

13. *The Religious Factor,* pp. 17-22.

14. *Ibid.,* pp. 69-73.

15. Lenski's view that the religious subcommunities have the characteristics of status groups is relevant here. For the relationships that hold between fraternities, and so on, and "status groups" in the stratification system may be similar to those between religious associations and the religious subcommunities. In a heterogeneous, mobile, and changing society, overlapping memberships and participation may add to the complexity of the system.

16. See the discussion of attitudes on foreign affairs, *The Religious Factor,* pp. 169-170.

17. Lenski found it unnecessary to separate white Protestants by denomination. Other studies have shown similar findings.

18. On the issue of segregated schools, those least likely to favor segregation were highly involved in the churches, marginally involved in the subcommunity among both Protestants and Catholics. See *The Religious Factor,* p. 173, table 32.

19. We are not pointing to a change *away from* associationalism but to a change *within* associationalism and the concomitant development of norms corresponding to the change.

20. Obviously the amount and rate of change vary from place to place and from one organization to another. Yet the "bureaucratic rationale" or "metaphysical pathos" seems more and more the same in all kinds of situations. See Alvin W. Gouldner, "Metaphysical Pathos and the Theory of Bureaucracy," in Seymour M. Lipset and Neil J. Smelser (eds.), *Sociology: The Progress of a Decade* (Englewood Cliffs: Prentice-Hall, 1961), pp. 80-89.

21. "Voluntarism: The Political Functions of an Antipolitical Doctrine," *Industrial and Labor Relations Review,* XV (1962).

22. In the debate over fair employment practices a standard defense has been this appeal to "private rights." One may, of course, reply that where associa-

tions incorporate, whether for profit or not, they have already placed themselves within the public domain, accepted constraint on their actions, and asked protection. The issue is, however, how far the law reaches—i.e., what kinds of relationships hold between economic associations and political ones.

23. This is Whyte's "social ethic" (*The Organization Man*) and Riesman's "other-directedness" (*The Lonely Crowd*).

24. The most interesting study of this phenomenon, stressing the kinds of conflicts involved and the pressures against "public controversy," is Kenneth Underwood's *Protestant and Catholic* (Boston: Beacon Press, 1957).

25. Daniel R. Miller and Guy E. Swanson, *The Changing American Parent* (New York: John Wiley & Sons, 1958).

26. S. M. Lipset, M. A. Trow, and J. S. Coleman, *Union Democracy* (Glencoe: The Free Press, 1956).

27. The objection here is not to some of the specific positions which POAU takes but to the "ideology" of the movement. In brief, no rigid "once for all time" line of demarcation can be defined, even by appeal to history. Relationships change with changing balances of forces in the community and with changing situations in religious knowledge on the part of the population.

28. In addition to Dahrendorf, cited above, see also S. M. Lipset, "Political Sociology," in *Sociology Today*, edited by Robert K. Merton, Leonard Broom, and Leonard S. Cottrell, Jr. (New York: Basic Books, 1959).

29. In *Union Democracy*, cited above.

30. Lewis Coser, *The Functions of Social Conflict* (Glencoe: The Free Press, 1956).

## II. ASSOCIATIONAL THOUGHT IN EARLY CALVINISM

### Frederick S. Carney

1. "Introduction" to Otto von Gierke, *Political Theories of the Middle Age*, translated by Maitland (Cambridge: Cambridge University Press, 1900), p. ix. This translation is of section 11 of the third volume of *Das deutsche Genossenschaftsrecht*, which volume is entitled (appropriately enough in light of Maitland's observation above) *Die Staatsund Korporationslehre des Altertums und des Mittelalters und ihre Aufnahme in Deutschland* (Berlin: Weidmann, 1881).

2. See the fourth volume of Gierke's *Das deutsche Genossenschaftsrecht* (Berlin: Weidmann, 1913), sections 14-18 of which have been translated by Ernest Barker as *Natural Law and the Theory of Society* (Cambridge: Cambridge University Press, 1934, 2 vols.; 1950, 1 vol.). See also his *Johannes Althusius und die Entwicklung der naturrechtlichen Staatstheorien* (Breslau: Koebner, 1880), which has been translated by Bernard Freyd as *The Development of Political Theory* (New York: W. W. Norton, 1939).

3. John W. Allen, *A History of Political Thought in the Sixteenth Century* (London: Methuen and Co., 1928), especially pp. 302-331.

4. The relation of both Calvin and these early Calvinists to the medieval world is much more complex than Allen indicates. Calvin's political thought has decisive medieval elements in it. Furthermore, the Calvinists borrowed not so much from Occam and other publicists, as Allen suggests, as from Bartolus and other legists. See section II of this essay.

5. Junius Brutus, *Vindiciae contra tyrannos* (Edinburgh [Basle?], 1579). An English translation was made by William Walker with the title *A Defence of Liberty Against Tyrants* (London: Simmons and Ibbitson, 1648). This translation was republished with an historical introduction by Harold Laski (London: G. Bell and Sons, 1924). For a much needed new translation, see my forthcoming volume *Early Protestant Political Thought* in A Library of Protestant Thought (Oxford University Press). Page references hereafter, however, are to the Laski republication of Walker's translation.

6. Theodore Beza (?), *De jure magistratuum* (n.p., 1576). Henri-Louis Gonin has provided a translation under the title *Concerning the Rights of Rulers* (Capetown: H.A.U.M., 1956).

7. Francis Hotman, *Franco-Gallia* (Geneva: Stoeris, 1573). This was translated into English, while retaining the Latin title, by Robert Viscount Molesworth (London: Goodwin, 1711). It is to be noted that this translation unfortu-

nately does not contain the augmented material of later editions of the *Franco-Gallia.*

8. ———, *Questionum illustrium* (Paris: Stephanus, 1573).

9. George Buchanan, *De jure regni apud Scotos* (Edinburgh: Rosseus, 1579). Several English translations have been made, the best of which is by Robert MacFarlan and is entitled *The Rights of the Crown in Scotland.* This is bound together with Samuel Rutherford's *Lex, Rex* (Edinburgh: Oliver and Boyd, 1843).

10. John Ponet, *Shorte Treatise of Politike Power* (London [?], 1556). Page references hereafter, however, are to the London 1642 edition.

11. Peter Martyr Vermigli, *Loci communes* (London: Kingston, 1576). There is a translation by Anthony Marten under the title *The Common Places of Peter Martyr* (London: B.L., 1583).

12. ———, *Commentaria in epistolam S. Pauli ad Romanos* (3rd ed.; Basle: Perna, 1668). This was translated as *Commentary on Romans* by "H.D." (London, 1568).

13. Jerome Zanchius, *De lege Dei,* in *Opera* (n.p., Gamonetus, 1613), Vol. IV.

14. ———, *Commentarius in epistolam ad Ephesios,* in *Opera,* Vol. VI.

15. Johannes Althusius, *Politica* (3rd ed.; Herborn, 1614). For an abridged translation of this work, see my *Politics of Johannes Althusius* (Boston: Beacon Press, 1964; London: Eyre and Spottiswoode, 1965). See also the valuable Introduction Carl J. Friedrich provided for his Latin Edition of Althusius' *Politica* (Cambridge: Harvard University Press, 1932), pp. xv-xcix.

16. ———, *Dicaelogicae* (Frankfurt: Corvinus, 1618).

17. Samuel Rutherford, *Lex, Rex* (London: Field, 1644). It is subtitled *The Law and the Prince.* Page references hereafter will refer to a later edition (Edinburgh: Oliver and Boyd, 1843), which is bound together with MacFarlan's translation (*Rights of the Crown in Scotland*) of Buchanan's *De jure regni apud Scotos.*

18. Althusius, *Politics,* p. 12. Note that page references to early Calvinist writings employed in this essay are, for the convenience of the English reader, (1) to the translations listed in the footnotes the first time they are mentioned, or (2) in the absence of such translations, to the Latin (or English) editions as listed.

19. The church is not a separate association for Althusius. Rather he affirms that the city, province, and commonwealth each has two forms of communication and two modes of administration, the ecclesiastical and the secular. (*Ibid.,* pp. 50-55, 69-73, 154-169.)

20. Zanchius, *Ad Ephesios,* p. 231.

21. Vermigli, *Common Places,* Part IV, p. 227. Rutherford, however, is not altogether happy with this analogy, largely because of the patriarchal use to which it had been put by English royalists. While he does not deny a commonality within the family and the commonwealth of the principles and procedures of government, he wants to make clear that "a father is a father by generation, . . . but a prince is a prince by the free suffrages of a community." (*Op. cit.,* pp. 62-64.)

22. Brutus, *op. cit.,* pp. 157 f.

23. Beza, *op. cit.,* p. 70.

24. Vermigli, *Common Places,* Part II, p. 379. This reference is to a chapter Vermigli devotes to the fifth commandment, which is subtitled "The Honoring of Superiors." His notion that the fifth commandment pertains to all superiors, and not just to parents, agrees with similar interpretations by Calvin and a large number of medieval commentators. See Calvin's treatment of this commandment not only in his *Institutes,* II, viii, 35-38, but also in his *Commentaries on the Last Four Books of Moses.* Thus while some writers construe the fifth commandment to pertain also to magistrates, Ponet argues that Romans 13 pertains also to parents. (*Op. cit.,* p. 20.)

25. E.g., Brutus, *op. cit.,* pp. 75 *et passim;* Zanchius, *De lege Dei,* pp. 216-219; Beza, *op. cit.,* pp. 51 f., 83.

26. Zanchius, *De lege Dei,* pp. 218 f.

27. Buchanan, *op. cit.,* p. 278; Brutus, *op. cit.,* p. 204; Beza, *op. cit.,* p. 71.

28. Althusius, *Politics,* pp. 108 f.; Brutus, *op. cit.,* p. 98.

29. Vermigli, *Common Places,* Part IV, pp. 17-21.

30. No claim is here made that these early Calvinists were unique in their acknowledgment of associational continuity. Aristotle, in discussing one of the forms of kingly rule, says "as household management is the kingly rule of a house, so kingly rule is the household management of a city, or of a nation, or of many nations." (*Politics*, 1285b 32.) See also James I, "The Trew Law of Free Monarchies," *Political Works* (London: Barker and Bill, 1616), which *Works* were reprinted (Cambridge: Harvard University Press, 1918) with an introduction by Charles H. McIlwain; Sir Robert Filmer, *Patriarcha* (London: Chiswell, 1680). On the other hand, this position does distinguish them from a number of writers in the history of political thought who did not recognize such associational continuity. However, even among writers, such as James I and Filmer, with whom they could agree on the *fact* of associational continuity, they often disagreed vehemently about the *nature* of it.

31. "While medieval federalism started from the unity of the whole, Althusius takes his stand entirely on the basis of natural-law individualism. He derives all social unity from a process of association which proceeds, as it were, from the bottom upwards. He regards the contract of society (i.e., the principle of partnership) as the creator of the whole system of public law and order (both in the parts, or earlier stages, of the state, and in its total and final structure)." (Gierke, *Natural Law and the Theory of Society*, p. 71.)

32. Gierke writes of Althusius' completed doctrine with obvious disappointment when he declares that, "in spite of every effort to attain the idea of a true and organic group being by the use of the Teutonic conception of 'fellowship,' there is a final failure to make either the state or the corporation a whole which is really one, and can assert itself against the individual in the strength of its own existence." (*Ibid.*, p. 76.) Note also the following passage from another work by Gierke: "This man [Althusius], excelling all others of his school of thought in the intensity of his sense of right, and equalling them in his zeal for liberty, had a doctrine of his own which, if it prepared the way for the destructive political theory culminating in Rousseau, yet in many respects laid a foundation for the constructive theory of the constitutional state." (*The Development of Political Theory*, p. 33.)

33. Althusius, *Politics*, p. 23. It is interesting to note that William Perkins, alone among the early Calvinists I have read, writes of the family largely in terms of a contract of marriage, and thus emphasizes voluntaristic elements. If he had approached the family less from the standpoint of engagement and marriage, and more from the standpoint of birth and nurture, would he have been less unusual among these early Calvinists? Nevertheless, he opened his volume with the statement that "the family is a natural and simple society," and proceeded to set forth various limits that any rightful marriage contract (and marriage) must recognize. *Christian Oeconomie* (London: Kingston, 1609).

34. *Politics*, p. 29.

35. *Ibid.*, p. 69. "The precepts of the Decalogue are included [in politics] to the extent that they infuse a vital spirit into the association and symbiotic life that we teach, that they carry a torch before the social life that we seek, and that they prescribe and constitute a way, rule, guiding star, and boundary for human society. If anyone would take them out of politics, he would destroy it; indeed, he would destroy all symbiosis and social life among men. For what would human life be without the piety of the first table of the Decalogue, and without the justice of the second." (*Ibid.*, p. 8.) See also pp. 17, 42, 47, 55, 75 f., 93, 136-144.

36. *Ibid.*, p. 69.

37. See his chapters entitled "The Ephors and Their Duties" and "Tyranny and Its Remedies." (*Ibid.*, pp. 87-114, 185-194.) See also his *Dicaelogicae*, III, 16, 6.

38. Rutherford, *op. cit.*, p. 1.

39. Rutherford refers directly to Althusius on a number of occasions in *Lex, Rex*.

40. Buchanan, *op. cit.*, p. 240 *et passim*. This analogy of the physician with the ruler is also employed by Ponet, *op. cit.*, p. 9; Brutus, *op. cit.*, p. 96.

41. The idea of the leader of an association being its guardian or trustee is quite common to the associational thought of early Calvinists, largely because the implied relation between guardian (*tutor*) and ward (*pupillus*) admirably

conveyed the notion of responsibility involved in their teleological concerns. See Hotman, *Quaestionum illustrium,* pp. 13 f.; Rutherford, *op. cit.,* p. 69; Beza, *op. cit.,* p. 30; Brutus, *op. cit.,* p. 99; Althusius, *Politics,* pp. 89, 102, 104-106, 193.

42. Buchanan, *op. cit.,* p. 249.

43. Ernest Barker wrote, "I am inclined to think that book iv, chapter xx, section 31 of the *Institutes* is one of the seed-beds of modern liberty." "A Huguenot Theory of Politics," in *Church, State, and Education* (Ann Arbor: University of Michigan, 1957), p. 84.

44. Benedict Aretius, *Commentarii in novum testamentum* (Paris: Preux, 1607), Acts 5:29; David Pareus, *Commentarius in epistolam ad Romanos* (Geneva: Chovet, 1617), ch. 13; Hotman, *Franco-Gallia,* pp. 63-77; Ponet, *op. cit.,* p. 7; Rutherford, *op. cit.,* p. 95; Brutus, *op. cit.,* pp. 127 ff., 207 ff.; Vermigli, *Common Places,* IV, pp. 324 f.; *Commentary on Romans,* ch. 13; Buchanan, *op. cit.,* p. 276; Beza, *op. cit.,* p. 48.

45. Jean Bodin, *De la Republique* (Paris: DuPuys, 1576), I, 4.

46. *Ibid.* Note also the following statement from the same chapter by Bodin: "I hold that the natural affection of parents for their children is incompatible with cruelty and abuse of power."

47. *Ibid.,* III, 7.

48. *Ibid.*

49. *Ibid.*

50. For a discussion of collegia that should be prohibited in principle, see Althusius, *Dicaelogicae,* I, 133. They are, for the most part, groups organized for purposes of monopoly or restraint of trade, sexual or alcoholic license, or religious heresy. The last category is also discussed by Zanchius, *De lege Dei,* p. 713. On the problem of religious toleration, see Zanchius, *ibid.,* pp. 795-803; Althusius, *Politics,* pp. 72 f., 167-169.

51. Bartolomew Keckermann, a Calvinist professor in far-off Danzig, provides the only exception to this statement that I have thus far encountered in my studies of this early period of Calvinism. He argued that "a prince should not permit any collegium to be organized by his subjects over which he does not exercise his authority through some person designated by himself." (*Systema disciplinae politicae* [Hanover: Antonius, 1607], I, 15.)

52. Bodin, *op. cit.,* I, 8-10.

53. Brutus, *op. cit.,* pp. 118 ff., 124 ff., 197; Buchanan, *op. cit.,* pp. 273 ff.; Althusius, *Politics,* pp. 4 f., 10, 65 ff., 87 ff.; Hotman, *Franco-Gallia,* pp. 63 ff.; *Quaestionum illustrium,* pp. 1 ff.; Rutherford, *op. cit.,* pp. 77 ff.

54. Unfortunately, William Walker's translation of Brutus, *Vindiciae contra tyrannos* (published as *Defence of Liberty Against Tyrants*), very often renders *populus* with a plural verb although the Latin original almost always employs a singular. This is to misconceive the people as individuals (or groups) rather than as an organized community. Walker made his translation many decades after the original was published, and during a time when the individualist interpretation of the foundations of society was widely advocated in England. Was he attempting by his translation to persuade Englishmen of the modernity of the *Vindiciae?*

55. Bodin, *op. cit.,* VI, 4. See also Claude Seyssel, *La Grand Monarchie de France* (Paris: Chaudière, 1519), I, 4; William Barclay, *De regno et regali potestate* (Paris: Chaudière, 1600), IV, 10.

56. Beza, *op. cit.,* pp. 36 ff.; Brutus, *op. cit.,* pp. 109 ff., 213; Rutherford, *op. cit.,* p. 146; Vermigli, *Commentary on Romans,* ch. 13; *Common Places,* IV, p. 325; Ponet, *op. cit.,* pp. 51 f.; Althusius, *Politics,* p. 190. Buchanan, however, is somewhat more ready than these others to authorize actions by private citizens against tyrants. (*Op. cit.,* p. 281.)

57. Ponet, *op. cit.,* p. 3.

58. *Ibid.,* p. 50.

59. Althusius, *Politics,* p. 135.

60. *Ibid.,* p. 136.

61. Rutherford, *op. cit.,* p. 1.

62. Zanchius, *De lege Dei,* p. 190.

63. Gierke, *Political Theories of the Middle Age,* p. 6. See also Gierke, "The Idea of Corporation," tr. by F. Kolegar in *Theories of Society,* ed. by Talcott Parsons *et al.* (New York: The Free Press of Glencoe, Inc., 1961), Vol. I

pp. 611-626. This translation is of Section 12 of the third volume of *Das deutsche Genossenschaftsrecht* (Berlin: Weidmann, 1881).

64. For further discussion of the relation of Althusius to Bartolus, see my unpublished dissertation, "The Associational Theory of Johannes Althusius" (University of Chicago, 1960), especially pp. 91-95 and 100-105. For some suggestions on the relation of Brutus to Bartolus, see Ernest Barker, *op. cit.*, pp. 74 *et passim*. On Bartolus himself, see C. N. S. Woolf, *Bartolus of Sassoferrato* (Cambridge: Cambridge University Press, 1913).

65. Gierke is in error when he says, "Althusius goes so far that neither in his political nor in his juristic works does he quote any text of the *Corpus juris canonici* or mention a single canonist among the many authors cited." (*The Development of Political Theory*, p. 69.) To the contrary, canon law is several times alluded to by Althusius in his *Politics*, and he cites therein several canonists, especially Covarruvias, Panormitanus, and Lancellot.

66. "Running through the glosses of the previous centuries were two separate doctrines on Church unity. The more conspicuous one, which has usually been regarded as the canonistic doctrine *par excellence,* insisted that the unity of the whole Church could be secured only by a rigorous subordination of all members to a single head, and to make the subordination effective, it developed the familiar theory of papal sovereignty. But side by side with this there existed another theory, applied at first to single churches, and then at the beginning of the fourteenth century, in a fragmentary fashion, to the Roman Church and the Church as a whole, a theory which stressed the corporate association of the members of a Church as the true principle of ecclesiastical unity, and which envisaged an exercise of corporate authority by the members of a church even in the absence of an effective head." (Brian Tierney, *Foundations of the Conciliar Theory* [Cambridge: Cambridge University Press, 1955], p. 240.) Note also: "The conciliar theory, one might say, sprang from the impregnation of Decretist ecclesiology by Decretalist corporation concepts." (*Ibid.,* p. 245.)

67. See Althusius, *Politics,* pp. 12 f., 18-20, 22 f., 28 f., 34, 61 f.

68. See Buchanan, *op. cit.,* pp. 280 ff.; Rutherford, *op. cit.,* pp. 54 ff.; Brutus, *op. cit.,* pp. 175 ff.; and Althusius, *Politics,* pp. 5, 116 ff., 123.

69. See Brutus, *op. cit.,* pp. 71 ff., 89 ff.; Vermigli, *Common Places,* Part II, pp. 582 ff.; Rutherford, *op. cit.,* pp. 56 *et passim;* and Althusius, *Politics,* 157 ff.

70. See the excellent discussion of private and public law tendencies as applied to political theory in Maitland, *op. cit.,* pp. xxviii ff. See also Gierke, "The Idea of Corporation," *loc. cit.*

71. Gierke presents an interesting list of passages from Cicero in which an entirely non-Roman law conception of *societas* is obviously intended. See *Political Theories of the Middle Age,* pp. 187 f.

72. Edmund Burke makes an interesting Ciceronian play on the notions of contract, partnership, and society in the following passage: "Society is indeed a contract. Subordinate contracts for objects of mere occasional interest may be dissolved at pleasure—but the state ought not to be considered as nothing better than a partnership agreement in a trade of pepper and coffee, calico or tobacco, or some other such low concern, to be taken up for a little temporary interest, and to be dissolved by the fancy of the parties. It is to be looked on with reverence, because it is not a partnership in things subservient only to the gross animal existence of a temporary and perishable nature. It is a partnership in all science, a partnership in all art, a partnership in every virtue, and in all perfection. As the ends of such a partnership cannot be obtained in many generations, it becomes a partnership not only between those who are living, but between those who are living, those who are dead, and those who are to be born. Each contract of each particular state is but a clause in the great primeval contract of eternal society." (*Reflections on the Revolution in France* [Chicago: Henry Regnery, 1955], pp. 139 f.)

73. Althusius, *Politics,* p. 22. See also pp. 12 f.

74. At first glance it might seem that the sacraments and other liturgical aspects of a religious covenant would constitute an exception (by way of addition) to this statement that a religious covenant is essentially what is required of an association by its very nature and circumstances seen as an act of commitment to God. But see Vermigli's suggestion distinguishing between the substance and accidents of a covenant, in *Common Places,* Part II, p. 583. Note also his state-

ment that "we are bound to true godliness and sound faith, even if there were no [religious] covenant to bind us." (*Ibid.*, p. 585.)

75. Brutus, *op. cit.*, p. 81.

### III. THE RELIGIOUS BACKGROUND OF THE IDEA OF A LOYAL OPPOSITION

#### George H. Williams

1. For example, a number of utterances of Richard Cardinal Cushing on the Council have expressly insisted that the parties in the basilica of St. Peter's are not to be likened to parliamentary parties of government and loyal opposition because, after forthright debate and due deliberation and voting, the minority always accepts as inspired the voice of the majority (*major et sanior pars*) and gives inward as well as conformist consent. The same point was made successively in Boston by Leo Cardinal Suenens and Franziskus Cardinal König; but the former, in his address under the auspices of the Paulist Fathers on May 6, 1964, made clear his own reason for rejecting the parliamentary parallel, namely, that in all the parliaments he knew of the party members had made up their minds on every public issue and maneuver before entering the chamber and that consequently debate and deliberation was only a form, in contrast to the authentic dialogue of the Council, convoked each day in the name of the Holy Spirit. See further below at n. 69. It is one purpose of the present sketch to show that precisely this conception of parliamentary debate lies deep in British and American parliamentary theory and usage and hence that the idea of the loyal opposition could also have Catholic conciliar significance.

2. T. C. Hansard, *Parliamentary Debates*, new series, XV (London: Parliamentary Proceedings . . ., 1827), cols. 135 and 137. See also Lord Broughton, *Recollections of a Long Life* (London: J. Murray, 1909-11), III, 129-131.

3. Siegfried Landshut, "Formen und Funktionen der parlamentarischen Opposition," and Dolf Sternberger, "Über parlamentarische Opposition," both essays edited by Gottfried Eisermann, *Wirtschaft und Kultursystem* (Zurich/Stuttgart: E. Rentsch, 1955), essays 12 and 17; Kurt Kluxen, *Das Problem der politischen Opposition* (Freiburg/Munich: Alber, 1956), and Ingeborg Bode, *Der Ursprung und Begriff der parlamentarischen Opposition* (Stuttgart: Fischer, 1962). The most comprehensive treatment of the theory, but primarily the history of the formative period of the emergence of the two-party system, is that of Archibald S. Foord, *His Majesty's Opposition, 1714-1830* (Oxford: Clarendon Press, 1964). An English essay on the subject that goes into the religious antecedents is the Romanes Lecture of G. M. Trevelyan, *The Two-Party System in English Political History* (Oxford: Clarendon Press, 1926).

4. Douglas Horton alludes to this episode in his *Vatican Diary 1963: A Protestant Observes the Second Session of Vatican Council II* (Philadelphia/Boston: The United Church Press, 1964), pp. 189 f. The episode was reviewed at the special meeting of the World Council of the Churches at Rammelsberg in Germany on July 27, 1964, when several observers of constituent bodies discussed the impact of the Vatican Council on the World Council of the Churches. For a very positive view of the ecclesiological significance of councils, see several of the recent writings by Peter Meinhold, *Der evangelische Christ und das Konzil* (Freiburg: Herder-Bücherei, 1962); *Konzile der Kirche in evangelischer Sicht* (Stuttgart: Kreuz-Verlag, 1962); with Abbot Laurentius Klein, *Über Wesen und Gestalt der Kirche* (Freiburg: Herder-Bücherei, 1963). In all three of these works it is recognized that on the Protestant side the history of councils has been seen too much in terms of law and jurisdiction, too little in terms of theology and more specifically of ecclesiology. The three works constitute a notable effort to reassess the significance of the idea of a general council for Lutheranism and the Reformed Tradition.

5. The address in French was printed in *Osservatore Romano*, December 5, 1963.

6. Eugen Rosenstock-Huessy, *Out of Revolution: Autobiography of Western Man* (New York: William Morrow, 1938), pp. 437-442.

7. John T. McNeill, *Unitive Protestantism: The Ecumenical Spirit and Its Persistent Expression* (rev. ed.; Richmond, Va.: John Knox Press, 1964), esp. pp. 89-129, 225-254.

8. Richard Marshall translated and published the *Defensor Pacis* of Marsilius of Padua in 1535, as part of Henry's defense of his reformation, but the sections of the work which spoke in terms of a republican form of secular government were carefully excised from this edition.

9. *Loc. cit.*, p. 46; cited by Franklin Le Van Baumer, "Christopher St. German," *American Historical Review*, XLII (1936/37), 638.

10. *Op. cit.*, Diiii; cited by Baumer, *op. cit.*, pp. 637 f.

11. Christopher St. German, *Doctor and Student* (London, 1530), ed. by W. Muchall (Cincinnati, 1874), p. 72.

12. Ernst Kantorowicz, *The King's Two Bodies; A Study in Mediaeval Political Theology* (Princeton: Princeton University Press, 1957), pp. 223-32. The sources of the Henrician theory of the *corpus republicae mysticum* include, among others, Sir John Fortescue (d. 1476), but Henry was the first to combine body politic *and ecclesiastic*. In contrast, Reginald Cardinal Pole argued the traditional view that the *corpus ecclesiae mysticum* was a divine, supra-national entity which could not be incorporated into any human body politic.

13. Cf. St. German's statement in *The Power of the Clergy*, Ch. VI: "For it is not to presume that so many noble princes and their counseyle, ne the lordes, and the nobles of the realme, ne yet the Commons gathered in the sayde parlymente wolde fro tyme to tyme renne in so great offence of conscyence as is the brekynge of the lawe of god"; cited by Baumer, *op. cit.*, pp. 648 f.

14. St. German, *op. cit.*, p. 279, cited by Baumer, *op. cit.*, p. 646.

15. The relationship of the imperialized kingship of Henry VIII and his reformation Parliament has been admirably worked out by a Japanese scholar, P. A. Sawada, in an unpublished thesis at the University of Bonn, "The Henrician Theory of the General Council and the Becoming of *Imperium Angliae*." I am grateful to the Rev. Prof. J. P. Dolan, under whose influence the dissertation got started, for making it possible for me to consult this study. He has himself expressed an interest in examining the extent to which Gallican ideas influenced the English tradition of loyal Opposition and suggests also the persistence of the influence of the twelfth-century canonists.

16. Chapuys to Charles V, November 13, 1530, *Calendar of State Papers, Spanish*, IV:1, No. 492, p. 798.

17. E. Hall, *The Union of the two illustre-famelies of Lancestre and Yorke* (London, 1548), ccv, as quoted by Eric Kemp, *Counsel and Consent: Aspects of the Government of the Church as Exemplified in the History of the English Provincial Synods* (London: S.P.C.K., 1961), p. 153.

18. H. Gee and W. Hardy, *Documents Illustrative of English Church History* (London/New York: Macmillan & Co., 1896), No. XLVIII, pp. 176-186.

19. *Ibid.*, No. LI, pp. 195-200.

20. St. German, *op. cit.*, Giiii[b]-Gvi[b]; cited by Baumer, *op. cit.*, p. 650.

21. John More's mentor, Bishop Stephen Gardiner of Winchester, had, of course, been presumably maintaining that the Holy Spirit was present only in a General Council. For the whole text of the interrogation, see James Gardiner, *Letters and Papers, Foreign and Domestic, of the Reign of Henry VIII* (London: Public Record Office, 1885), VIII, No. 592, p. 224 (S.P. 1/92, foll. 68-70 as quoted in Sawada, *op. cit.*, note 106).

22. Giberti from Cambrai, 27 April 1537. *Letters and Papers*, XII:1, No. 1053, p. 481.

23. Cf. Raymond Albright, "Conciliarism in Anglicanism," *Church History*, XXXIII (1964), 3-22.

24. As early as 1531 the claim was made for Henry by the Duke of Norfolk. Duke of Norfolk to Imperial Ambassador, Eustace Chapuys, *Letters and Papers*, V, No. 45, p. 19. Henry himself said to the Cistercian abbot of Chailly that he was *rex, imperator*, and even *Papa* for England. Letter of Chapuys to Charles, 31 July 1531. *Letters and Papers*, V, No. 361, p. 168. By 1533 the doctrine of the *translatio imperii* was enacted by Parliament. See R. Koebner, "'The Imperial Crown of the Realm,' Henry VIII, Constantine the Great, and Polydore Vergil," *Bulletin*, Institute of Historical Research, XXVI (1953), 29-52. But Henry's claim to being *imperator in regno suo* was not the same as to claim to be a universal *Imperator Romanorum*. His was an *imperium merum*.

25. *A Protestation of the King, Council, and Clergy* (1537), 115.

26. *A Treatise in Defense of the Reformation* (1539); cf. *Letters and Papers,*

XIV; 1, No. 376, pp. 144 f. (S.P. 6/3 foll. 79-85, as cited by Sawada, *op. cit.,* note 116).

27. British Museum, Cleop. E VI, vol. 330$^{r-v}$; Parker Society, Cranmer's *Miscellaneous Writings and Letters,* ed. by J. E. Cox (Cambridge: University Press, 1846), pp. 463 f. For Cranmer's conciliarism *in extenso,* see McNeill, *op. cit.,* pp. 225-254.

28. *Writings and Disputations of Thomas Cranmer . . . Relative to the Sacrament of the Lord's Supper,* edited for the Parker Society by J. F. Cox (Cambridge, 1844), II, 27, 174, 180, 190 f., 196, 217, 223.

29. Presumably Cranmer, during the June-July session of Parliament in 1536, "Thynges necessary as it seemeth to be remembered."

During his trial under Mary Tudor in 1556 Cranmer reaffirmed his conciliarism and appealed to the authority of a "free General Council." But he insisted even in his mortal extremity under the Counter-Reformation examiners on "a holy general council, lawfully gathered in the Holy Ghost" that would be "above the Pope." (*Miscellaneous Writings and Letters,* pp. 224 f.)

30. "Quid ad regiam majestatem?", *Letters and Papers,* XIX:2, No. 484, p. 273.

31. As an unusual Congregational anglican one may instance here Henry Burton (1578-1648), who in his *Protestation Protested* (July, 1641) opposed the vowing of the parliamentary Protestation of May 3, 1641 against "popery" in the national Church on the ground that there should still be freedom for even more tender consciences to proceed further to "separate" from the uncleanness of nominal Christianity (II Corinthians 6:17; cf. Isaiah 52:11); and accordingly, he argued for a national Church regularly reformed by Parliament and at the same time for independent churches or congregations under Christ "the King of saints," that is, for the more scrupulous Puritans, whose ministers would be maintained freely by the members "wholly without any compulsion (as is used in Tithes)." Burton's proposal was accepted in principle in the ecclesiastical settlement after the Glorious Revolution.

32. On this, see among other recent works, G. L. Mosse, *The Struggle for Sovereignty in England from the Reign of Queen Elizabeth to the Petition of Right* (East Lansing, Mich.: University Press, 1950).

33. Alexander Dunlap Lindsay, noting that the Bolshevik maxim "no opposition party and no opposition within the party" is the antithesis of democracy, suggests that the nonconformist conscience in the seventeenth century was the ultimate source of the conscience in political opposition in the evolution of English political institutions. He was surely right in pointing to the great debate between Levellers in the armies and Oliver Cromwell and Henry Ireton for the government at the grand council of officers in Putney in October, 1647, as a major contribution to the development of the English understanding of the role of the nonconformist conscience. Although Cromwell could not agree with the representatives of the Levellers on continuous or specific consent of the governed in workaday politics, he was in agreement with them in their democratic belief in the individual conscience and in their expectation that through discussion and mutual correction God's will would prevail. Lindsay quotes Cromwell on this point: "Truly we have heard many speaking to us [in the Putney Debate]; and I cannot but think that in many of those things God hath spoke to us. I cannot but think that in most that have spoke there hath been some things of God laid forth to us; and yet there hath been several contradictions in what hath been spoken. But certainly God is not the author of contradictions." See *The Essentials of Democracy* (London: Oxford University Press, 1929), p. 18 (and for the Bolshevik maxim, p. 35). I have rendered Cromwell's statement according to the critically edited text of A. S. P. Woodhouse, *Puritanism and Liberty: Being the Army Debates (1647-9)* (2nd ed.; Chicago: University of Chicago Press, 1951), p. 104. See further, L. F. Solt, *Saints in Arms: Puritanism and Democracy in Cromwell's Army* (Palo Alto: Stanford University Press, 1959).

34. Woodhouse, *op. cit.,* text, p. 23.

35. *Ibid.,* p. 17, italics mine.

36. This is the sentence following immediately upon the quotation from Cromwell by Lindsay, above at n. 33.

37. *Ibid.,* text, p. 105. All the matter in square brackets is supplied by Wood-

house except the very first and also the first enclosure after the first ellipsis; italics mine.

38. Rosenstock-Huessy, *Out of Revolution,* p. 344: "It was the insight into the inevitability of opposition in heaven which overcame the reluctance of human brains to tolerate opposition on earth. When we find the Leader of the Opposition legally established in the Canadian constitution, we should not forget that the discoveries of the astronomer had to give man a glimpse of the revolution of the stars before he was bold enough to legalize human opposition." See also especially pp. 332-347. On cosmic Toryism see also below, n. 44.

39. Caroline Robbins, *The Eighteenth-Century Commonwealthman: Studies in the transmission, development and circumstance of English liberal thought from the Restoration of Charles II until the War with the Thirteen Colonies* (Cambridge: Harvard University Press, 1959), pp. 4 and *passim.*

40. For the most comprehensive study of Bolingbroke, see the forthcoming Harvard dissertation of Isaac Kramnick, "Bolingbroke: An Augustan Political Theorist," Cambridge, 1965.

41. Henry St. John Viscount Bolingbroke, *Works* (London, 1754), II, p. 32; Dublin ed., 1793, II, p. 4.

42. *Ibid.; ibid.*

43. *Ibid.,* pp. 32-38; *ibid.,* pp. 4-11.

44. On Bolingbroke's Deism, see Walter M. Merrill, *From Statesman to Philosopher: A Study in Bolingbroke's Deism* (New York: Philosophical Library, 1949).

45. *Works* (London), III, p. 30; Dublin, III, pp. 30 f.

46. *Ibid.,* p. 29; *ibid.,* p. 30.

47. *Ibid.,* p. 17; *ibid.,* p. 18.

48. *Ibid.,* p. 18; *ibid.,* p. 19.

49. It is of lexicographical interest that, while in Britain, Germany, etc., the phrase is always "His Majesty's Opposition," in all American dictionaries and in general American usage it is always with the supplement "His Majesty's *Loyal* Opposition." A conjecture that Ralph Waldo Emerson in his *English Traits* might have been the originator of the Americanization of the phrase proved wrong.

In the American domestication of the English parliamentary phrase and institution it will be borne in mind that the Founding Fathers of the Republic felt especially at home in England with those called there the Real Whigs, the Commonwealthsmen who were familiar with the canon of Leveller-Independent literature going back to the Putney Debates. See Robbins, *op. cit.,* on Whig Canon, p. 4 and *passim;* on the Founding Fathers and the Real Whigs, pp. 19 ff., 82, 330, 347. It will be further borne in mind that while Americans inherited the British two-party system and for a while continued to use one of the Old World party labels, American party history knows also two other types of party: the ideological party of the Continent (only a recessive model) and the distinctively American type of a coalition party (with conventions reconciling sectional and class differences, as distinguished from coalition government). On the Methodist influence in the rise of the Labour Party, see Maldwyn Edwards, *Methodism and England: A Study of Methodism in Its Social and Political Aspects . . . 1850-1932* (London: The Epworth Press, 1943); Ernest R. Taylor, *Methodism and Politics 1791-1851* (Cambridge: University Press, 1935).

50. See above, n. 3, for the recent West German literature.

51. Bolingbroke, above at n. 46.

52. Compare the usage in "Catholic" France where *église* is reserved for the once established Church, *temple* for the Protestant meetinghouse.

53. See below, n. 61.

54. H. F. Lovell Cocks, *The Nonconformist Conscience* (London: Independent Press, 1943); Horton Davies, *The English Free Churches* (London/New York: Oxford University Press, 1952); Ernest A. Payne, *The Free Church Tradition in the Life of England* (3rd ed.; London: SCM Press, 1951).

55. Stephen Neill and Ruth Rouse, *A History of the Ecumenical Movement 1517-1948* (Philadelphia: The Westminster Press, 1954).

56. See below, n. 59.

57. Feodor Dostoievsky, *Diary*: "The Roman Catholic Church fights in the name of Caesar." See below at n. 58. Dostoievsky saw a continuity between

the man-god Apollo, Caesar, Roman Catholicism, the French Revolution, and secular socialism. This he contrasted with the Orthodox conception of the God-Man, Christ.

58. "By accepting that third counsel of the mighty spirit, you [Jesus] could have accomplished all that man seeks on earth, that is to say, whom to worship, to whom to entrust his conscience, and how at last to unite all in a common, harmonious, and incontestable ant-hill, for the need of universal unity is the third and last torment [temptation] of man. Mankind as a whole has always striven to organize itself into a world state. There have been many great nations with great histories, but the more highly developed they were, the more unhappy they were, for they were more acutely conscious of the need for the world wide union of men." (*Op. cit.*, David Magarshak translation [Penguin Classics, 1958], I, p. 302.) In the evolution of this Dostoievskian figure it is of interest that originally the authoritarian was not a Catholic prelate. See Georges Florovsky, "Die Sackgassen der Romantik," part 3, *Orient und Occident*, IV (1930), 14-37.

59. At the meetings of the American Society of Church History at Philadelphia in December, Florovsky documented his convictions in a paper entitled "The Authority of the Ancient Councils and the Traditions of the Fathers," in which he showed that the modern Western historiography of the ancient councils has been written out of the presuppositions of Western conciliarism. He therein shows that what would appear to have been the prototype of all councils, the Apostolic Council in Acts 15 with its phrase "It seemed good to us and the Holy Spirit," was not, in fact, regarded anciently as the model of the ecumenical councils, but rather, and much later, of course, of the Latin councils of the Conciliar Age. Florovsky's single most incisive expression of an Orthodox theory of the Church and the ecumenical encounter is "Sobornost: The Catholicity of the Church," *The Church of God: An Anglo-Russian Symposium*, ed. by E. L. Mascall (London: S.P.C.K. Press, 1934), pp. 51-74; see also below at n. 65. The present writer has brought together all of Florovsky's writings on this and kindred subjects in "Georges Vasilievich Florovsky," *Greek Orthodox Theological Review*, XI (1965), especially pp. 81-86.

60. The present writer has elsewhere written on what he considers the three levels of ecumenism in Catholicism not here discussed: ethically motivated international good will, interfaith solidarity, and intrafaith (intra-Christian) ecumenism: *Dimensions of Catholic Ecumenism*, Occasional Papers, I (The Hague: International Association for Liberal Christianity and Religious Freedom, 1966), 48 pp.

On the Roman Catholic side, one of the most helpful clarifications of the various postures in the ecumenical encounter is that of Gustave Thils, La "Théologie Oecuménique": Notion, Formes, Démarches, 2nd ed., Bibliotheca Ephemeridum Theologicarum Lovanensium, VIII (1963). He distinguishes four historic phases and present-day levels of encounter, extending from (1) hostile controversy (*oppositions massives*), through (2) existential confrontation, to (3) the search for common foundations, with close attention to identical meanings concealed beneath differences in terminology (*le souci des equivalences*) in (4) radical intuitions into the overarching principles of particular systems and trends.

61. In the contemporary situation the term "Third Force" designates the Pentecostals, Adventists, etc. (over against Catholicism and main-line Protestantism, Orthodoxy remaining undistinguished). The term was first used in this sense by Henry Pitney Van Dusen, reflecting on the global mission, to describe the world-embracing action of zealous groups growing in part out of the Free Church tradition but independent of the present main-line Protestant bodies. See "Will Lund Be Ecumenical?," *The Christian Century*, LXIX (July 23, 1952), 848-851. He subsequently refined his definition. See his *Christianity on the March* (New York: Harper & Row, 1963).

The term "Third Force" designates the changing congeries of groups, depending upon the observer and the century. On the significance of another Third Force, the Evangelicals within sixteenth-century Catholicism and the left wing of the Protestant Reformation, seen from the perspective of a Catholic interested both in civil liberty and in the ecumenical dialogue, see Friedrich Heer, *Die Dritte Kraft: Der europäische Humanismus zwischen den Fronten des konfessionellen Zeitalters* (Frankfurt a/M : S. Fischer Verlag, 1959). A similar study by Herman van Gelder, *The Two Reformations of the Sixteenth Century* (The Hague: Marinus Nijhoff, 1961), does not draw any present-day political or ecumenical inference from his Second, i.e., the Evangelical Humanist Reformation (Erasmianism, Evangelical Rationalism, etc.), contrasted with the Protestant and the Counter-Reformation. Cf. the present writer's more inclusive "Radical Reformation" contrasted with the "Magisterial" and the Counter-Reformation, *The Radical Reformation* (Philadelphia: The Westminster Press, 1962), introduction.

62. "Planimetrical" is used by Georges Florovsky somewhat disparagingly to designate the usual ecumenicity in space in contrast to the ecumenicity in time with its consensus of the ages.

63. One is here reminded of James L. Adams' "The Uses of Diversity," Convocation Address, Harvard Divinity School *Bulletin,* LI (1957/58), No. 7, pp. 47-64.

64. It should be remembered that Parliament even in the age of the Second Reformation of England acted like the Henrician Reformation Parliament: the Westminster Assembly of Divines with its Westminster [Presbyterian] Confession was constitutionally a creature of the Puritan Parliament, and not an independent synod as was the Assembly of the Kirk in Scotland.

65. Georges Florovsky, "Obedience and Witness," in Robert C. Mackie and Charles C. West, eds., *The Sufficiency of God: Essays in Honour of W. A. Visser 't Hooft* (London: SCM Press, 1963), p. 62.

66. It should be immediately added with respect to the World Council of Churches that, although constitutionally the constituent churches are formally equal, ecclesiologically they do not need to consider themselves equal. Secretary Visser 't Hooft made this explicit at the World Assembly in Amsterdam: "Nothing in the official documents contains the slightest suggestion that the Council takes its stand on an ecclesiology according to which each Church is to think of itself as one of the many *equally* true churches. Ecumenism does not mean ecclesiological relativism or syncretism." Despite the want of complete mutual recognition as complete or true churches, the constituent bodies of the World Council took the momentous decision "to stay together." To covenant to remain together on the same platform is the beginning of significant parliamentary debate and the constellation of a loyal opposition.

67. One may compare here, significantly, the application of the idea of a loyal opposition to Catholic education in Leslie Dewart, "Academic Freedom and Catholic Dissent," *Commonweal,* LXXX (April 3, 1964), 33-36, especially pp. 39 f.: "Freedom of conscience and the individual's duty to the whole Church require a 'loyal opposition,' that is, an opposition grounded upon the very legitimacy of the authority and upon whatever continuity the ruler may have preserved with the faithful under his command. . . ." "Even more, under certain circumstances the Christian's duty to the Church may require him, all the while remaining subject to authority and disposed to the strictest obedience, actually to *oppose* 'the guidance of the Church.'"

68. *The Ecumenist,* I (April/May, 1963), 62.

69. "The Council and Church Unity," *Criterion,* III (Spring, 1964), 10.

70. Reported in the *Osservatore Romano* of 18 February 1950.

71. Karl Rahner, S.J., *Free Speech in the Church* (London/New York: Sheed & Ward, 1959), p. 14; a translation of *Das freie Wort in der Kirche* (Einsiedeln: Johannes-Verlag, 1953).

72. *Ibid.,* p. 23.

73. *Documentazione Olandese del Concilio,* 15 September 1965, p. 3.

74. Something of this kind of thinking, drawn particularly from the left wing of the Reformation, is suggested by Franklin Littell, "The Work of the Holy Spirit in Group Discussion," *Mennonite Quarterly Review,* XXXIV (1960), 75 ff.

75. The Greek term is, of course, our word "heresies."

76. See, e.g., S. L. Greenslade, *Schism in the Early Church* (London: SCM Press, 1953), and Walter Bauer, *Rechtgläubigkeit und Ketzerei im ältesten Christentum* (Tübingen: Mohr, 1934). It was still within Jewry that Rabbi Gamaliel argued in the council that, if the followers of the new Way were of God, the others "might even be found opposing God" (Acts 5:33-39).

77. *Sanior* was often a medieval canonist's euphemism for a minority with the power.

IV. THE MEANING OF "CHURCH" IN ANABAPTISM AND ROMAN CATHOLICISM

*Michael Novak*

1. Ronald Knox, *Enthusiasm* (London: Oxford University Press, 1950), pp. 590-591.

2. See the lead article in the London *Tablet,* March 28, 1964.

3. The most thorough study is George Huntston Williams, *The Radical Reformation* (Philadelphia: The Westminster Press, 1962).

4. See Franklin H. Littell, *The Anabaptist View of the Church* (2nd ed.; Boston: Starr King Press, 1958), Ch. V, "The Changing Reputation of the Anabaptists."

5. See Williams, *op. cit.*

6. See Littell, *op. cit.,* Introduction: "A Working Definition of 'Anabaptist.'"

7. See, e.g., E. Belfort Bax, *The Rise and Fall of the Anabaptists* (London: Swan Sonnenschein & Company, 1903; New York: The Macmillan Company, 1903).

8. See Norman Cohn, *The Pursuit of the Millennium* (New York: Harper & Brothers [Torchbook Series], 1961).

9. See George Huntston Williams, *Spiritual and Anabaptist Writers,* Vol. XXV of Library of Christian Classics (Philadelphia: The Westminster Press, 1957), pp. 136-144.

10. See William R. Estep, *The Anabaptist Story* (Nashville, Tenn.: Broadman Press, 1963), p. 99, quoting from John Horsch, *The Hutterian Brethren* (Goshen, Ind.: Mennonite Historical Society, 1931).

11. Not long before Troeltsch published *The Social Teaching of the Christian Churches,* Leo XIII was asking for a renewal of Thomistic studies, on the grounds that the historical understanding of St. Thomas was of a very low level. In choosing Thomism as representative of a basic type of Christian society, Troeltsch seems (a) to have overrated the influence of Thomism as compared with other elements (such as the Latin jurists) in late medieval society and (b) to have given a very inadequate presentation of such fundamental matters as the relation of nature and grace in Aquinas. In twentieth-century Catholicism, Thomistic studies have proceeded far beyond the Thomism sketched by Troeltsch, and other approaches to philosophy and to theology also have increased in importance. Troeltsch's first description of the "church type" (Harper's Torchbook edition, 1960, vol. 2, p. 461) does not appear to fit either medieval Catholicism or contemporary Catholicism (especially not the latter) with much success.

12. Robert Friedmann, *Hutterite Studies* (Goshen, Ind.: Mennonite Historical Society, 1961), p. 6.

13. *Ibid.*

14. *Ibid.,* p. 7.

15. *Ibid.,* p. 9.

16. *Ibid.*

17. *Ibid.,* p. 10.

18. *Ibid.,* p. 12, quoting H. Richard Niebuhr, *The Social Sources of Denominationalism* (New York: Henry Holt and Company, 1929), p. 39.

19. *Ibid.,* p. 38.

20. *Ibid.,* p. 7, quoting from an unpublished paper of Roland H. Bainton. Although Professor Bainton is often credited with inventing the term, John T. McNeill used it publicly two months before Bainton's article appeared. In a telephone conversation on June 21, 1964, a typescript of which Prof. D. B. Robertson has been kind enough to furnish me, Prof. Bainton added: "But now there is somebody in the *Mennonite Quarterly Review* who pointed out that neither of us created it, and that he had run into it in earlier works; and I am sure I did not get it out of McNeill; I got it from somebody else who had invented it. As a matter of fact, Luther uses the expression, except that he inverts the direction— the Catholics on the left and 'Schwärmer' on the right. But he said that he took the middle of the road, between these other two. . . . The term 'left-wing' I saw

somewhere else before I used it or McNeill used it; I don't remember where, and as I say, I got the idea out of Luther."

21. Roland H. Bainton, "The Left Wing of the Reformation," *Journal of Religion*, XXI (1941), 124-134.

22. See Littell, *op. cit.*, and *The Free Church* (Boston: Starr King Press, 1957).

23. Friedmann, *op. cit.*, p. 30.

24. *Ibid.*

25. *Ibid.*, p. 31.

26. *Ibid.*

27. *Ibid.*, p. 38.

28. *Ibid.*, p. 32.

29. *Ibid.*, p. 33.

30. *Ibid.*, p. 34.

31. *Ibid.*

32. *Ibid.*

33. *Ibid.*, p. 35.

34. *Ibid.*, p. 36.

35. *Ibid.*, p. 37.

36. *Ibid.*, p. 38.

37. See, e.g., Williams, *Spiritual and Anabaptist Writers.*

38. *The Mennonite Encyclopedia* (1955), I, p. 534, quoting from "The Catholic Periodical for the St. Bernard Pastorate of Frankfurt," VI (1932), No. 3. This encyclopedia article gives a quite narrow, legalistic view of Roman Catholicism, and errs in describing the Catholic teaching on the sacraments. Unhappily, the article in *The Catholic Encyclopedia* (1907), I, pp. 445-446, is even less adequate; it links the Anabaptists by association with the Donatists, overlooks the doctrines of religious liberty and discipleship, and gives disproportionate attention to Thomas Müntzer and the Münster revolt—a seriously misleading article.

39. Littell, *The Free Church*, p. 131.

40. Littell, *Anabaptist View of the Church*, pp. 62-64.

41. *The Free Church*, p. 74. Littell also quotes Troeltsch (*Social Teaching*, Vol. I [Macmillan, 1931], p. 445) on the stultifying effect of the spiritualizers of Christianity, whose champions "desire the spiritual interpretation of the Gospel, and the universality of a Christianity of the people, without the compromises of the Church and without concealing the purely Divine element in the institutional character of the Church. Its champions desire the ethical radicalism of a Society which is built upon the ideal of the Gospel, without the narrowness and pettiness of the sect. It is, however, impossible to carry the 'spirit of the Gospel' into practice without some opportunistic restriction to that which is practically possible, and without the resolve not to allow the best to be the enemy of the good." (Littell, p. 80.)

42. *Ibid.*, p. 116.

43. *Ibid.*, p. 118.

44. *Ibid.*, pp. 125-126.

45. *Ibid.*, p. 66.

46. Littell, *Anabaptist View of the Church*, p. 85.

47. *Ibid.*, p. 84.

48. *Ibid.*

49. *Ibid.*

50. *Ibid.*, p. 85.

51. *Ibid.*, p. 84.

52. *Ibid.*, p. 85.

53. *Ibid.*

54. *Ibid.*, p. 86.

55. *Ibid.*, pp. 85-86.

56. *Ibid.*

57. *Ibid.*, p. 92.

58. *Ibid.*, p. 93.

59. *Ibid.*

60. *Ibid.*, p. 94, quoting from Menno Simons, *Meditation on the Twenty-fifth Psalm*, Preface (c. 1537).

61. Littell, *The Free Church*, p. 130, quoting from Karl Barth, MSS. for Commission I of the World Council of Churches (April 1947).

62. *Ibid.*, p. 127.
63. *Ibid.*
64. *Ibid.*
65. *Ibid.*
66. *Ibid.*, p. 149.
67. *Ibid.*, pp. 149-150.
68. *Ibid.*, Chs. IV and VI: "The Free Church and 'American Religion' " and "The Free Church and Its Discipline."
69. *Ibid.*, p. 93.
70. *The Documents of Vatican II,* Walter M. Abbott, S.J. (ed.), (New York: Guild Press, 1966), pp. 14-37.
71. See Michael Novak, *The Open Church* (New York: The Macmillan Company, 1964), chs. 10-11.
72. *Ibid.*, ch. 20, for the first such occasion.

V. HOBBES'S THEORY OF ASSOCIATIONS IN THE SEVENTEENTH-CENTURY MILIEU

### D. B. Robertson

1. *New York Times,* January 9, 1964, p. 10.
2. Cf. Max Weber's note about America being "the association-land par excellence." "Max Weber's Proposal for Sociological Study of Voluntary Associations," unpublished translation by E. C. Hughes, from Weber's "Geschaftsbericht," *Verhandlungen des ersten deutschen Sozialogentages,* vom 19-22 Oktober, 1910 in Frankfurt a/M, Tübingen, 1911, pp. 52-60. Of course, de Tocqueville had already described this phenomenon a long time before.
3. Weber, for instance, in this same piece points out that a German town of as many as 30,000 was, in his time, likely to have as many as 300 such groups listed in the telephone directories. Edmond Cahn notes that the ancient Athenians "considered it one of the elementary features of their constitution," and Aristotle saw association as that which "shaped and defined a human being." (Edmond Cahn, *The Predicament of Democratic Man* [New York: The Macmillan Company, 1961], p. 99.)
4. See John Timbs, *Clubs and Club Life in London* (London: Chotto and Windus, 1898). Timbs has a note on the origin of clubs and a listing of more than 100 "clubs." There is a brief history and description of clubs in the *Encyclopaedia Britannica,* 11th edition, Volume 6, pp. 564-568. See also *The Oxford Classical Dictionary* (Oxford: The Clarendon Press, 1949), pp. 204-205, for a brief description of Greek and Roman clubs.
5. Edmond Cahn, *The Moral Decision* (Bloomington: Indiana University Press [a Midland Book], 1959), p. 157.
6. Cahn, *Predicament of Democratic Man,* p. 98.
7. Thomas Hobbes, *Leviathan* (New York: The Liberal Arts Press, 1958), Part II, ch. 29, p. 261. This edition of *Leviathan* will be referred to unless otherwise indicated.
8. Some scholars trace "Benefit Clubs" or "Friendly Societies" to the period following the Norman Conquest. Sir Frederic M. Eden, however, makes out a good case for what he called "modern Friendly Societies" having been in existence in pre-Norman times, organized especially to help those in need. (*The State of the Poor* [3 volumes; London: J. Davis, 1797], Vol. I, Ch. III, pp. 590-632).
9. For a general survey of this problem, see Robert A. Nisbet, *The Quest for Community* (New York: Oxford University Press, 1953).
10. Rudolph Sohm, *Outlines of Church History* (Boston: Beacon Press, 1958), p. 156. This line of thinking, of course, is developed in the works of Weber and Troeltsch, among other places.
11. G. P. Gooch calls Hobbes "the least English of our three great political thinkers." (In *Hobbes* [London: Humphrey Milford Amen House, Proceedings of the British Academy], Volume XXV, 1939, p. 3.) R. G. Collingwood, on the contrary, in *The New Leviathan* (Oxford: The Clarendon Press, 1936), p. 266, claims Hobbes as the "most English of Englishmen" in his "classical politics," because he (Hobbes) reflects in his writings very clearly English experience in the political and social life of the time. Perhaps this is true in terms of Hobbes's own

immediate period, but it is not true in terms of the future course of Anglo-Saxon history, which is better represented by the Levellers and later in the century by Locke. A more specifically "Christian" and popular treatment of the subject ten years later, under the same title, was by Paul Hutchinson. His work was intended to be a warning to Christian citizens against the encroachments of Big State or Leviathan. See Paul Hutchinson, *The New Leviathan* (New York: Willett, Clark & Co., 1946).

12. Leo Strauss, *The Political Philosophy of Hobbes* (Chicago: The University of Chicago Press [Phoenix Edition], 1963), pp. 63 ff.

13. Strauss (*op. cit.*, p. 59) says that ". . . Hobbes was from the outset a decided upholder of the monarchy and a decided opponent of democracy, and he kept to this opinion throughout his whole life." While Strauss does rest this statement on Hobbes's own words, he nevertheless qualifies the point by his references to the "legal equivalence" of democracy (*ibid.*, pp. 57-58). Hobbes's emphasis upon *de facto* government would seem to support the same qualification. "His final theory is that every effective rule is *eo ipso* legitimate" (*ibid.*, p. 68). Then there is Strauss's statement that the artificial state ". . . in principle may with equal justification be democratic, aristocratic, or monarchic . . . Originally he considered democracy as the primary form of the artificial state" (*ibid.*, p. 63). But—and here is our special concern for Hobbes's mature view about political life—by the time *Leviathan* appeared, this view was long gone. It seems puzzling, though, that the first statement is made without qualification.

14. In *Three Discourses, The English Works of Thomas Hobbes of Malmesbury*, collected and edited by Sir William Molesworth (London: John Bohn, 1839), Vol. IV, Part I, pp. 1-76; in his conclusion to this discourse, he says, "Thus have we considered the nature of man so far as was requisite for the finding out the first and most simple elements wherein the compositions of politic rules and laws are lastly resolved" (p. 76). See also *Leviathan*, Part I, especially the first 12 chapters.

15. A. E. Taylor, *Thomas Hobbes* (London: Archibald Constable & Co., Ltd., 1908), pp. 55-75.

16. F. C. Hood, *The Divine Politics of Hobbes* (Oxford: The Clarendon Press, 1964), p. 74. This view is shared by one of the earlier writers on Hobbes: G. C. Robertson, *Hobbes* (London: William Blackwood & Sons, 1886), pp. 51-52.

17. Introduction to *Leviathan*, p. 23.

18. *Ibid.*, p. 24. See also Richard Peters, *Hobbes* (Harmondsworth: Penguin Books, Ltd., 1956), pp. 76 ff. and p. 154.

19. *English Works*, Vol. III, pp. xi, xii.

20. *Leviathan*, p. 106.

21. Sanford Lakoff says that "Hobbes recapitulates the argument of Calvin in political terms, except that he makes several substitutions." (Sanford Lakoff, *Equality in Political Philosophy* [Cambridge: Harvard University Press, 1964], p. 73.)

22. *English Works*, Vol. II, p. 7.

23. *Ibid.*, p. ii.

24. *Ibid.*

25. *Leviathan*, p. 107.

26. *English Works*, Vol. II, p. 9.

27. *Leviathan*, p. 109.

28. Sheldon Wolin, *Politics and Vision* (Boston: Little, Brown & Company, 1960), ch. 8.

29. *Ibid.*, p. 243.

30. H. R. Trevor-Roper, "The General Crisis of the 17th Century," *Past and Present*, No. 16 (November 1959), pp. 31-33.

31. One of Trevor-Roper's critics, E. H. Kossman, in a subsequent issue of *Past and Present*, No. 18 (November 1960), pp. 8-9, notes that he seems to contradict himself on the point in the end—at least that there was "general gloom."

32. For example, William Walwyn, one of the Leveller leaders, wrote: "Seeing God hath so blest that which has been done, as thereby to cleer the way, and to afford an opportunity which these 600 years has been desired, but could never be attained, of making this a truly happy and wholly Free Nation . . ." (*A*

*Manifestation,* reprinted in William Haller and Godfrey Davies, *The Leveller Tracts* [New York: Columbia University Press, 1944], p. 277.)

33. Christopher Hill, *Puritanism and Revolution* (London: Secker and Warburg, 1958), p. 277.

34. *Leviathan,* Ch. XXI.

35. John Bowle, *Hobbes and His Critics* (New York: Oxford University Press, 1952), p. 172.

36. For a survey of this subject in Western history, see J. W. Gough, *The Social Contract* (Oxford: The Clarendon Press, 1936).

37. For a variety of treatments and interpretations of "natural law," following are some suggestions: J. L. Adams, "The Law of Nature: Some General Considerations," *The Journal of Religion,* XXV, No. 2 (April 1945), 88-96; there is a brief historical survey by Georges Gurvitch in *Encyclopedia of the Social Sciences;* Otto von Gierke, of course (with Ernest Barker's introduction), is a perpetual resource on this subject: *Natural Law and the Theory of Society, 1500-1800* (Boston: Beacon Press, 1957), Appendix by Ernst Troeltsch. Following are some of the books in which chapters or sections related to a discussion of Hobbes and the subject are to be found: E. G. Catlin, *Thomas Hobbes* (Oxford: Basil Blackwell, 1922), pp. 36-39; J. W. Gough, *op. cit.,* Ch. VIII; F. C. Hood, *The Divine Politics of Thomas Hobbes* (Oxford: The Clarendon Press, 1964), Chs. VII-VIII; C. B. Macpherson, *The Political Theory of Possessive Individualism* (Oxford: The Clarendon Press, 1962), pp. 17 ff., 68-70; S. I. Mintz, *The Hunting of Leviathan* (Cambridge: Cambridge University Press, 1962), pp. 26-28; Richard Peters, *Hobbes* (London:Penguin Books, 1956), pp. 169-170, 173-176, 204-205; E. J. Roesch, *The Totalitarian Threat* (New York: Philosophical Library, 1963), several sections; Strauss, *op. cit.,* several sections; Howard Warrender, *The Political Philosophy of Hobbes* (Oxford: The Clarendon Press), Chs. III-IV, VII, X, XII; Wolin, *op. cit.,* pp. 262-265. Hobbes discusses the subject in *Leviathan,* Chs. XIII-XV, among other places.

38. *Leviathan,* p. 142.

39. J. L. A. speaks of a "synthetic definition," *op. cit.,* p. 95. Nisbet is simply wrong in equating Hobbes's view of natural law with "the 17th-century views of natural law." (R. A. Nisbet, *The Quest for Community* [New York: Oxford University Press, 1953], p. 131.)

40. *Leviathan,* p. 109.

41. *Ibid.,* p. 110.

42. *Ibid.,* p. 130. Hobbes states his "laws of nature" as obligations on men, but he says that "They are but conclusions or theorems concerning what conduces to the conservation and defense of themselves, whereas law, properly, is the word of him that by right has command over others." (*Ibid.,* p. 132.)

43. W. W. Kulski, in "Comments," H. D. Lasswell and Harlan Cleveland, *The Ethic of Power* (New York: Harper & Brothers, 1962), p. 290.

44. In "The Political Act as an Act of Will," *The American Journal of Sociology,* LXIX, No. 1 (July, 1963), 1-6.

45. *Ibid.,* p. 1.

46. *Ibid.,* p. 2.

47. *Ibid.,* p. 1.

48. "The Distortion of Political Theory: the XVIIth Century Case," *Journal of the History of Ideas,* XXV, No. 3 (July-September 1964), 323-332.

49. *Leviathan,* p. 173.

50. Hill, *op. cit.,* p. 282.

51. Hill (*ibid.,* p. 283) relates his description of Hobbes here to the "burning question" of the day, the predicament of the small proprietor, whose existence still depended upon status rather than contract. Hill notes that the struggle here involved was a moral one as well as a socio-economic matter, concluding that "Now here Hobbes was making contract the basis of morality!" To Hill this is decisive for an understanding of Hobbes. "Nowhere is the fundamentally 'bourgeois' nature of Hobbes's approach to the state and to morality more apparent than in this, the foundation of both." Hill is not the first nor the last to see Hobbes in this light. A recent and very suggestive book is by Professor C. B. Macpherson: *The Political Theory of Possessive Individualism, Hobbes to Locke.* He says that "the model of a possessive market society, and no other, does correspond in essentials to modern competitive societies . . . and that that model and

no other does meet the essential requirements of Hobbes's society" (p. 61). Also, "It is only a society as fragmented as a market society that can credibly be treated as a mechanical system of self-moving individuals" (p. 79). An interesting statement of an opposed view is found in Nisbet (*op. cit.*, pp. 138 ff.). Nisbet catalogues several points of specific antagonism against the "middle class" in Hobbes's thought. Any evidence of Hobbes's identity with this class, he says, ". . . is because he could see that this class, by reason of the very absence of any sense of *noblesse oblige*, could never become, as the older aristocracy had been, a threat to the unity of the political state" (p. 139).

52. *Leviathan*, p. 105.

53. *Ibid.* For a discussion of "equality" in Hobbes's thought, see Macpherson (*op. cit.*, pp. 74-78, 83-85, 87-90).

54. Macpherson, *op. cit.*, p. 88.

55. *Leviathan*, p. 105.

56. *Ibid.*

57. *Ibid.*, p. 270.

58. *Ibid.*

59. Noted by Hill (*op. cit.*, p. 279) in agreeing with Clarendon on the "radical" nature of Hobbes's attack upon the aristocracy.

60. *Leviathan*, p. 260. Noted by Hood (*op. cit.*, pp. 104-105).

61. *Leviathan*, p. 271.

62. Hood, *op. cit.*, p. 105.

63. I am not yet prepared to follow altogether Macpherson's thesis of "possessive individualism" as it applies to the Levellers, and the implication that they shared such kindred "individualism" with Hobbes. The fact that in their "programmatic statements" they qualify the principle of universal manhood suffrage, in, for instance, their "Third Agreement," I take for the time being (along with other interpreters—notably Franck and Schenck), as a concession to political expediency. My hesitancy is based on two points: (1) the heavy emphasis of the Levellers on equality as an aspect of natural law; (2) the sort of "individualism" so well documented by Macpherson takes no account of Leveller associational emphases. In fact, the word "association" does not appear in his index! Further, he neglects one of the most fundamental elements of Leveller doctrine— the meaning of "vocation." Christopher Hill, in his review of Macpherson's book (*Past and Present*, No. 24, pp. 86-89), goes overboard in his acceptance of Macpherson's thesis. He states at the end of his review of the book the obvious! Macpherson's thesis "cannot be laughed off or ignored." There is no need to argue this point; Macpherson's masterful delineation of this connecting theme in various representatives of the age will be a resource for some time to come. But there were, after all, other connecting themes. Macpherson and Hill both emphasize the importance of *not* overemphasizing one aspect of the picture. All right. Let's don't!

64. There is little doubt that Hobbes prepared a solid foundation for a radical individualism, but that he should be cited as a contributor to the development of "democracy" takes a bit of doing! Yet Nisbet (*op cit.*, p. 138) contributes this bland statement, that "It is not the totalitarian state that Hobbes gives us but the necessary political environment of the natural system of liberty which was to become identified later with the Enlightenment in France and England."

65. Gierke, *Natural Law and the Theory of Society*, p. 60.

66. *Ibid.*

67. *Ibid.*

68. *Leviathan*, p. 108. Hobbes clearly had little knowledge of the American Indians. There was no group that "had no government."

69. "The Political Act as an Act of Will," *op. cit.*, p. 1.

70. See W. Friedmann, *Legal Theory* (3rd ed.; London: Stevens & Sons, Ltd., 1953), p. 397.

71. Quoted by Nisbet (*op. cit.*, p. 118). Apparently during the period of the Republic, groups operated more freely.

72. See J. C. Ayer, *A Source Book for Ancient Church History* (New York: Charles Scribner's Sons, 1939), p. 21.

73. See Otto von Gierke, "The Idea of Corporation," tr. by F. Kolegar, in *Theories of Society*, ed. by Parsons, Shils, Naegele & Pitts (New York: The Free

Press of Glencoe, Inc., 1961), I, 611-626. P. W. Duff, *Personality in Roman Private Law* (Cambridge: Cambridge University Press, 1938), traces all the complexities of the rise of the "fiction" theory and its relationship to the "concession" theory and of their "reception" (or non-reception) in England.

74. For the historic importance of this legal conception, see two earlier articles by H. J. Laski, "The Personality of Associations," *Harvard Law Review,* XXIX, No. 4 (February 1916), 404-426, and "The Early History of the Corporation in England," *Harvard Law Review,* XXX, No. 6 (April 1917), 575.

75. F. W. Maitland, Introduction to his translation of Otto von Gierke, *Political Theories of the Middle Age* (Boston: Beacon Press, 1958), p. xxx. Maitland's associate, Sir Frederick Pollock, in an essay entitled "Has the Common Law Received the Fiction Theory of Corporations?" does not agree with Maitland's judgment. He thinks one has to distinguish between "occasional borrowing" and "serious reception of the doctrine." (*Essays in the Law* [London: Macmillan & Co., 1922], pp. 151 ff.)

76. *Ibid.,* p. xxxi.

77. *Ibid.,* p. xxix.

78. Quoted in David Fellman, *The Constitutional Right of Association* (Chicago: University of Chicago Press, 1963), pp. 99-100. One argument about Englishmen's rights of assembly, not directly provided for, is that they are derivable from individual liberty and the right of free speech. See J. M. Jarrett and V. A. Mund, "The Right of Assembly," *New York University Law Quarterly Review,* IX, No. 1 (September 1931), p. 3. Beyond that, these authors, constitutional specialists, argue that the Englishman's right of assembly has substantial foundations in common law and in statutory law.

79. A specifically stated "constitutional right" to associate, it is clear, does not necessarily guarantee actual and functional group life in a state. Consider, for instance, the "legal guarantee" of voluntary associations under the Soviet Constitution: Article 126 of the Constitution reads: "In conformity with the interests of the working people, and in order to develop the organizational initiative and political activity of the masses of the people, citizens of the U.S.S.R. are guaranteed the right to unite in social organizations: trade unions, co-operative societies, youth organisations, sport and defence organisations, cultural, technical and scientific societies; and the most active and politically conscious citizens in the ranks of the working class, working peasants and working intelligensia voluntarily unite in the Communist Party of the Soviet Union . . ." Cited under "Legal Situation," in *The Trade Union Situation in the U.S.S.R.,* Report of Mission from the International Labour Office (Geneva: La Tribune de Genève, 1960), p. 41. A case somewhat more nearly in the Anglo-Saxon tradition is the Indian Constitution of 1949, which specifically guarantees the right of freedom of association.

80. Cahn, *The Predicament of Democratic Man,* p. 99.

81. *The Federalist* (New York: The Modern Library, 1937), papers 10 and 51.

82. *Ibid.,* Article 10, p. 54.

83. Gaillard Hunt, *The Writings of James Madison, 1790-1802,* Vol. VI (New York: G. P. Putnam's Sons, 1906), p. 86, on "Parties," and pp. 106 ff., on "A Candid State of Parties."

84. Mr. Roy Branson, in "A Note on Madison's Use of the Words Majority, Party and Faction" (2 pages, unpublished), explores the question of whether Madison moved toward a new definition of "faction" or to a positive appreciation of their function even in terms of his original definition.

85. See R. A. Horn, *Groups and the Constitution* (Stanford: Stanford University Press, 1956), p. 1. See also M. R. Konvitz, *First Amendment Freedoms* (Ithaca: Cornell University Press, 1963).

86. *Gibson v. Florida Legislative Investigating Committee, United States Reports,* Vol. 372 (Washington: U.S. Government Printing Office, 1963), pp. 557-558.

87. Konvitz, *op. cit.,* p. 158. Without this right (of association), other rights would be nugatory. Horn (*op. cit.,* p. 1) affirms as the "central theme" of his book "that freedom of association is one of the most important civil liberties guaranteed by the Constitution of the United States . . ."

88. *Leviathan,* p. 106.
89. *Ibid.,* p. 261.
90. As Croom Robertson says: "Nor does history confirm the timorous thought of Hobbes, that all the woes of anarchy are instantly present as the inevitable alternative to tame endurance of the most arbitrary acts of quiescence." (*Op. cit.,* p. 232.)
91. *Leviathan,* p. 181.
92. *Ibid.*
93. *Ibid.*
94. *Ibid.,* p. 186.
95. *Ibid.,* pp. 186-188.
96. *Ibid.,* p. 189. See also Gierke, *Natural Law,* p. 80.
97. *Ibid.,* p. 181.
98. *Ibid.,* p. 191.
99. *Ibid.*
100. *Ibid.,* p. 189.
101. *Ibid.,* p. 192.
102. Strauss, *op. cit.,* p. 71. Basil Willey, *The Seventeenth Century Background* (New York: Doubleday & Co., Inc. [Anchor Book], 1955), observes that "in Hobbes the appearance, at least, of orthodoxy was somehow preserved."
103. Strauss, *op. cit.,* p. 71.
104. R. M. Grant, *A Short History of the Interpretation of the Bible* (New York: The Macmillan Company, 1963), pp. 145-146.
105. *English Works,* Vol. III, pp. 697-698.
106. Thomas Hobbes, *Behemoth,* ed. by William Molesworth (New York: Burt Franklin [Research and Source Works Series, No. 38], 1963), p. 5.
107. *Ibid.*
108. *Ibid.*
109. See G. L. Burr, "Liberals and Liberty Four Hundred Years Ago," *The Proceedings of the Unitarian Historical Society,* III (1933), Part I, pp. 8-11.

VI. THE VOLUNTARY PRINCIPLE IN RELIGION AND RELIGIOUS FREEDOM IN AMERICA

### *Robert T. Handy*

1. Martin E. Marty, "Protestantism Enters Third Phase," *The Christian Century,* LXXVIII (January 18, 1961), 72.
2. For a full discussion, see Anson Phelps Stokes, *Church and State in the United States* (3 vols.; New York: Harper & Brothers, 1950); for brief introductions, see Sidney E. Mead, *The Lively Experiment: The Shaping of Christianity in America* (New York: Harper & Row, 1963), Ch. II, "From Coercion to Persuasion: Another Look at the Rise of Religious Liberty and the Emergence of Denominationalism"; H. Shelton Smith, Robert T. Handy, and Lefferts A. Loetscher, *American Christianity: An Historical Interpretation with Representative Documents,* I (New York: Charles Scribner's Sons, 1960), Ch. VIII, "Religion in the Struggle for Freedom."
3. Winthrop S. Hudson, *The Great Tradition of the American Churches* (New York: Harper & Brothers, 1953), p. 48; see pp. 49-55. See also Ralph Barton Perry, *Puritanism and Democracy* (New York: Vanguard Press, 1944), and A. S. P. Woodhouse, *Puritanism and Liberty* (2nd ed.; Chicago: University of Chicago Press, 1951).
4. Hugh Hastings (ed.), *Ecclesiastical Records, State of New York,* Vol. III (Albany: J. B. Lyon Co., 1902), p. 1910.
5. L. F. Greene (ed.), *The Writings of the Late Elder John Leland* (New York: G. W. Wood, 1845), p. 182.
6. Quoted by Stokes, *op. cit.,* I, 207.
7. Alice M. Baldwin, *The New England Clergy and the American Revolution* (Durham: Duke University Press, 1928), p. 80.
8. William Henry Foote, *Sketches of Virginia, Historical and Biographical* (Philadelphia: William S. Martien, 1850; Richmond: John Knox Press, 1966, indexed), p. 322.
9. See Mead, *The Lively Experiment,* Ch. VII, "Denominationalism: The Shape of Protestantism in America."

416 VOLUNTARY ASSOCIATIONS

10. *The Works of William E. Channing, D.D.* (11th complete edition; Boston: Geo. E. Channing, 1849), I, 282 f.
11. Quoted by Stow Persons, *American Minds: A History of Ideas* (New York: Henry Holt & Co., 1958), p. 160.
12. Charles Beecher (ed.), *Autobiography, Correspondence, Etc., of Lyman Beecher, D.D.* (2 vols.; New York: Harper & Brothers, 1864), I, 344.
13. Perry Miller *et al., Religion and Freedom of Thought* (Garden City: Doubleday & Co., 1954), pp. 15 f.
14. James Fulton Maclear, " 'The True American Union' of Church and State: The Reconstruction of the Theocratic Tradition," *Church History,* XXVIII (1959), 56 f. This is a very useful article; on several grounds I believe that some such word as "theocentric" would better describe the tradition than does the word "theocratic."
15. Alexis de Tocqueville (Philips Bradley, ed.), *Democracy in America* (2 vols.; New York: Alfred A. Knopf, 1945), I, 303.
16. Edwards A. Park (ed.), *Writings of Professor B. B. Edwards, with a Memoir* (2 vols.; Boston: John P. Jewett & Co., 1853), I, 490.
17. David S. Schaff, "The Movement and Mission of American Christianity," *American Journal of Theology,* XVI (1912), 63, 65.
18. de Tocqueville, *op. cit.,* I, 263 f.
19. Francis J. Grund, *The Americans in their Moral, Social and Political Relations,* I, 281, as quoted in Stokes, *op. cit.,* I, 782 f.
20. Charles G. Finney, *Lectures to Professing Christians* (New York: John S. Taylor, 1837), p. 90.
21. Will Herberg, *Protestant-Catholic-Jew: An Essay in American Religious Sociology* (Garden City: Doubleday & Co., 1955), p. 212.
22. Quoted by Winfred E. Garrison, *The March of Faith: The Story of Religion in America Since 1865* (New York: Harper & Brothers, 1933), p. 210.
23. André Siegfried (tr. H. H. Hemming and Doris Hemming), *America Comes of Age* (New York: Harcourt, Brace & Co., 1927), p. 33.
24. Robert T. Handy, "The American Religious Depression, 1925-1935," *Church History,* XXIX (1960), 3-16.
25. Charles Fiske, *The Confessions of a Puzzled Parson* (New York: Charles Scribner's Sons, 1928), p. 191.
26. Herberg, *Protestant-Catholic-Jew,* pp. 139 f.
27. See, e.g., Edward Duff, S.J., *The Social Thought of the World Council of Churches* (New York: Association Press, 1956), especially pp. 276-282, and John C. Bennett (ed.), *Christian Social Ethics in a Changing World* (New York: Association Press, 1966).
28. See A. F. Carillo de Albornoz, *Roman Catholicism and Religious Liberty* (Geneva: World Council of Churches, 1959), and the Declaration on Religious Freedom of the Second Vatican Council, *Dignitatis Humanae,* promulgated by Pope Paul VI on December 7, 1965.

VII. THE POLITICAL THEORY OF VOLUNTARY ASSOCIATION
IN EARLY NINETEENTH-CENTURY GERMAN LIBERAL THOUGHT

*Georg G. Iggers*

1. Herbert B. Adams, *The Germanic Origin of New England Towns* in *Johns Hopkins University Studies in Historical and Political Science,* I, No. 2 (Baltimore: Johns Hopkins Press, 1882), 13. On the theory of the Germanic origin of American liberties, see Amales Tripathi, *Evolution of Historiography in America, 1870-1910* (Calcutta, 1956), pp. 28-42; Harvey Wish, *The American Historian. A Social-Intellectual History of the American Past* (New York: Oxford University Press, 1960), pp. 182-183; on Henry Adams' criticism of the Germanists, see Oscar Cargill, "The Medievalism of Henry Adams," in *Essays and Studies in Honor of Carleton Brown* (New York: Oxford University Press, 1940), pp. 310-319.
2. Heinrich von Treitschke, "Die Freiheit," *Preussische Jahrbücher,* VII (1861), 382.
3. A. D. Lindsay, *The Modern Democratic State,* I (New York: Oxford University Press, 1947), 115.

4. Ernst Troeltsch, *Protestantism and Progress,* tr. W. Montgomery (Boston: Beacon Press, 1958), p. 121; cf. A. D. Lindsay, *op. cit.,* p. 118.

5. Cf. Franz Schnabel, *Deutsche Geschichte im neunzehnten Jahrhundert,* 4th ed., I (Freiburg i. b., 1948), 83-88.

6. Arnold Rose, *Theory and Method in the Social Sciences* (Minneapolis: University of Minnesota Press, 1954), p. 73.

7. Ernest Barker, "Translator's Introduction" in Otto von Gierke, *Natural Law and the Theory of Society, 1500 to 1800* (Cambridge: Cambridge University Press, 1934), I, lxxxvii.

8. *Ibid.,* p. 76. In German, Otto von Gierke, *Das deutsche Genossenschaftsrecht* (Graz, 1954), p. 350. For studies of German corporatist thought in more recent periods, see Ellsworth Faris, Jr., *German Corporatism and Its Social Background, 1800-1860* (Dissertation, University of Chicago, 1950) and Ralph H. Bowen, *German Theories of the Corporate State; with Special Reference to the Period 1870-1919* (New York: McGraw-Hill, 1947).

9. For a discussion by Gierke of theories of voluntary association in eighteenth-century Germany see "The Atomistic Conception of the Nature of Associations in Eighteenth-Century Germany," Barker, pp. 124-127.

10. For discussions of Humboldt's political thought see S. A. Kähler, *Wilhelm von Humboldt und der Staat* (München, 1927); Friedrich Meinecke, "Wilhelm von Humboldt und der deutsche Staat," *Die neue Rundschau;* and Georg G. Iggers, *Historicism in Germany. The Rise and Decline of a Tradition of Historical and Political Thought,* ch. 3, "Wilhelm von Humboldt" (book in preparation).

11. Wilhelm von Humboldt, *Ideen zu einem Versuch die Grenzen der Wirksamkeit des Staats zu bestimmen* (to be cited hereafter as *Ideas*) in *Gesammelte Schriften* (Berlin, 1903-1936), I, 106.

12. *Ibid.,* p. 109.

13. See *ibid.,* Chapters III, VI, VII, VIII.

14. See *ibid.,* I, 247. Cf. *ibid.,* p. 200: "Far from bringing about harmful consequences, societies and associations are one of the surest means of furthering and accelerating the education of men. The best one might expect from the state in this respect would be a directive that every moral person or society be viewed only as an association of its members at every given moment and that therefore nothing prevent it to decide according to its pleasure by majority vote about the use of its common energies and means."

15. *Ibid.,* I, 236.

16. *Ibid.,* I, 200.

17. Lindsay, *op. cit.,* p. 117.

18. Virginia Declaration of Rights; cf. Lindsay, *op. cit.,* p. 122.

19. *Gesammelte Schriften,* I, 126-127.

20. "Ideen über Staatsverfassung, durch die neue französische Constitution veranlasst," *ibid.,* I, 79-80.

21. *Ideas, ibid.,* I, 137.

22. Leonard Krieger, *The German Idea of Freedom* (Boston: Beacon Press, 1957), p. 168.

23. *Ideas,* in *Gesammelte Schriften,* I, 243.

24. *Briefwechsel zwischen Schiller und Wilhelm von Humboldt,* ed. A. Leitzmann (Berlin, 1900), p. 50.

25. Gerhard Ritter in *Stein, eine politische Biographie* (Stuttgart, 1931) stresses the conservative, restorative elements in Stein's thought, his desire to create a corporate society adjusted to modern conditions. Max Lehmann in *Freiherr von Stein,* 3 vols. (Leipzig, 1902-1905), tends to view Stein more as a man of the Enlightenment.

26. "Denkschrift über Preussens ständische Verfassung (4. Februar 1819)" (to be cited hereafter as "1819 Memorandum") in Wilhelm von Humboldt, *Eine Auswahl aus seinen politischen Schriften* (to be cited as *Auswahl*), ed. Siegfried Kähler (Berlin, 1922), p. 169.

27. *Ibid.,* p. 171.

28. *Ibid.,* p. 191.

29. *Ibid.,* pp. 204-212.

30. "Denkschrift über die deutsche Verfassung" (to be cited hereafter as "1813 Memorandum") in *Auswahl,* p. 91.

31. *Über die Aufgabe des Geschichtsschreibers* (Berlin, 1822), p. 16.

32. "1813 Memorandum," *Auswahl*, p. 90.

33. *Ibid.*, p. 89.

34. Cf. Gunther Eyck, "English and French Influences on German Liberalism Before 1848," *Journal of the History of Ideas*, XVIII (1957), 313-341; Georg G. Iggers, *op. cit.*, Ch. V, "The Political Historians."

35. Even Rotteck's colleague Karl Welcker, more of an admirer of Montesquieu than of Rousseau, was sympathetic to English institution.

36. See P. A. Pfizer, *Gedanken über das Ziel und die Aufgabe des deutschen Liberalismus* (Tübingen, 1832).

37. Friedrich Christoph Dahlmann, *Geschichte der englischen Revolution* (Leipzig, 1844) and *Geschichte der französischen Revolution* (Leipzig, 1845).

38. Dahlmann, *Die Politik auf den Grund und das Mass der gegebenen Zustände zurückgeführt* (Berlin, 1924); see *ibid.*, p. 85, regarding natural rights, p. 112 regarding the judiciary.

39. *Ibid.*, pp. 84-85; cf. p. 55.

40. Cf. *ibid.*, p. 55.

41. Cf. *ibid.*, pp. 55-56.

42. *Ibid.*, p. 56.

43. *Ibid.*, pp. 258-265.

44. *Ibid.*, pp. 268-279; regarding Quakers and Moravian Brethren, see p. 271.

45. *Ibid.*, p. 271.

46. *Ibid.*, p. 192; discussion of Locke, pp. 191-192; Rousseau, pp. 194-196; American Declaration of Independence, p. 196; French Declaration, p. 197.

47. *Ibid.*, p. 133.

48. *Ibid.*, p. 200.

49. *Ibid.*, pp. 53-54.

50. Droysen to W. A. A. Arendt, Berlin, July 31, 1831, *Briefwechsel,* ed. Rudolf Hübner (Stuttgart, 1929), I, 38: "I would like to ask the pleasure of depicting Hegel as the philosopher of the Restoration and if at all possible of accompanying him to Cherbourg." Cherbourg was the port from which Charles X embarked for England after the 1830 Revolution. Cf. Wolfgang Hock, *Liberales Denken im Zeitalter der Paulskirche. Droysen und die Frankfurter Mitte* (Münster, 1957), pp. 14-16.

51. However, Droysen was by no means a "Hegelian." He was very deeply impressed by Hegel's concept of the state as a moral end and Hegel's conception of history as the development of reason. This in a sense is the theme of his own *Historik,* ed. Rudolf Hübner (München, 1937). Nevertheless, he developed a theory of historical knowledge which emphasized the basic difference between history and the sciences, criticized Hegel for misunderstanding the nature of history, and emphasized that the state was an ethical institution but not the one concrete manifestation of the ethical idea. Cf. Hock, *op. cit.*, and Iggers, *op. cit.*

52. Georg Wilhelm Hegel, *The Philosophy of Law,* in *Selections,* ed. J. Loewenberg (New York: Charles Scribner's Sons, 1929), p. 443.

53. See Jean Jacques Rousseau, *The Social Contract* (New York: Carlton House, n.d.).

54. Georg Wilhelm Hegel, *Grundlinien der Philosophie des Rechts,* 2nd ed. in *Sämtliche Werke,* ed. Georg Lasson, VI (Leipzig, 1921), 196 f. (to be cited hereafter as *S.W.*).

55. Rousseau, quoted in Otto Vossler, *Rousseaus Freiheitslehre* (Göttingen, 1963), pp. 188-189, 237, 239.

56. Rousseau, *The Social Contract and Discourses* (London, 1913), p. 25.

57. Hegel, *Philosophie der Weltgeschichte* in *S.W.*, VIII (Leipzig, 1920), 90.

58. Hegel, *Philosophie des Rechts* in *S.W.*, VI, 42.

59. Quoted from Hegel, *Selections, op. cit.*, p. 399; cf. *Philosophie der Weltgeschichte* in *S.W.*, VIII, 127.

60. *Philosophie der Weltgeschichte* in *S.W.*, VIII, 126.

61. *Social Contract*, p. 25.

62. Johann G. Droysen, "Preussen und Deutschland (1847)," in *Politische Schriften,* ed. Felix Gilbert (München, 1933), p. 114.

63. *Historik, op. cit.*, p. 261.

64. *Ibid.*, p. 259.

65. *Ibid.,* pp. 261-262.
66. *Ibid.,* p. 261; cf. "Preussen und Deutschland," *op. cit.,* p. 116.
67. *Ibid.,* p. 114.
68. *Historik, op. cit.,* p. 266.
69. Cf. Ernst Troeltsch, *The Social Teaching of the Christian Churches,* tr. Olive Wyon (New York: The Macmillan Company, 1931), II, 550.
70. Otto von Gierke, *Das deutsche Genossenschaftsrecht,* I (Graz, 1954), 882-883. This is a photographic reproduction of the first edition, 4 volumes (Berlin, 1868-1913).
71. For a bibliography of Gierke's writings, see Erik Wolf, *Grosse Rechtsdenker der deutschen Geistesgeschichte* (Tübingen, 1951), pp. 704-706.
72. Cf. Heinrich Heffter, *Die deutsche Selbstverwaltung im 19. Jahrhundert* (Stuttgart, 1950), pp. 525-530. The term *Genossenschaft* is extremely difficult to translate. Its dictionary meanings would include "fellowship," "association," "co-operative society," and others. Gierke, Carl Friedrich observed, nowhere defined the term clearly "but traced its evolution in contrast with its antithesis *Herrschaft. Genossenschaft* is found where several human beings realize the ends of the group through some form of cooperation of their several wills, while *Herrschaft* is found where group ends are realized through subordination of the wills of the members under one or several commanding wills." ("Gierke, Otto von," *Encyclopedia of the Social Sciences,* VI [New York: The Macmillan Company, 1931], 655.) See also Gierke, *Das deutsche Genossenschaftsrecht,* I, 12. In its purest form, the *Genossenschaft* was for Gierke a peculiarly Teutonic institution with its roots in the primeval past. See *ibid.,* I, 3.
73. Cf. Wolfgang Friedmann, *Legal Theory* (London: Stevens & Sons, Ltd., 1949), p. 172.
74. Cf. Heffter, *op. cit.,* p. 528.
75. Cf. Friedmann, *op. cit.,* p. 174.
76. Carl Schmitt, Hugo Preuss, *Sein Staatsbegriff und seine Stellung in der deutschen Staatslehre* (Tübingen, 1930), p. 12.
77. Cf. Heffter, *op. cit.,* pp. 751-759. For a bibliography see Hugo Preuss, *Staat, Recht und Freiheit. Aus 40 Jahren deutscher Politik und Geschichte,* ed. Theodor Heuss (Tübingen, 1926), pp. 583-588.

VIII. RAUSCHENBUSCH'S VIEW OF THE CHURCH
AS A DYNAMIC VOLUNTARY ASSOCIATION

*Donovan E. Smucker*

1. Walter Rauschenbusch, *A Theology for the Social Gospel* (New York: The Macmillan Company, 1917), p. 122.
2. Rauschenbusch, "Why I Am a Baptist," published originally in *The Rochester Baptist Monthly,* XX (1905-1906). Reprinted as a pamphlet from *The Colgate-Rochester School Bulletin,* December 1938.
3. *Ibid.,* p. 11.
4. Walter Rauschenbusch, *Christianity and the Social Crisis* (New York: The Macmillan Company, 1907), pp. 192-193. The quoted sentence is from Émile de Laveleye, *Protestantism and Catholicism in Their Bearing on the Liberty and Prosperity of Nations,* p. 34.
5. *Ibid.,* p. 193.
6. *Ibid.*
7. C. H. Moehlman, "Who is Walter Rauschenbusch?", *Crozer Quarterly,* XXIII, January 1946.
8. Richard Heath, *The Captive City of God* (London: Headley Brothers, 1905), p. 26.
9. *Ibid.,* pp. 47-48.
10. *Ibid.,* pp. 90-91.
11. *Ibid.,* p. 93.
12. *Ibid.,* p. 120.
13. *Ibid.,* p. 145.
14. *Ibid.,* p. 94.
15. Émile de Laveleye, *op. cit.,* pp. 27-28.
16. *Ibid.,* p. 29.

17. *Ibid.*

18. Vedder was also the author of *Balthasar Hübmaier* and in general was widely informed regarding Anabaptist materials of fifty years ago. His chapter on the Anabaptists in *Socialism and the Ethics of Jesus* (New York: The Macmillan Company, 1914) recommends Kautsky, Bax, and Heath as bibliography.

19. Henry C. Vedder, *Socialism and the Ethics of Jesus* (New York: The Macmillan Company, 1912), pp. 475-476.

20. *Ibid.*, p. 492. Others listed here: Peabody, Shailer Mathews, Ely, Campbell, Stelzle, C. R. Brown, Hodges, Reichert, Thompson, and Spargo.

### IX. A NOTE ON CREATIVE FREEDOM AND THE STATE IN THE SOCIAL PHILOSOPHY OF NICOLAS BERDYAEV

#### Douglas Sturm

1. Frederick C. Conybeare, *Russian Dissenters* (Cambridge: Harvard University Press, 1921).

2. Serge Bolshakoff, *Russian Nonconformity* (Philadelphia: The Westminster Press, 1950), p. 18.

3. On Russian thought of this period see V. V. Zenkovsky, *A History of Russian Philosophy*, tr. George L. Kline (New York: Columbia University Press, 1953), 2 vols.; Nicolas V. Riasanovsky, *Russia and the West in the Teaching of the Slavophiles* (Cambridge: Harvard University Press, 1952); and Nicolas Berdyaev, *The Russian Idea* (London: Geoffrey Bles, 1947).

4. Zenkovsky, *op. cit.*, Vol. II, p. 763.

5. See especially *The Russian Idea, op. cit.*, and *Dream and Reality*, translation by Katharine Lampert (London: Geoffrey Bles, 1950).

6. Nicolas Berdyaev, *Spirit and Reality*, tr. George Reavey (London: Geoffrey Bles, 1946), p. 33.

7. Berdyaev, *Freedom and the Spirit*, tr. Oliver Fielding Clarke (London: Geoffrey Bles, 1948), pp. 121 f.

8. Berdyaev, *Truth and Revelation*, tr. R. M. French (London: Geoffrey Bles, 1953), p. 71.

9. Berdyaev, *The Meaning of the Creative Act*, tr. Donald A. Lowrie (London: Victor Gollancz, 1955), p. 151 (italics in the original).

10. Berdyaev, *The Beginning and the End*, tr. R. M. French (London: Geoffrey Bles, 1952; New York: Harper & Brothers [Torchbook Series], 1957), p. 174.

11. Berdyaev, *The Divine and the Human*, tr. R. M. French (London: Geoffrey Bles, 1949), p. 143.

12. *The Beginning and the End*, p. 62.

13. *The Meaning of the Creative Act*, pp. 320-322.

14. Berdyaev, *The Destiny of Man*, tr. Natalie Duddington (London: Geoffrey Bles, 1954), pp. 78, 79.

15. See, for instance, *Slavery and Freedom*, tr. R. M. French (London: Geoffrey Bles, 1944), pp. 43, 254; *Solitude and Society*, tr. George Reavey (London: Geoffrey Bles, 1947), pp. 47, 151; and *The Divine and the Human*, p. 122.

16. Berdyaev, *The Realm of Spirit and the Realm of Caesar*, tr. Donald A. Lowrie (New York: Harper & Brothers, 1952), p. 99.

17. This is clearly Berdyaev's position, which makes it difficult to understand Reinhold Niebuhr's criticism of Berdyaev in his review of *The Russian Idea.* Niebuhr writes: "A part of the claim [made by Berdyaev] of the superiority of Russian spirituality over the West is derived from the illusion that it is possible to dispense with legal safeguards of both order and freedom so long as perfect love is achieved. This perfect love is not ever achieved in man's collective relationships; and it is a utopian illusion to expect such a consummation. . . . The freedom and the community which is implied in the Christian love commandment must be at least partially secured by law." (*Religion in Life*, Vol. XVIII, No. 2, Spring 1949.) This criticism is as quoted, with approval, by Will Herberg, *Four Existentialist Theologians* (Garden City: Doubleday and Co., 1958, Anchor Book Series, p. 15).

18. Here we may observe that Zenkovsky concludes, as a result of his analysis of Berdyaev's scheme of three kinds of ethics, that "Berdyaev recognizes not *three,* but only *two,* stages in ethical evolution," the ethics of redemption being

omitted on the basis of Berdyaev's assertion in *The Destiny of Man,* pp. 109 and 123, that "the ethics of redemption is in every way opposed to this world. . . . The gospel cannot serve as a basis for the state, the family, the economic life." (*A History of Russian Philosophy,* Vol. II, p. 769.) However, Zenkovsky too easily discounts the relevance of the ethics of redemption in Berdyaev's thought, even concerning man's associational life. Berdyaev does apply this ethic to "this world." In *Slavery and Freedom,* pp. 142 f., for instance, he writes that, "if it is good for individual people to repent and be humbled, it would be still better for communities, states, nations, and churches, to enter upon the path of repentance and humility" for "the arrogance of an individual person is not so terrible as the arrogance of a nation, a state, a class or of an ecclesiastical confession." The point that Berdyaev wishes to make is that, in a world of sin, the ethics of redemption *alone* cannot serve as a basis for man's social existence. It must be complemented by the ethics of law, and completed by the ethics of creativeness.

19. *The Destiny of Man,* p. 111.

20. *The Meaning of the Creative Act,* pp. 256 f., 270.

21. Will Herberg (*op. cit.,* p. 14) has described Berdyaev's social philosophy as deriving from his "ethic of meonic freedom." This is in error. Berdyaev's social philosophy derives from his total scheme of ethics, which culminates in his "ethic of creative freedom." As we have observed in our analysis of Berdyaev's concept of freedom, creative freedom is a synthesis of meonic freedom and freedom as an end. Perhaps Herberg goes wrong when he writes of "creative non-being" (p. 9). Non-being, which is meonic freedom, is not creative, but is only the possibility of creativeness. Creativeness among men involves the interaction of the already created world, man (including his meonic freedom, genius, talents), and God.

22. It should be noted that Berdyaev is not always consistent in his use of the terms society and community. But the conceptual distinction is always clear.

23. *The Beginning and the End,* p. 129.

24. *Ibid.,* p. 127.

25. *The Realm of Spirit and the Realm of Caesar,* p. 122.

26. See *Slavery and Freedom,* pp. 106, 202-203, and *The Realm of Spirit and the Realm of Caesar,* pp. 97-99.

27. *Slavery and Freedom,* p. 215.

28. *The Meaning of the Creative Act,* p. 290.

29. *The Divine and the Human,* p. 122.

30. "Every man has it in his power to become a personality, and . . . must be afforded every opportunity of achieving this end." (*Solitude and Society,* p. 129.)

31. *The Realm of Spirit and the Realm of Caesar,* p. 83.

32. *Ibid.,* p. 114.

33. These latter are the cultural values. Culture, in Berdyaev's interpretation, is composed of values that are higher and "more spiritual" than the merely economic. That is, cultural values are less dependent than economic values upon the material-natural dimension of existence for their realization. However, the difference between economic values and cultural values is not absolute. On occasion in his writings, Berdyaev even includes technics and economics among the achievements of culture (for instance, *The Meaning of the Creative Act,* p. 323). Generally, however, he distinguishes between economic activities, on the one hand, and cultural activities, including the activities of philosophy, science, art, literature, music, morals, and religion, on the other.

34. *The Realm of Spirit and the Realm of Caesar,* p. 113.

35. *Slavery and Freedom,* p. 219.

36. *The Realm of Spirit and the Realm of Caesar,* p. 113. At the same time, Berdyaev insists that the laboring man be given as great an opportunity as possible to be creative, to determine his own actions and judgments at firsthand, and to realize the freedom of his spirit. This is difficult in those positions in which economic activity has become almost completely mechanized and routinized, but nonetheless individuality and originality ought to be provided for even at the expense of economic efficiency. See *Slavery and Freedom,* pp. 220-221, and *The Destiny of Man,* p. 216.

37. *The Destiny of Man,* p. 195.

38. *Slavery and Freedom*, p. 151.
39. *The Meaning of the Creative Act*, p. 277.
40. *Slavery and Freedom*, p. 150.
41. *The Destiny of Man*, pp. 195-196.
42. *The Beginning and the End*, p. 217.
43. *The Realm of Spirit and the Realm of Caesar*, p. 113.
44. *Solitude and Society*, p. 145.
45. *Slavery and Freedom*, pp. 210, 148.
46. *Ibid.*, pp. 209-212.
47. *Ibid.*, pp. 152, 210-211, 218-219.
48. *The Destiny of Man*, pp. 207 f., 210.
49. On this subject, see Berdyaev's chapter entitled "The Lure and Slavery of Revolution" in his *Slavery and Freedom*, pp. 189-200, and his discussion on pp. 207-212 in *The Destiny of Man*. In his *Christianity and Class War* (tr. Donald Attwater; New York: Sheed and Ward, 1935), pp. 79-83, Berdyaev discusses the meaning of violence. He argues that those men that defend the *status quo* in some situations are often guilty of a greater degree of violence than those men that counsel war or revolution. Berdyaev instances the deprivation of elementary economic rights as coercion and violence as great if not greater than the coercion and violence necessary to alter the societal-political structure in order to achieve a more equitable economic situation. On this basis, he states that class war must not be repudiated, although it must be subordinated to the principle of personality and spirit and be purged of any notion of vengeance.
50. *The Realm of Spirit and the Realm of Caesar*, pp. 85, 156, 160. See the entire chapter entitled "Nationalism and the Unity of Mankind" in this volume, pp. 149-160.
51. *The Destiny of Man*, p. 201.
52. *Solitude and Society*, pp. 137 f.
53. *Ibid.*, p. 137. See also *The Meaning of the Creative Act*, p. 278.
54. *Slavery and Freedom*, p. 148.
55. *The Beginning and the End*, p. 227.
56. *The Meaning of the Creative Act*, p. 290.
57. *The Destiny of Man*, p. 196.
58. *Slavery and Freedom*, p. 140.
59. *Ibid.*, p. 148.
60. The proposition that the state may and ought to be creative is not novel. The position is expressed in such varied books as William Ernest Hocking's *Man and the State* (New Haven: Yale University Press, 1926); R. M. MacIver's *The Web of Government* (New York: The Macmillan Co., 1947); and Yves R. Simon's *Philosophy of Democratic Government* (Chicago: University of Chicago Press, 1951). On the other hand, compare Max Weber's statement: "The state's absolute end is to safeguard (or to change) the external and internal distribution of power. . . . It is absolutely essential for every political association to appeal to the naked violence of coercive means. . . . It is only this very appeal to violence that constitutes a political association in our terminology. The state is an association that claims the monopoly of the *legitimate use of violence*, and cannot be defined in any other manner." (*From Max Weber: Essays in Sociology*, tr. Gerth and Mills [London: Routledge & Kegan Paul Ltd., 1948], p. 334.)
61. *Slavery and Freedom*, p. 151.
62. With this recasting of Berdyaev's valuation of the state, the significance of the thirteenth chapter of Paul's letter to the Romans is more than "purely historical and relative," as Berdyaev asserts in *The Realm of Spirit and the Realm of Caesar*, p. 70. Indeed, the thirteenth chapter of Romans and the seemingly contradictory thirteenth chapter of the Revelation to John, the latter of which is given a nod of appreciation by Berdyaev in the same passage, are reconcilable as referring to different faces of the state.
63. *Slavery and Freedom*, p. 8.
64. See Chapter VII, pp. 142-155, of *The Russian Idea*.
65. *Slavery and Freedom*, p. 11.
66. *Dream and Reality*, p. 46.

**X. MISSIONARY SOCIETIES AND THE DEVELOPMENT OF OTHER FORMS OF ASSOCIATIONS IN INDIA**

*Richard W. Taylor*

1. Reinhard Bendix (*Max Weber: An Intellectual Portrait* [London: Heinemann, 1960], pp. 291 ff.) tends toward a triangular model rather than the quadrangular one suggested here.

2. This is not to deny that the Absolutes of different schools, such as those of the vedantists, the Kashmir shivites, and the grammarians, often seem not fully commensurate.

3. This interpretation of S. Natarajan in *A Century of Social Reform in India* (Bombay: Asia Publishing House, 1959; see especially pp. 5-6 )is the more telling because it seems to be made grudgingly.

4. Edward Thompson, *The Making of the Indian Princes* (London: Oxford University Press, 1943), pp. viii, 144-145.

5. See M. S. Gore, "Historical Background of Social Work in India," being Part I of *Social Welfare in India* (issued on behalf of the Planning Commission, Government of India, New Delhi, 1955), especially pp. 6 f.

6. Kenneth Ingham, *Reformers in India 1793-1833* (Cambridge: Cambridge University Press, 1956), pp. 57-58.

7. Church Missionary Society, MSS.: "North India. Letters," Vol. I, fo. 19. Cited by Ingham, *ibid.*, p. 60.

8. *Missionary Register,* 1822, p. 73; 1824, p. 49; and 1828, p. 112. Cited by Ingham, *op. cit.*, pp. 60-61.

9. Ingham, *op. cit.*, p. 82.

10. *Ibid.*, p. 95. See also pp. 84-95.

11. A. R. Desai, *Social Backgrounds of Indian Nationalism* (Bombay: Oxford University Press, 1948), especially pp. 120-130. D. F. Pocock, "Notes on the Interaction of English and Indian Thought in the 19th Century," in *Journal of World History,* IV-4 (1958), pp. 833-848, elaborates Desai's treatment.

12. See M. N. Srinivas, "A Note on Sanskritization and Westernization" in *Far Eastern Quarterly,* XV, 4 (August, 1956), and his earlier book referred to therein which I do not have at hand at the moment.

13. J. N. Farquhar, *Modern Religious Movements in India* (London: Macmillan & Co., 1915, 1924), p. 108.

14. *Ibid.*, p. 77.

15. See Wint in Sir George Schuster and Guy Wint, *India and Democracy* (London: Macmillan & Co., 1941), pp. 104-105.

16. Common group rites of the extended family group are far from rare. These are well treated in village context by A. C. Mayer, *Caste and Kinship in Central India* (Berkeley and Los Angeles: University of California Press, 1960). Such rites, however, are hardly congregational worship in the sense here used.

17. See N. C. Chaudhuri, *The Autobiography of an Unknown Indian* (London: Macmillan & Co., 1951), p. 479.

18. M. M. Begg in a personal interview with Creighton Lacy on January 29, 1960. Prof. Lacy has very kindly shared his manuscript *India's Social Conscience.* Cf. Richard W. Taylor and M. M. Thomas, *Mud Walls and Steel Mills* (New York: Friendship Press, 1963), ch. 3.

19. Pocock, *op. cit.*, p. 843, says just this.

20. See *ibid.*, p. 839, for citation of Farquhar and Mayhew on this. Pocock goes on to note that the introduction of Christian ethics has survived and that neo-Hinduism has been shaped largely by Ram Mohan Roy.

21. Mohandas Gandhi, *Autobiography,* Chs. XV and XX, and *Satyagraha,* Chs. XIII and XXXIII. The forthcoming Harvard thesis by Chandran Devanesan will throw more light on this.

22. L. S.S. O'Malley, *Modern India and the West* (London: Oxford University Press, 1941), p. 684.

23. Chaudhuri, *op. cit.*, pp. 107 ff.; also see pp. 198 f.

24. Natarajan, *op. cit.*, p. 8.

25. This treatment in terms of communications theory was suggested by Arthur H. Cole, "The Relations of Missionary Activity to Economic Development"

in *Economic Development and Cultural Change,* IX, No. 2 (January 1961), 120-127.

26. See Richard W. Taylor, "Christ's Folk in North India" in *Religion and Society,* X, No. 4 (December 1963), 16-24.

27. L. W. Brown, *The Indian Christians of St. Thomas* (Cambridge: Cambridge University Press, 1956), p. 109.

28. In India the major part of the budgets of most Christian educational institutions comes from the state. This also helps to modify the dependence of the principal on the hierarchy—and to increase such dependence on the state education department.

29. Some of these "movements" have been: World Literacy Incorporated, with grants of money and persons; the Danforth Foundation, with grants for teacher education abroad; the Oberlin-Shansi Foundation with help of all three kinds; and the Theological Education Fund.

30. In fields outside of higher education some typical "movements" impinging on the Indian church include: War on Want; Food for India; the group around Mason Olcott; and World Vision, Inc.

31. This was the case even when the comity agreement in Canada at the time of church union gave all the ex-Presbyterian area in North India to the United Church of Canada.

32. A group of the Disciples of Christ in Mid-India is typical.

33. See the newsletter of the National Association edited by J. J. Russell of Melrose, Mass., which includes quotations of letters from the Rev. A. Aachariah of Nagercoil and other news of this situation.

34. That most of those in India concerned for the future of the church think such movements irresponsible, at least, is perhaps not fully relevant to this study.

35. Bishop James K. Mathews, formerly of the staff of the Methodist Board of Missions with responsibility for India, is able to pinpoint the coming into the American discussion of this Indian device.

36. The best treatment of this to date would seem to be that of Lloyd I. Rudolph and Susanne Hoeber Rudolph, "The Political Role of India's Caste Associations" in *Pacific Affairs,* XXXIII, No. 1 (March 1960), 5-22.

37. Edgar Thurston, *Castes and Tribes of Southern India* (7 vols.; Madras: Government Press, 1909), VI, 364-376. The material on the "bosom controversy" is largely cited from G. T. Mackenzie, *Christianity in Travancore* (1901), while the *Madras Mail* (1907) is cited for the giving up of palm tapping.

38. J. H. Hutton, *Caste in India* (Bombay: Oxford University Press, 1946, 1951), pp. 99 ff., reiterates this observation with respect to both classical caste governments and more recent caste associations. He also cites in this connection Sir Wm. Sleeman, *Rambles and Recollections of an Indian Official* (1844), Vol. I, p. 61; L. S. S. O'Malley, *Indian Caste Customs* (1932), pp. 52 ff.; and E. A. H. Blunt, *The Caste System of Northern India* (1931), pp. 104, 106, 125.

39. These studies comprise several dozen M. A. "research papers" in the Department of Sociology of the Nagpur University.

40. On this change see P. D. Devanandan and M. M. Thomas (eds.), *The Changing Pattern of Family in India* (Bangalore: Christian Institute for the Study of Religion and Society, 1960).

41. That the model of the natural family is basic to Indian natural associations was well pointed out by Sir Henry Maine in his Rede Lecture. Henry Sumner Maine, *The Effects of Observation of India on Modern European Thought* (London: John Murray, 1875). On page 20 Maine writes, "A new sect, increasing in numbers and power, becomes a new caste. . . . In Western Europe, if a natural group breaks up, its members can only form a new one by voluntary association. In Central India they would recombine on the footing and on the model of a natural family."

42. A. I. Mayhew, "The Christian Ethic and India" in L. S. S. O'Malley (ed.), *Modern India and the West* (London: Oxford University Press, 1941), pp. 305-337 and especially p. 333, where the Rt. Rev. V. S. Azariah is cited. See also Mrs. H. Grey, "The Progress of Women" in O'Malley (ed.), *ibid.,* pp. 445-483, and especially the statement of Dr. Muthulakshmi Reddi on p. 455.

43. See J. N. Farquhar, *op. cit.,* pp. 25, 80.

44. Both the need for and dearth of such associations for lonely younger intellectuals has been noted by Edward A. Shils in his recent work on India.

45. This friendlessness is particularly well reflected in the appendix of G. Morris Carstairs, *The Twice-Born* (Bloomington: Indiana University Press, 1958; London: Hocart), and in Carstairs, "Rorschachs of 40 high caste Hindu and 10 Moslem men from Delwara, Udaipur, India," in *Microcard publications of primary records in culture and personality,* Vol. 1, No. 6.

XI. THE COMMUNAUTÉ DE TRAVAIL

### Verne H. Fletcher

There is, to our knowledge, no satisfactory study of the *Communauté de Travail* in English. The only account we have, in fact, is that of C. H. Bishop (4): appreciative, even enthusiastic, but rather loosely written, imprecise, subjective. A further drawback, which of course is not the author's fault, is that the early hopes of the movement and the present reality are far from coinciding and, as we have further pointed out, it is in the evolution of the movement that our principal lessons are to be learned. Bishop is the sole source for the accounts given by Fromm (18) and by Kahler (26), and they cannot very well rise above their source. Infield (25) leans heavily on Bishop. The only addition here, a slight one, is his report on the "cooperative potential" testing which he carried out in several of the communities. A brief but accurate impression of the early days can be gained from Gordon R. Taylor (39).

No over-all study exists in French either. The DuTeil work (14) is about the best for the early period, but his point of view is completely "Barbu" and many would not agree with his interpretation. For the evolution and crises of the last decade we have Meister (33) and Desroche (10). Otherwise we depend chiefly on the publications of the *Entente Communautaire* (15) and upon impressions gained from visits to various communities and to the *Entente* in the years 1952-1953 and again in the fall of 1961.

(1) Berneri, Marie L., *Journey Through Utopia* (Boston: Beacon Press, 1950). The quotation is from page 3.

(2) Bestor, Arthur E., Jr., *Backwoods Utopias: The Sectarian and Owenline Phases of Communitarian Socialism in America: 1663-1829* (Philadelphia: University of Pennsylvania Press, 1950).

(3) ———, "The Evolution of the Socialist Vocabulary," *Journal of the History of Ideas,* IX (June 1948), 259-302.

(4) Bishop, Claire Huchet, *All Things Common* (New York: Harper & Brothers, 1950).

(5) Buber, Martin, *Paths in Utopia,* tr. R. F. C. Hull (Boston: Beacon Press, 1958).

(6) ———, "Three Theses of a Religious Socialism," in *Pointing the Way* (New York: Harper & Brothers, 1957), p. 112.

(7) Desroche, Henri, and Meister, Albert, *Une Communauté de travail de la banlieue parisienne* (Paris: Editions de Minuit, 1955).

(8) Desroche, Henri, "Communities of the Past in France," *Cooperative Living,* IV (Spring 1953), 12-15.

(9) ———, "Dissidences religieuses et socialismes," *L'Année sociologique,* 1952, pp. 393-429.

(10) Desroche, Henri *et al., Études sur la tradition française de l'association ouvrière* (Paris: Editions de Minuit, 1956).

(11) Desroche, Henri, *Les Shakers américains: d'un néo-christianisme à un pré-socialisme?* (Paris: Editions de Minuit, 1955). While writing on the Shakers, Desroche gives such a broad perspective that the book may be consulted for indications on the entire American movement plus its pre-history in Europe. For a summary of this book see our review in *Journal of Religion,* XXXVI (October 1956), 276-279.

(12) ———, "Socialisme et sociologie du christianisme," *Cahiers Internationaux de Sociologie,* XXI (July 1956), 149-167.

(13) ———, "Sociogenèse du processus coopératif," *Communauté* (August 1954), pp. 1-5.

(14) DuTeil, Roger, *Communauté de travail l'expérience révolutionnaire de Marcel Barbu* (Paris: Presses Universitaire de France, 1949).

(15) Entente communautaire, *Communauté,* bi-monthly organ of E. C. 1948-1962. Also occasional reports, brochures, surveys, etc.

(16) Friedmann, Georges, "Lettre-préface," *Archives internationales de sociologie de la coopération,* I (January-June 1957), 4.

(17) ———, *Le Travail en miettes* (Paris: Gallimard, 1956).

(18) Fromm, Erich, *The Sane Society* (New York: Rinehart and Co., 1955), pp. 306-320.

(19) Gide, Charles, *Communist and Cooperative Colonies,* tr. E. F. Row (New York: Thomas Y. Crowell, 1928).

(20) Gourot, Jean, "La Communauté Boimondau," *Esprit,* XIX (April 1951), 540-561.

(21) Gurvitch, Georges, *Déterminismes sociaux et liberté humaine* (Paris: Presses Universitaires de France, 1955), p. 11.

(22) Haubtmann, Pierre, *Marx et Proudhon: leurs rapports personnels: 1844-47* (Paris: Economie et Humanisme, 1947), p. 16.

(23) Holloway, Mark, *Heavens on Earth: Utopian Communities in America: 1680-1880* (New York: Library Publishers, 1951). The quotation is from page 19.

(24) Infield, Henrik, *Cooperative Communities at Work* (London: Kegan Paul, 1947).

(25) ———, *Utopia and Experiment* (New York: F. A. Praeger, 1955), pp. 185-203.

(26) Kahler, Erich, *The Tower and the Abyss: An Inquiry into the Transformation of the Individual* (New York: George Braziller, 1957), pp. 282-297.

(27) Lasserre, Georges, "Coopération et syndicalisme," *Esprit,* XIX (November 1951), 731-736.

(28) Lebret, L. J., and Desroches, H. Ch., *La Communauté Boimondau,* "Documents Economie et Humanisme," No. 4 (L'Arbresle, Rhône: Editions Economie et Humanisme, 1946).

(29) Lefebvre, Henri, *Les Classiques de la liberté: Marx* (Geneva: Edition des Trois Collines, 1947), pp. 217-218.

(30) LeRoy, Maxime, *Histoire des idées sociales en France,* Vol. I and Vol. II (Paris: Gallimard, 1946-50).

(31) Maitron, Jean, *Histoire du mouvement anarchiste en France de 1880-1914* (Paris: Société Universitaire d'Editions et de Librairie, 1951).

(32) ———, "Milieux libres," *Esprit,* XIX (April 1951), 529-546.

(33) Meister, Albert, *Les Communautés de travail: bilan d'une expérience de propriété et de gestion collectives* (Paris: Entente Communautaire, 1958).

(34) ———, *Coopérative d'habitation et sociologie de voisinage* (Paris: Editions de Minuit, 1957).

(35) Moix, Candide, *La Pensée d'Emmanuel Mounier* (Paris: Editions du Seuil, 1951).

(36) Nordhoff, Charles, *The Communistic Societies of the United States* (New York: Harper & Brothers, 1875).

(37) Noyes, John H., *History of American Socialisms* (Philadelphia: Lippincott, 1870).

(38) Perroux, François, *Communauté* (Paris: Presses Universitaires de France, 1942).

(39) Taylor, Gordon R., "Experiment in Living: the Communities of Work," *World Review,* LIV (November 1949), 45-49.

XIII. A NEW PATTERN OF COMMUNITY

*Franklin H. Littell*

1. See Francis R. Allen and Hornell Hart et al., *Technology and Social Change* (New York: Appleton-Century-Crofts, 1957), pp. 455-473.

2. See *From State Church to Pluralism* (New York: Doubleday & Co., 1962), *passim.*

3. Charles R. Adrian, *Governing Urban America* (New York: McGraw-Hill Book Co., 1955), pp. 16-17.

4. John Osman, "A City is a Civilization," in Robert Lee (ed.), *Cities and Churches: Readings on the Urban Church* (Philadelphia: The Westminster Press, 1962), p. 75.

5. *Professional Life as Christian Vocation.* Papers of the Ecumenical Institute, III (Geneva: Oikumene, n.d.), p. 26.

6. Louis Wirth, "Urbanism as a Way of Life," in Lee, *op. cit.,* p. 33.

7. Lines from "The Deserted Village," by Oliver Goldsmith (1728-1774).

8. See "The City," one of a series of Interviews on the American Character (Santa Barbara, Calif.: Fund for the Republic, 1962), p. 25.

9. Joseph Story, *Commentaries on the Constitution* (5th ed.; Boston: Little, Brown & Co., 1891), par. 1873.

10. Line from "Miniver Cheevy," by Edwin Arlington Robinson (1869-1935).

11. Robert E. Park, "The City," in Lee, *op. cit.,* p. 48.

12. Robert C. Wood, *Suburbia: Its People and Their Politics* (Boston: Houghton Mifflin Co., 1959), p. 95.

13. C. Delisle Burns, *Political Ideals* (London: Oxford University Press, 1917), p. 45.

14. J. G. Russell, *Late, Ancient, and Medieval Population* (Philadelphia: American Philosophical Society, 1958), p. 6.

15. "Democratic Discipline and Professional Responsibility," in C. Scott Fletcher (ed.), *Education: The Challenge Ahead* (New York: W. W. Norton & Co., 1962), pp. 122-134.

16. A. D. Lindsay, *The Essentials of Democracy* (Philadelphia: University of Pennsylvania Press, 1929), p. 36.

17. From David Gascoyne, "A Wartime Drum," in *Contemporary Verse,* edited by Kenneth Allott (Baltimore: Penguin Books, Inc.), p. 249.

18. Richard Crossman (ed.), *The God That Failed* (New York: Harper & Brothers, 1949), p. 228.

19. Chapter 5 in Franklin H. Littell, *The German Phoenix* (New York: Doubleday & Co., 1960).

20. See "Can America Adopt the Evangelical Academy?" in *The Christian Scholar,* XLIII, No. 1 (March 1960), pp. 39-45.

21. See the argument in Luther's "Letter to the Christian Nobility of the German Nation," in *Three Treatises* (Philadelphia: Muhlenberg Press, 1943).

XIV. THE CRISIS OF THE CONGREGATION: A DEBATE

*Gabriel Fackre*

1. Thomas Wieser, "A New Ecumenical Discussion on the Congregation," *The Ecumenical Review,* XVI, No. 2 (January 1964), 153-157; *Concept VIII* (November 1964), papers from the Department on Studies in Evangelism, World Council of Churches, pp. 3, 4, 24; *Concept V* (September 1963), p. 5; *Concept VII* (May 1964), pp. 5, 33. Because of the abundance of different working groups, conferences, and individuals reporting in this up-to-the-minute mimeographed account of the ongoing discussion, reference will be made only to page numbers.

2. There has been an explosion of literature on this subject in the past few years. Our principle of selection in the documentation is twofold: (1) A sampling of the most recent commentary; (2) some of the landmark writing. While there is limited reference to periodicals, it should be noted that there is a lively running debate on the issues raised here in such periodicals as *Concept, Renewal, Laity, Christian Comment, The Ecumenical Review, Letters to Laymen, Social Action, Christianity and Crisis,* and *The Christian Century.*

3. E. R. Wickham, *Encounter with Modern Society* (New York: The Seabury Press, 1964), pp. 68-83; Martin E. Marty, "Death and Birth of the Parish," in Martin E. Marty, editor and author with Paul R. Biegner, Roy Blumhorst, and Kenneth R. Young, *Death and Birth of the Parish* (St. Louis: Concordia, 1964), pp. 10-13; *Concept III* (January 1963), p. 25; *Concept V,* pp. 17, 41.

4. Colin W. Williams, *What in the World?* (New York: Office of Publication and Distribution, National Council of the Churches of Christ in the U.S.A.,

1964), pp. 13-18; Mark Gibbs and T. Ralph Morton, *God's Frozen People* (Philadelphia: The Westminster Press, 1965), pp. 101-102; Horst Symanowski, *The Christian Witness in an Industrial Society* (Philadelphia: The Westminster Press, 1964), pp. 44-48, translated by George H. Kehm, introduction by Robert Starbuck; *Concept III*, pp. 19-20; *Concept V*, pp. 19-20, 34.

5. Colin W. Williams, *Where in the World?* (New York: Office of Publication and Distribution, National Council of the Churches of Christ in the U.S.A., 1963), p. 7; Peter L. Berger, *The Noise of Solemn Assemblies* (Garden City, N. Y.: Doubleday & Co., Inc., 1961), pp. 37-38; Marty in DBP, p. 18; *Concept V*, pp. 32-33.

6. Gibson Winter, *The New Creation as Metropolis* (New York: The Macmillan Company, 1963), pp. 66-67; George W. Webber, *The Congregation in Mission* (New York: Abingdon Press, 1964), pp. 21-22, 25; EWMS, p. 55; *What in the World?*, pp. 8-10; GFP, p. 41; CWIS, p. 47.

7. Hugh C. White, Jr., and Robert C. Batchelder, *Mission to Metropolis: a Total Strategy,* Occasional Paper No. 7 on Christian Faith and Industrial Society of the Detroit Industrial Mission, pp. 8-9; EWMS, pp. 36-38, 106-108; CWIS, pp. 37-38; NSA, pp. 38, 103-104; NCAM, pp. 6-12, 16-17, 29-30, 57, 126; CIM, p. 32; *Concept V*, pp. 23, 26, 36.

8. EWMS, pp. 122-123; Marty in DBP, p. 21; GFP, pp. 38, 41-44, 69-74; NSA, pp. 37-38; MMTS, pp. 4-6.

9. NCAM, pp. 12-13, 29-30; *Concept V*, pp. 17, 21; *Concept VII*, p. 14.

10. J. Archie Hargraves, "Go Where the Action Is: The Church and Urbanization," *Social Action,* XXX, No. 6 (February 1964), 15-35; Stephen C. Rose, "Twenty Questions: The Urban Training Center for Christian Mission," brochure interpreting the Urban Training Center for Christian Mission, Chicago, Ill. (no date).

11. Marty in DBP, pp. 23, 29; CWIS, pp. 33-36; NCAM, pp. 5-8, 67, 125, 140-141; CIM, p. 101; *Concept VII*, p. 40.

12. NCAM, *passim.*

13. Dietrich Bonhoeffer, *Prisoner for God,* edited by Eberhard Bethge, translated by Reginald H. Fuller (New York: The Macmillan Company, 1961), pp. 146-149, 156-160, 171; Langdon Gilkey, *How the Church Can Minister to the World Without Losing Itself* (New York: Harper & Row, 1964), pp. 32-47; William Stringfellow, *My People Is the Enemy* (New York: Holt, Rinehart and Winston, 1964), pp. 147-149; Gabriel J. Fackre, *The Pastor and the World* (Philadelphia: United Church Press, 1964), pp. 11-28; *What in the World?*, pp. 44-46; NCAM, 13-19, 25-32.

14. PFG, pp. 146-147, 156-160.

15. J. A. T. Robinson, *Honest to God* (Philadelphia: The Westminster Press, 1963), pp. 23, 36-39, 92; *What in the World?*, pp. 59-60; NCAM, p. 117; PFG, pp. 156, 158-159.

16. Stephen C. Rose, "The Way Ahead," *Renewal,* III, No. 9 (December 1963), 2-15; Gerhard Lenski, *The Religious Factor* (Garden City, N. Y.: Doubleday & Co., Inc. [Anchor Books], 1963), pp. 59-60; Hans Joachim Margull, "Evangelism in Ecumenical Perspectives," *The Ecumenical Review,* XVI, No. 2 (January 1964), 133-145; Marty in DBP, pp. 25-26; *What in the World?*, p. 105; GFP, pp. 90-92; *Where in the World?*, pp. 10, 12, 28, 59; NSA, pp. 33-104, 129, 157-171; NCAM, pp. 13, 22-24, 48, 127, 134-135; HCCMWWLI, pp. 16-26; *Concept IV* (April 1963), p. 26; *Concept V*, p. 31; *Concept VII*, pp. 3-7.

17. Jean Bosc, *The Kingly Office of the Lord Jesus Christ* (Edinburgh: Oliver & Boyd, 1959), p. 43 ff.

18. GFP, pp. 33, 44-49, 119-123, 133-137; *Where in the World?*, p. 12; NSA, pp. 161-171, 176-177; NCAM, pp. 19, 31, 33, 64, 77; HCCMWWLI, pp. 41-43, 129-131.

19. William C. Clebsch, *Contemporary Perspectives on Word, World, and Sacrament,* published by Division of College and University Work, National Lutheran Council and Division of College Work, Protestant Episcopal Church, 1962; J. C. Hoekendijk, "The Church in Missionary Thinking," *International Review of Missions,* XVI, No. 163 (July 1952), 324-336; Wilhelm Andersen, *Towards a Theology of Mission* (London: SCM Press, 1955), pp. 36-40; NCAM, pp. 50-51, 73-78; *Concept V*, p. 4; *Concept VII*, p. 4.

20. Note the titles of such recent books as *What in the World?, Where in the World?, The Nun in the World, The Pastor and the World, The Secular Meaning of the Gospel, The Secular Relevance of the Church, The Secular City.*

21. Hendrikus Berkhof, *The Doctrine of the Holy Spirit* (Richmond, Va.: John Knox Press, 1964), pp. 94-105; Lewis Mudge, *One Church: Catholic and Reformed* (Philadelphia: The Westminster Press, 1963), pp. 58-76; Joseph Sittler, "Urban Fact and the Human Situation," *Challenge and Response in the City*, edited by Walter Kloetzli (Rock Island, Ill.: Augustana Press), pp. 17-20; Hans Joachim Margull, "Structures for Missionary Congregations," *The International Review of Missions*, Vol. 52 (1963), 442-443; Robert Spike, "The Metropolis: Crucible for Theological Reconstruction," in *The Church and the Exploding Metropolis*, edited by Robert Lee (Richmond, Va.: John Knox Press, 1965), pp. 37-42; Kathleen Bliss, *We the People* (Philadelphia: Fortress Press, 1964), pp. 102-105, 114-115; EWMC, pp. 27-30; GFP, pp. 178-180; *What in the World?*, pp. 21-22, 29, 47, 51-55, 62; CWIS, pp. 66, 114; NCAM, pp. 42, 46, 52, 55, 79; CIM, pp. 56-57; PFG, pp. 153-154, 166, 168-169; *Concept VII*, pp. 3-8, 43; MPIE, pp. 94-99.

22. George Todd, "The Saints Are Destined to Be Urban Men," *Social Action, op. cit.*, pp. 47-48; Robert Strom, "God's Work Is in the World: A New Freedom for Ministry," *Renewal*, III, No. 7 (October 1963), 10-12; J. Archie Hargraves, *Stop Pussyfooting through a Revolution* (The Stewardship Council of the United Church of Christ; in cooperation with the Board of Homeland Ministries, 1963), pp. 2-3; HTG, pp. 64-83; CWIS, pp. 39, 66, 113-114; *Concept VII*, p. 24; *What in the World?*, pp. 21-22, 29, 40-47, 51-55, 62.

23. Paul L. Lehmann, *Ethics in a Christian Context* (New York: Harper & Row, 1963), pp. 74-101; CWIS, pp. 130, 141, 148; CIM, pp. 48-73; PFG, pp. 179-180.

24. Harvey Cox, "The Church in East Germany," *Letters to Laymen:* Journal of the Christian Faith and Life Community in Austin, Texas, X, No. 5 (May/June 1964), 3; *What in the World?*, p. 54; CWIS, pp. 64-67, 99, 122; PFG, pp. 124-125, 142-143; HTG, pp. 94-104.

25. EWMS, pp. 38-40; *What in the World?*, pp. 50-55; NCAM, p. 1-2; PFG, pp. 146-147, 160.

26. Howard Moody, *The Fourth Man* (New York: The Macmillan Company, 1964), pp. 33-50; Neil, in Stephen Charles Neil and Hans-Reudi Weber, *The Layman in Christian History* (Philadelphia: The Westminster Press, 1963), pp. 18-19; EWMS, pp. 45-49; *What in the World?*, pp. 21, 52-53, 62; CWIS, pp. 64-67, 99, 122; NCAM, pp. 2-3, 5-6, 11, 59, 61, 72-73, 80, 85, 89, 90, 112-114, 133; Hargraves, *Social Action, op. cit.*, p. 27; Spike in CEM, p. 37; WTP, pp. 16, 93; CIM, pp. 36, 50; *Concept VII*, pp. 23.

27. Robert Raines, *Reshaping the Christian Life* (New York: Harper & Row, 1964), p. 48; EWMS, pp. 98-103; *What in the World?*, p. 11; GFP, pp. 178-180; CWIS, pp. 66, 99; *Where in the World?*, p. 15; Lewis Mudge, *Is God Alive?* (Philadelphia: United Church Press, 1963), pp. 31-34; PFG, pp. 168-169; Spike in CEM, pp. 34-38. The stress upon involvement as the posture of learning is also described as "the listening ministry": *What in the World?*, p. 82; GFP, pp. 20-21; CWIS, pp. 50, 54, 65, 99; *Where in the World?*, pp. 85-86, 94; NSA, p. 152; NCAM, pp. 18, 53, 55, 60, 62, 70-72, 106; CIM, pp. 11-12, 142-143, 172; *Concept VII*, pp. 3-7 (Hoekendijk), p. 25.

28. On the general plea for new forms: World Council of Churches, Division of World Mission and Evangelism, *A Tent-Making Ministry* (Geneva: World Council of Churches, 1963); Gordon Cosby, "Not Renewal but Reformation," *Renewal*, III, No. 3 (April 1963), 4-6; EWMS, pp. 79-81; DBP, pp. 28-30; *What in the World?*, pp. 13, 24; GFP, p. 43; NCAM, p. 58; *Where in the World?*, pp. 69-70; PFG, p. 140; *Concept V*, p. 29; *Concept VII*, p. 2. The plea for new forms to replace the obsolete establishment makes strange bedfellows. Members of the Ku Klux Klan see their para-parochial activity as the expression of the new hope of mission needed for a new day. (See Harold H. Martin and Kenneth Fairly, "We've Got Nothing to Hide," *The Saturday Evening Post*, January 30, 1965, p. 28.) A recurring note in the quest for new forms is the assertion that "the church *is* obedience" and without obedience the church becomes an "heretical structure": Mrs. Porter Brown, "The Church is Obedience," *Ecumenical Institute*

*Newsletter,* Vol. 1, No. 4 (November 1964), 1, 3, 8; *What in the World?,* pp. 89-92; *Where in the World?,* pp. 82-83, 97; NCAM, p. 143; SPTAR, p. 3. Clues for the new style of a new form are "servanthood" and "holy worldliness": Gibson Winter, "Christendom in Metropolis," *Christianity and Crisis,* XXII, No. 20 (November 26, 1962), 206-211; Hans-Reudi Weber, *Salty Christians* (New York: The Seabury Press, 1963), pp. 45-49; EWMS, pp. 12-13; *Where in the World?,* pp. 26, 31; NCAM, pp. 18, 32-33, 54, 86, 89; Don Benedict, "Structures for the New Era," *Renewal,* III, No. 7 (October 1963), p. 6; HTG, pp. 84-104.

29. *What in the World?,* pp. 69-73, 94.

30. Cameron Hall, editor, *On-the-Job Ethics* (New York: Department of the Church and Economic Life, Division of Christian Life and Work, The National Council of the Churches of Christ in the U.S.A., 1963); Madeleine Barot and Ralph Young, editors, *Laity,* No. 14 (November 1962), "Christians in Power Structures"; Robert Spike, "The Uses of Leisure Time," *Renewal,* III, No. 8 (November 1963), p. 4; EWMS, pp. 18-19, 40-42, 122-125; *What in the World?,* pp. 74-79; CWIS, pp. 38-43; *Where in the World?,* pp. 83-84; NCAM, p. 125; *Concept VII,* p. 29.

31. *What in the World?,* pp. 73-74, 105; *Where in the World?,* pp. 84, 100; *Concept VII,* p. 29.

32. Carolyn Childs, "The Coffee House Form of Witness," unpublished manuscript for Union Theological Seminary Seminar (New York), "New Forms of Witness in Urban Society," George William Webber, instructor; John D. Perry, "The Coffee House Ministry," *The Christian Century,* LXXXII, No. 6 (February 6, 1965), 180-184; Gabriel J. Fackre and Herbert R. Davis, "Encounter and Pip's Place," *United Church Herald,* Vol. 7, No. 4 (February 15, 1964), 17-19, 34.

33. Ernest W. Southcott, *The Parish Come Alive* (New York: Morehouse-Gorham Co., 1956), pp. 44-68; David C. Orr, *The House Church* (Glasgow: The Iona Community, n.d.); Elizabeth O'Connor, *Call to Commitment* (New York: Harper & Row, 1963), pp. 83-91; "The Church in the House," *Laity,* No. 3 (April 1957), pp. 37-70.

34. CWIS, pp. 111, 113; *Where in the World?,* pp. 33-34; NCAM, pp. 20, 27; PFG, pp. 73, 97, 122-125, 140, 144, 163-164, 166-167; HTG, pp. 136-137; Hargraves, *Social Action, op. cit.,* p. 31. The conception of mission as making and keeping life human is allied to the protest against "churchification": J. C. Hoekendijk, "The Call to Evangelism," unpublished study paper for World Council of Churches Working Groups exploring "The Missionary Structure of the Congregation," p. 7; CWIS, pp. 35, 54-56; Spike in CEM, p. 38; Margull, *Ecumenical Review, op. cit.,* pp. 137-139; *Concept V,* p. 35; *Concept VII,* p. 23.

35. Lee J. Gable, *Church and World Encounter* (Philadelphia: United Church Press, 1964); Hans-Ruedi Weber, ed., *Signs of Renewal* (Geneva: Department on the Laity, World Council of Churches, 1957); *What in the World?,* pp. 24-25; NSA, pp. 149-157.

36. Oberkirchenrat Flohr, *et al.,* "Der Dienst der Evangelischen Akademien im Rahmen der kirchlichen Gesamtaufgabe," *Zeitschrift für Evangelische Ethik,* Heft, 6/1963, p. 375; GFP, pp. 138-152; NCAM, pp. 124-125; MMTS, pp. 9-10.

37. See *Kirchridge Contour, The Coracle.*

38. Henrik F. Infield, *The American Intentional Communities: Study in the Sociology of Cooperation* (Glen Gardner, N. J.: Glen Gardner Community Press, 1955), especially the description of Gould Farm, pp. 73-109; Henry Winthrop, "Ethics and Technics in Social Reconstruction," *Darshana International,* III, No. 1 (January 1963), 61-81; James Luther Adams, "Bruderschaften, geistliche," Weltkirchen Lexikon herausgegeben von Franklin H. Littell und Hans Hermann Walz, pp. 182-185.

39. CWIS, pp. 80-88; Hargraves, *Social Action, op. cit.;* PW, pp. 74-75; *Concept VII,* p. 40; *Concept IV,* pp. 22-23; *Concept V,* p. 38; *Concept VIII,* pp. 2-7, 24-29; *Concept VII,* pp. 29, 30, 31, 41.

40. *What in the World?,* pp. 78-81; PW, pp. 55-58.

41. *Concept VIII,* pp. 2-7, 24-29.

42. EWMS, pp. 98-103; CWIS, pp. 55-56; *What in the World?,* pp. 91-92; NSA, pp. 147-149; NCAM, pp. 25, 68-73, 92; PFG, p. 123; Benedict, *Renewal, op. cit.,* p. 5. There is current an interesting discussion on the pros and cons of

new shapes of sacramental life emerging in the secular setting. See EWMS, pp. 113-121; NCAM, pp. 129-130; Hargraves, *Social Action, op. cit.,* p. 25; Robert Spike, "The Tension between Social Action and Cultural Analysis," *Letters to Laymen,* Vol. 8, No. 8 (September 1962), 7.

43. Arthur Thomas, "The Meaning of the Summer for the Church," "A Missionary Presence in Mississippi, 1964," *Social Action,* XXXI, No. 3 (November 1964), 19-23; *What in the World?,* pp. 82-92; CWIS, pp. 55-56; NCAM, pp. 85, 105, 128.

44. NCAM, p. 54; Cosby, *Renewal, op. cit.,* pp. 5-6.

45. Robert Strom, "God's Work in the World: A New Freedom for Ministry," *Renewal,* III, No. 7 (October 1963), 10-12; CWIS, pp. 24-25, 85, 87, 100, 104, 126-128; NCAM, pp. 8-11, 19, 26, 32-33, 46-47, 63, 72, 92-98, 123.

46. Bruce E. Knox, "What and Where in the World? Some Notes on 'The Sycamore Community,'" *Focus,* Vol. 1, No. 2 (October 1954), 1-3; CIM, pp. 132-133; RCL, pp. 37-38, 133; CTC, *passim.*

47. Abram Kardiner and Lionel Ovesey, *The Mark of Oppression* (Cleveland: The World Publishing Company [Meridian Books], 1962).

48. Reinhold Niebuhr, *The Nature and Destiny of Man,* Vol. I, *Human Nature* (New York: Charles Scribner's Sons, 1945); RF, p. 3.

49. RF, p. 10; Roger Mehl, *Society and Love* (Philadelphia: The Westminster Press, 1964), pp. 20-35; MPIE, p. 43.

50. Daniel Jenkins, *Beyond Religion* (Philadelphia: The Westminster Press, 1962), p. 45; MPIE, pp. 85-96.

51. *Concept V,* pp. 3, 14; *Concept VII,* pp. 17, 20, 36, 46, 50.

52. Dietrich Bonhoeffer, *Ethics,* translated by Neville Horton Smith and edited by Eberhard Bethge (New York: The Macmillan Company, 1955), p. 198; Roger Lloyd, *Ferment in the Church* (New York: Morehouse-Barlow Co., 1964), pp. 116-121; PW, pp. 41, 53; *Concept VII,* p. 11.

53. *Concept V,* p. 4; *Concept VII,* p. 49; RCL, pp. 41-47; SL, pp. 20-35, 39, 74, 121, 152, 172, 176, 211; WTP, p. 129.

54. Markus Barth, "Critique of Gibson Winter, New Creation as Metropolis," *Concept VIII* (November 1964), pp. 30-32, is a two-page summary of an important and extended analysis by Barth of the Winter volume (available in mimeographed form as "The Latest Church Ideology" [January 1965]); *Concept VII,* pp. 15-17, 24.

55. *Concept VII,* pp. 15-17.

56. Abbe G. Michonneau, *Revolution in a City Parish* (Westminster, Md.: The Newman Press, 1961), pp. 13-16; Peter L. Berger, "Letter on the Parish Ministry," *The Christian Century,* LXXXI, No. 18 (April 29, 1964), 550; Glen W. Trimble, "Church Strategy in a World of Cities," *Information Service,* XLIII, No. 10 (May 9, 1964), 1-3; Truman Douglass, "I Believe in the Local Church," *United Church Herald,* Vol. 7, No. 16 (September 15, 1964), 16; CIM, pp. 200-201; *Concept VII,* pp. 18-21; WTP, pp. 125-127; PW, p. 48.

57. Hendrik Kraemer, *A Theology of the Laity* (Philadelphia: The Westminster Press, 1959), p. 41; Douglass, *United Church Herald, op. cit.,* p. 16; PW, p. 48.

58. GFP, pp. 114-115; CIM, pp. 149-150; MMTS, p. 7.

59. Wallace Fisher, *From Tradition to Mission* (Nashville: Abingdon Press, 1965); SPTAR, pp. 7-12, 33-44; DBP, pp. 43-96.

60. DBP, 99-163; Hillel Black, "This Is War," *The Saturday Evening Post,* Vol. 237 (January 25, 1964), 60-63.

61. PW, pp. 47-48; *Concept VIII,* p. 36.

62. Peter Berger, "The Christian in the Structures of Modern Society," an unpublished address at North American Conference, "The Churches in Mission," sponsored by the Department on Studies in Evangelism, World Council of Churches, Yale Divinity School (September 9-12, 1963), pp. 6-9; PW, p. 47.

63. GFP, p. 61.

64. Arthur C. Clarke, "Everybody in Instant Touch," *Life,* Vol. 57, No. 13 (September 25, 1964), 118-131.

65. DEARKG, pp. 375-384; Douglass, *United Church Herald, op. cit.,* p. 5.

66. Dietrich Bonhoeffer, *The Communion of Saints* (New York: Harper &

Row, 1963), pp. 157-160, 170; HCCMWWLI, pp. 100-103; WTP, p. 112; PW, pp. 46-47.

67. Fackre and Davis, *United Church Herald, op. cit.*, p. 34.

68. "Renewal in the Churches," *Union Seminary Quarterly Review,* XVI, No. 3 (March 1961), entire issue; DBP, pp. 31-33.

69. See public statements made by Hubert Humphrey, Everett Dirksen, and Richard Russell following the passage of the civil rights legislation of 1964.

70. Lesslie Newbigin, *The Household of God* (New York: Friendship Press, 1960), pp. 55-57, 66-68, 84, 86, 110-112; James Gustafson, *Treasure in Earthen Vessels* (New York: Harper & Row, 1961), pp. 49-112; J. Robert Nelson, *The Realm of Redemption* (London: Epworth Press, 1951), pp. 79, 166, 168; William Stringfellow, *Free in Obedience* (New York: The Seabury Press, 1964), pp. 101-102; Hans Küng, *The Council, Reform and Reunion,* tr. by Cecily Hastings (New York: Sheed and Ward, 1961), pp. 12-36; Trevor Huddleston, *The True and Living God* (London: Collins [Fontana Books], 1964), pp. 73-83, 94; DBP, p. 33; HCCMWWLI, pp. 75-77, 105-127; PW, pp. 43-45; TTM, pp. 48-58; WTP, pp. 18, 78-80, 138; *Concept III,* p. 7; *Concept VII,* pp. 9-12; RCL, p. 9.

71. Dietrich Bonhoeffer, *Life Together,* translated with introduction by John W. Doberstein (New York: Harper & Brothers, 1954), pp. 25-30, 37-39; GFP, p. 185; DHS, pp. 51-55; PW, pp. 45-46; HG, pp. 22-24, 56, 74-75; MPIE, p. 90.

72. DHS, pp. 54-55; HG, p. 74; PW, pp. 44-45; OCCR, p. 44.

73. "The Finality of Jesus Christ in the Age of Universal History," *Bulletin,* VIII, No. 2 (Autumn 1962), Division of Studies, World Council of Churches, pp. 6-10, 33, 41; MPIE, pp. 93-99; TTM, pp. 45-58; TLG, pp. 75-83; BR, pp. 82-83.

74. TL, p. 150.

75. RR, p. 1.

76. Marcus Barth in *Concept VIII,* p. 31; *Concept VIII,* p. 32. To be mentioned here also is the danger of glib "Lo here, lo there" identifications of the working of God: *Concept VII,* p. 44; MPIE, p. 91.

77. Marcus Barth in *Concept VIII,* p. 30-31; *Concept VII,* pp. 9-10.

78. Marcus Barth in *Concept VIII,* p. 36.

79. Colin Williams, "Evangelism and the Congregation," *Ecumenical Review,* XVI, No. 2 (January 1964), 150; DBP, p. 32; HCCMWWLI, pp. 26-27; DHS, pp. 40-41; PW, p. 47; Berger, *Christian Century, op. cit.,* p. 549; Douglass, *United Church Herald, op. cit.,* p. 15.

80. Fred Hoskins, "Equipping God's People," *The Chicago Theological Seminary Register,* Vol. LII, No. 3 (March 31, 1962), 3, 6-7; DHS, p. 116; HCCMWWLI, pp. 26-27; BR, pp. 108-110; Berger, *Christian Century, op. cit.,* pp. 549-550.

81. Vladimir Lossky, *The Mystical Theology of the Eastern Church* (London: James Clarke & Co., Ltd., 1957), *passim; Concept VII,* pp. 8-12.

82. RCL, p. 22; *Concept VII,* pp. 8, 10, 29; PW, p. 48.

83. Daniel Jenkins, "The Christian and This World," *Social Action,* XXIX, No. 5, pp. 8-10; CIM, pp. 78, 84, 63, 144-145; BR, p. 46; HCCMWWLI, pp. 74-98; PW, pp. 28-38.

84. Howard Fuller, "The Local Church Pastor and the Urban Revolution," *Urban Timepiece,* Vol. 1, No. 1 (May 1964), 1, 4, 5; WTP, pp. 122-125; PW, pp. 31-32, 35-38.

85. FO, p. 106; RCL, pp. 7, 9; *Concept VII,* p. 9.

86. Bruce Hunt, "A Chicago Experiment," *Renewal,* IV, No. 9, pp. 12-14; EWMS, pp. 123-125; DBP, pp. 34-39; WTP, p. 127; MMTS, pp. 6-10; DEARKG, pp. 375-384; Douglass, *United Church Herald, op. cit.,* pp. 14-16; *Concept VIII,* pp. 2-7, 24-29.

XVII. JAMES LUTHER ADAMS: A BIOGRAPHICAL AND INTELLECTUAL SKETCH

*Max L. Stackhouse*

1. James Luther Adams, *Taking Time Seriously* (Glencoe, Ill.: The Free Press, 1957), p. 27.

2. S. A. Ashe, *History of North Carolina* (Greensboro, N.C.: C. L. Van Noppen, 1925-), III, 57 ff. Here we have a characterization of his great-uncle

as a true gentleman of the South. Beyond that, the written sources are of things JLA remembers, although his memory is voluminous and accurate. See "How My Mind Has Changed," *The Christian Century,* LVI, No. 36 (September 6, 1939), 1067-1070, and as reprinted in the collected essays *Taking Time Seriously,* assembled for him when he left Chicago to come to Harvard. Also available was the manuscript "Notes on the Evolution of My Social Concerns," a paper delivered to the American Society of Christian Social Ethics. I should like to thank Adams' good friend, J. Bryan Allin, in particular, and several contributors to this volume who have been of great help in extending personal impressions and knowledge beyond the scope of the present writer.

3. D. W. Soper, *Men Who Shape Belief* (Philadelphia: The Westminster Press, 1953).

4. Edmund Gosse, *Father and Son* (New York: Charles Scribner's Sons, 1925).

5. *Ibid.* This writing is mentioned almost in passing in *Hound and Horn,* V, 4, pp. 695 ff. When asked about this book, Professor Adams nodded and said, "My childhood."

6. *Taking Time Seriously,* p. 11.

7. Max Weber, *Sociology of Religion* (Boston: Beacon Press, 1963).

8. Based on some notes, saved by Mr. Allin, in JLA's handwriting. Mr. Allin has also guided my research in other invaluable ways.

9. From information sent by Mr. Allin.

10. *Taking Time Seriously,* p. 12.

11. *Ibid.,* p. 15.

12. The Greenfield Group, for example, spent nearly a year on Ernst Troeltsch, an experience that has had lasting effect on JLA. Not only does he give the only known Troeltsch seminar in the country, but he is responsible for the series on Troeltsch in the first two issues of the *Journal for the Scientific Study of Religion* and he has in preparation the most complete translation of Troeltsch's writings yet collected. One might also add that several students of his have been influenced by his interest in Troeltsch.

13. John F. Hayward, *Existentialism and Religious Liberalism* (Boston: Beacon Press, 1962).

14. *Taking Time Seriously,* p. 17. Not therein related is the very critical speech made by JLA at graduation concerning the intellectual chastity of Harvard Divinity School, a speech evoking no small response.

15. G. H. Williams (ed.), *The Harvard Divinity School* (Boston: Beacon Press, 1954), pp. 180 f. This passage was written by James Luther Adams.

16. *Ibid.,* p. 181.

17. Financed, incidentally, in part by the Billings prize for preaching, an annual award given at the Divinity School. When asked by the author what he preached on, Adams recalled that he almost forgot about the contest entirely. In fact, he was on his way downtown in the subway when, reaching into his bookbag to find some reading material, he found his sermon from the previous Sunday. It reminded him of the contest, so he got off at the next stop, took the next car back to Harvard Square, and ran to the chapel. Slipping in the back door, he saw that there were still several to speak. He sat down with the others and took the last turn. He remembers only one phrase from the sermon, "smothering the cross with lilies in the name of piety," but it was evidently more memorable than the one sentence, for he won the entire bag; no second or third prize was given that year.

18. See Liston Pope's now classic study of churches in milltowns and how their constituents influence their theological ethics and church policy (*Millhands and Preachers;* New Haven: Yale University Press, 1942).

19. See *Irving Babbitt: Man and Teacher,* edited by F. Manchester and O. Shepard (New York: G. P. Putnam's Sons, 1941), especially Chapter XXI by James Luther Adams and J. Bryan Allin. Also influential, though less so, during this period were Kittredge and Lowes.

20. *Taking Time Seriously,* p. 13.

21. *Hound and Horn,* pp. 696 ff.

22. *Ibid.*

23. Rudolf Otto, *Kingdom of God and Son of Man* (London: Lutterworth Press, 1938).

24. *Taking Time Seriously,* p. 18. It was also during this stay in Paris that he had a chance to visit Father Georges Florovsky at the Russian Academy (later to become Adams' colleague at Harvard). While there he also became acquainted with Nicolas Berdyaev. On one occasion Adams engaged him in conversation about Capitalism, Communism, and Catholicism. Berdyaev launched forth with the view that the corruption and gangsterism in America resulted directly from the secularizing Calvinist influence in the history of this country. When Adams told him that Legs Diamond and the Chicago hoods were, for the most part, Roman Catholic, that great Roman Catholic funerals were held after the gangsters shot each other up, he could not believe it and almost fell off his chair. It not only was impossible for him to comprehend, he was also embarrassed for having been propounding a pet theory about the lineage from Calvinism to Capitalism to gangsterism.

25. Adams' familiarity with these and other aspects of Roman Catholic thought served him well when he became an official Observer at Vatican Council II. (Two students of Adams, who are contributors to this volume, were also associated with Vatican Council II, Professor George H. Williams and Michael Novak.)

26. See his translation of the first chapter of *Le Christianisme et la Paix,* Edition "Je Sers," Paris, 1933, which appeared in the *Protestant Digest,* June 1939, pp. 16 f. As with various other European writers, Adams has made numerous manuscript translations of the writings of Philip, for the use of students.

27. Henry Nelson Wieman, *The Directive in History* (Boston: Beacon Press, 1949).

28. Paul Tillich, *The Protestant Era* (Chicago: University of Chicago Press, 1948).

29. See Ira Blalock, Jr., "James Luther Adams' Philosophy of History," a forthcoming article in *Proceedings of the Unitarian Historical Society.* See also in the present volume the chapter by James D. Hunt entitled "Voluntary Associations as a Key to History" and James D. Hunt, "James Luther Adams and His Demand for an Effective Religious Liberalism," unpublished Ph.D. Dissertation, Syracuse University, 1965.

30. In this regard it is interesting to note the following statement by him in a letter to the author: "When Karl Barth writes on Mozart, he reveals a concern that seems to me to be quite in order for a theologian, though I would say that his 'image' of Mozart is as much a lopsided 'construct' as is Kierkegaard's."

31. See J. L. Adams, "Notes on the Study of Gould Farm," *Cooperative Living,* VII, No. 1 (Winter 1955-56).

32. He once wrote in a memo to the author: "I have always studied by a method of opening myself in succession to the writings of a major figure. I think every student (including the minister) should be working through a single writer systematically at every period of his life."

# INDEX